Pathway to the Profession:

From Law School to Lawyer

New York State Bar Association Continuing Legal Education publications are intended to provide current and accurate information to help attorneys maintain their professional competence. Publications are distributed with the understanding that NYSBA does not render any legal, accounting or other professional service. Attorneys using publications or orally conveyed information in dealing with a specific client's or their own legal matters should also research original sources of authority.

We consider the publication of any NYSBA practice book as the beginning of a dialogue with our readers. Periodic updates to this book will give us the opportunity to incorporate your suggestions regarding additions or corrections. Please send your comments to: CLE Publications Director, New York State Bar Association, One Elk Street, Albany, NY 12207.

TABLE OF CONTENTS

Attorney Professionalism

Technology and the Law

Law Practice

Legal Writing

Contracts

Evidence

Trial Practice

Marketing You and Your Practice

Personal Development

Foreword

On behalf of myself and the 75,000 members of the New York State Bar Association—Congratulations! You've made it through law school, and in a few short months you will join the ranks of attorneys licensed to practice in New York. This is an honor and a privilege, and we welcome your entry into the profession. And we want you to know that the New York State Bar Association will be with you at every step in your career.

The NYSBA is a professional association dedicated to helping attorneys hone their skills as lawyers and develop as members of a noble profession. The NYSBA offers educational and networking opportunities, free and low-cost legal research plans, and practice-oriented reference materials. Membership in the NYSBA puts you in contact with colleagues and mentors who will help you stand out from the crowd and have a well-rounded approach to the profession.

The NYSBA's mission includes cultivating the science of jurisprudence; elevating the standard of integrity, honor, professional skill and courtesy in the legal profession; and cherishing and fostering a spirit of collegiality among its members. It is these core values that brought about the *Pathway to the Profession* program. *Pathway* is founded on the belief that if current attorneys help the next generation of attorneys, the practice of law will be better—and more fulfilling—for all. It was developed to provide support to law schools and students, and to help new attorneys transition into practice. *Pathway*'s tailored programs are designed to complement existing curriculum and create new opportunities for ongoing academic experience and exposure.

Aside from *Pathway*, one of the key ways to ensure your success as a new attorney—and to elevate standards and foster collegiality—is to become involved in one or more of the NYSBA's practice-specific Sections or Committees, as well as the Young Lawyers Section. Speaking from my own experience, NYSBA membership proved invaluable after I graduated from law school, The Bar Association not only offered educational programs, relevant resources and benefits, but also—particularly through Section and Committee membership—an introduction to New York's leading attorneys, both in and outside of my area of practice. Many of them started as valued contacts, but became lifelong friends. NYSBA gave me the opportunity to work not only with the finest attorneys in New York State but with some of the finest people I would ever know. Involvement in the organized bar made me realize every day that being an attorney *is* a noble profession, one that serves the public good, and one that is both rewarding and satisfying. Getting involved in the bar will help you keep your passion for the law, and the justice system, alive and burning bright.

In that vein, I'd like to share some advice: Demonstrate hard work and diligence in all you do. Understand the culture of your work environment, learn who the players are, and emulate those who deserve your respect and admiration. Be nice to the administrative, technical and paralegal staff because they will save you time and time again. Be involved and approach all your work with enthusiasm. Your attitude and appearance will matter. Work on a variety of projects, as many as you can get your hands on. You might discover an interest in an area you didn't expect. If you want to be successful, do everything to the best of your ability; others are watching and taking note. Love what you do and believe in what you are doing.

That said, we offer you *Pathway to the Profession: From Law School to Lawyer*, a compilation of substantive materials on topics such as legal writing and legal research, motion practice, attorney professionalism, and marketing; all this to help make your transition from student to professional as seamless as possible. The materials are culled from the NYSBA's extensive archive of articles on these topics. We hope you find them useful and informative.

In law school, one learns about the law, but not necessarily how to practice. So, consider this a guide book to the practice of law. New York practice and New York law remain the gold standard for lawyers throughout the world, and the NYSBA and I want to ensure that, after graduation, you have all the tools you need at your disposal to become a successful member of the New York legal community. And, as always, the New York State Bar Association and its 120-member staff are here to help you achieve that success.

On behalf of the NYSBA's 75,000 members, once again, I congratulate you and welcome you to the New York State Bar Association.

David P. Miranda
President
New York State Bar Association
2015–2016

PATHWAY TO THE PROFESSION: FROM LAW SCHOOL TO LAWYER

NYSBA RESOURCES

FAQ

Below are frequently asked questions regarding the benefits of membership in the New York State Bar Association (NYSBA), as well as additional questions our Member Resource Center receives from members. Detailed information regarding these topics can be found at **www.nysba. org** or by calling our Member Resource Center at 800.582.2452.

NYSBA MEMBERSHIP FAQS

Q How much does it cost to join NYSBA if I am a newly admitted attorney?

A Membership in NYSBA is free for your first year of practice; you get free membership in the Young Lawyer's Section too. Membership in the other NYSBA Sections is also either free for the first year or available at a discounted rate.

Please note, it is important to contact NYSBA to make sure we have up-to-date contact information so you can receive these benefits.

Q I had free legal research on Westlaw and Lexis when I was in law school. Does NYSBA provide access to legal research?

A Yes. NYSBA has entered into a partnership with Fastcase and WoltersKluwers (LoislawConnect) to provide NYSBA members with access to legal research tools. Through Fastcase, members have free and unlimited access to the following libraries: N.Y. Court of Appeals, A.D. Decisions, Misc. Decisions, N.Y. Consolidated Laws, N.Y.C.R.R., N.Y.S. Constitution, U.S. Code, 2d Circuit Decisions, and Supreme Court Decisions.

Through LoislawConnect, NYSBA members have access to recent cases in several libraries as well as access to NYSBA Ethics Opinions. The full LoislawConnect library is also available at exclusive NYSBA member discounts. Also provided through Loislaw are email alerts of new cases (NYSBA/Loislaw CaseAlert service); members choose one of 20 areas of practice and new cases are emailed to the address specified.

Q What other substantive research/informational tools are available to NYSBA members?

A One of the most important benefits of NYSBA membership is exclusive access to substantive, practical content. The following publications are available to all NYSBA members in print, online and through the NYSBA Periodicals app (available for Apple and Android devices).

NYSBA Journal: Substantive articles and columns on the law, law practice, legal writing and ethics.

New York State Law Digest: Monthly wrap-up of significant Court of Appeals cases and statutory developments. Between issues, check the NYSBA website for online alerts of breaking news.

State Bar News: News of the Association, its initiatives and its members, with regular columns on tech and law practice management as well as Section and Committee highlights.

Sections: NYSBA's Sections are also an invaluable source of substantive content. By joining one (or more) of NYSBA's 25 Sections you gain access to Section newsletters and journals (available in an online, searchable format going back to 2000), access to Section seminars and meetings, and online access to discussions and blogs and a practice-area specific communities.

Q **Does NYSBA offer additional benefits such as health and malpractice insurance?**

A USI Affinity, the exclusive sponsored provider of insurance programs for NYSBA members, offers a broad spectrum of comprehensive, competitive insurance plans to meet the unique needs of NYSBA members, their firms, and their employees. These include medical, dental and vision policies; prescription drug coverage; disability insurance; home and auto insurance; and professional liability coverage. NYSBA members also enjoy deep discounts on a wide range of products and services.

Q **I need a job. Can NYSBA help?**

A Job postings are available at **www.nysba.org/jobs**, NYSBA's Career Center. In addition, NYSBA and NYSBA Sections offer numerous networking and career development events.

Q **What are some additional benefits of NYSBA Membership?**

A NYSBA offers exclusive discounts on many services and products which, in many cases more than pay for the cost of membership. You can find a full list of benefits at **www.nysba.org/memberbenefits**.

Here are just a few:

CLE: NYSBA is one of the leading providers of CLE in New York State. CLE seminars are provided live and in a variety of other formats. Of particular note is that members save $400 on the 16-credit Bridge the Gap CLE program.

CLIO: A legal practice management program that is optimized to meet the needs of solo practitioners and small firms. Cloud-hosted, secure and easy-to-use, Clio keeps your valuable practice data at your fingertips and frees you of your office server.

Reference Books: Practical and practice-oriented, written by attorneys for attorneys.

NYSBA Practice Forms and Form Products: Downloadable and on CD.

NYSBA FAQs:

In addition to questions you may have about the benefits of NYSBA membership, we are also including some of the most frequently asked questions regarding the practice of law in New York State.

BAR EXAM & RECIPROCITY

Q Who administers the New York State Bar Exam and determines attorney reciprocity?

A The New York State Board of Law Examiners does both. You can contact them at 518.453.5990, www.nybarexam.org.

Q Does NYSBA give me the results from the Bar Exam?

A The Board of Law Examiners publishes the results and emails them to candidates. Contact them at 518.453.5990, www.nybarexam.org.

ATTORNEY REGISTRATION (LICENSING) & IDENTIFICATION

Q Does NYSBA license attorneys to practice in New York?

A NYSBA is not the official New York Bar and is not responsible for attorney licenses or registration. Please contact the NYS Office of Court Administration (OCA), the official licensing/registration unit at 212.428.2800, www.nycourts.gov.

Q Do I need to remain a member of the Association in order to keep my license?

A Although the benefits provided by NYSBA membership are ex-tremely valuable, membership in NYSBA is voluntary. If you have any questions about your license contact the OCA at 212.428.2800, www.nycourts.gov.

Q Does membership in NYSBA entitle an attorney to practice in New York?

A NYSBA is not the official New York Bar and is not responsible for attorney licenses or registration. Please contact the NYS Office of Court Administration (OCA), the official licensing/registration unit at 212.428.2800, www.nycourts.gov.

Q As a licensed attorney, how often do I pay my NYSBA membership dues versus my licensing fees?

A NYSBA membership dues are paid annually, and the amount varies based on the number of years you are admitted to practice. Licensing fees with the NYS Office of Court Administration (OCA) are mandatory and are paid biennially by all attorneys engaged in the active practice of law. For information regarding NYSBA membership dues, call 800.582.2452. For information regarding OCA licensing fees, call 212.428.2800.

ATTORNEY SEARCH & VERIFICATION / CERTIFICATES OF GOOD STANDING

Q Can NYSBA verify whether an attorney is a member in good standing of the New York Bar?

A NYSBA is not the official New York Bar and is not responsible for attorney licenses or registration. Please contact the NYS Office of Court Administration (OCA), the official licensing/registration unit: 212.428.2800, www.nycourts.gov.

Q Can I run a search on NYSBA website for a New York attorney that I am trying to locate?

A You can search for an attorney at the OCA website: www.nycourts.gov

Q How does a licensed attorney obtain a Certificate of Good Standing?

A Letters or Certificates of Good Standing can be obtained from the Appellate Department where the attorney was admitted to practice.

1st Department (Manhattan) call 212.340.0400.

2nd Department (Brooklyn) call 718.875.1300.

3rd Department (Albany) call 518.471.4777.

4th Department (Rochester) call 585.530.3100.

If you do not know which Appellate Division the attorney was admitted in, you may obtain this information from the NYS Unified Court System's website: www.nycourts.gov.

COURT IDENTIFICATION/SECURE PASS

Q Does the licensing body, the OCA, administer bar cards?

A No. Upon admission to the bar, the Appellate Division does not furnish an ID card, nor does New York have bar numbers. However, Secure Pass ID card applications can be picked up at any New York state courthouse and are available to any attorney in order to gain access into New York courthouses. Additional information can be found at http://www.nycourts.gov/attorneys/registration/securepass.shtml

EARNING CLE CREDITS; REPORTING REQUIREMENTS

The Office of Court Administration (OCA) has a very detailed and informative FAQs section on its website, which contains all the information you need to comply with the mandatory CLE requirements. Go to http://www.nycourts.gov/attorneys/cle/newattorney_faqs.shtml.

Here are a few of the most frequently asked questions:

Q How do I keep track when I start earning CLE credits?

A As a member of NYSBA, if you take a program with us, we automatically upload the credits earned in your profile under credit tracker. Just log in to our website to check on the number of credits you have earned. You can also add any credits earned from other CLE programs, for example from a county or other bar association. Once you've completed your first two-year reporting period (16 credits per year, for a total of 32 credits), and you start earning credits from NYSBA CLE webcasts and DVDs, we will automatically track those credits for you as well.

Q Does NYSBA submit my credits to the CLE Board when my reporting cycle ends?

A NYSBA does not report your credits for you. We provide the CLE credit tracker as a tool so you can make sure you have the credits you need and you can check against the certificates you have.

Q Are there any restrictions on the programs I can take as a newly admitted attorney?

A Newly admitted attorneys must complete 16 credits per year, for a total of 32 credits, in the first two-year reporting period. During this period, attorneys must attend live programs that are transitional in nature. Transitional courses are designed to help newly admitted attorneys develop a foundation in the practical skills, techniques and procedures that are essential to the practice of law. The sponsoring organization will be able to tell you which of its courses are transitional.

NYSBA offers a wide array of transitional programs, including our Practical Skills Series, writing seminars, starting a practice in New York, lessons on ethics and civility and the CPLR Update. Go to our website, **www.nysba.org** and click on CLE for a calendar.

Newly admitted attorneys may not receive credit for viewing webcasts, downloads and DVDs or listening to CDs or other audio files. Attendance at interactive video conferencing of live programs, such as NYSBA's "Bridge the Gap," which originates in New York City and is video conferenced to Albany and Buffalo, is allowed, however.

Q Where can I find the mandatory CLE rules for New York?

A These are available at our website, **www.nysba.org**. Click on the CLE tab, scroll to CLE Information, Policies and Order Forms, and click on Mandatory CLE Rules for New York State. A more detailed discussion of the rules and requirements can be found on the OCA website: http://www.nycourts.gov/attorneys/cle/newattorney_faqs.shtml.

MORE ABOUT THE NEW YORK STATE BAR ASSOCIATION

A visit to our website, **www.nysba.org**, will answer most of your questions about NYSBA and provide contact information for answers to more specific inquiries.

Here are a few of the most frequently asked questions.

Q Is NYSBA part of state government?

A NYSBA is a private voluntary membership organization administered by attorneys who are elected by the membership. While the Association does lobby the Legislature on issues involving proposed laws, it does so strictly as a private party. NYSBA also issues ethics opinions on many areas of practice, but these opinions are not official state rules.

Q As a newly admitted attorney, I'll likely have a question or two about ethics, court rulings and general matters of practice management. How can NYSBA help me find the answers?

A The best way is to join one or more of NYSBA member-only online communities. Once you join a community, you will have colleagues and resources to help guide you on your way. In fact, the document resources of all communities will likely have information that will be helpful to you.

A number of helpful resources are right on our website. Go to www. nysba.org and click on the Professional Conduct link. This will take you to the Professional Conduct Resources for New York Attorneys page, which has links to all NYSBA Ethics Opinions from 1964 to the present, the New York Rules of Professional Conduct with Comments, resources for marketing your practice, rules and guidance on attorney advertising and business development, and more detailed information on ethics and escrow accounts, and ethics and the Interest on Lawyers Account.

Q I'd like to start my own practice. Does NYSBA have any resources for newly solo practitioners?

A Start at our website, **www.nysba.org**, and click on the Practice Resources link. You can also call NYSBA at 518.463.3200 and ask for the Law Practice Management department.

I FORGOT . . .

Q I forgot my password. How do I log in?

A For Login assistance, please call NYSBA's Member Resource Center at 800.582.2452. Our telephone hours are Monday-Friday, 8:00 a.m. – 4:45 p.m.

Two Member Benefits Offer Assistance With Every Lawyer's Daily Practice

Highlighted below are two of the Association's premier exclusive member benefits: LoislawConnect CaseAlert Service and Fastcase Legal Research. Both can help members succeed in their daily practices.

LoislawConnect CaseAlert

The NYSBA/LoislawConnect LawWatch CaseAlert Service is a free member benefit that allows members who sign up to receive email alerts of new cases in one of 20 areas of practice. The New York State Bar Association was the first bar association in the country to provide this service.

This is how it works: several pre-selected searches, each relevant to a particular area of the law, have been assigned to the practice areas. Members may elect to receive email alerts in one area of their choice.

When a new decision that matches the search terms in the selected area is published, an excerpt from the case will be automatically emailed to the member. In that email, a link will be provided that allows free access to the full text of the case.

Practice areas are antitrust, business, commercial, corporate, criminal, elder, entertainment, environmental, family, health, immigration, insurance, intellectual property, international, labor, municipal, real property, tax, torts, trusts and estates law.

For more information, visit www.nysba.org/casealert.

Fastcase

State Bar members can take advantage of free legal research service from Fastcase. Members receive free and unlimited access to the following libraries: New York Court of Appeals, Appellate Division decisions, miscellaneous decisions, New York Consolidated Laws, New York Codes Rules and Regulations (N.Y.C.R.R.), New York State Constitution, U.S. Code, 2d Circuit decisions and Supreme Court decisions.

Members who prefer unlimited access to the full Fastcase law library—which includes all federal and state research—can receive an 80 percent discount off the regular price of $995 (that means members pay just $195 per year).

The State Bar's newly admitted attorney members receive free access to the full Fastcase research libraries for the first two years after being admitted. For more information, visit www.nysba.org/fastcase.

Search Tips

Fastcase knows the difference between a generally authoritative case and a case that is authoritative for a specific search.

Just about every legal research service will give subscribers some idea of how authoritative a case is—meaning how many times other cases have cited to it. That's useful to some extent, but what if a member wants to know the most authoritative cases for a specific issue? Fastcase has that covered.

When a search is run, look at the search results on the far right side of the screen. Under the Authority Check header, notice two columns: "Entire Database" and "These Results." The number under "Entire Database" means how many times the case has been cited by all other cases in the Fastcase database.

That's a useful tool; but the magic is really in the "These Results" number. That number reflects how many times the cases for the member's specific search have been cited by the current search results. In other words, Fastcase can display which cases are the most frequently cited cases for any specific search.

Search by Party Name

Fastcase allows subscribers to easily look up cases by party name. Select as much information as is known, type the party names and search away. Simply navigate to the search caselaw page, select the known information about the case (date range, jurisdiction, etc.), then click search.

If unsure about the exact spelling of the name, consider pairing this feature with a wildcard operator (*) to match alternative spellings of the party names. Litig* returns cases containing the words litigator, litigation, litigious, litigants, etc. Eat* returns cases containing the words eat, eaten, eatery, eaters, eating, etc. In short, it searches all the various ways a court can phrase any particular word.

Search by Jurisdiction

Fastcase can filter search results by jurisdiction. Simply run a search, then change the Jurisdiction dropdown to any court. When a list of case law searches is generated, subscribers can filter the list to cases from just one jurisdiction. For example, search all federal appellate courts for "felony murder." Well over 1,000 results will be found.

If interested in seeing only cases from a specific Circuit Court of Appeals mentioning that phrase, don't re-run the search, simply select the circuit from the jurisdiction filter at the top, left-hand side of the screen. The results will change from 1,000+ to far fewer as the results from the initial search in other jurisdictions are temporarily hidden. Instantly return to the full list by selecting "All Jurisdictions" from the drop-down Jurisdiction filter.

Customer Support

Also free to active State Bar members is @Fastcase, live-chat assistance with a research associate. The Fastcase customer outreach team is an important part of the company's mission to help members work harder and smarter.

To access live chat, just select Live Help from the Help menu at the top of the screen. A Live Chat window will open. Type in a question and wait for a Fastcase customer support associate to respond.

Members who cannot attend any of the three monthly Fastcase webinars can check out their training page for short video tutorials, one-page cheat sheets, and more. Go to www.fastcase.com/support/. Fastcase offers three different training webinars (Introduction to Fastcase, Advanced Legal Research on Fastcase and Boolean Searching on Fastcase). Sign up for them at www.fastcase.com/webinars.

This article originally appeared in the September/October 2014 NYSBA *State Bar News*.

Ethics Opinions

The Association's Professional Ethics Committee was established in 1952. Its main purpose is to "answer inquiries as to whether conduct of a member of the legal profession complies with the applicable New York rules or legal or judicial ethics..." Since its formation, the Committee has issued more than 1,000 formal opinions, all of which are available on the Association's web site under Professional Conduct. It has also issued numerous informal opinions, which are sent only to the inquirer and are confidential. While the Committee's opinions are not binding on disciplinary authorities, they are often cited as the opinions of experts in the interpretation of the Rules.

Any attorney may seek an opinion. The inquiry must seek advice about the conduct of the inquirer, as the Committee will not offer advice on the conduct of an attorney other than the person making the inquiry. In addition, the question must concern the future conduct of the inquirer. Fundamentally, the purpose of the service is to guide attorneys as to how to proceed when faced with an ethical question. It should be noted that the advice given is limited to ethical questions governed by the Rules of Professional Conduct. The Association does not advise attorneys on questions of law.

Any attorney seeking advice should submit his or her request to ethics@nysba.org. If there is a previous opinion of the Committee that answers the question, the inquirer will be referred to that opinion. If there is no precedential opinion, the request will be sent to the Professional Ethics Committee, which will consider the matter and issue an opinion. Opinions usually take several months. If immediate advice is needed and there is no precedent, the inquirer will be referred to a member of the committee who will discuss the matter with the inquirer. That member will give guidance, although that guidance would not constitute an opinion.

Lawyer Assistance Program

Statement of Purpose

The New York State Bar Association Lawyer Assistance Program (LAP) provides education and confidential assistance to lawyers, judges and law students who are affected by substance abuse, stress, depression or other mental health issues. Its goal is to assist in the prevention, early identification and intervention of problems that can affect professional conduct and quality of life.

Confidentiality

All LAP services are confidential and protected under Section 499 of the Judiciary Law as amended by Chapter 327 of the Laws of 1993.

LAP Services Are Confidential, Voluntary, Free and Include:

- Early identification of impairment;

- intervention and motivation of impaired attorneys to seek help;

- assessment, evaluation and development of an appropriate treatment plan;

- referral of impaired attorneys to community resources, self-help groups, outpatient counseling, detoxification and rehabilitation services;

- information and referral for depression; and

- training programs on alcoholism, drug abuse and stress management.

Lawyer Referral: Good for Lawyers, Clients

By Brandon Vogel

When Donna Chin moved from New Jersey to Ithaca, New York, she wanted to change the focus of her law practice after receiving a master of laws degree.

So, she joined the New York State Bar Association. She also joined the Lawyer Referral and Information Service (LRIS) panel as a way to build her nonprofit practice. She was not disappointed.

"It helped bring me into the local courts," said Chin, who concentrates her practice in appeals, formation of nonprofits and compliance for businesses. "It has been a positive experience. It's a good way for solo and small firm lawyers to build a client base, diversify their practice and do good. For me, it allowed me to practice the law that I choose to do now."

Chin's experience reflects that of other solo and small-firm practitioners who have used the LRIS to expand their practice and client roster.

Chin is a member of the Committee on Lawyer Referral Service, which oversees LRIS operations. "It does good programs for the public and the public that need representation," said Chin.

Public Service

"Lawyer Referral services are the best way for the uninformed consumer to access an experienced attorney to address his or her legal matter," said Committee Chair Anna K. Christian of Albany (Boies, Schiller & Flexner LLP).

Lawyers who are State Bar members pay an annual fee of $75 to be listed on the panel for referrals. Non-members pay $125 to be listed. If a panel lawyer is retained by a referred client, the lawyers pay LRIS 10 percent of their fee for cases billed at $500 or more.

Christian is proud of the LRIS mission to serve the public needing legal services, and to provide panel lawyers with carefully screened clients. Notably, the LRIS reacted quickly in the aftermath of recent natural disasters—Hurricane Irene and Superstorm Sandy—recruiting attorneys from across the state to assist those requiring legal guidance with their insurance carriers, Federal Emergency Management Agency (FEMA) applications and other legal issues.

The LRIS seeks out and responds to unmet legal needs for New York citizens, creating a mutual benefit for the attorneys who become panel members of the service, and the clients in need of legal referrals.

For example, LRIS, with committee oversight, created a Veterans Panel reduced cost program in November 2013 to help veterans with a broad range of legal matters, including obtaining federal benefits, military discharge upgrades, adoptions and family law and bankruptcy. More than 250 attorneys around the state will have participated when the program ends on November 30.

Building a Client Base

By mid-October, LRIS had received more than 11,500 calls from the public in 2014. Of those requests, 2,355 were referred to a lawyer (about 20.4 percent).

Lawyer Referral and Information Service

Founded:
1981

Number of phone calls by mid-October in 2014:
11,531

Number of referrals by mid-October in 2014:
2,355

Most frequent referrals:
Negligence and tort (11 percent); matrimonial and divorce (6.8 percent); and criminal law (5.35 percent).

Counties served: 44
Allegany, Cattaraugus, Cayuga, Chautauqua, Chemung, Chenango, Clinton, Columbia, Cortland, Delaware, Essex, Franklin, Fulton, Genesee, Greene, Hamilton, Herkimer, Jefferson, Lewis, Livingston, Madison, Montgomery, Niagara, Oneida, Ontario, Orleans, Oswego, Otsego, Rensselaer, St. Lawrence, Saratoga, Schenectady, Schoharie, Schuyler, Seneca, Steuben, Tioga, Tompkins, Ulster, Warren, Washington, Wayne, Wyoming, Yates

---

Elena Jaffe Tastensen of Saratoga Springs (Law Office of Elena Jaffe Tastensen, PLLC) benefited from the LRIS during her early years as a solo practitioner. After working as an assistant district attorney in New York County and as an attorney for the New York State Consumer Protection Board in Albany, Tastensen set up her own firm 10 years ago in Saratoga Springs. She concentrates her practice in family and matrimonial law, as well as criminal law.

She is enthusiastic about her experience as a member of the LRIS Panel. "It is absolutely a worthwhile experience," said Tastensen. "The LRIS really helped me grow my practice. Now that I have been in business for myself for more than 10 years, it's still a great way to find new clients."

She appreciates that attorneys can specify which areas they practice in and the kind of cases they can take. "It is a win-win," said Tastensen. "Attorneys get referrals for their practice. Clients get an attorney who is experienced in that area of law."

Frank M. Putorti, Jr. of Schenectady (Law Office of Frank M. Putorti, Jr.) won a medical malpractice case that was referred to him through the LRIS last year. It was one of the largest cases ever to come through the LRIS.

He noted that some clients call LRIS because they have been turned down by other attorneys. "I would like to see more clients go through LRIS because I think it's a good service," said Putorti. "Every lawyer should try it. It's a good thing."

Lawyers interested in joining the LRIS panel can find an application and more information at www.nysba.org/lawyerreferral.

BRANDON VOGEL is NYSBA's Social Media and Web Content Manager.

This article originally appeared in the November/December 2014 NYSBA *State Bar News*.

Lawyer Assistance Program: New Study Presents New Possibilities for Lawyer Well-Being

By Patrick McKenna and Patricia Spataro

What is the difference between a happy lawyer and an unhappy lawyer? Sounds like the beginning of a bad lawyer joke, doesn't it? But, the fact that many lawyers are very unhappy is nothing to joke about; it is a serious issue confronting the profession.

According to a study done by Florida State University Professors Lawrence Krieger and Kennon Sheldon, the results of which are compiled in a report released in February entitled, "What Makes Lawyers Happy: Transcending the Anecdotes with Data from 6,200 Lawyers," the difference between being a happy lawyer and an unhappy one lies in attitudes and values.

Krieger and Sheldon discovered that lawyers who find a career path that allow them some control over their daily work, the opportunity to connect with colleagues and to do work they feel competent doing are most likely to be happy and enjoy practicing law.

In fact, feeling connected, competent and autonomous was nearly four times more predictive of happiness than income, and five times more predictive than class rank. Similarly, lawyers who valued meaningful work were significantly happier and less prone to depression than lawyers with higher incomes.

In other words, the intrinsic value of service to others will facilitate a happy career much more so than the extrinsic value of a big paycheck.

Misplaced priorities early in the career of a lawyer can send a person down the wrong path. Once upon a time, the goal of being a high-income attorney was to enable a person to live well. But now, the outstanding debt that new lawyers are saddled with after law school makes considering money more of a necessity.

This can drive new lawyers into jobs that compromise their emotional needs. Life as a lawyer is demanding and stressful. Starting off on the wrong foot can only make matters worse. But, as you can see, there are many factors driving career path decisions.

As we've known for some time, the stress of being a lawyer can jeopardize a lawyer's mental health. It contributes to the high rate of alcoholism and depression experienced by members of the profession. Krieger and Sheldon's study clearly directs attorneys to guard their emotional well-being; and in doing so, they have a better shot at a happy career.

The trove of new data and findings may facilitate a shift in the legal profession toward a more proactive and positive approach to developing and supporting lawyer well-being. The Krieger-Sheldon Report is the largest and most detailed study of its type.

To place the report in historical context, it is instructive to review other lawyer well-being studies. The obvious recurring theme is that the legal profession has a serious and prevalent well-being problem that is manifesting in a growing number of maladies, behaviors and habits.

But, while these studies conclude that far too many lawyers are dangerously unhealthy and unhappy and professional implications are dire, little is offered by way of solution. Despite a broad consensus that this downward trajectory in well-being bodes ill for the entire profession, we are fighting it mainly by identifying and responding to individual crises.

It seems to be human nature to ignore problems until they are so out of proportion that denying them is no longer possible. The suggestions that prevention and early intervention as solutions emerging from this study are like fresh air for lawyer assistance.

For 25 years, NYSBA's Lawyer Assistance Program (LAP) has been a strong proponent of preventing problems. We are grateful to Krieger and Sheldon for proving our theory and clarifying that what's important has more to do with intrinsic values than extrinsic motivators. The results of this study will give our message of self-care more credibility.

The LAP remains steadfast in our mission to help those in crisis. But, we are very excited about having facts and proven strategies to promote well-being as a way not only to prevent serious mental health problems but, also, to enhance the quality of work life for lawyers.

PATRICK MCKENNA is a member of the NYSBA Lawyer Assistance Committee and the Judicial Wellness Committee.

PATRICIA SPATARO is the Director of the NYSBA Lawyer Assistance Program and can be reached at 800-255-0569.

This article originally appeared in the September/October 2014 NYSBA *State Bar News.*

No Matter Your Interests, Pro Bono Opportunities Abound

By Gloria Herron Arthur

Finding a pro bono project that suits your interests, needs and skill may be easier than you think.

Not every pro bono matter requires a long-term time commitment. There are plenty of short-term projects available assisting unrepresented litigants, such as an attorney-for-the day program or an evening brief advice and referral clinic.

Not a litigator? You don't have to be. Volunteer to explain court forms or assist a self-help litigant fill out a petition. On the other hand, if you desire a more intense pro bono opportunity, perhaps an appeal is just right for you, or handling a class action lawsuit. But whatever your preference, first, you have to get started.

Where to Start?

• Bar associations

The New York State Bar Association, the New York City Bar Association, Volunteers of Legal Services and Pro Bono.net jointly sponsor the online Pro Bono Opportunities Guide for Lawyers in New York State. Go to www.nysba.org/PBNET. This easy-to-use guide can be searched by county or by the substantive law area in which the volunteer wishes to serve.

The State Bar has several committees and sections that sponsor pro bono opportunities. For example, the Committee on Courts of Appellate Jurisdiction, in collaboration with The Legal Project and the Rural Law Center of New York, operates a pro bono appeals program in the Third and Fourth Departments.

The appeals program is designed to assist persons of modest means who do not qualify for assigned appellate counsel, whether they are taking or responding to an appeal. Preference is given to cases that may have a broad impact and involve the essentials of life, such as Family Court matters, education cases, family stability, health, housing, personal safety, public benefits, and subsistence income. For more information on the Appellate Pro Bono Project, go to www.nysba.org/probonoappeals.

Some of the larger county bar associations, such as the New York City, Nassau/Suffolk, Westchester, Albany, Onondaga, Monroe and Erie county bars, also offer a diverse range of pro bono opportunities. There are needs in veterans benefits, eviction defense, debtor/creditor projects, and mortgage foreclosure advice clinics. Don't be discouraged if these are not your usual areas of practice because training is available.

Another added benefit is that your pro bono work may qualify you to earn continuing legal education (CLE) credit. For more information, go to www.nycourts.gov and click on the link for Pro Bono.

• Legal services programs that serve low-income persons

Civil legal services programs across the state not only welcome volunteers but frequently offer free CLE training programs in core poverty law topics to attorneys who promise to accept a pre-screened case referral.

The State Bar regularly co-sponsors CLE pro bono recruitment programs in the Capital District with local legal services providers in domestic violence, landlord tenant cases, bankruptcy, Lesbian, Gay, Bisexual, Transgendered and Questioning issues and a host of other topics. The Capital District encompasses the Third and Fourth Judicial Districts.

To identify legal services providers in your area, visit www.LawHelpNY.org. This site can be searched by county and/or subject matter and briefly describes the legal services provided by the program.

• Volunteer attorney court programs

Under the supervision of court staff, volunteer attorneys can spend just a few hours, a full day or part of a day in a courthouse providing brief legal advice and assistance to self-represented litigants in consumer debt cases, family matters (e.g., custody, visitation and child support), landlord-tenant cases, matrimonials and uncontested divorce. The court system will provide free training with CLE credits. For more information on court-sponsored volunteer attorney programs, go to www.nycourts.gov and click on Pro Bono.

This brief listing of potential opportunities is not exclusive. For further help in locating a pro bono opportunity in your area, perhaps we can be of assistance. Contact the Department of Pro Bono Affairs at www.nysba.org/probono.

GLORIA HERRON ARTHUR is NYSBA's Pro Bono Director.

This article originally appeared in the May/June 2014 NYSBA *State Bar News.*

PATHWAY TO THE PROFESSION: FROM LAW SCHOOL TO LAWYER

THE PRACTICE OF LAW IN NEW YORK STATE

The Practice of Law in New York State

An Introduction for Newly-Admitted Attorneys

INTRODUCTION

This pamphlet is designed to assist persons seeking to practice law in New York, as well as newly-admitted attorneys, in learning about the court system, the requirements for admission to the bar, membership in the bar and practice in New York state. The pamphlet also contains a listing of some useful reference works and addresses.

The Court System

The court system in New York State, organized about 200 years ago, is generally divided along territorial lines. The courts in the state are listed below, starting with the court of highest authority:

1. Court of Appeals

2. Appellate Division of Supreme Court

3. Appellate Term of Supreme Court

4. Supreme Court

5. Court of Claims

6. Commercial Division

7. Litigation Coordinating Panel

8. Family Court

9. Surrogate's Court

10. County Courts

11. Problem-Solving Courts

12. Local Courts

* The following is reprinted from *The Courts of New York* (NYSBA 2015). This section is based on a publication of the Committee on Courts and the Community of the New York State Bar Association (1987) entitled *The Courts of New York State*. (See, also, relevant provisions of the New York State Constitution [especially Article VI]; the Judiciary Law; the Civil Practice Law and Rules and the Criminal Procedure Law [especially about appeals]; the various court acts including the Family Court Act, the Surrogate's Court Procedure Act, the Court of Claims Act, the New York City Criminal Court Act, the New York City Civil Court Act, the Uniform City Court Act, the Uniform District Court Act, the Uniform Justice Court Act, and relevant court rules.)

a. New York City Courts

b. Other City Courts

c. District Courts

d. Justice Courts

New York courts, with the exception of justice courts, are financed by the state and are administered by the Office of Court Administration under the authority of the Chief Judge of the State of New York. Each of these courts is discussed more fully below. The New York State Unified Court System (www.nycourts.gov) has links to individual court websites that provide decisions, court rules, the names of judges and court forms.

Court of Appeals

Founded in 1846, the Court of Appeals is the highest court in the state and the court of last resort for most cases. It is generally the ultimate authority on questions of law in New York State. Although a few cases involving questions of federal law or the United States Constitution eventually may be taken to the United States Supreme Court, these are rare. The Court of Appeals hears both criminal and civil appeals. (The distinctions between criminal and civil cases are discussed in later sections.)

This court, which convenes in Albany, consists of six associate judges and one Chief Judge, who also serves as Chief Judge of the state and chief judicial officer of the unified court system. All judges of this court are appointed by the governor, with the advice and consent of the state senate, from a list prepared by a nonpartisan nominating commission.

In 1869, the court was reorganized to comprise the current seven-judge panel. Judges were for the most part elected to the position, although the governor would appoint a replacement for a vacancy due to death or resignation. The last time judges were elected to the Court of Appeals was in 1974; since then, they have been appointed by the governor.

Appeals in civil cases must first be heard in one of the appellate divisions of the state's Supreme Court before being taken to the Court of Appeals. However, cases involving only questions of a statute's constitutionality may go directly to the Court of Appeals from the trial court. In cases that come through the Appellate Division, the appellant generally must obtain permission to appeal to the Court of Appeals. The only instances in which a case will automatically be sent to the Court of Appeals are when two justices of the Appellate Division dissent or a state or federal constitutional question is presented.

Except when a death sentence is involved, criminal cases must be appealed to the Appellate Division or Appellate Term first, and special permission must be obtained before the case may be taken to the Court of Appeals.

In addition to hearing appeals, the Court of Appeals is responsible for determining policy for the administration of the state's court system and for adopting rules governing the admission of attorneys to the bar.

Appellate Division of Supreme Court

The Appellate Division of the Supreme Court is the intermediate appellate court of the state. It hears civil and criminal appeals, reviewing the record established at trial in lower courts.

Created by the state constitution in 1894 and established in 1896, the Appellate Division was intended to be one court, whose departments would never sit together. It is divided geographically into four departments throughout the state; each department is responsible for hearing most appeals from the courts within its geographical area.

Justices of the Appellate Division are appointed by the governor from among Supreme Court justices. The number of justices on a hearing panel in a department will vary between four and five, depending on the caseload. The actual number of justices in each department is far higher—for example, there are currently about 20 justices in the Second Department.

Each department of the Appellate Division is responsible for admitting to practice and disciplining attorneys within its respective geographical region.

Although the Court of Appeals is the only court in the state whose decisions are binding on all of the state's lower courts, at times the decision of one appellate court will be binding on lower courts not within its geographical area. This occurs when there is no ruling from the appellate court in the trial court's own department. If two departments have different rulings on the same matter the lower courts must each follow their department's ruling.

Appellate Term of Supreme Court

The four departments of the Appellate Division are divided further into 13 judicial districts (see chart and map starting on page 22). The Appellate Term of the Supreme Court is unique to the First (New York County, the Bronx) and Second Judicial Departments (Kings, Queens, Staten Island, Nassau, Suffolk, Rockland, Westchester, Putnam, Dutchess and Orange Counties). The Appellate Term, which is composed of justices of the Supreme Court chosen by the Chief Administrator of the Courts with approval of the presiding justice of the Appellate Division, hears appeals from local and county courts. At least two and no more than three justices will preside in any case.

Supreme Court

The Supreme Court is the statewide trial court with the broadest jurisdiction, hearing both criminal and civil cases. It can hear virtually any type of case brought before it, with the exception of claims against the state, which must be brought in the Court of Claims.

The Supreme Court's practically unlimited jurisdiction makes its caseload correspondingly heavier than that of other courts. Consequently, attempts are generally made throughout the state to divide the workload among the Supreme Court and the lower courts of limited jurisdiction.

One area in which the Supreme Court must be involved, however, is in proceedings to end a marriage, because it is the only court that can grant a divorce, annulment or separation.

The Supreme Court is divided into 13 judicial districts statewide, and justices are elected in each district for terms of 14 years.

Family Court

The Family Court was established in 1962 to replace the Children's Court and New York City's Domestic Relations Court. The Family Court handles most cases involving youths between the ages of eight and 16 who are charged with offenses that would be crimes if committed by adults.

It also hears cases involving family disputes and child custody, determines support payments for families, handles adoptions, and may even determine the parentage of a child through paternity proceedings.

Family Court deals with all types of family problems except termination of a marriage, which the Supreme Court handles (see above). Family Court judges serve for 10-year terms. Outside New York City, they are elected; within the city of New York, such judges are appointed by the mayor.

Surrogate's Court

The Surrogate's Court is responsible for all matters relating to the property of deceased persons and to guardianships. Whether or not a person leaves a valid will, all claims on the estate brought by heirs, legatees or creditors are handled by the Surrogate's Court.

Judges of this court are elected in each county for terms of 10 years (14 years in New York City). Matters commonly dealt with in the Surrogate's Court include the probate of wills; the appointment and control of executors, administrators and trustees; adoptions; and the final settlement of estates.

County Court

A county court exists in each county of the state outside New York City (see "Local Courts" below for the equivalent in New York City). Judges are elected for 10-year terms, with the number of judges varying according to population. County Court judges preside over both criminal and civil cases.

Although the County Court's jurisdiction over criminal matters is almost unlimited (as is the Supreme Court's), its jurisdiction in civil cases is more restricted. Money claims in cases to be tried in this court may not exceed $25,000.

In sparsely populated counties, a single judge may be responsible for the Family Court, Surrogate's Court and County Court. In other counties, two judges may share the responsibility for these three courts or may be elected to only one or two of the courts. In the more populous counties outside New York City, different judges usually are elected to preside solely in the County Court, Family Court and Surrogate's Court.

Specialized Courts and Parts

1.   Court of Claims

Judges of the Court of Claims have the sole responsibility for hearing claims brought against the state of New York or certain state agencies. They are appointed by the governor, with the advice and consent of the state senate, for terms of nine years.

2.   Commercial Division

This division handles complicated commercial cases as part of the Supreme Court of New York State (www.nycourts.gov/courts/comdiv/).

In order for a matter to be heard in the Commercial Division, the case must be a commercial case and must meet a monetary threshold that varies depending on the county or district. The following are considered commercial cases:

1.   Where out of a business deal one or more of the following arises:

    a.   Breach of contract or fiduciary duty

    b.   Fraud or misrepresentation

    c.   Business tort

2.   Transactions governed by the Uniform Commercial Code

3.   Transactions involving commercial property

4.   Shareholder derivative actions

5.   Commercial class actions

6.   Business transactions involving commercial banks

7. Internal affairs of business organizations

8. Malpractice by accountants and legal malpractice out of representation in commercial matters

9. Environmental insurance coverage

10. Commercial insurance coverage

Without consideration of the monetary threshold, the following matters are included:

1. Dissolution of corporations, partnerships, LLCs, LLPs

2. Applications to stay or compel arbitration and affirm or disaffirm arbitration awards and related conjunctive relief pursuant to CPLR Article 75 involving any of the foregoing commercial issues

Commercial Divisions are located in eight counties—Albany, Kings, Nassau, New York, Onondaga, Queens, Suffolk and Westchester—and in the Seventh and Eighth Judicial Districts (www.nycourts.gov/rules/trial courts/202.shtml#70).

3.   Litigation Coordinating Panel

This panel receives and resolves applications for the coordination of litigation that is pending in more than one judicial district of the state but applies to pre-trial proceedings only. Its purpose is to facilitate the consistent and efficient resolution of cases. The panel is located in the Supreme Court, Civil Branch, of New York County but can hear applications from New York County or elsewhere around the state (www.nycourts.gov/courts/1jd/supctmanh/LCP/LCP-Index.shtml).

Problem-Solving Courts

Problem-solving courts are divided into the following:

1.   Adolescent Diversion Parts

Adolescent Diversion Parts handle matters concerning 16- and 17-year-old adolescents who have committed nonviolent crimes (www.nycourts. gov/courts/problem_solving/adp/index.shtml).[1]

2.   Community Courts

Community courts combine conventional punishments with alternative sanctions and on-site treatment and training. The court collaborates with citizens, criminal justice agencies, businesses, local civic organizations, government entities, and social service providers. The goal is to provide a type of neighborhood-focused problem solving (www.nycourts.gov/courts/problem_solving/cc/home.shtml).

---

1.   As of this writing, there is ongoing discussion about possibly raising the age of criminal responsiblity to 18.

3. Domestic Violence Courts

Domestic violence courts adjudicate criminal offenses involving intimate partners (www.nycourts.gov/courts/problem_solving/dv/home.shtml).

4. Drug Treatment Courts

The basic concept behind drug treatment courts is to invoke a dramatic intervention by the court in cooperation with an entire team including the defense, prosecution, treatment, education, and law enforcement. In return for a promise of a reduced sentence, appropriate nonviolent addicted offenders are given the option of entering voluntarily into court-supervised treatment (www.nycourts.gov/courts/problem_solving/drugcourts/overview.shtml).

5. Integrated Domestic Violence Courts

This court brings before a single judge the multiple criminal, family (civil) and matrimonial (divorce) disputes for families where domestic violence is an underlying issue (www.nycourts.gov/courts/problem_solving/idv/home.shtml).

6. Mental Health Courts

These courts handle criminal cases involving defendants with mental illness and focus on providing offenders with the support needed in order to avoid future criminal behavior (www.nycourts.gov/courts/problem_solving/mh/home.shtml).

7. Sex Offender Courts

The purpose of sex offender courts is to enhance public safety by preventing further victimization with early intervention and post-disposition monitoring (www.nycourts.gov/courts/problem_solving/so/home.shtml).

8. Veteran's Courts

A Veterans Treatment Court/Track is a separate court calendar within an existing drug treatment or mental health court that provides veteran defendants suffering from addiction, mental illness and/or co-occurring disorders with linkages to community-based services as well as local, state and federal agencies specializing in veteran's affairs (www.nycourts.gov/courts/problem_solving/vet/index.shtml).

9. Youthful Offender Domestic Violence Courts

These courts handle exclusively domestic violence cases involving defendants aged 16 through 19 (www.nycourts.gov/courts/problem_solving/yo/home.shtml).

Local Courts

1.   New York City Courts

In New York City, two courts have responsibilities different from those of courts elsewhere in the state. The Civil Court of the City of New York can hear civil matters involving amounts that do not exceed $25,000, as well as cases up to that amount involving real property within New York City. The judges of this court have citywide jurisdiction and are elected for 10-year terms.

The Housing Part of this court hears landlord-tenant cases and promotes enforcement of housing codes. This part is staffed by judges appointed for five-year terms by the administrative judge of the Civil Court.

A Small Claims Part hears cases brought by private individuals for amounts up to $5,000. The rules of this part of the court encourage informal and simplified procedures. A Small Claims Part is designed to make it easier for a person to sue for small amounts of money without having to be represented by an attorney (similar small claims parts are authorized for the other city, district and justice courts in the state).

The Commercial Claims Part of the New York City Civil Court is where certain business entities may bring small claims actions (similar commercial small claims parts are authorized for the other city and district courts in the state).

The Criminal Court of New York City has jurisdiction only over criminal matters. It can try all criminal cases except felonies, and it may conduct preliminary hearings in felony cases. Criminal court judges also serve as magistrates and can issue warrants of arrest. They are appointed by the mayor of New York City for 10-year terms.

2.   Other City Courts

Each of the 61 cities outside New York City has its own city court, and each has both criminal and civil jurisdiction.

In criminal matters, the city court can try cases involving misdemeanors or minor violations, and it can hear preliminary matters in felony cases. A city court also can hear civil cases involving not more than $15,000, as well as landlord-tenant disputes.

Judges of city courts must be attorneys who have been licensed to practice law in New York State for at least five years. They are elected by voters in their respective cities for terms of 10 years, or six years in the case of part-time judges.

Some city courts also have a Small Claims Part, which can hear matters for amounts of up to $5,000.

3.   District Courts

District courts currently exist only in Nassau and Suffolk Counties, where they have limited jurisdiction over both civil and criminal cases.

In criminal matters, the district court can try all offenses except felonies, and it can hear preliminary matters in felony cases. In civil matters, the court is limited to cases involving claims for $15,000 or less. It also may hear some matters concerning liens on property and landlord-tenant disputes.

Judges of this court, who must be lawyers, are elected by district voters for terms of six years.

4. Justice Courts

Justice courts consist of town and village courts. The judges of these courts, often formerly referred to as justices of the peace, need not be lawyers, although they must meet special training requirements. They are elected to four-year terms by the locality they serve.

Justice courts can hear both criminal and civil cases, but their jurisdiction in both instances is severely limited. In criminal matters, justice courts can try misdemeanors, traffic cases and minor violations, and can conduct preliminary proceedings in felony cases.

In civil matters, justice courts may hear cases where no more than $3,000 worth of property or money is in dispute. Also, landlord-tenant cases may be heard there, regardless of the amount of rent involved. A justice court may not decide a case involving title to real property.

5. Judicial Conduct Commission

The state constitution provides for a Commission on Judicial Conduct, which has the authority to impose sanctions, from admonition to removal, on judges and justices of state and local courts and to retire them for disability, subject to review by the Court of Appeals.

6. Alternative Methods of Dispute Resolution

Alternative dispute resolution (ADR) is an umbrella term used to describe a variety of processes and techniques to resolve disputes. The unified court system has developed a number of pilot ADR programs for different types of cases throughout the state. Experimentation has been encouraged in the courts at every level using mediation, arbitration, neutral evaluation and summary jury trials. Furthermore, given New York's extraordinary size and diverse regions, each of these initiatives is tailored to the particular community and court environment in which it operates. The Community Dispute Resolution Centers Program, administered by the Office of Court Administration, and available in all 62 counties of the state, provides financial support to nonprofit organizations that offer dispute resolution services. Community dispute resolution centers offer mediation and some arbitration services as an alternative to criminal, civil and Family Court litigation. In addition to providing dispute resolution services, many of the centers offer a variety of educational, facilitative and preventive services in their communities that help people to manage and resolve conflicts before they reach the court system

NEW YORK STATE JUDICIAL SYSTEM
CIVIL APPEALS STRUCTURE

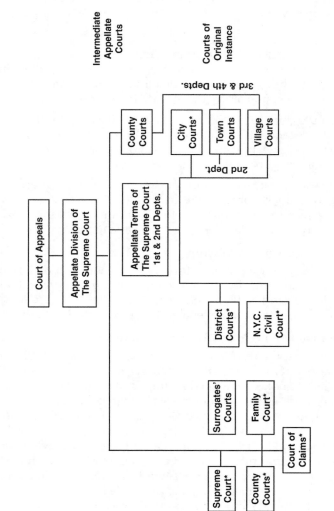

Intermediate Appellate Courts

Courts of Original Instance

Court of Appeals

Appellate Division of The Supreme Court

Appellate Terms of The Supreme Court 1st & 2nd Depts.

County Courts

City Courts*

Town Courts

Village Courts

3rd & 4th Depts.

2nd Dept.

District Courts*

N.Y.C. Civil Court*

Surrogates' Courts

Family Court*

Court of Claims*

Supreme Court*

County Courts*

*Appeals from judgments of courts of record of original instance that finally determine actions where the only question involved is the validity of a statutory provision under the New York state or United States Constitution may be taken directly to the Court of Appeals.

Source: State of New York Office of Court Administration.

NEW YORK STATE JUDICIAL SYSTEM
CRIMINAL APPEALS STRUCTURE

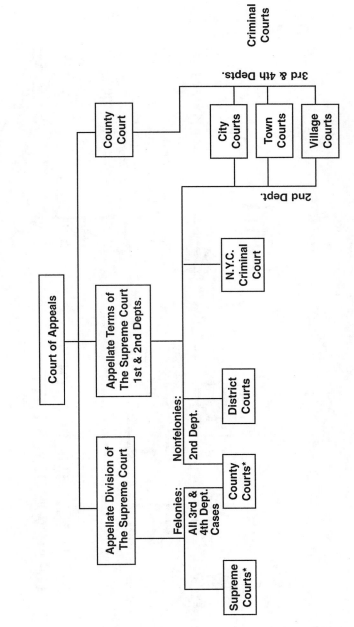

*Appeals involving death sentences must be taken directly to the Court of Appeals.

Source: State of New York Office of Court Administration.

C. Map and Chart of New York State Judicial Districts*

(New York County) I
(Kings Counties) II
(Nassau & Sufflok Counties) X
(Queens County) XI
(Bronx County) XII
(Richmond County) XIII

JUDICIAL DISTRICTS OF NEW YORK STATE

*This map and chart are reprinted from page 57 of the 2009 New York Lawyers Diary and Manual.

New York State Counties by Judicial Department and District

FIRST DEPARTMENT
First Judicial District
New York

Twelfth Judicial District
Bronx

SECOND DEPARTMENT
Second Judicial District
Kings

Ninth Judicial District
Dutchess
Orange
Putnam
Rockland
Westchester

Tenth Judicial District
Nassau
Suffolk

Eleventh Judicial District
Queens

Thirteenth Judicial District
Richmond

THIRD DEPARTMENT
Third Judicial District
Albany
Columbia
Greene
Rensselaer
Schoharie
Sullivan
Ulster

Fourth Judicial District
Clinton
Essex
Franklin
Fulton
Hamilton
Montgomery
Saratoga
Schenectady
St. Lawrence
Warren
Washington

Sixth Judicial District
Broome
Chemung
Chenango
Cortland
Delaware
Madison
Otsego
Schuyler
Tioga
Tompkins

FOURTH DEPARTMENT
Fifth Judicial District
Herkimer
Jefferson
Lewis
Oneida
Onondaga
Oswego

Seventh Judicial District
Cayuga
Livingston
Monroe
Ontario
Seneca
Steuben
Wayne
Yates

Eighth Judicial District
Allegany
Cattaraugus
Chautauqua
Erie
Genesee
Niagara
Orleans
Wyoming

D. Auxiliary Programs and Court-Related Agencies*

APPELLATE AUXILIARY OPERATIONS

State Reporter
State Board of Law Examiners
Candidate Examination Program
Candidate Fitness Program
Attorney Discipline Program
Assigned Counsel Program
Attorneys for Children Program
Mental Hygiene Legal Service Program

COURT-RELATED AGENCIES

Commissioners of Jurors and New York City County Clerks
Supreme and County Court Libraries
Lawyers' Fund for Client Protection
IOLA Fund of the State of New York
Judicial Conduct Commission
New York State Judicial Institute

Appellate Auxiliary Operations

The Appellate Auxiliary Operations include the State Reporter, State Board of Law Examiners, Candidate Fitness Program, Assigned Counsel Program, Law Guardian Program, Attorney Discipline Program and the Mental Hygiene Legal Service Program. With the exception of the State Reporter and the State Board of Law Examiners, which are operated under the direction of the Court of Appeals, all of the above programs are administered under the supervision of the presiding justices of each of the Appellate Division.

State Reporter

The State Reporter is the chief executive officer of the New York State Law Reporting Bureau which operates under the general supervision of the Court of Appeals. Pursuant to statutory mandate, the New York State Law Reporting Bureau edits and headnotes the decisions of the New York courts, and supervises their publication in weekly Advance Sheets, bound volumes, and an online computer retrieval database of the Official New York Law Reports. The New York State Law Reporting Bureau makes available all opinions and memoranda decisions handed down by the Court of Appeals, Appellate Divisions and Appellate Terms, and publishes selected opinions of the *nisi prius* courts which contain holdings of precedential significance or address matters of public interest [go to www.nycourts.gov/reporter where unpublished trial court writings are available, or call (518) 453-6900]. The State Reporter also prepares the *Official New York Law Reports Style Manual* which sets forth citation

---

* The following is largely taken from *Structure of the Courts* (1986) produced by the State of New York Unified Court System.

guidelines for use in judicial opinions and in legal writings submitted to the New York courts.

State Board of Law Examiners

The State Board of Law Examiners runs the Candidate Examination Program under the general supervision of the Court of Appeals. The board determines, by examination or credential review, whether a candidate for the bar is qualified to practice law in New York state. The board insures that only competent persons, sufficiently learned in the law, are permitted to practice in New York state. For more information, see page 31 of this booklet, or go to the State Board of Law Examiners Web site www.nybarexam.org.

Candidate Fitness Program

The Candidate Fitness Program determines whether candidates possess the demonstrated ethical character required in order to be admitted to the bar. The Candidate Fitness Program is administered by the Appellate Division Departments, in conjunction with their Committees on Character and Fitness.

Attorney Discipline Program

Through the Attorney Discipline Program, appointed committees conduct investigations of alleged attorney misconduct, impose confidential discipline (which, depending on the Judicial Department, may include letters of caution, and oral and written admonitions) and, in more serious cases, prosecute charges before the Appellate Division, which proceedings may result in public censure, suspension or disbarment of the attorney. The purpose of the program is to protect the public, deter attorney misconduct, and preserve the reputation of the bar

*   *   *

The following programs provide services, including counsel, to those unable to obtain such services themselves.

Section 35 of the Judiciary Law—Assigned Counsel Program

Section 35 of the Judiciary Law established an Assigned Counsel Program which provides legal services to persons alleged to be mentally ill, mentally defective, narcotics addicts or children in certain custody proceedings; provides indigents before the courts with medical and psychiatric examination services, and provides legal services to indigents in certain kinds of proceedings when such services cannot be provided through other sources. (Public defender and legal service agencies also provide legal services for persons accused of crimes and others; see also County Law article 18B and other provisions such as Family Court Act § 261, Surrogate's Court Procedure Act § 403-a, and Civil Practice Law and Rules § 1102).

Attorneys for Children Program

The general purpose of the Attorneys for Children Program is to provide counsel to minors in certain proceedings in Family Court, such as juvenile delinquency, persons in need of supervision, and child protective proceedings. In addition, the court has the discretion to appoint an attorney in any proceeding when such representation will serve the purposes of the Family Court Act.

Mental Hygiene Legal Service Program

The Mental Hygiene Legal Service Program (MHLS) ensures that mentally disabled persons who are under care that restricts their freedom are afforded due process of the law. In carrying out this responsibility, the MHLS provides or procures legal counsel for patients in judicial proceedings concerning confinement, care and treatment.

Court-Related Agencies

Commissioner of Jurors and New York City County Clerks

The Commissioner of Jurors' Offices are responsible for supplying the trial courts with prospective jurors and for the management of a variety of functions related to discharging this responsibility, including summoning and qualification of citizens for jury services, the maintenance of juror service records, and the operation of juror assembly rooms.

In New York City, the five county clerks serve as commissioners of jurors and also perform a variety of non-jury functions including among others, the maintenance of Supreme Court case records, the qualification of notary publics and commissioners of deeds, the filing of corporation and business certificates, and the processing of passports. Outside the city of New York, county clerks are elected county-paid officials, who, in addition to many non-court functions, maintain County Court and Supreme Court records.

Supreme and County Court Law Libraries

The law libraries serve as major legal research centers and often serve as the only legal resources available to the local bench, bar and public.

Lawyers' Fund for Client Protection*

The Lawyers' Fund for Client Protection—previously the Clients' Security Fund—is a state agency financed principally by a $60 share of each lawyer's $375 biennial registration fee. The Fund receives no revenues from the IOLA program, or from state tax revenues.

---

* See Section on Client Funds (infra) for more information on the Lawyers' Fund for Client Protection and IOLA.

The Fund is administered pro bono publico by a board of trustees appointed by the judges of the state Court of Appeals. There are seven trustees: currently five lawyers and two business executives.

The trustees are authorized to reimburse law clients for money or property that is misappropriated by a member of the bar in the practice of law. Since the Fund's inception in 1982, the Fund has restored more than $132 million to victims of dishonest conduct in the practice of law.

To qualify for reimbursement, the loss must involve the misuse of clients' money or property in the practice of law. The trustees cannot settle fee disputes, compensate clients for malpractice or neglect, or reimburse losses from activities unrelated to an attorney-client relationship. Awards of reimbursement are generally made after a lawyer's disbarment, and where it appears that the lawyer cannot make restitution.

Typical losses reimbursed by the Fund include the theft of estate and trust assets; down payments and the proceeds in real property transactions; debt collection proceeds; personal injury settlements; and money embezzled from clients in investment transactions arising from an attorney-client relationship and the practice of law.

Financial sanctions against attorneys during litigation or imposed by court rules for engaging in frivolous conduct are made payable to the Fund. The Fund is also provided notice of any dishonored checks drawn upon an attorney's trust, escrow or special account.

The Fund's governing statutes are sections 97-t of the State Finance Law and 468-b of the Judiciary Law. The trustees' regulations are published in 22 NYCRR Part 7200. By Appellate Division rules and the trustees' regulations, lawyers who assist claimants before the Fund cannot charge legal fees.

The Fund's offices are located at 119 Washington Avenue, Albany, New York 12210. Telephone (518) 434-1935, or (800) 442-3863. The Fund's Web site, www.nylawfund.org, contains information about the Fund, frequently asked questions about the Fund and its procedures; the trustees' regulations; reimbursement claim forms; recent annual reports; and consumer and lawyer publications.

IOLA

IOLA is the acronym for "Interest on Lawyer Accounts." Pursuant to State Finance Law § 97-v and Judiciary Law § 497, lawyers and law firms are required to establish interest-bearing trust accounts for clients' funds that are nominal in amount, or are expected to be held for a short period of time making it impractical to account for income on individual deposits. The interest earned will be forwarded directly by the financial institutions to the IOLA Fund for the following purposes: (a) to award funds to organizations providing legal assistance to the poor throughout the state; and (b) to grant awards to programs for the improvement of the admin-

istration of justice in New York state. More information can be obtained
by writing to Interest On Lawyer Account Fund of the State of New York,
11 East 44th Street, Suite 1406, New York, NY 10017, or telephoning (646)
865-1541 or (800) 222-IOLA. Attorneys must enroll new IOLA accounts
with the IOLA fund via its website: www.iola.org.

Judicial Conduct Commission

The state constitution provides for a Commission on Judicial Conduct with authority to determine discipline, from admonition to removal,
of judges and justices of state and local courts and to retire them for
disabilities, subject to review by the Court of Appeals. Contact information: 61 Broadway, New York, NY 10006, (646) 386-4800, cjc@cjc.ny.gov.
Website address: www.cjc.ny.gov.

New York State Judicial Institute

The Judicial Institute provides a forum for judicial scholarships,
including continuing education and seminars, as well as programs with
other state and federal judicial systems. Contact information: 84 North
Broadway, White Plains, NY 10603, (914) 824-5800.

E.   Overview of Administrative Structure of Court System

The following description of court administration is taken, in large
part, from pages 136-138 of the *New York Legal Research Guide* by Ellen M.
Gibson (published by William S. Hein & Co., Inc., Buffalo, NY, 1988).

Court Administration

Court administration is governed by article VI, section 28, of the
New York Constitution and sections 210 through 217 of the Judiciary
Law. The present administrative structure is the result of constitutional
amendments and legislation which went into effect in the 1960's and
1970's.

The Chief Judge and the Administrative Board of the Courts. New
York has had the framework for "a unified court system" since 1961. The
chief judge of the Court of Appeals is the Unified Court System's chief
judicial officer and chair of the Administrative Board of the Courts. In
addition to the chief judge, members of the Administrative Board of the
Courts are the presiding justices from each judicial department. The chief
judge, after consultation with the board, establishes standards and administrative policies applicable to the Unified Court System. These must
be approved by the Court of Appeals.

The Chief Administrator of the Courts. The chief administrator of
the courts is appointed by the chief judge with the advice and consent
of the board. If the chief administrator is a judge or justice in the Unified
Court System, he or she holds the title of chief administrative judge. The
chief administrator supervises the administration and operation of the
Unified Court System.

The chief administrator's annual report to the governor on the activities of the Unified Court System is the best source for statistics on the courts and for current descriptions of the court structure and administration. Additional useful information included in the annual report are the number of registered attorneys by county and judicial department, personnel and budgetary information on the court system, a summary of educational and training programs conducted during the year, and a summary of legislation sponsored by the chief administrator. The current series of annual reports covers 1978 to date. Prior to 1978, the above-described annual information on the court system was published in the annual reports of the Administrative Board of the Judicial Conference (1962-1977), the Judicial Conference (1955-1961), and the annual reports of the Judicial Council (1934-1954).

Office of Court Administration. The Office of Court Administration (OCA) was established in 1974. The OCA assists the chief administrator in the operation of the unified court system. Its responsibilities include budget preparation and management of the unified court system, attorney registration, and administration of the Community Dispute Resolution Centers Program. The OCA counsel's office has an important legislative role. Its legal staff assists the legislative advisory committees on civil practice, criminal law and procedure, the Surrogate's Court, and Family Court.

The Judicial Conference. The Judicial Conference is a large advisory body composed of: the chief judge of the Court of Appeals; the presiding Appellate Division justice and one Supreme Court justice from each of the four judicial departments; representative judges from the other courts; and representatives from the state bar. The chairpersons and ranking minority members of the Senate and the Assembly Committees on the Judiciary and Committees on Codes are ex officio members of the Judicial Conference.

The Judicial Conference studies and makes recommendations for changes in laws and rules relating to civil, criminal and family law practice. The Judicial Conference also advises the chief administrator of the courts on education programs for the judicial and non-judicial personnel of the unified court system. When requested to do so, it consults with the chief judge and chief administrator on the operation of the court system. Many of the functions now performed by the Administrative Board of the Courts were performed by the Judicial Council (from 1934-1954) and the Judicial Conference (from 1955-1977).

F.   Federal Court

There are four United States District Courts in New York State as follows:

Southern District

The Southern District covers the counties of Bronx, New York, Dutchess, Orange, Putnam, Rockland, Sullivan and Westchester.

Eastern District

The Eastern District covers the counties of Kings, Queens, Nassau, Suffolk and Richmond.

Western District

The Western District covers the counties of Allegany, Cattaraugus, Chautauqua, Chemung, Erie, Genesee, Livingston, Monroe, Niagara, Ontario, Orleans, Schuyler, Seneca, Steuben, Wayne, Wyoming and Yates.

Northern District

The Northern District covers the counties of Albany, Broome, Cayuga, Chenango, Clinton, Columbia, Cortland, Delaware, Essex, Franklin, Fulton, Greene, Hamilton, Herkimer, Jefferson, Lewis, Madison, Montgomery, Oneida, Onondaga, Oswego, Otsego, Rensselaer, St. Lawrence, Saratoga, Schenectady, Schoharie, Tioga, Tompkins, Ulster, Warren and Washington.

* * *

The United States Court of Appeals for the Second Circuit, covering Connecticut, New York and Vermont, is located in the United States Court House, 40 Foley Square, New York, New York 10007.

Both the United States Court of International Trade and the United States Tax Court also have courtrooms in New York City. The United States Bankruptcy Court sits in numerous locations throughout New York state; it is territorially divided along lines similar to the United States District Courts.

II.   Admission to the New York State Bar*

A.   Admission on Examination**

In general, after graduating from an approved law school, you must gain admission to the New York State Bar in order to practice law. Such applicants for admission are required to possess good moral character and fitness and successfully complete a written examination.

---

* Admission to the New York State Bar is generally governed by the following statutes and court rules: Judiciary Law §§ 53, 56, 90, 460-468-a, 478, 484; CPLR article 94; Rules of the Court of Appeals, 22 NYCRR Part 520; Rules of the Appellate Divisions: First Department: Part 602; Second Department: Part 690, 692; Third Department: Part 805; Fourth Department: § 1022.9, 1022,34; Part 1029.

**The following is largely reprinted from *Law as a Career in New York State* (1989) published by the New York State Bar Association.

ADMINISTRATIVE STRUCTURE

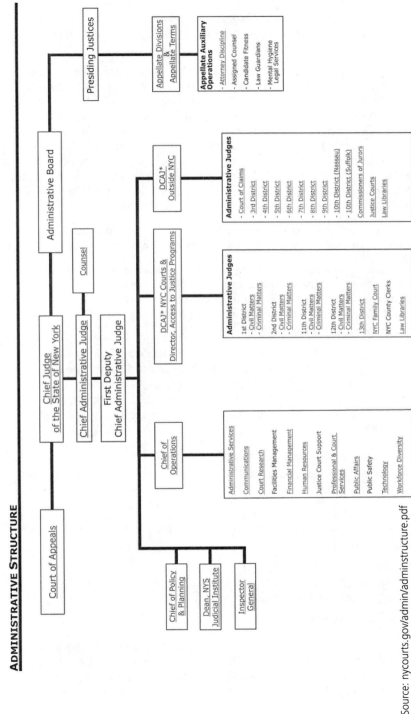

Source: nycourts.gov/admin/adminstructure.pdf

*DCAJ - Deputy Chief Administrative Judge

Chart provided by Office of Court Administration.

The written exam in New York state is administered by the State Board of Law Examiners and is given twice each year, in February and July.

The two-day examination includes the Multistate Bar Examination which is a multiple-choice, day-long test that covers subjects applicable in all states. Another part is a full-day exam consisting mainly of essay questions which require application of New York state law to a series of complex fact patterns. One Multistate Performance Test (MPT) question (a national exam) has been added in lieu of one of the former six essay questions. In addition to the New York State Bar Exam, an applicant must also take and pass the Multistate Professional Responsibility Examination (MPRE), which deals with professional responsibility issues. The MPRE can be taken prior to or after graduation from law school.

For more information about the New York bar examination see the Web site of the State Board of Law Examiners: www.nybarexam.org.

Following passage of the bar exam, the applicant is certified for admission to a Committee on Character and Fitness in one of the four Departments of the Appellate Division of State Supreme Court. He or she must file an application for admission to the bar with the appropriate Appellate Division Department.

Each applicant has a personal interview with the Character and Fitness Committee. After the Character and Fitness Committee recommends to the Appellate Division that the applicant be admitted to the practice of law in New York state, upon approval by the court, formal swearing-in ceremonies are then conducted by a Department of the Appellate Division.

B.   Admission Without Examination

In general, to be admitted to the New York state bar without examination, an applicant must:

1. Be currently admitted to the bar of at least one other jurisdiction which would similarly admit a New York state attorney to its bar without examination;

2. Have actually practiced, for at least five of the seven years immediately preceding the application, in one or more jurisdictions where admitted to practice;

3. Be over 26 years of age;

4. Have the necessary legal education to qualify applicant for admission without examination (have an approved American law school juris doctorate degree); (the legal education must be certified by the State Board of Law Examiners; $400 fee); and

5. Satisfy the Appellate Division that he or she possesses the character and general fitness requisite for an attorney and counselor-at-law by submitting an application to the appropriate Appellate Division Committee on Character and Fitness; also requires an interview by the Committee on Character and Fitness.

For further information on the legal education requirement, see the Web site of the State Board of Law Examiners: www.nybarexam.org. For further information on the other requirements, contact the admissions office of the appropriate Department of the Appellate Division. In general, each Appellate Division Department handles the applications of persons having residence or full-time employment within the geographical boundaries of the department; the Third Judicial Department (which is centered in Albany) also is responsible for applicants who neither reside in nor have full-time employment in New York state.

C. Legal Consultants, In-House Counsel Pro Hac Vice, Student Legal Practice

Legal consultants are foreign attorneys with offices in New York state licensed to give legal advice on the law of the foreign country in which they have been admitted (see Judiciary Law § 53; Court of Appeals Rules, Part 521). In-house counsel are attorneys who, though not admitted to the NY bar, are employed full time in New York by a non-governmental corporation, partnership, association, or other legal entity that is not itself engaged in the practice of law or the rendering of legal services outside such organization. Application to register as an In-house counsel must be made with the Appellate Division of the Supreme Court (see Court of Appeals Rules, Part 522; Rules of the Chief Administrator, Part 118). *Pro hac vice* admissions for particular causes are generally reserved to the discretion of the particular court in which the admission is sought (see Court of Appeals Rules, Section 520.11). *Pro hac vice* admissions for specified time periods are also available for certain students and employees of certain legal aid societies and government entities (see also, Court of Appeals Rules, Part 520.11[a] [2]). Student legal practice is governed by Judiciary Law §§ 478 and 484 and relevant Appellate Division rules.

D. Oath of Office

Upon being admitted to practice in the state of New York, each applicant is required to swear (or affirm) the following constitutional oath of office (see Judiciary Law § 466 and NY Const. art. XIII § I):

> I do solemnly swear that I will support the Constitution of the United States, and the New York Constitution, and that I will faithfully discharge the duties of the office of attorney and counselor at law of the Supreme Court of the state of New York according to the best of my ability.

III. Membership in the New York State Bar

Please note that admission to the New York state bar does not constitute membership in the New York State Bar Association, which is a voluntary organization. Unlike some other states, New York state does not have an "integrated bar." However, membership in the New York State Bar Association and other local bar associations is recommended. For further information, please contact New York State Bar Association, Membership Services, One Elk Street, Albany, New York 12207, phone: (518) 487-5577; e-mail: membership@nysba.org.

A. Attorney Registration and Fees

Section 468-a of the Judiciary Law and 22 NYCRR Part 118 of the Rules of the Chief Administrator of the Courts require the biennial registration of all attorneys admitted in the State of New York, whether they are resident or non-resident, active or retired, or practicing law in New York or anywhere else. All attorneys are required to renew their attorney registration every two years, within 30 days after the attorney's birthday. The fee for this registration is $375.00 (of which $60.00 is earmarked to support the Lawyers' Fund for Client Protection, $50.00 is deposited in the Indigent Legal Services Fund, $25.00 in the Legal Services Assistance Fund, and the remainder in the Attorney Licencing Fund). No fee is required from an attorney who certifies that he or she is "retired" from the practice of law (see, section III C, *infra*).

New York does not have an inactive status as may be available in other jurisdictions and attorneys who fail to comply with the registration requirements are subject to referral for disciplinary action by the Appellate Division.

Newly-admitted attorneys are required to file an initial registration and pay the $375 fee prior to taking the constitutional oath of office. Information and forms are provided to new attorneys in conjunction with the admission process. Thereafter, the Office of Court Administration automatically sends the necessary forms to enable attorneys to comply with the requirement after the initial registration. For further information contact the Attorney Registration Unit at the Office of Court Administration, P.O. Box 2806, Church Street Station, New York, New York 10008; via e-mail to attyreg@nycourts.gov; or by phone at (212) 428-2800.

B. Address Changes and Name Changes

Attorneys admitted to the New York state bar are required to inform the Attorney Registration Unit of address changes within 30 days of the change. Changes may be submitted electronically at www.nycourts.gov/attorneys, via email to attyreg@nycourts.gov, or by mail to Office of Court Administration, P.O. Box 2806, Church Street Station, New York, NY 10008.

Name changes must be made at the Appellate Division department of admission. For instructions, contact the court directly: 1st Department

(NYC) (212) 340-0400; 2nd Department (Brooklyn) (718) 875-1300; 3rd Department (Albany) (518) 471-4778; and 4th Department (Rochester) (585) 530-3100.

C. Retirement or Resignation

There is no provision for an "inactive" or out-of-state status in the attorney registration rules which would excuse an attorney from filing a biennial registration. All attorneys admitted to the New York state bar whether they are resident or non-resident, active or retired, or practicing law in New York or anywhere else must file a registration every two years, and if actively practicing law anywhere, pay the biennial fee. No fee is required for attorneys who can certify that they are "retired" from the practice of law. Part 118.1(g) of the Rules of the Chief Administrator, as follows, defines for the purposes of registration both the "practice of law" and the term "retired." The definition of "retired" also includes full-time judges and attorneys engaged only in pro bono legal activities:

> 118.1(g) Each registration statement filed pursuant to this section shall be accompanied by a registration fee of $375. No fee shall be required from an attorney who certifies that he or she has retired from the practice of law. For purposes of this section, the "practice of law" shall mean the giving of legal advice or counsel to, or providing legal representation for, particular body or individual in a particular situation in either the public or private sector in the State of New York or elsewhere, it shall include the appearance as an attorney before any court or administrative agency. An attorney is "retired" from the practice of law when, other than the performance of legal services without compensation, he or she does not practice law in any respect and does not intend ever to engage in acts that constitute the practice of law. For purposes of section 468-a of the Judiciary Law, a full-time judge or justice of the Unified Court System of the State of New York or of a court of any other state or of a federal court, shall be deemed "retired" from the practice of law. An attorney in good standing, at least 55 years old and with at least 10 years experience, who participates without compensation in an approved pro bono legal services program, may enroll as an "attorney emeritus."

Part 118.1(g) was amended in January 2010 to include an additional status of Attorney Emeritus. This program has been established by the Unified Court System, in cooperation with the organized bar, legal services providers and other members of the legal community, to encourage retired attorneys to volunteer their legal skills on a pro bono basis to assist low-income New Yorkers who cannot afford an attorney.

To be eligible as an Attorney Emeritus you must be an attorney in good standing who is at least 55 years of age and has practiced law for a minimum of 10 years. By enrolling as an Attorney Emeritus you indicate your willingness to perform a minimum of 30 hours of pro bono legal services each year under the auspices of a qualified legal services organization in New York.

Because filing a biennial registration is required whether you are resident or non-resident, active or retired, or practicing law in New York or anywhere, the only way avoid this obligation is to "resign" from the New York State bar, in which case the attorney would no longer be entitled to practice law in New York state or hold him or herself out as a member of the New York state bar. Resignation applications should be made to the Appellate Division Attorney Admissions Department. Attorneys who are the subject of disciplinary proceedings may be able to resign but such resignations result in orders of disbarment, removal, or striking the attorney's name from the roll of attorneys; each Appellate Division Department has rules governing such "disciplinary" resignations.*

D.   Certificates of Good Standing

Upon admission to the bar, the Appellate Division does not furnish an "ID card," nor does New York have "bar numbers," like some other jurisdictions. However, if the need arises for an attorney to obtain documentation of admission to the bar and/or of good standing, each Appellate Division can provide a "certificate of good standing" to attorneys admitted to the bar of the State of New York, provided that the attorney is registered and is in "good standing" (i.e., not under disciplinary sanction). The attorney seeking such a certificate should contact the Appellate Division Attorney Admissions Department.

There is, however, an ID card program administered by the Unified Court System (Secure Pass) that allows holders to enter New York State courthouses without having to pass through magnetometers. Secure Pass ID cards are available to any New York attorney. Program guidelines can be viewed at: http://www.nycourts.gov/attorneys/registration/secure-pass.shtml.

Secure Pass applications can be picked up at any trial-level New York state courthouse.

E.   Continuing Legal Education Is Mandatory in the State of New York

The Administrative Board of the Courts approved a Mandatory Continuing Legal Education (MCLE) requirement, which became effective December 31, 1998 for all attorneys admitted to the New York Bar.

---

* Rules of the Appellate Division, First Department (§ 603.11), Second Department (691.9), Third Department (806.8), and Fourth Department (1022.25).

Newly admitted attorneys (those within their first two years of admission to the Bar) must complete a minimum of 32 hours of accredited transitional continuing legal education (CLE) courses by the second anniversary of their admission to the New York Bar, with at least 16 completed before the first anniversary of admisssion and another 16 completed between the first and second anniversaries. The 16 credit hours must be in specific categories of credit: 3 credit hours in ethics and professionalism, 6 credit hours in skills, and 7 credit hours in law practice management and/or areas of professional practice. The courses attended must be in the traditional live classroom format or the fully interactive videoconference format.

Experienced attorneys (those admitted to the New York Bar more than two years) are required to complete a minimum of 24 credit hours of accredited CLE courses every two years, of which at least 4 credit hours must be in the ethics and professionalism category. Unlike newly admitted attorneys, experienced attorneys may complete CLE programs in any format, and may also earn credit through other CLE activities, such as teaching CLE courses, authoring legal research-based publications or providing pro bono legal services.

New York attorneys must certify to their CLE compliance at the time of their biennial attorney registration, and must keep their certificates of attendance for at least four years from the date of the course, in case of audit.

Attorneys who do not practice law in New York throughout their biennial CLE reporting cycle may be exempt from the CLE requirement. All members of the New York Bar are presumed to be practicing law in New York unless otherwise shown; the burden of proof is on the individual attorney. Lawyers who are exempt from New York's CLE requirement, but are required to comply with the CLE requirements of another juristiction, must comply with those requirements and certify that compliance on the biennial registration statement.

Additional information on the New York's CLE program may be found on the Unified Court System website at: www.nycourts.gov/attorneys/cle, or obtained by calling the New York State Continuing Legal Education Board at: (212) 428-2105, or for callers outside of New York City, toll-free at: (877) NYS-4CLE. Questions about CLE requirements may also be directed to the CLE Board via email at: cle@nycourts.gov.

The New York State Bar Association is certified by the New York State Continuing Legal Education Board as an accredited provider of Continuing Legal Education in the State of New York. The state bar association offers more than 200 for-credit live CLE seminars each year, held in locations throughout the state, and more than 40 live programs in five days at the state bar association's Annual Meeting.

NYSBA members attend the Association's CLE programs at discounted prices. For more information on NYSBA CLE seminars, including pricing, call: (800) 582-2452 or (518) 463-3724. Access our website at: www.nysba.org and point to the CLE navigation button.

F.   Pro Bono Activities

Beginning in 2013, all applicants seeking admission to the New York bar will be required to perform at least 50 hours of law-related pro bono service prior to taking the oath of office.

Following admission to the bar the following goals are encouraged.

The Rules of Professional Conduct (Part 1200 Joint Rules of the Appellate Divisions), adopted on April 1, 2009, now contain the following:

RULE 6.1:
Voluntary Pro Bono Service

Lawyers are strongly encouraged to provide pro bono legal services to benefit poor persons.

(a) Every lawyer should aspire to:

(1) provide at least 20 hours of pro bono legal services each year to poor persons; and

(2) contribute financially to organizations that provide legal services to poor persons.

(b) Pro bono legal services that meet this goal are:

(1) professional services rendered in civil matters, and in those criminal matters for which the government is not obliged to provide funds for legal representation, to persons who are financially unable to compensate counsel;

(2) activities related to improving the administration of justice by simplifying the legal process for, or increasing the availability and quality of legal services to, poor persons; and

(3) professional services to charitable, religious, civic and educational organizations in matters designed predominantly to address the needs of poor persons.

(c) Appropriate organizations for financial contributions are:

(1) organizations primarily engaged in the provision of legal services to the poor; and

(2) organizations substantially engaged in the provision of legal services to the poor, provided that the donated funds are to be used for the provision of such legal services.

(d) This Rule is not intended to be enforced through the disciplinary process, and the failure to fulfill the aspirational goals contained herein should be without legal consequence.

G. Secure Pass ID Cards

Secure Pass IDs are available to all New York attorneys. The ID Card is a voluntary program and will allow holders to enter New York State courthouses without having to pass through magnetometers, while maintaining the highest level of security for the facility.

All applicants must pay a $25.00 processing fee and undergo a thorough application process, including an electronic criminal history search. Applications for Secure Pass IDs are available at most trial-level New York State courthouses. All applications must appear in person to both apply for and pick up the completed card.

IV. Practice in New York State

A. Conduct of Attorneys

1. Rules of the Appellate Divisions

In general, the conduct of attorneys is overseen by the Appellate Division Departments and the disciplinary committees. Each Appellate Division has its own relevant rules ** and attorneys are advised to direct questions concerning the rules to them. In general, if you practice within geographical boundaries of, or were admitted by, a particular Appellate Division, you are subject to that department's jurisdiction for conduct and disciplinary purposes.

2. The New York Rules of Professional Conduct

The New York Rules of Professional Conduct have been adopted by the Appellate Divisions of the New York State Supreme Court and are published in the Joint Rules of the Appellate Division (22 NYCRR 1200.0). The Appellate Divisions have not adopted the Preamble, Scope and Comments, which are published solely by the New York State Bar Association to provide guidance for attorneys in complying with the Rules. Where a conflict exists between a Rule and the Preamble, Scope or a Comment, the Rule controls.

Copies of the New Rules of Professional Conduct (with Comments) are available from the New York State Bar Association, One Elk Street, Albany, New York 12207. To place an order, you may call the Association's CLE Department at: (800)582-2452. You may also download the Code for free on NYSBA's Web site. The following is the preamble and scope as adopted by the New York State Bar Association and a listing of the Rules.

** Rules of the Appellate Division, First Department, Part 603; Second Department, Part 691; Third Department, Part 806; Fourth Department, Part 1022.

PREAMBLE:
A LAWYER'S RESPONSIBILITIES

[1] A lawyer, as a member of the legal profession, is a representative of clients and an officer of the legal system with special responsibility for the quality of justice. As a representative of clients, a lawyer assumes many roles, including advisor, advocate, negotiator, and evaluator. As an officer of the legal system, each lawyer has a duty to uphold the legal process; to demonstrate respect for the legal system; to seek improvement of the law; and to promote access to the legal system and the administration of justice. In addition, a lawyer should further the public's understanding of and confidence in the rule of law and the justice system because, in a constitutional democracy, legal institutions depend on popular participation and support to maintain their authority.

[2] The touchstone of the client-lawyer relationship is the lawyer's obligation to assert the client's position under the rules of the adversary system, to maintain the client's confidential information except in limited circumstances, and to act with loyalty during the period of the representation.

[3] A lawyer's responsibilities in fulfilling these many roles and obligations are usually harmonious. In the course of law practice, however, conflicts may arise among the lawyer's responsibilities to clients, to the legal system and to the lawyer's own interests. The Rules of Professional Conduct often prescribe terms for resolving such conflicts. Nevertheless, within the framework of the Rules, many difficult issues of professional discretion can arise. The lawyer must resolve such issues through the exercise of sensitive professional and moral judgment, guided by the basic principles underlying the Rules.

[4] The legal profession is largely self-governing. An independent legal profession is an important force in preserving government under law, because abuse of legal authority is more readily challenged by a profession whose members are not dependent on government for the right to practice law. To the extent that lawyers meet these professional obligations, the occasion for government regulation is obviated.

[5] The relative autonomy of the legal profession carries with it special responsibilities of self governance. Every lawyer is responsible for observance of the Rules of Professional Conduct and also should aid in securing their observance by other lawyers. Neglect of these responsibilities compromises the independence of the profession and the public interest that it serves. Compliance with the Rules depends primarily upon the lawyer's understanding of the Rules and desire to comply with the professional norms they embody for the benefit of clients and the legal system, and, secondarily, upon reinforcement by peer and public opinion. So long as its practitioners are guided by these principles, the law will continue to be a noble profession.

SCOPE

[6] The Rules of Professional Conduct are rules of reason. They should be interpreted with reference to the purposes of legal representation and of the law itself. Some of the Rules are imperatives, cast in the terms "shall" or "shall not." These Rules define proper conduct for purposes of professional discipline. Others, generally cast in the term "may," are permissive and define areas under the Rules in which the lawyer has discretion to exercise professional judgment. No disciplinary action should be taken when the lawyer chooses not to act or acts within the bounds of such discretion. Other Rules define the nature of relationships between the lawyer and others. The Rules are thus partly obligatory and disciplinary and partly constitutive and descriptive in that they define a lawyer's professional role. Many of the Comments use the term "should." Comments do not add obligations to the Rules but provide guidance for practicing in compliance with the Rules. The Rules state the minimum level of conduct below which no lawyer can fall without being subject to disciplinary action.

[7] The Rules presuppose a larger legal context shaping the lawyer's role. That context includes court rules and statutes relating to matters of licensure, laws defining specific obligations of lawyers, and substantive and procedural law in general. The Comments are sometimes used to alert lawyers to their responsibilities under such other law.

[8] The Rules provide a framework for the ethical practice of law. Compliance with the Rules, as with all law in an open society, depends primarily upon understanding and voluntary compliance, secondarily upon reinforcement by peer and public opinion and finally, when necessary, upon enforcement through disciplinary proceedings. The Rules do not, however, exhaust the moral and ethical considerations that should inform a lawyer, for no worthwhile human activity can be completely defined by legal rules.

[9] Furthermore, for purposes of determining the lawyer's authority and responsibility, principles of substantive law external to these Rules determine whether a client-lawyer relationship exists. Most of the duties flowing from the client-lawyer relationship attach only after the client has requested the lawyer to render legal services and the lawyer has agreed to do so. But there are some duties, such as that of confidentiality under Rule 1.6, that attach when the lawyer agrees to consider whether a client-lawyer relationship shall be established. See Rule 1.18. Whether a client-lawyer relationship exists for any specific purpose can depend on the circumstances and may be a question of fact.

[10] Under various legal provisions, including constitutional, statutory and common law, the responsibilities of government lawyers may include authority concerning legal matters that ordinarily reposes in the client in private client-lawyer relationships. For example, a lawyer for a government agency may have authority on behalf of the government to decide whether to agree to a settlement or to appeal from an adverse judgment. Such authority in various respects is generally vested in the attorney general and the state's attorney in state government, and in their federal counterparts, and the same may be true of other government law officers. Also, lawyers under the supervision of these officers may be authorized to represent several government agencies in intragovernmental legal controversies in circumstances where a private lawyer could not represent multiple private clients. These Rules do not abrogate any such authority.

[11] Failure to comply with an obligation or prohibition imposed by a Rule is a basis for invoking the disciplinary process. The Rules presuppose that disciplinary assessment of a lawyer's conduct will be made on the basis of the facts and circumstances as they existed at the time of the conduct in question and in recognition of the fact that a lawyer often has to act upon uncertain or incomplete evidence of the situation. Moreover, the Rules presuppose that whether discipline should be imposed for a violation, and the severity of a sanction, depend on all the circumstances, such as the willfulness and seriousness of the violation, extenuating factors and whether there have been previous violations.

[12] Violation of a Rule should not itself give rise to a cause of action against a lawyer nor should it create any presumption in such a case that a legal duty has been breached. In addition, violation of a Rule 5 does not necessarily warrant any other nondisciplinary remedy, such as disqualification of a lawyer in pending litigation. The Rules are designed to provide guidance to lawyers and to provide a structure for regulating conduct through disciplinary agencies. They are not designed to be a basis for civil liability. Furthermore, the purpose of the Rules can be subverted when they are invoked by opposing parties as procedural weapons. The fact that a Rule is a just basis for a lawyer's self-assessment, or for sanctioning a lawyer under the administration of a disciplinary authority, does not imply that an antagonist in a collateral proceeding or transaction has standing to seek enforcement of the Rule. Nevertheless, because the Rules do establish standards of conduct by lawyers, a lawyer's violation of a Rule may be evidence of breach of the applicable standard of conduct.

[13] The Comment accompanying each Rule explains and illustrates the meaning and purpose of the Rule. The Preamble and this note on Scope provide general orientation. The Comments are intended as guides to interpretation, but the text of each Rule is authoritative.

TABLE OF CONTENTS

22 NYCRR 1200.0 Rules of Professional Conduct.

Transactions with Persons Other Than Clients
Rule 4.1: Truthfulness in statements to others
Rule 4.2: Communication with person represented by counsel
Rule 4.3: Communicating with unrepresented persons
Rule 4.4: Respect for rights of third persons
Rule 4.5: Communication after incidents involving personal injury or
    wrongful death

Law Firms and Associations
Rule 5.1: Responsibilities of law firms, partners, managers and supervi-
    sory lawyers
Rule 5.2: Responsibilities of a subordinate lawyer
Rule 5.3: Lawyer's responsibility for conduct of nonlawyers
Rule 5.4: Professional independence of a lawyer
Rule 5.5: Unauthorized practice of law
Rule 5.6: Restrictions on right to practice
Rule 5.7: Responsibilities regarding nonlegal services
Rule 5.8: Contractual relationship between lawyers and nonlegal profes-
    sionals

Public Service
Rule 6.1: Voluntary pro bono service
Rule 6.2: [Reserved]
Rule 6.3: Membership in a legal services organization
Rule 6.4: Law reform activities affecting client interests
Rule 6.5: Participation in limited pro bono legal service programs

Information About Legal Services
Rule 7.1: Advertising
Rule 7.2: Payment for referrals
Rule 7.3: Solicitation and recommendation of professional employment
Rule 7.4: Identification of practice and specialty
Rule 7.5: Professional notices, letterheads, and signs

Maintaining the Integrity of the Profession
Rule 8.1: Candor in the bar admission process
Rule 8.2: Judicial officers and candidates
Rule 8.3: Reporting professional misconduct
Rule 8.4: Misconduct
Rule 8.5: Disciplinary authority and choice of law

Additional joint Appellate Division rules cover Cooperative Business Arrangements Between Lawyers and Non-Legal Professionals (Part
1205); Statement of Client's Rights (Part 1210); Written Letter of Engagement (Part 1215); Mediation of Attorney-Client Disputes (Part 1220); Fee
Arbitration (Part 1230); Dishonored Check Reporting Rules for Attorney
Special, Trust and Escrow Accounts (Part 1300); Procedure for Attorneys
in Domestic Relations Matters (Part 1400); and Continuing Legal Education (Part 1500).

Advice on Ethical Questions

An attorney may obtain ethical guidance regarding questions concerning the attorney's own professional conduct by writing to the New York State Bar Association, Committee on Professional Ethics, One Elk Street, Albany, NY 12207, (518) 487-5694 fax, ethics@nysba.org e-mail. Opinions of the committee are advisory and are rendered only to attorneys concerning their own conduct, not the conduct of another attorney. The committee does not pass upon questions of law or on matters which are in litigation—such matters are within the authority of the court to determine. The committee does not consider hypothetical inquiries nor questions which have also been presented to another bar.

The committee's determinations are either in the form of an informal letter response, which is sent to the inquiring attorney only, or a formal advisory opinion which is published.

If emergency guidance on an ethical question is needed, an attorney may telephone (518) 487-5691. Following appropriate screening to insure the committee has not previously rendered a formal opinion on the issues, an attorney may then be referred for telephone guidance to a member of the committee for an informal, non-binding opinion.

An attorney who works for state government in any capacity is also bound by Public Officers Law §§ 73, 73-a and 74, which govern business and professional activities, require financial disclosure, and set a code of ethics for state employees. These standards apply in addition to the New York Rules of Professional Conduct. An attorney may obtain ethical guidance about the application of the Public Officers Law ethics provisions by writing to the New York State Commission on Public Integrity. If the question is one of first impression, the commission will issue a formal advisory opinion acted upon by the full commission, which opinion will be published with identifying detail omitted. Otherwise, an informal opinion letter will be supplied. Inquiries should be forwarded to the New York State Commission on Public Integrity: 540 Broadway, Albany, NY 12207, (518) 408-3976, cpi@nyintegrity.org e-mail.

Published Ethical Opinions

All of the formal opinions issued by the Committee on Professional Ethics, together with an index, are available on the Association's Web site: www.nysba.org/ethics. A free mobile app is also available that allows you to search the complete database of opinions and will provide you notification of new opinions; visit www.nysba.org/ethicsapp.

* * *

3.   Client Funds

The following is a partial reprint of *A Practical Guide to Attorney Trust Accounts and Recordkeeping* available from The Lawyers' Fund for Client Protection.

What are a lawyer's ethical obligations regarding client funds?

A lawyer in possession of client funds and property is a fiduciary.[1] The lawyer must safeguard and segregate those assets. This obligation applies, as well, to money and property of non-clients coming into a lawyer's possession in the practice of law. They must be preserved, and cannot be commingled with the lawyer's personal and business assets.

A lawyer is also obligated to notify a client when client funds are received by the lawyer; provide appropriate accountings; and disburse promptly all funds and property to which the client is entitled.

Non-cash property belonging to a client should be clearly identified as trust property and secured in the lawyer's safe or safe deposit box.

What is an attorney trust account?

It is a "special" bank account, usually a checking or savings account, for clients' money and other escrow funds that a lawyer holds in the practice of law. A lawyer may have one account, or several, depending on need.

Attorney trust accounts must be maintained in banks and trust companies located within New York state. Out-of-state banks may be used only with the prior and specific written approval of the client or other beneficial owner of the funds.

In all cases, lawyers can only use banks that have agreed to furnish dishonored check notices to the Lawyers' Fund for Client Protection pursuant to statewide court rules. (22 NYCRR Part 1200, Rule 1.15 (b) (1). The Dishonored Check Notice Reporting Rules are reported at 22 NYCRR Part 1300.)

An attorney trust account should never be overdrawn and should not carry overdraft protection.

Withdrawals from an attorney trust account must be made to named payees, and not to cash. And only members of the New York bar can be signatories on an attorney trust account.

The trust account must be specially designated with one of three required titles: Attorney Trust Account, Attorney Special Account, or Attorney Escrow Account. These required titles may be further quali-

---

1.   Rules of Professional Conduct [22 N.Y.C.R.R. 1200.0] rule 1.15.

fied with other descriptive language. For example, an attorney can add "IOLA Account" or "Closing Account" below one of the required titles.

These accounts must be maintained separately from the lawyer's personal and business accounts, as well as from other fiduciary accounts, like those maintained for estates, guardianships, and trusts.

What is the purpose of an attorney trust account?

To safeguard clients' funds from loss, and avoid the appearance of impropriety.

The attorney trust account is a depository for all funds belonging to clients and other persons in the practice of law.

Funds belonging partly to a client and partly to a lawyer, presently or potentially, must also be deposited in the trust account. The lawyer's portion may be withdrawn when due, unless the client disputes the withdrawal. In that event, the funds must remain intact until the dispute with the client is resolved.

What about bank service charges?

A lawyer may deposit funds into the attorney trust account which are necessary to maintain the account, and to pay bank service charges.

Should interest-bearing accounts be used?

It depends on the size of the clients' funds, how long the funds will be held, interest rates, bank fees, and administrative costs, among other things. See the discussion about IOLA accounts on following page.

What about large amounts that will be held a long time?

Where the amount and expected holding period of a client's funds make it obvious that the interest that will be earned will exceed the administrative costs (both bank fees and reasonable costs incurred by the lawyer in the connection with administering the account), a lawyer may have a fiduciary obligation to invest.[2] In that circumstance, the lawyer should consult with the client, and invest the funds in the manner directed by the client. Preferably, the client should execute a writing that will make it clear exactly what fees and costs will be charged against the interest earned.

If client funds are invested, lawyers may use a separate interest-bearing account for each client, or pooled accounts in banks which have the capability to credit interest to individual client sub-accounts. Lawyers may also allocate interest on an attorney trust account to individual clients and other beneficial owners, and may charge the beneficial owners

---

2. See NYSBA, Comm. on Prof. Ethics, Ops. 554 (1983), 575 (1986); Assoc. Bar, NYC, Comm. on Prof. & Jud. Ethics, Op. 1986-5 (1986).

the reasonable cost of doing so, but neither legal nor administrative fees may be measured by the interest earned on a client's money.[3] Again, it would be prudent to have the arrangements set forth in writing.

A lawyer should be mindful of income tax reporting requirements, and consider using the client's social security or federal tax identification number on the account.

What about small deposits, or ones held briefly?

Client funds that cannot earn net interest for the client are called "qualifying funds" and ones that can earn net interest for the client are called "non-qualifying funds." By statute and regulation, lawyers enjoy a safe harbor for the determination of whether client funds are "qualifying." Client funds are "qualifying" if, in the sole discretion and judgment of the attorney or law firm, they are too small in amount, or are reasonably expected to be held for too short a time, to earn income for a client or third person in excess of the costs incurred to secure such income.[4] Lawyers may not be held liable in damages or to answer for a charge of professional misconduct if they deposit money into an IOLA account in their good faith judgment that they are qualified funds.[5]

What is IOLA?

IOLA is the acronym for the New York Interest On Lawyer Account Fund. IOLA uses interest on attorney trust accounts (which interest could not otherwise be available to clients) to fund non-profit agencies in New York which provide civil legal services to low-income persons and programs to improve the administration of justice.

Attorney participation in IOLA is mandatory in two senses. First, every lawyer who handles client funds must maintain an IOLA account. Second, the lawyer must use an IOLA account for qualifying funds, unless he or she uses an account which will generate, compute and pay net interest to the client.[6] A New York lawyer may not place qualifying funds in a non-IOLA account that does not pay net interest to the client.

A lawyer's participation in IOLA has no income tax consequences for the lawyer, or for the client. In addition, IOLA assumes the cost of basic bank service charges and fees on the account, but not charges or fees for special banking services.

IOLA's offices are located at: 11 East 44th Street, Suite 1406, NY, NY, 10017, telephone: (646) 865-1541, or (800) 222-IOLA. Web site: www.iola. org.

---

3.   NYSBA Op. 532 (1981).
4.   21 N.Y.C.R.R. § 7000.2(e).
5.   Judiciary Law § 497(5); 21 N.Y.C.R.R. § 7000.8(b).
6.   Judiciary Law § 497(4); 21 N.Y.C.R.R. § 7000.8(a).

Can lawyers retain interest on attorney trust accounts?

No. A lawyer, as a fiduciary, cannot profit on the administration of an attorney trust account. All interest earned on the account belongs to the law clients and persons whose money generated the interest.[7]

Are there special rules for down payments?

Yes. A buyer's down payment, entrusted with a seller's attorney pending a closing, generally remains the property of the buyer until title passes. The lawyer/escrow agent serves as a fiduciary, and must safeguard and segregate the buyer's down payment in a special bank account.

The purchase contract should make provision for depositing the down payment in a bank account, the disposition of interest, and other escrow responsibilities.

A 1991 statute[8] codifies the fiduciary obligations of lawyers and realtors who accept down payments in residential purchases and sales, including condominium units and cooperative apartments.

The statute requires that the purchase contract identify the escrow agent and the bank where the down payment will be deposited pending the closing. It also permits a lawyer to use an IOLA account in appropriate transactions.

Are other bank accounts needed?

Yes. A practitioner needs a professional business account as a depository for legal fees, and to pay operating expenses. A typical designation is *Attorney Office Account*. Lawyers also need special accounts when they serve as fiduciaries for estates, trusts, guardianships and the like.

Where are advance legal fees deposited?

This depends upon the lawyer's fee agreement with the client. If the advance fee becomes the lawyer's property when it is paid by the client, the fee should be deposited in the firm's business account, and not in the attorney trust account.

If, on the other hand, the advance fee is to remain client property until it is earned by the lawyer, it should be deposited in the attorney trust account, to be withdrawn by the lawyer as it is earned.[9]

In either event, a lawyer has a professional obligation to refund unearned legal fees to a client whenever the lawyer completes or withdraws from a representation, or the lawyer is discharged by the client.[10]

---

7. NYSBA, Ops. 532 (1981), 582 (1987); NYC Op. 81-86 (1981).
8. General Business Law, Article 36-C, §§ 778, 778-a.
9. Rules of Professional Conduct rule 1.16(e) (22 N.Y.C.R.R. 1200.0).
10. Rules of Professional Conduct rule 1.15(f) (22 N.Y.C.R.R. 1200.0).

And advances from clients for court fees and expenses?

This also depends upon the lawyer's fee agreement with the client. If the money advanced by the client is to remain client property until it is used for specific litigation expenses, it should be segregated and preserved in the attorney trust account, or a similar special account.

How are unclaimed client funds handled?

If a lawyer cannot locate a client or another person who is owed funds from the attorney trust account, the lawyer should seek a judicial order to fix the lawyer's fees and disbursements, and to deposit the client's share with the Lawyers' Fund for Client Protection.[11]

What happens when a sole signatory dies?

The Supreme Court has authority to appoint a successor signatory for the attorney trust account. The procedures are set forth in court rules adopted in 1994.[12]

What accounting books are required?

No specific accounting system is mandated by court rule, but a basic trust accounting system for a law firm consists of a trust receipts journal, a trust disbursements journal, and a trust ledger book containing the individual ledger accounts for recording each financial transaction affecting that client's funds.

At a minimum, each client's ledger account should reflect the date, source, and a description of each item of deposit, as well as the date, payee, and purpose of each withdrawal.

Many practitioners find that the so-called "one-write" or "pegboard" manual systems provide an efficient and economical method of trust accounting.[13] There are also approved computer software packages for law office trust accounting.[14]

Internal office controls are essential. It is good business practice to prepare a monthly reconciliation of the balances in the trust ledger book, the lawyer's trust receipts and disbursements journals, the account checkbook, and bank statements.

What bookkeeping records must be maintained?

Every lawyer and law firm must preserve, for seven years after the events they record, copies of all:

---

11.   Rules of Professional Conduct rule 1.15(g) (22 N.Y.C.R.R. 1200.0).
12.   Rule 1.15(g); 22 NYCRR § 1200.15(g).
13.   Vendors include Eastern Systems, Inc., Safeguard Business Systems, Inc., and McBee One-Write Bookkeeping Systems.
14.   Contact the NYSBA Law Practice Management Department, One Elk Street, Albany, NY 12207, (800) 699-5636, or the ABA's Legal Technology Resource Center, 321 N. Clark St., Chicago, Ill. 60654, (312) 988-5465 for guidance on resources in these areas.

— books of account affecting all attorney trust and office operating accounts;

— client retainer and fee agreements;

— checkbooks and check stubs, bank statements, prenumbered canceled checks and duplicate deposit slips;

— statements to clients showing disbursements of their funds;

— bills and statements rendered to clients;

— records showing payments to other lawyers or non-employees for services rendered; and

— retainer and closing statements filed with the Office of Court Administration.

In the event that a law firm dissolves, appropriate arrangements must be made for the maintenance of the firm's records, either by a former partner or the successor law firm. In the absence of an agreement, the local Appellate Division has the authority to impose an arrangement.[15]

How are these rules enforced?

All records required to be maintained by the rules of the Appellate Division Departments may be subpoenaed in a disciplinary proceeding under section 90 of the Judiciary Law.

Lawyers are also required to certify their familiarity and compliance with Rule 1.15 as part of the biennial registration form filed with the Office of Court Administration.

What are the consequences of noncompliance?

A lawyer who does not maintain the accounts and records required of Rule 1.15 is subject to disciplinary action under section 90 of the Judiciary Law.

What losses are covered by the Lawyer's Fund?

The New York Lawyers' Fund for Client Protection—previously the Clients' Security Fund—is financed by a $60 share of each lawyer's $375 biennial registration fee. The fund receives no revenues from the IOLA program or from state tax revenues.

The fund is administered pro bono publico by a board of trustees appointed by the state Court of Appeals.[16] Since the fund's inception in 1982, the trustees have restored more than $91 million to victims of dishonest conduct in the practice of law.

---

15. Rules of Professional Conduct rule 1.15(h) (22 N.Y.C.R.R. 1200.0).
16. Judiciary Law § 468-b; State Finance Law § 97-t.

The fund is authorized to reimburse law clients for money or property that is misappropriated by a member of the bar in the practice of law. Awards are generally made after a lawyer's disbarment and where it appears that the lawyer cannot make restitution.

To qualify for reimbursement, the loss must involve the misuse of law clients' money or property in the practice of law. The trustees cannot settle fee disputes, or compensate clients for malpractice or neglect.

Typical losses reimbursed include the theft of estate and trust assets; down payments and the proceeds in real property transactions; debt collection proceeds; personal injury settlements; and money embezzled from clients in investment transactions.

The fund's offices are located at 119 Washington Avenue, Albany, New York 12210. Telephone (518) 434-1935 or (800) 452-3863. Web site: www.nylawfund.org

Another valuable resource available from the New York State Bar Association's CLE Department is the book entitled *Attorney Escrow Accounts— Rules, Regulations and Related Topics* (2015, Fourth Edition), (800) 582-2452, www.nysba.org/CLE.

* * *

4.　Advertising and Solicitation

Attorneys should be aware of and consult the provisions of the New York Rules of Professional Conduct that pertain to advertising, publicity, professional notices, letterheads, offices, signs, and solicitation, and the relevant provisions of article 15 of the Judiciary Law. (See, also, General Business Law § 337 [advertising to procure divorces]; and Not-for-Profit Corporation Law § 301 [5] [use of the word "lawyer" in corporate name].)

5.　Compensation of Attorneys

The most basic statutory statement of attorney compensation is found at Judiciary Law § 474:

> The compensation of an attorney or counsellor for his services is governed by agreement, express or implied, which is not restricted by law.

Attorneys should also be aware of and consult the remainder of Judiciary Law § 474 and other relevant provisions of article 15 of the Judiciary Law, General Obligations Law § 5-701(10), and relevant provisions of the New York Rules of Professional Conduct.

Reasonable contingency fees for attorneys in cases involving a personal injury or wrongful death, other than medical, dental or podiatric malpractice, are found in: 22 NYCRR § 603.7, 22 NYCRR § 691.20(e),

22 NYCRR § 806.13 and § 1022.31. Judiciary Law § 474-a details the fee schedule which must be used for contingent fee cases in claims for medical, dental or podiatric malpractice cases.

6. Mandatory Letter of Engagement

Attorneys should be aware that as of March 4, 2002, they must provide a letter of engagement or written retainer agreement where the fee to be charged is $3,000 or more. (22 N.Y.C.R.R. pt. 1215). These rules do not apply to domestic relations matters covered by 22 N.Y.C.R.R. pt. 1400 or to cases "where the attorney's services are of the same general kind as previously rendered to and paid for by the client." The letter of engagement must explain the scope of the representation, the fees and expenses to be charged and provide notice of the client's right to arbitration. [22 N.Y.C.R.R. § 1215.1(b).]

Attorneys employed in a contingent fee matter must, promptly after employment, "provide the client with a writing stating the method by which the fee is to be determined," including percentages and how expenses are to be deducted. Upon conclusion of the matter, the attorney is to provide the client with a further written statement setting forth the recovery, the remittance and method of determination. [Rules of Professional Conduct rule 1.5(c); see 22 N.Y.C.R.R. §§ 603.7(e), 691.20(e), 806.13, 1022.31.]* For attorneys practicing in the 1st and 2nd Departments, retainer and closing statements in contingency fee matters must also be filed with OCA.

7. Attorney-Client Fee Dispute Resolution Program

Many bar associations in New York have long provided for arbitration and mediation of attorney-client fee disputes. Part 137 of the Rules of the Chief Administrator establishes a statewide Attorney-Client Fee Dispute Resolution Program which is administered by bar associations and district administrative judges' offices throughout the state. Local fee dispute resolution programs are approved by the Board of Governors and the appropriate Presiding Justice of the Appellate Division. Arbitration under Part 137 is mandatory for an attorney if requested by a client. Awards are final and binding unless de novo review is sought as provided by the rule. It applies where representation commenced on or after January 1, 2002, to attorneys who undertake to represent a client in most civil matters. Although the rules provide for arbitration as a primary means of resolving fee disputes, mediation is also available. For more information: Web: www.nycourts.gov/feedispute; Email: feedispute@nycourts.gov; Toll-free: (877) 333-7137 or Mail: Board of Governors, Office of Court Administration, 25 Beaver Street, Room 885, New York, NY 10004.

---

* Paragraph largely reprinted from page 22, *Pitfalls of Practice* (2d ed. 2002) published by the New York State Bar Association.

8.   Judiciary Law § 470**

Attorneys practicing in New York state should be aware of Judiciary Law § 470, which states:

> A person, regularly admitted to practice as an attorney and counselor, in the courts of record of this state, whose office for the transaction of law business is within the state, may practice as such attorney or counselor, although he resides in an adjoining state.

For further explanation of this statute, attorneys should read the decided cases which have interpreted it, especially, *Schoenefeld v State of New York* (2011 WL 3957282 [United States District Court for the Northern District of New York, 2011]) (*see also,* Brennan, "Repeal Judiciary Law § 470," *NYSBA Journal*, January 1990).

9.   Standards of Civility

Preamble

The New York State Standards of Civility for the legal profession set forth principles of behavior to which the bar, the bench and court employees should aspire. They are not intended as rules to be enforced by sanction or disciplinary action, nor are they intended to supplement or modify the Rules Governing Judicial Conduct, the New York Rules of Professional Conduct and its Disciplinary Rules, or any other applicable rule or requirement governing conduct. Instead they are a set of guidelines intended to encourage lawyers, judges and court personnel to observe principles of civility and decorum, and to confirm the legal profession's rightful status as an honorable and respected profession where courtesy and civility are observed as a matter of course. The standards are divided into four parts: lawyers' duties to the court and court personnel; judges' duties to lawyers, parties and witnesses; and court personnel duties to lawyers and litigants.

As lawyers, judges and court employees, we are all essential participants in the judicial process. That process cannot work effectively to serve the public unless we first treat each other with courtesy, respect and civility.

Lawyers' Duties to Other Lawyers, Litigants and Witnesses

1. Lawyers should be courteous and civil in all professional dealings with other persons.

    A. Lawyers should act in a civil manner regardless of the ill feelings that their clients may have toward others.

**A challenge to § 470 is presently on appeal in Federal District Court.

B. Lawyers can disagree without being disagreeable. Effective representation does not require antagonistic or acrimonious behavior. Whether orally or in writing, lawyers should avoid vulgar language, disparaging personal remarks or acrimony toward other counsel, parties or witnesses.

C. Lawyers should require that persons under their supervision conduct themselves with courtesy and civility.

2. When consistent with their clients' interest, lawyers should cooperate with opposing counsel in an effort to avoid litigation that has already commenced.

A. Lawyers should avoid unnecessary motion practice or other judicial intervention by negotiating and agreeing with other counsel whenever it is practicable to do so.

B. Lawyers should allow themselves sufficient time to resolve any dispute or disagreement by communicating with one another and imposing reasonable and meaningful deadlines in light of the nature and status of the case.

3. A lawyer should respect the schedule and commitments of opposing counsel, consistent with protection of their client's interests.

A. In the absence of a court order, a lawyer should agree to reasonable requests for extensions of time or for waiver of procedural formalities when the legitimate interests of the client will not be adversely affected.

B. Upon request coupled with the simple representation by counsel that more time is required, the first request for an extension to respond to pleading ordinarily should be granted as a matter of courtesy.

C. A lawyer should not attach unfair or extraneous conditions to extensions of time. A lawyer is entitled to impose conditions appropriate to preserve rights that an extension might otherwise jeopardize, and may request, but should not unreasonably insist on, reciprocal scheduling concessions.

D. A lawyer should endeavor to consult with other counsel regarding scheduling matters in a good faith effort to avoid scheduling conflicts. A lawyer should likewise cooperate with opposing counsel when scheduling changes are requested, provided the interests of his or her client will not be jeopardized.

E. A lawyer should notify other counsel and, if appropriate, the court or other persons at the earliest possible time when hearings, depositions, meetings or conferences are to be canceled or postponed.

4. A lawyer should promptly return telephone calls and answer correspondence reasonably requiring a response.

5. The timing and manner of service of papers should not be designed to cause disadvantage to the party receiving the papers.

   A. Papers should not be served in a manner designed to take advantage of an opponent's known absence from the office.

   B. Papers should not be served at a time or in a manner designed to inconvenience an adversary.

   C. Unless specifically authorized by law or rule, a lawyer should not submit papers to the court without serving copies of all such papers upon opposing counsel in such a manner that opposing counsel will receive them before or contemporaneously with the submission to the court.

6. A lawyer should not use any aspect of the litigation process, including discovery and motion practice, as a means of harassment or for the purpose of unnecessarily prolonging litigation or increasing litigation expenses.

   A. A lawyer should avoid discovery that is not necessary to obtain facts or perpetuate testimony or that is designed to place an undue burden or expense on a party.

   B. A lawyer should respond to discovery requests reasonably and not strain to interpret the request so as to avoid disclosure of relevant and non-privileged information.

7. In depositions and other proceedings, and in negotiations, lawyers should conduct themselves with dignity and refrain from engaging in acts of rudeness and disrespect.

   A. Lawyers should not engage in any conduct during a deposition that would not be appropriate in the presence of a judge.

   B. Lawyers should advise their clients and witnesses of the proper conduct expected of them in court, at depositions and at conferences, and, to the best of their ability, prevent clients and witnesses from causing disorder or disruption.

   C. A lawyer should not obstruct questioning during a deposition or object to deposition questions unless necessary.

   D. Lawyers should ask only those questions they reasonably believe are necessary for the prosecution or defense of an action. Lawyers should refrain from asking repetitive or argumentative questions and from making self-serving statements.

8. A lawyer should adhere to all express promises and agreements with other counsel, whether oral or in writing, and to agreements implied by the circumstances or by local customs.

9. Lawyers should not mislead other persons involved in the litigation process.

   A. A lawyer should not falsely hold out the possibility of settlement as a means for adjourning discovery or delaying trial.

   B. A lawyer should not ascribe a position to another counsel that counsel has not taken or otherwise seek to create an unjustified inference based on counsel's statements or conduct.

   C. In preparing written versions of agreements and court orders, a lawyer should attempt to correctly reflect the agreement of the parties or the direction of the court.

10. Lawyers should be mindful of the need to protect the standing of the legal profession in the eyes of the public. Accordingly, lawyers should bring the New York State Standards of Civility to the attention of other lawyers when appropriate.

Lawyers' Duties to the Court and Court Personnel

1. A lawyer is both an officer of the court and an advocate. As such, the lawyer should always strive to uphold the honor and dignity of the profession, avoid disorder and disruption in the courtroom, and maintain a respectful attitude toward the court.

   A. Lawyers should always speak and write civilly and respectfully in all communications with the court and court personnel.

   B. Lawyers should use their best efforts to dissuade clients and witnesses from causing disorder or disruption in the courtroom.

   C. Lawyers should not engage in conduct intended primarily to harass or to humiliate witnesses.

   D. Lawyers should be punctual and prepared for all court appearances; if delayed, the lawyer should notify the court and counsel whenever possible.

2. Court personnel are an integral part of the justice system and should be treated with courtesy and respect at all times.

Judges' Duties to Lawyers, Parties and Witnesses

1. A judge should be patient, courteous and civil to lawyers, parties and witnesses.

   A. A judge should maintain control over the proceedings and insure that they are conducted in a civil manner.

B. Judges should not employ hostile, demeaning or humiliating words in opinions or in written or oral communications with lawyers, parties or witnesses.

C. Judges should, to the extent consistent with the efficient conduct of litigation and other demands on the court, be considerate of the schedules of lawyers, parties and witnesses when scheduling hearings, meetings or conferences.

D. Judges should be punctual in convening all trials, hearings, meetings and conferences; if delayed, they should notify counsel when possible.

E. Judges should make all reasonable efforts to decide promptly all matters presented to them for decision.

F. Judges should use their best effort to insure that court personnel under their direction act civilly toward lawyers, parties and witnesses.

Duties of Court Personnel to the Court, Lawyers and Litigants

Court personnel should be courteous, patient and respectful while providing prompt, efficient and helpful service to all persons having business with the courts.

A. Court employees should respond promptly and helpfully to requests for assistance or information.

B. Court employees should respect the judge's directions concerning the procedures and atmosphere that the judge wishes to maintain in his or her courtroom.

10. Assistance Available

If you, or a colleague in the legal community, suffer from depression or substance abuse (alcohol or drugs) to a degree significant enough to adversely affect your work and those about you, there is help available. For the New York State Bar Association's lawyer assistance program, call (800) 255-0569; for the lawyer assistance program of the Association of the Bar of the City of New York, call (212) 302-5787. Their advice is free and confidential. Several county bar associations offer similar services.

B. Unauthorized Practice

At present, there is no single place to turn in New York State for a definition of the practice of law and what may constitute the unauthorized practice of law in New York State. However, attorneys are referred to the provisions of article 15 of the Judiciary Law (especially §§ 478 and 484). Investigation and prosecution of allegations of unauthorized practice are handled by the Attorney General's office (Judiciary Law §§ 476-a to 476-c). Unauthorized practice may subject the violator to misdemeanor prosecution (Judiciary Law § 485) or contempt of court (Judiciary Law § 750[b]). (See, also, Judiciary Law §§ 16, 250).

C. Partnerships and Professional Corporations

In addition to the "solo" practice of law, attorneys form partnerships and professional corporations to engage in the practice of law. In New York state, attorneys forming such entities should consult, at least, New York's Partnership Law (New York has adopted the Uniform Partnership Act) and Article 15 (Professional Service Corporations) of the Business Corporation Law. Contact information: Department of State Division of Corporations, State Records and Uniform Commercial Code, 99 Washington Avenue, 6th Floor, Albany, NY 12231, www.dos.state.ny.us/corps/mission.html.

D. Judiciary Law Article 15

Because of the frequency of references to Judiciary Law article 15 in this pamphlet, its sections are listed below (outline from Book 29, Judiciary Law, McKinney's Consolidated Laws of New York, Annotated):

460. Examination and admission of attorneys.

460-a. Disclosure with respect to loans made or guaranteed by the New York state higher education services corporation.

460-b. Applications for special arrangements.

461. Compensation of state board of law examiners; appointment and compensation of employees.

462. Annual account by state board of law examiners.

463. Times and places of examinations.

464. Certification by state board of successful candidates.

465. Fee for examinations and for credential review for admission on motion; disposition; refunds; funds.

466. Attorney's oath of office.

467. Registration of attorneys.

468. Official registration of attorneys to be kept by the chief administrator of the courts.

468-a. Biennial registration of attorneys.

468-b. Clients' Security Fund of the State of New York.

469. Continuance where attorney is member of legislature.

[469-a. Renumbered.]

470. Attorneys having offices in this state may reside in adjoining state.

471.   Attorney who is judge's partner or clerk prohibited from practicing before him or in his court.

472.   Attorney who is surrogate's parent or child prohibited from practicing before him.

473.   Constables, coroners, criers and attendants prohibited from practicing during term of office.

474.   Compensation of attorney or counsellor.

474-a. Contingent fees for attorneys in claims or actions for medical, dental, or pediatric malpractice.

474-b. Attorney retainer statements.

475.   Attorney's lien in action, special or other proceeding.

475-a. [Notice of attorney's lien prior to commencement of action; service and contents.]

476.   Action against attorney for lending his name in suits and against person using name.

476-a. Action for unlawful practice of the law.

476-b. Injunction to restrain defendant from unlawful practice of the law.

476-c. Investigation by the attorney-general.

477.   Settlement of actions for personal injury.

478.   Practicing or appearing as attorney-at-law without being admitted and registered.

479.   Soliciting business on behalf of an attorney.

480.   Entering hospital to negotiate settlement or obtain release or statement.

481.   Aiding, assisting or abetting the solicitation of persons or the procurement of a retainer for or on behalf of an attorney.

482.   Employment by attorney of person to aid, assist or abet in the solicitation of business or the procurement through solicitation of a retainer to perform legal services.

483.   Signs advertising services as attorney at law.

484.   None but attorneys to practice in the state.

485.   Violation of certain preceding sections a misdemeanor.

486.   Practice of law by attorney who has been disbarred, suspended, or convicted of a felony.

486-a. Conviction for felony of person who is an attorney and counselor at law; notice thereof to be given by clerk to appropriate appellate division of the supreme court.

487. Misconduct by attorneys.

488. Buying demands on which to bring an action.

489. Purchase of claims by corporations or collection agencies.

490. Limitation.

491. Sharing of compensation by attorneys prohibited.

492. Use of attorney's name by another.

493. Attorneys forbidden to defend criminal prosecutions carried on by their partners, or formerly by themselves.

494. Attorneys may defend themselves.

495. Corporations and voluntary associations not to practice law.

496. Statement to be filed by organizations offering legal services.

497. Attorneys fiduciary funds; interest-bearing accounts.

498. Professional referrals.

499. Lawyer assistance committees.

This content is a slighly revised version of the NYSBA pamphlet *The Practice of Law in New York State: An Introduction for Newly-Admitted Attorneys,* **originally published in 2012.**

PATHWAY TO THE PROFESSION: FROM LAW SCHOOL TO LAWYER

PREPARING FOR PRACTICE

How to Find a Job in State Government

I. Research

Job seekers must first identify substantive areas of public policy and law that are of interest. With well over 100 agencies, commissions, divisions, boards and authorities to choose from, it would certainly help in a job search to narrow down the field of options. To do this, it is necessary to discover the statutory purposes of as many units of state government as possible, and the current policy trends, goals and focus of these units. The following list of reference materials about New York State government would be a good place to begin:

- Legislative Manual (published annually)

- New York State Statistical Yearbook (published annually)

- Directory of State Agencies (published by the New York State Department of State)

- The Red Book (published annually)

- From the New York State Web site at http://www.ny.gov/ there are links to the various agencies, offices and authorities

Once you have narrowed your search, and before writing a cover letter or going to an interview, it is important to learn about the policy and program priorities for those agencies/offices that interest you. The following documents will help you with this task:

- Annual Message of the Governor to the Legislature on the State of the State (available online)

- Annual Reports prepared by each agency, commission and authority detailing office structure, recent accomplishments and goals

- The New York Red Book

Taking all of this background information into an interview will certainly provide you with a competitive advantage, as you will be able to demonstrate an interest in and knowledge of the work for which you are applying.

II. Types of Legal Job Titles

There are several ways to secure a full-time job with state government. The most common method is by taking an exam administered by the Department of Civil Service. While the Department of Civil Service calls this an exam, it is not a traditional test, but rather a questionnaire which can be completed at home, at your leisure. This exam is designed to evaluate (rank) each applicant based upon his or her training and experience. The questionnaire asks for information on the courses taken in law school and the types of job experience and training you have had to date. The answers (recorded on a computer sheet by the applicant) are then fed into a computer.

When an agency is seeking to fill an attorney position, it requests a list of candidates from Civil Service. In order to obtain a list from the Opportunities in Public Service Legal Specialty Areas Exam, the agency is asked to complete a similar questionnaire which describes the type of training and experience required for a particular job. A list is then generated by the Department of Civil Service, which ranks those whose profile may match the agency's needs. The Civil Service Law requires the agencies to hire for each position from the top three candidates on the list. If a candidate declines an interview or refuses to accept employment, the agency may go to the fourth name on the list, and so on.

III. Employment Classifications

The Civil Service Law provides for different "classes" of employment within state government. The most common "classes" are competitive, noncompetitive and exempt. If you are in a "competitive" title, it means you have been hired from the civil service exam lists described previously. This classification offers state employees the most protection under the law. For example, if you are a competitive class attorney for an agency that is disbanded, under Civil Service Law you will be given a preference in filling similar jobs in other agencies.

If a position is classified as "exempt," it is filled by agency appointment independent of any civil service list. The Civil Service Law states that this class includes "all other offices or positions for which the Civil Service Commission has determined it is not practicable to fill by competitive or non-competitive examination." If you are hired to fill an exempt position, your salary level does not have to mirror the Attorney Traineeship Schedule, and job retention is at the discretion of the agency appointing authority. Therefore, this classification does not enjoy the same job protection as a competitive title.

If a position is classified as "noncompetitive," this means it is not in the "exempt" class, but the Civil Service Commission finds it is not practicable to ascertain the merit and fitness of applicants by competitive examination. For example, many attorneys who are litigators for the state may be classified as "noncompetitive," since it is not always practicable to test their litigation/trial skills. The Department of Civil Service adopts minimum qualifications for appointments to noncompetitive positions. As with "exempt" positions, "noncompetitive" positions are not filled from any civil service list. With the exception of some attorneys in the noncompetitive class who may be in policy-making positions, after approximately one year most noncompetitive attorneys receive the benefit of a set of tenure protections (exempt class attorneys do not receive these protections).

Law students who obtain part-time/temporary employment with state agencies while they are in school are generally classified as noncompetitive legal aides or exempt legal aides/interns. There is no civil service exam for law students who are seeking part-time, nonpermanent employment.

IV. Albany Law School's Government Field Placement Programs

The Government Law Center (GLC) and the Clinic & Justice Center co-sponsor a government field placement program for Albany Law School students during the fall, spring and summer academic semesters. Students earn three academic credits for working ten to fifteen hours per week at a participating government law office, and participating in a weekly class. This experience differs from traditional clinical programs since it requires students to apply their legal skills in a different manner as they work on legal aspects of significant public policy issues. Internships that involve essentially traditional legal skills are not part of this program. Students participating in this program are supervised closely by an attorney at the agency where they are assigned.

Albany Law School also offers a "Semester in Government Program." This is a unique opportunity for law students to spend 30 hours per week working in a New York State government agency or the legislature, under the supervision of a government lawyer/mentor. Students are required to attend the weekly field placement seminar, as well as a weekly three-hour course in government ethics at Albany Law School. A total of 12 academic credits are awarded for this program. This is the only full-time government law experience for law students in New York State government.

Participating in internship experiences such as these will help with the Opportunities in Public Service Legal Specialty Areas Exam administered by the Department of Civil Service. Since the exam is designed to evaluate applicants based upon training and experience, the experience gained through an internship can be invaluable.

V. State Ethics Law Regarding Students

Subdivision 8 of § 73 of the Public Officers Law provides that a person who has been employed with the state cannot, for a period of two years after leaving state employment, appear or practice before the agency with which he or she was employed, or receive compensation for any work rendered on behalf of any person or entity in relation to any case or proceeding before that agency. In effect, the law prohibits state employees from leaving their agency and then representing a private client in a matter before that agency for a period of two years after the end of their service.

Many students have asked if this regulation would apply to them working for a state agency part-time during law school or as interns. The New York State Commission on Public Integrity issued an Advisory Opinion on January 10, 1991 (Op. 91-1), which distinguishes between a "student" and an "employee" for purposes of the two-year post-employment restrictions. The Commission held that the restrictions do not apply to students so long as students meet the following four requirements: (1) the student must be enrolled full-time as a student in an accredited course of study or on seasonal recess therefrom; (2) the student cannot work half-time or more per week during the school year; (3) a student may not work full-time for more than 120 days (four months) during the summer vacation period; and (4) the student cannot receive any state employee benefits, such as medical, retirement or vacation benefits or have any right to re-employment. Advisory Opinion 09-02, issued on February 3, 2009, references Advisory Opinion No. 91-01 and reaffirms the four criteria to be considered when determining whether post-employment restrictions apply to a student, or not.

If you are not currently a full-time student, then the New York State Public Officers Law would apply when you obtain public sector employment. It would be a good idea to become acquainted with the provisions of this law prior to accepting employment. A guide to the law produced by the New York State Commission on Public Integrity is reprinted at the end of this book. The Joint Commission on Public Ethics (JCOPE) replaced the former New York State Commission on Public Integrity pursuant to the Public Integrity Reform Act (L.2011, ch. 399). Consult the JCOPE website, www.jcope.ny.gov, for any updates on the guide of post-employment restrictions.

VI.   Conclusion

Public sector employment with New York State can be very rewarding. As each agency is unique, so are the functions of the various offices of counsel. It is important to do your research and be prepared in order to write informative cover letters that capture the reader's attention, to engage in substantive discussion during the interview process and to determine which agencies best meet your goals.

This article originally appeared in *Legal Careers in NYS Government*, 10th Ed. (NYSBA, 2012).

Legal Education and the Future of the Legal Profession

Seeking Quality, Employers Target Skilled Law Grads

When it comes right down to it, all the hand-wringing over the quality of legal education—practical lessons vs. theoretical, two years of study vs. three, the bar exam vs. reality—all boils down to one simple question.

Can Graduates Do the Job?

The answer often depends on what employers need. And what employers need depends on the size of the firm, the type of law they practice and whether they have the resources to invest in training lawyers in the specialty work their firms provide.

The State Bar's Task Force on the Future of the Legal Profession, in its 2011 report, struggled with the question in making recommendations for changes to law school curriculum. "What is practice ready," the report asked, "in a profession where there is a myriad of practice types in the law firm setting and an apparent preference in the legal marketplace for specialist practitioners?"

And, what do non-firm employers look for in their first-year hires? What about those seeking quality employees within the judiciary, district attorney offices or nonprofit or legal aid practices?

Writers Mark Mahoney and Brandon Vogel took the challenge. Below, their reports from the employment front lines of private and public practice.

Law Firms Differ Over Skills Needed By Grads

By Mark Mahoney

Apparently, there are as many different answers to the question—what is practice ready?—as there are types of law firms.

John P. Amershadian, president of Hodgson Russ LLP, said his firm is not looking for law schools to produce specialists, but rather to graduate lawyers who are willing to work hard and are trained to learn.

"I think there's too much recent focus on this idea that they ought to know particular things about a substantive area of law. I don't expect them to," said Amershadian, whose 197-year-old firm employs more than 200 lawyers in six Northeastern cities. "I'd much rather they spend their time learning how to learn, learning how to research, learning how to analyze, than I want them to know particular substantive rules. They'll learn that here, or in any law firm."

He said he wants graduates to come out of law school with the ability to take on a project and figure out how to approach it.

He admitted that because of the size of his firm, he has the luxury of time in bringing new associates up to speed on specific areas of law. He said if he were a solo practitioner, he would "probably take a different attitude toward this."

On the Front Lines

Tucker Stanclift, founding partner at Stanclift, Ludemann and Mc-Morris PC in Glens Falls, has that different attitude, in large part out of necessity.

Stanclift said his small-town firm of eight attorneys is seeking graduates who understand the fundamentals of the frontline practice of law. He suggested law schools focus less on theory and more on practical skills.

"I'm an in-the-trenches practitioner. The fundamentals of the frontline practice of law aren't always about the theoretical," he said. "I think most people can learn what they need to learn in law school in about a year-and-a-half. As practitioners, we spend as much time, if not more, trying to unteach them some of the things they learned in law school."

Among the other qualities sought by law firms in new hires were a track record of performance, people skills, a personality that fits the culture of the firm they're joining, and energy and ambition, according to a 2013 article by Sumita Dalal, CEO and founder of the legal education website, FindMyLawTutor.

Other sources suggested that law schools should focus on transnational studies to serve the growing global market, management skills, good writing and more clinical work.

New attorneys are still struggling to find work, as demand for new associates remained stagnant in the fall of 2013, following a five-year trend, according to a survey conducted by the National Association for Law Placement (NALP).

"We have seen some bobbling in recruiting volumes this past fall, with some numbers that point to increased recruiting volumes and some that suggest decreased volume," NALP Executive Director James Leipold said in a prepared statement. "In any event, most of the markers that we track have more or less flat-lined for the last several years."

That puts added pressure on law schools to graduate attorneys who fit in with what law firms need.

Stanclift—a former chair of the State Bar's Young Lawyers Section and a member of the Future of the Legal Profession task force—suggested that law schools teach and train graduates in much the same way medical schools prepare doctors, with residency requirements before being licensed to practice.

"There's very little comprehension of first-year associates about the practical application of the things you teach in law school," he said. "Where I think prospective new associates are lacking is in knowledge about the practice of law, about the fundamentals of the business of the law, and not the theoretical that is being taught in the classroom."

Stanclift also said law schools should spend more time teaching students the business end of lawyering.

"The fundamentals of basic business are not being taught in law school. They don't teach it to you," he said. "I think we are doing a disservice to our future profession by not explaining to them that this is a business as well as a profession. 'Sale' is not a four-letter word."

Amershadian agreed that law schools could do a better job teaching about the business of law.

"Everybody in law school ought to take an accounting class," he said.

Business acumen among new grads was listed as a top need by administrators of law firms in recent articles on the subject. Some law professionals quoted said that while new lawyers do not need to know profit-and-loss or get involved in billing, they do need to understand the business side of legal work.

Stanclift said law school debt has forced graduates to look for high-paying jobs in order to pay off their loans, which can average $125,000 or more.

"There are only a few of those jobs compared to the population," he said. "If you want to work in Glens Falls, you're not going to make $150,000 your first year out of law school. You'd be lucky to make that 10 years out of law school."

Amershadian said he didn't see new associates focusing on getting jobs to repay their loans. But he is losing new attorneys to the in-house legal teams of corporations, including some of his own clients.

He said he hoped the specialized training his firm provided would come back to help his firm in referrals and business from those former associates.

Amershadian also complimented the latest crop of law school grads for their willingness to buck a common view of today's young people in terms of their questionable work ethic and unwillingness to put in long hours.

He said the youngest lawyers are eager to work and often put in the longest hours, well aware of their good fortune in finding full-time employment in a difficult economy.

MARK MAHONEY is the former Associate Director of NYSBA's Media Services and Public Affairs Department.

What District Attorneys, Judges Prize in Lawyers
By Brandon Vogel

If Justice Deborah H. Karalunas were ever a law school dean, she would require students to take a writing-intensive course each semester.

"You can never do enough to improve your writing skills," said Karalunas, presiding justice of the Onondaga County Supreme Court, Commercial Division, and past chair of the Judicial Section. "That is key to being a good clerk and lawyer."

As a former partner at Bond Schoeneck & King and as a judge for the last 12 years, Karalunas knows exactly what it takes to succeed as a clerk and what she wants in a law clerk.

"Strong analytical and research skills are the most important skills for a clerk," said Karalunas. "I also want someone who is a clear and concise writer. A law clerk must be reliable and cooperative, efficient, flexible and responsive to critique. A law clerk must understand the importance of keeping confidences."

Karalunas works closely with law students. "I think law students should be instructed on the differences between computer research and book research. Each has distinct advantages," said Karalunas. "Sometimes young lawyers do not appreciate the benefits of book research."

For example, Karalunas said, "When researching a statutory provision, sometimes it is easier to find 'the answer' in the McKinney's head-notes than on the computer."

Hon. Victoria A. Graffeo, senior associate judge of the Court of Appeals, noted that the Court of Appeals attracts "very highly qualified applicants" for clerkships. She hires clerks who have had prior legal experience.

She considers three characteristics the most important for judicial clerkships. "First is the analytical acumen to properly identify issues and conduct thorough research. Second are excellent writing skills and clarity of expression, as well as the ability to concisely present the issues," said Graffeo. "Lastly, it is good judgment, which comes with time and experience."

DAs as Employers

The right fit is the most important consideration for John M. George, first deputy district attorney of the Westchester County District Attorney's Office, when he hires a new assistant district attorney.

With the economic decline, there are a greater number of applicants for available assistant district attorney positions. George acknowledged that law graduates now compete with admitted attorneys who have lost their jobs or are looking to make a lateral move.

"In the past, we liked to have a freshman class and bring them up together as a class," said George. "We have been somewhat forced to hire admitted attorneys" because DA offices need people with some practical experience.

George said his office is "looking for people with academic proficiency, legal intelligence, and who are well-rounded. Really, we need someone who is going to fit in with the team and see public service as a noble cause."

Law schools are still fulfilling their mission of teaching "how to think like lawyers, read a case and interpret what they see," he said.

"Law schools have come forward with more practical experiences for law students," said George. "That's important. The real world is sometimes at odds with the academic world."

In Warren County, District Attorney Kathleen B. Hogan said she hires a number of summer interns, a few of whom have gone on to serve as assistant district attorneys in Warren County. Hogan has successfully referred interns to other district attorneys' offices because she can vouch for their good work and skills.

"The most important thing we look for is unwavering integrity," said Hogan. "We look for people with integrity, and who are bright."

BRANDON VOGEL is NYSBA's Social Media and Web Content Manager.

This article originally appeared in the May/June 2014 NYSBA *State Bar News.*

PATHWAY TO THE PROFESSION: FROM LAW SCHOOL TO LAWYER

ATTORNEY PROFESSIONALISM

Can Attorney Behavior Outside the Office Lead to Disciplinary Action?

To the Forum:

I have always been curious about what conduct outside of legal practice could potentially affect my ability to practice law. Recently, for whatever reason, I have done a number of things that some people have told me are unbecoming. For example, last year my home suffered damage after Super Storm Sandy. My insurance claim listed not only items of direct loss, but also some items that needed repair even before the storm, but which "may" have been exacerbated by it. In addition, I currently own real estate for investment. Several of these properties display numerous building code violations and fines. Lastly, a month or so ago, I submitted an application for a bank loan, and I may have said on the application that I attended Yale Law School, rather than my true alma mater, "Yala" Law School.

My question for the Forum: Do any of these constitute violations of the Rules of Professional Conduct that could lead to disciplinary charges?

Sincerely,
Risk E. Behavior

Dear Risk E. Behavior:

Although we suspect that there are some who may believe that a firm divide should exist between the personal and professional lives of an attorney, the fact is that we are officers of the Court with specific ethical and legal responsibilities. Attorneys should know that they are representatives of our profession and that conduct outside the practice of law can result in disciplinary action.

While this may seem basic, lawyers should be mindful of Rule 8.4 of the Rules of Professional Conduct which states that "a lawyer or law firm shall not engage in illegal conduct that adversely reflects on the lawyer's honesty, trustworthiness or fitness as a lawyer…" *See* Rule 8.4(b). Furthermore, "a lawyer or law firm shall not engage in conduct involving dishonesty, fraud, deceit or misrepresentation…" *See* Rule 8.4(c).

The question whether an attorney's conduct outside of a professional practice can be subject to disciplinary action has been subject to much debate. In New York, conduct or dishonesty in an attorney's business or personal dealings may give rise to a level warranting professional discipline. *See* Hal R. Lieberman, *Discipline for 'Private Conduct': Rationale and Recent Trends*, N.Y.L.J., Feb 19, 2013, p. 3, which gives several examples where attorneys were disciplined for certain acts of misconduct outside of their respective legal practices, including:

- falsely accusing a state trooper of having uttered anti-Semitic slurs against him, and reaffirming those accusations on more than one occasion, in an attempt to get out of a speeding ticket;

- willfully refusing, in violation of court orders, to timely pay child support;

- pursuing vexation litigation as a "party-litigant, not as an attorney";

- telling the coexecutor under a will executed by the lawyer's uncle that the lawyer needed a power of attorney ("POA") from the uncle to reinstate dormant bank accounts but instead used the POA to restructure, and to attempt to restructure, his uncle's accounts for the lawyer's personal benefit; and

- fraudulently occupying a rent-regulated apartment for two years after the death of the tenant of record.

Id. (internal citations omitted).

Suspensions were deemed an appropriate sanction for an attorney who pled guilty to possessing and engaging in the distribution of narcotics (*see In re Silberman*, 83 A.D.3d 95 (1st Dep't 2009)) as well as for another attorney who pled guilty to operating a motor vehicle under the influence of alcohol and leaving the scene of an accident (*see In re Clarey*, 55 A.D.3d 209 (2d Dep't 2008), *cited in* Lieberman, *supra*, at p. 3). A more drastic penalty—immediate disbarment—was imposed where an attorney was convicted of forging a medical prescription form (*see In re Felsen*, 40 A.D.3d 1257 (3d Dep't 2007)); in another case an attorney's conviction for felony assault resulted in automatic disbarment (*see In re Ugweches*, 60 A.D.3d 125 (1st Dep't 2009)). Lieberman, *supra*.

This year, an attorney was disciplined for impersonating someone on a dating website that resulted in criminal charges (*see In re O'Hare*, 968 N.Y.S.2d 394 (1st Dep't July 17, 2013)), and another for disregarding an order of protection by sending text messages to an estranged spouse (*see In re Knudsen*, 109 A.D.3d 94 (1st Dep't 2013)). Outside of this state, one disciplinary authority cited an attorney for violating the equivalent of Rule 8.4(c) by misrepresenting the condition of his home in connection with alleged water damage which occurred in his basement. *See* Edward J. Cleary, *Accountability or Overkill: Disciplining Private Behavior*, available at http://www.mnbar.org/benchandbar/2001/feb01/prof-resp.htm.

The situations presented in your inquiry, though perhaps not as egregious as the conduct noted above, could potentially subject you to disciplinary action. Here's why.

"[A]ny lawyer who commits a 'serious crime,' as defined in the stat-ute, is subject to professional discipline whether or not the conviction has anything to do with the attorney's law practice." *See* Hal R. Lieberman and Richard Supple, *Private Conduct and Professional Discipline*, N.Y.L.J., July 23, 2002, p. 20; *see also* Judiciary Law § 90(4)(d).

Judiciary Law § 90(4)(d) defines the term "serious crime" as

> any criminal offense denominated a felony under the laws of any state, district or territory or of the United States which does not constitute a felony under the laws of this state, and any other crime a necessary element of which, as determined by statutory or common law definition of such crime, includes interference with the administration of justice, false swearing, misrepresen-tation, fraud, willful failure to file income tax returns, deceit, bribery, extortion, misappropriation, theft, or an attempt or conspiracy or solicitation of another to com-mit a serious crime.

Inflated insurance claims are likely a crime under New York Penal Law §§ 176.00–176.35. Whether it is a mis-demeanor or a felony will de-pend on the amount of money involved but should you be convicted of a felony, you would be subject to automatic disbarment under Judiciary Law § 90(4)(a). At a minimum, there is also the possibility of automatic suspension from practice under Judiciary Law § 90(4)(f), which provides that

> [a]ny attorney and counsellor-at-law convicted of a seri-ous crime, as defined in paragraph d of this subdivision, whether by plea of guilty or nolo contendere or from a verdict after trial or otherwise, shall be suspended upon the receipt by the appellate division of the supreme court of the record of such conviction until a final order is made pursuant to paragraph g of this subdivision.

Lawyers should not submit inflated insurance claims. It subjects you to possible disciplinary action, almost certainly jeopardizing your profes-sional career in the short term and possibly permanently.

Turning to your real estate with numerous building code violations and fines, although your obvious neglect of these properties may not be something that would get you prosecuted for a serious crime, why are you taking the risk that someone might file a complaint against you? The kind of conduct you describe could be viewed as conduct reflecting on your "honesty, trustworthiness or fitness as a lawyer." Therefore, if you do engage in a business which would subject you to scrutiny by adminis-trative authorities, you would be well advised to comply with all neces-sary regulations, especially building codes.

The false statement in your loan application that you went to Yale Law School instead of "Yala" Law School is something that you most certainly realize was not the right thing to do. Obviously, you know that you had an obligation to be completely accurate when you applied for a loan and that any material misstatement in the application could be a federal criminal offense (*see* 18 U.S.C § 1014 (2013)), which would be likely to result in disciplinary action. Furthermore, as discussed above, at a minimum, an act of misrepresentation, fraud or deceit qualifies as a serious crime under Judiciary Law § 90(4)(f) that would subject you to automatic suspension from practice and could even result in automatic disbarment under Judiciary Law § 90(4)(a). As we have stated above, you would be wise not to engage in any action of misrepresentation, fraud or deceit, such as misstating where you went to law school, since it would place your professional career at risk.

Although this should go without saying, an attorney should never make any inaccurate disclosure of information concerning himself or herself because even an attorney's misrepresentation of his or her own professional background can result in discipline. Indeed, one jurisdiction has disciplined an attorney for misrepresenting which law school he attended on the resume he sent to a prospective employer. *In re Hadzi-Antich*, 497 A.2d 1062 (D.C. 1985). In another jurisdiction, an attorney was suspended from practice for three years for falsifying grades on his law school transcript. *In re Loren Elliotte Friedman*, 2009 Ill. Atty. Reg. Disc. LEXIS 75, *aff'd*, 2010 Ill. Atty. Reg. Disc. LEXIS 126 (Ill. 2010).

Attorneys "should know better" even when acting outside the office. We are not setting an unreachable bar, but only wish to remind attorneys that when dealing with others, even outside of the attorney-client relationship, it is necessary for attorneys to always act with common sense and candor in their dealings outside of their professional world.

Sincerely,
The Forum by

Vincent J. Syracuse, Esq.
Matthew R. Maron, Esq.,
Tannenbaum Helpern Syracuse & Hirschtritt LLP

This article originally appeared in the October 2013 *NYSBA Journal*.

Court Appearance

To the Forum:

I graduated law school last year and was just admitted to the bar. With very few job prospects out there for young attorneys, I decided to hang out my own shingle. Lately I have encountered judges and counsel who give me strange looks when they see me in court or at a meeting. I have also lost a few clients and have come to realize, I am not sure why, that this may have something to do with my appearance. I never really understood the need for attorneys to dress formally. So I dress pretty much the way I did in law school. I don't wear a tie when I am in court. I usually enjoy sporting a nice pair of expensive jeans and then top them off with some brightly colored shoes. Some of the judges that I have appeared before have openly commented not only on my informal dress but also my piercings and a few visible tattoos. To me, the way I dress is an expression of my basic rights to free speech. It is the quality of my arguments that should count, not the way I dress that should be important. I am the first member of my family to become a lawyer and do not have any mentors to help me. Do I have a professional obligation to wear a suit and tie when I am in court? What about meetings with clients or other lawyers?

Sincerely,
N.O. Fashionplate

Dear N.O. Fashionplate:

We all remember the famous scene in *My Cousin Vinny* where Vincent LaGuardia Gambini, Esq., makes his first appearance before the Honorable Chamberlain Haller wearing a leather jacket. When asked by the judge what he is wearing, Vinny says "I don't get the question," and answers "Um, I'm wearing clothes." In the iconic colloquy that follows, Judge Haller sternly sets us all straight about proper dress in the courtroom:

> Judge Haller: When you come into my court looking like you do, you not only insult me, but you insult the integrity of this court!

> Vinny: I apologize, sir, but, uh…this is how I dress.

> Judge Haller: The next time you appear in my court, you will look lawyerly. And I mean you comb your hair, and wear a suit and tie. And that suit had better be made out of some sort of…cloth. You understand me?

> Vinny: Uh yes. Fine, Judge, fine.

Hopefully, we all "get" what Judge Haller was saying to Mr. Gambini: appropriate dress is part of professional responsibility, especially when we go to court.

In the past two decades, the business community has experienced many changes in how people dress at the office and in other professional settings. Some attribute this to the technology sector (*see* Claire Cain Miller, *Techies Break a Fashion Taboo*, N.Y. Times, Aug. 3, 2012), which is almost completely dominated by younger entrepreneurs who believe that, like the typewriter, the "suit and tie" for men and business suits for women are relics of a foregone era. While many law offices have adopted business casual as the norm, the legal profession has held the line when it comes to traditional business attire in a professional setting, even though, more often than not, clients are more likely to dress in business-casual attire when meeting with their counsel.

We know that this may seem old-fashioned, but we should not overlook the fact that court proceedings are serious business. They are forums that address our basic freedoms and countless economic issues. How we dress in the courtroom is a sign of respect that should be consistent with the seriousness of what we do when we appear in court. Believe it or not, attorneys have shown up in court wearing jogging suits and sneakers; we can only wonder what they were thinking.

We attorneys should not dress in a manner that unnecessarily calls attention to ourselves or adopts a casual attitude about the importance of what we do and the judicial process. Former Chief Judge Judith S. Kaye put it best when she said that "[one's] dress should not be noticed [and we] should stand out for the quality of our presentation." *See* Ann Farmer, *Order in the Closet—Why Attire for Women Lawyers Is Still an Issue*, American Bar Association, Perspectives, Vol. 19, No. 2 (Fall 2010). Although Chief Judge Kaye's comments were focused on female attorneys, proper dress in the courtroom is *not* a gender issue, and *all* attorneys should follow her sage advice.

Perhaps anticipating what Judge Haller would say a few years later in *My Cousin Vinny*, a Florida court took on the issue in *Sandstrom v. State*, 309 So. 2d 17 (Fla. Dist. Ct. App. 1975), *cert. dismissed*, 336 So. 2d 572 (Fla. 1976), when a lawyer showed up in court wearing what appeared to be a white leisure suit (probably similar to what John Travolta wore in *Saturday Night Fever*), no tie and exposed chest hair. The court opined in *Sandstrom* that proper attire in the courtroom is an integral part of our judicial system. In the words of the court:

> The wearing of a coat and necktie in open court has been a long honored tradition. It has always been considered a contribution to the seriousness and solemnity of the occasion and the proceedings. It is a sign of respect. A "jacket and tie" are still required dress in many public

places. The Supreme Court of the United States by "Notice to Counsel" advises that appropriate dress in appearing before that court is conservative business dress. Would anyone question that includes a coat and necktie?

In our judgment the court's order requiring appellant to wear a tie in court was a simple requirement bearing a reasonable relationship to the proper administration of justice in that court. Appellant's dogged refusal to comply demonstrated a total lack of cooperation by counsel and was hardly befitting a member of the bar.

Id.

But how does one know what is appropriate, and what is not? While that may be a relatively easy task when we are talking about men wearing a suit and tie to court, we should also understand that appropriate standards are not always written in stone and, in fact, often change with the times. And, what is acceptable to some may not be acceptable to everyone. *Peck v. Stone*, 32 A.D.2d 506 (4th Dep't 1969), is a great example. In *Peck*, the trial court order prohibiting a female attorney from wearing a miniskirt in court resulted in a reversal by the Appellate Division. The court in *Peck* found that:

[T]he record fail[ed] to show that petitioner's appearance in any way created distraction or in any manner disrupted the ordinary proceedings of the court. There is no suggestion that petitioner's dress was so immodest or revealing as to shock one's sense of propriety. Neither is it urged by respondent that the continued appearance by petitioner, so garbed, would create any distraction. In fact, with understandable candor, respondent's counsel admitted that no such claim was made, and, further that her appearance did not create a disruptive condition. Furthermore the record demonstrates that during appellant's colloquy with the court she was at all times respectful, reserved and at no time could her demonstrated attitude in any manner be considered contrary to her ethical responsibilities as an officer of the court.

Id.

In re De Carlo, 141 N.J. Super. 42 (1976), is another example. Citing *Peck* and distinguishing *Sandstrom*, the appellate court reversed the lower court's contempt order that chastised a female attorney who wore gray wool slacks, a matching gray sweater and a green open-collared blouse in court, finding such attire "w[as] not of the kind that could be fairly labeled disruptive, distractive or depreciative of the solemnity of the judicial process so as to foreclose her courtroom appearance." Id. The following decade, a California appellate court held that the standard for appropriate courtroom attire was based on the test as to "whether it interfere[d] with courtroom decorum disrupting justice, that is, whether it tend[ed] to cause disorder or interference with or impede the functioning of the court." *See Jensen v. Superior Court*, 154 Cal. App. 3d 533 (1984) (reversal of lower court's refusal to permit plaintiff's attorney, who wore a turban, to appear at a hearing, unless the attorney showed he wore the turban for some "legitimate" purpose).

An opinion of the New York County Lawyers' Association Committee on Professional Ethics (the NYCLA Opinion) is also instructive and expresses the view that the Code of Professional Responsibility (the precursor to the current Rules of Professional Conduct (the RPC)) did not prohibit female attorneys "from wearing appropriately tailored pants suits or other pant-based outfits in a court appearance." *See* NYCLA Eth. Op. 688, 1991 WL 755944 (1991). In support of this view, the NYCLA Opinion cited to former Disciplinary Rules 1-102(A)(3) and (5) as well as 7-106(C)(6), respectively. Both of these rules are now codified (though slightly revised) as Rules 8.4(b)–(d) and 3.3(f)(2) of the RPC. Rule 8.4(d) of the RPC provides that "a lawyer…shall not engage in conduct that is prejudicial to the administration of justice." Furthermore, Rule 3.3(f) (2) of the RPC states that "[i]n appearing as a lawyer before a tribunal, a lawyer shall not engage in undignified or discourteous conduct."

More recently, at a Seventh Circuit Bar Association Meeting in 2009, a judge declared that for women "titillating attire was a huge problem, [and] a distraction in the courtroom" and that "[one should not] dress in court as if it's Saturday night and you're going out to a party." The same judge also frowned upon men "who sported loud ties, some with designs like smiley faces." *See* John Schwartz, *At a Symposium of Judges, a Debate on the Laws of Fashion*, N.Y. Times, May 22, 2009.

With all due respect to what you say is your need to express your rights of free speech, when it comes to proper dress there are some things best left at the door when you enter a courthouse. As officers of the court and members of the bar, we all have both a professional and an ethical obligation to dress in a professional manner when appearing in court. That means a suit and tie for men and an appropriate business suit for women. With regard to your tattoos and piercings, we would suggest that you do your best to remove any distracting jewelry before you appear before any judge, because such accessories cause unnecessary distraction and potentially interfere with courtroom decorum. *See, e.g., Peck*, 32 A.D.2d at 507–08; *see also Jensen*, 154 Cal. App. 3d at 537. It is hard to help you with your tattoos which may not be so easy to hide. We suggest that the next time you appear in court, you would be wise to make every effort to hide the more potentially distracting tattoos so that a judge may focus more closely on what you are saying rather than what you look like. For better or worse, human beings have a natural inclination to focus on what people look like, so based on how you describe yourself, we believe that you should limit how many visible tattoos people can see when you are in court.

As for your question concerning proper dress when meeting with clients or other lawyers, hopefully your own common sense should guide how you present yourself in those particular settings. As your client's counsel, you are in the best position to gauge your client's expectations. If, for example, you happen to represent a client who also shares your interest in piercings and tattoos, then it may be acceptable in limited circumstances to dress informally in the manner as you have described. However, when meeting with other lawyers (and potentially adverse parties) we strongly advise that you dress as if you were going to court. Many times an adversary and his or her client will scrutinize how the opposing party and lawyer present themselves, and you do not want to dress in a way that could potentially compromise the manner in which you would advocate for your client.

Remember, people rarely get criticized for overdressing, a view that was recently embraced by one notable pop culture figure. *See* Justin Timberlake, "Suit & Tie," on *The 20/20 Experience* (RCA Records 2013). However, those who dress down often face the risk of having their choice of clothing overshadow what they might be saying. To that end, use your best judgment deciding what to wear when you meet with a client. But when you go to court you have an obligation to present yourself in a respectful manner (which means appropriate business attire).

That said, we should all remember that the standards for appropriate dress are never stagnant and are likely to change with the times. It would be interesting to put this Forum in a time capsule and open it in 20 years. Will judges still wear robes, and will lawyers still wear business suits in court? We think so, but only time will tell.

Sincerely,
The Forum by

Vincent J. Syracuse, Esq.
Matthew R. Maron, Esq.
Tannenbaum Helpern Syracuse & Hirschtritt LLP

This article originally appeared in the May 2014 *NYSBA Journal*.

What Is Sanctionable Conduct?

To the Forum:

I am always conscious about running up unnecessary legal fees in litigation matters and I am acutely aware that, in this current economic climate, clients scrutinize legal bills more than ever. I recently succeeded in winning summary judgment on liability for my client in a breach of contract matter and the trial court subsequently directed a hearing on damages in which my adversary, David Delayer (Delayer), moved for a stay in the appellate court. The stay was granted, however, on the condition that Delayer's client post an undertaking. The day after the stay was granted, I emailed Delayer asking if his client would be posting the undertaking directed by the appellate court. His response was, "We have not made that determination as of yet." A few days later, at a conference before the trial court, Delayer said that his clients "were not seeking to obtain an undertaking." Since Delayer represented that he was not going to seek an undertaking, the trial court scheduled a damages hearing at the conference to occur in 30 days. The day after the conference and in preparation for the hearing, I served a document subpoena upon Delayer, which he moved to quash. That motion was argued a few days before the damages hearing and was granted in part by the trial court. The following morning, I was informed by Delayer that his client had posted the undertaking directed by the appellate court which it had required in order to stay the damages hearing. That afternoon, counsel for the insurance company (which issued the undertaking) informed me that Delayer had applied for the bond "weeks earlier." This is the first I had heard about the timing of the application for the bond, and from past experience I know that a bond is usually issued in a matter of days (if not the same day). Had I known that Delayer had applied for the bond weeks ago (and assuming it was issued shortly after he applied for it), then I would not have been forced to spend unnecessary time opposing his motion to quash since he likely knew weeks prior that the bond was issued, thereby staying the damages hearing.

I believe that Delayer's actions are unprofessional. At a minimum, Delayer's behavior is a clear example of uncivil (perhaps unethical) conduct motivated solely for the purpose of increasing my client's litigation expenses.

My questions for the Forum: Did my adversary act unprofessionally? Is Delayer's conduct sanctionable?

Sincerely,
A. Barrister

Dear A. Barrister:

What constitutes sanctionable conduct is one of the most hotly debated matters faced by the bench and the bar. Section 130-1 of the Rules of the Chief Administrator of the Courts, 22 N.Y.C.R.R. 130-1 (Rule 130-1 or Part 130) sets forth the provisions governing how costs and sanctions may be awarded by a court when it finds that a party or its attorney has acted in a manner warranting the imposition of costs or sanctions. Specifically, Rule 130-1.1 states:

> (a) The court, in its discretion, may award to any party or attorney in any civil action or proceeding before the court, except where prohibited by law, costs in the form of reimbursement for actual expenses reasonably incurred and reasonable attorney's fees, resulting from frivolous conduct as defined in this Part. In addition to or in lieu of awarding costs, the court, in its discretion may impose financial sanctions upon any party or attorney in a civil action or proceeding who engages in frivolous conduct as defined in this Part, which shall be payable as provided in section 130-1.3 of this Part. This Part shall not apply to town or village courts, to proceedings in a small claims part of any court, or to proceedings in the Family Court commenced under Article 3, 7 or 8 of the Family Court Act.

> (b) The court, as appropriate, may make such award of costs or impose such financial sanctions against either an attorney or a party to the litigation or against both. Where the award or sanction is against an attorney, it may be against the attorney personally or upon a partnership, firm, corporation, government agency, prosecutor's office, legal aid society or public defender's office with which the attorney is associated and that has appeared as attorney of record. The award or sanctions may be imposed upon any attorney appearing in the action or upon a partnership, firm or corporation with which the attorney is associated.

> (c) For purposes of this Part, conduct is frivolous if:

> > (1) it is completely without merit in law and cannot be supported by a reasonable argument for an extension, modification or reversal of existing law;

> > (2) it is undertaken primarily to delay or prolong the resolution of the litigation, or to harass or maliciously injure another; or

> > (3) it asserts material factual statements that are false.

Frivolous conduct shall include the making of a frivolous motion for costs or sanctions under this section. In determining whether the conduct undertaken was frivolous, the court shall consider, among other issues, (1) the circumstances under which the conduct took place, including the time available for investigating the legal or factual basis of the conduct; and (2) whether or not the conduct was continued when its lack of legal or factual basis was apparent, should have been apparent, or was brought to the attention of counsel or the party.

(d) An award of costs or the imposition of sanctions may be made either upon motion in compliance with CPLR 2214 or 2215 or upon the court's own initiative, after a reasonable opportunity to be heard. The form of the hearing shall depend upon the nature of the conduct and the circumstances of the case.

Although a full discussion of what constitutes sanctionable conduct could take up volumes of this *Journal*, it appears that the situation which you have described focuses primarily on the question of whether a potentially expensive delay caused by an adversary rises to the level of frivolous conduct and should be sanctioned. Rule 130-1.1(c)(2) notes that frivolous conduct includes actions which are "undertaken primarily to delay or prolong the resolution of the litigation, or to harass or maliciously injure another." Rule 130-1.1(c)(2). One example of sanctionable delay involved a law firm which had hindered the resolution of a litigation by twice moving for additional time to submit an appeal brief while withholding for many months information regarding a related settlement in another state that mooted the appeal and of the firm's intention to move to dismiss the appeal on that ground. *See Naposki v. First National Bank of Atlanta*, 18 A.D.3d 835 (2d Dep't 2005).

Of course, an analysis as to what constitutes sanctionable conduct would be incomplete without mentioning Rule 11 of the Federal Rules of Civil Procedure. Although the federal courts are often hesitant to order sanctions when faced with the allegation that a party or its counsel engaged in conduct intended to "cause unnecessary delay, or needlessly increase the cost of litigation..." (*see* Fed R. Civ. P. 11(b)(1)), Rule 11 is not by itself the only weapon to combat delay tactics by an attorney. 28 U.S.C.A. § 1927 states that

[a]ny attorney...who so multiplies the proceedings in any case unreasonably and vexatiously may be required by the court to satisfy personally the excess costs, expenses, and attorneys' fees reasonably incurred because of such conduct.

In *Wechsler v. Hunt Health Systems, Ltd.*, 216 F. Supp. 2d 347 (S.D.N.Y. 2002), the District Court granted sanctions pursuant to both Rule 11 and 28 U.S.C. § 1927 against a defense counsel who "on the eve of [a]... pre-trial conference to set a trial date...sought [a] procedurally unsound motion for summary judgment." *Id.* at 357. The court in *Wechsler* noted that such conduct by defense counsel "sought to needlessly delay th[e] action." *Id.* at 358.

Naposki and *Wechsler* show just two examples of how courts view delay tactics—they are not taken lightly. While we all know that delay and expense are often inevitable in litigation, smart lawyers recognize that they only create problems for themselves when they engage in delay tactics that include unnecessary motion practice (as seen in *Wechsler*) or discovery "undertaken primarily to delay or prolong the resolution of the litigation, or to harass or maliciously injure another." *See* Rule 130-1.1(c)(2).

We are sure that there are many members of our profession who would consider completely unprofessional Delayer's failure to inform you about the status of the bond in a timely manner. Certainly, many would view Delayer's conduct as violations of multiple provisions of the Standards of Civility (the Standards) (*see* 22 N.Y.C.R.R. § 1200, App. A). Part VI of the Standards provides that "[a] lawyer should not use any aspect of the litigation process...for the purpose of unnecessarily prolonging litigation or increasing litigation expenses." Furthermore, Part IX of the Standards states that "[l]awyers should not mislead other persons involved in the litigation process" and Part IX(b) provides that "[a] lawyer should not ascribe a position to another counsel that counsel has not taken or otherwise seek to create an unjustified inference based on counsel's statements or conduct."

You mentioned that you had emailed Delayer the day after the stay was granted by the appellate court asking if his client would be posting the undertaking directed by the appellate court and that Delayer claimed he had not made that determination. As you noted above, Delayer thereafter made a representation before the trial court that his clients "were not seeking to obtain an undertaking." It is entirely possible that Delayer misrepresented his position concerning the undertaking in his exchange with you (a potential violation of Rule 4.1 of the New York Rules of Professional Conduct (the RPC) which requires that "[i]n the course of representing a client, a lawyer shall not knowingly make a false statement of fact or law to a third person"). Of greater concern is that Delayer may have misrepresented himself before the trial court concerning the status of the undertaking. Such misstatement could amount to a violation of Rule 3.3(a)(1) of the RPC which states that "[a] lawyer shall not knowingly make a false statement of fact or law to a tribunal..."

If you had known that Delayer had actually received the undertaking earlier in time than he later told you, then you would not have had to operate under the assumption that the damages hearing was going forward as previously scheduled by the trial court and you would not have been forced to engage in an unnecessary discovery dispute in advance of the previously scheduled hearing date. By keeping you in the dark as to the status of the undertaking, Delayer's conduct likely caused you to incur unnecessary litigation expenses (a violation of Part VI of the Standards) and the position he took as to the undertaking may have been both misleading and contrary to what he represented to you in prior conversations (a violation of Part IX of the Standards).

Now, was Delayer's conduct sanctionable? Perhaps wanting to go in the other direction, one court recently answered this question in the negative. *Conason v. Megan Holding, LLC*, N.Y.L.J., May 7, 2013, at 22 (Sup. Ct., N.Y. Co. Apr. 18, 2013), was an action for alleged rent overcharges. The plaintiffs won summary judgment on liability. The court directed an assessment of damages by way of a hearing and ordered an award of attorney fees for the plaintiffs. The defendants sought a stay of the damages hearing in the Appellate Division and further perfected their appeal. The Appellate Division stayed the damages hearing on the condition that the defendants post an undertaking. The plaintiffs thereafter moved for costs in the form of attorney fees, claiming that the defendants failed to inform them they were applying for a bond, thus causing the plaintiffs unnecessary work in litigating a subpoena, among other motion practice. The court addressed the issue of whether a party could be sanctioned for failing to save its adversary money, noting doing so would cause no prejudice to itself. In the end, the court denied the plaintiffs' motion for costs and found that the conduct at issue was not sanctionable. The court stated that while Part 130 could expressly provide that failing to save an adversary money was sanctionable, it did not, and questioned where "to draw the line between mere discourtesy and sanctionable misconduct." In addition, the court found that a code of conduct prohibiting causing an adversary to waste money would be difficult to interpret and enforce.

The court in *Conason* apparently felt constrained by the fact that (unlike in Rule 11) there is no express language in Part 130 permitting an award of costs and sanctions when attorneys engage in conduct that unnecessarily adds to the cost of a case. Nevertheless the court expressed the view that attorneys potentially have both a moral duty and a heightened ethical duty not to engage in conduct that could result in one's adversary being forced to incur unnecessary litigation expenses. In the words of the court, "the day may come when the law takes a more moralistic, one might say 'holistic,' approach," adding that "we all gain when nobody is allowed gratuitously to cause another's loss." *Id.* Furthermore, the court embraced the idea that "[i]n normal civil society, the failure to save someone else money is bad form" and that "[w]hat in normal civil society is common courtesy may some day in law become ethical obligation." *Id.*

While counsel's tactics in *Conason* may not have risen to the level of sanctionable conduct, we can think of situations that might warrant a different result. Consider, for example, the adversary who insists that a deposition must be scheduled in a distant location on a holiday week, claiming that is the only place and time the witness will be available for the next six months. The fact, as discovered when the deposition is taken, is that the attorney knew full well that the witness was available in the adversary's home city for much of that time and there was no reason for the out-of-town deposition. Was the concealment of this fact frivolous conduct within the meaning of Part 130? We are sure that many of us would view it as such.

Although Delayer's conduct (which bears a striking resemblance to the conduct at issue in *Conason*) may not, at least in the view of one judge, have been sanctionable, it should be a cautionary tale for attorneys in their dealings with opposing counsel. The lesson to be learned is that the case law may not always keep pace with the conduct. Lawyers take a great risk when they engage in practices which delay cases and cause unnecessary litigation expense.

Sincerely,
The Forum by

Vincent J. Syracuse, Esq., and
Matthew R. Maron, Esq.,
Tannenbaum Helpern Syracuse & Hirschtritt LLP

This article originally appeared in the July/August 2013 *NYSBA Journal*.

When You Disagree with the Senior Partner

To the Forum:

I am a mid-level partner in a firm that is considered the leader in advising a particular industry. Across the relevant practice areas, the law as it applies to this industry is unsettled and developing, so our activity calls for a lot of judgment. Clients often rely on our advice almost as if our judgments were the law…which, of course, they are not, and that is the nub of my problem.

In particular, based on our longstanding advice and the strength of our firm's reputation, no one in the industry engages in a particular practice I will call "X." Last week, a new entrant to the industry ("Client") asked about "X," and when I gave the stock "no" answer, Client handed me a research paper written by another lawyer who has never had contact with this particular industry. I read the paper with some skepticism and discovered, to my surprise, that it utterly demolishes our long-held position and proves, conclusively in my judgment, that X is permissible.

My boss (whose name is on our firm's door) cannot find a hole in the newcomer's analysis but yet still insists that "we have our story and we are sticking to it." I am not sure whether he concedes that he has been wrong or refuses to consider that possibility, but his main concern is that our firm and those whom we have advised have too much invested in the status quo to consider a change. He points out that all the leading industry players have been able to operate successfully (though at some additional cost) without doing X, so there is little to gain in our telling everyone that we have been wrong all along. On the other hand, if we say yes only to Client, it will gain an unfair advantage over the others, and when word inevitably gets out we will look silly (or worse) and may lose a lot of business.

To complicate matters, Client insists that the reasoning that they and the new guy on the block have adduced in support of X is their proprietary information, insofar as it represents an ability to do something lucrative that the rest of the market has missed. Client has prohibited us from disclosing that anyone believes that X is permissible.

My boss has instructed me to tell Client that their other lawyer is mistaken and has no feel for this very specialized industry, and given our firm's reputation that might well be the end of the matter. But that will not be the end of the matter for me. I am not comfortable giving advice that I honestly believe to be wrong or in participating in what appears to me to be a cover-up. I have three questions:

1. May or must I tell Client my opinion, regardless of the directive from my senior partner?

2. Is Client within its rights in prohibiting our firm from disclosing to others the fact that someone has concluded that X is permissible (regardless of what we advise Client)?

3. If I leave my firm, may I disclose this sordid mess at least to justify why I am leaving or have changed my views, or am I bound to respect the firm's confidences even if they constitute, in my judgment, intentional malpractice?

Sincerely,
Painted into a Corner

Dear Painted:

We sincerely sympathize with your predicament. This is the sort of situation that has come increasingly to characterize legal practice as it shifts from a learned profession to a business, albeit both a heavily regulated and self-regulated business, with unique traditions that we still strive to uphold. Perhaps it was never really as quaint as we might prefer to think—Abe Lincoln made a lot of money representing railroads—but we hope you get the picture. And a general counsel of a company may have to face this type of pressure much more often than an outside advisor such as you.

Your first question—whether you may or must tell Client your personal opinion—turns in large part, in our view, on Client's relationship with you and with your firm.

If Client clearly relies principally on your senior partner's judgment or Client's main relationship is with another lawyer at your firm, your best course of action would be to ask that lawyer to convey the firm's position to Client. You do not have a duty to overrule the firm's consensus if you know that Client intends to rely on the firm's viewpoint as opposed to your own, but you also do not have a duty to be a shill for anyone. You cannot in good conscience be a mouthpiece for falsity, but as long as it is clear to you that Client is not asking specifically for *your* personal judgment, you can, if you want, pass the buck. We caution you that this may not endear you to your partners, who might see you as unwilling to "take responsibility," and, in any event, you will have no control over how the communication is presented and whether Client infers or is told that this is *your* conclusion.

As a result, the approach set forth in the preceding paragraph may not be the one you want to take. In that case, and certainly if you believe that Client wants to rely on *your* judgment, you would be on solid ground to advise Client truthfully that the firm's view is "no" but your personal view is "yes." One way this finds expression in complicated areas like taxation is a formulation like, "It may be correct and reasonable advisors might so conclude, but as a firm we do not feel comfortable issuing that opinion." You should not give in to the temptation to disclose why the firm's view differs from yours or to denigrate your senior partner's motivations, but you should feel free to tell Client that he can call your partners for further clarification. Obviously if you do this, you owe your partners and your firm the courtesy, if not the duty, of letting them know in advance what you intend to do so that they are not blindsided.

No matter how this plays out, you should be prepared for a potential showdown and for the possibility that you may need to find other employment rather soon. They may teach about that aspect of professional life in business school, but not in law school.

Turning to your second question—about who, in effect, owns the knowledge and the technology—we offer several observations. First, in view of the novelty of the conclusion that Client's other lawyer has reached and the important commercial implications, we believe Client has a right to insist that you and your firm *not* disclose this information.

As we have discussed many times before in the Forum, Rule 1.6 of the New York Rules of Professional Conduct (RPC) prohibits disclosure of confidential client information without the client's informed consent. Specifically, Rule 1.6(a) of the RPC states that "[a] lawyer shall not *knowingly* reveal confidential information, as defined in this Rule, or use such information to the disadvantage of a client or for the advantage of the lawyer or a third person…" (emphasis added). As defined by the RPC, confidential information "consists of information gained during or relating to the representation of a client, whatever its source, that is (a) protected by the attorney-client privilege, (b) likely to be embarrassing or detrimental to the client if disclosed, or (c) information that the client has requested be kept confidential" but "does not ordinarily include (i) a lawyer's legal knowledge or legal research or (ii) information that is generally known in the local community or in the trade, field or profession to which the information relates." *See id.*

Without even reaching the question of whether Client has a proprietary right in an item of intellectual property (the way Client might frame this), your discussions with Client, including his revelation to you of what the other lawyer had concluded, seem to be well within the scope of what is deemed "confidential information." *See id.*

Second, if your firm discloses and criticizes the other lawyer's conclusion, observers may come to think of your firm as a bully and question its motives. No private actor, regardless of how influential, should wrap itself in the mantle of "the system" and think that it has a duty to police what others do that overrides ethical and professional constraints.

On the other hand, no one "owns the law." If you happen to have had occasion to think about the law, for any reason, and another person asks you a question, you are free to answer it as you believe is correct. So, should your partners reconsider or if you free yourself from the bonds that connect you to them, you are well within the bounds of ethics and professionalism to give what you believe to be correct advice. But be vigilant not to cross the fuzzy line between answering a question when it is posed to you or is inherent in an analysis that you have been asked to do, and, on the other hand, volunteering information or inducing people to ask you that question.

Finally, the matter of confidentiality as to the legal conclusion and analysis, but still not as to details of your discussions with Client, will evaporate if and when there is general public awareness that someone says X is permissible. Our advice that you and your firm still tread carefully continues: fair comment, yes; calling out the attack dogs, no.

Your third question concerns the intersection of duty to clients and duty to partners. The answer is not all that difficult, though you may not be happy with it. Until the public becomes aware of the specifics, as noted in the preceding paragraphs, you cannot disclose the details to promote yourself or even to explain your departure. Depending on what actually happens, you can say something along the lines of, "I found myself disagreeing with my partners' professional judgment or risk evaluation on one or more matters," or even "I was forced out because I refused to counsel a client in a way that was contrary to my best professional judgment." But beware that it is a cold world out there, and in our experience it is far from certain that people will not think of these as self-serving statements. There is really not much else you can say without actually accusing your firm of malpractice, and the life of a whistleblower is lonely save for the excitement of potentially having to defend a defamation lawsuit.

Do you remember "The Game of Life" in its original form, before the advent of political correctness? There were spaces marked "Revenge," and with one spin of the wheel you could instantly win the game as a "Millionaire Tycoon" or go to the "Poor Farm." If you are prepared for long odds, consider how significant a breakthrough this is for Client. If you believe in each other and Client is prepared to provide enough business to anchor a practice, then hang out your own shingle, run with the innovation and grow with Client. Others have done worse in situations like this.

Sincerely,
The Forum by

Vincent J. Syracuse, Esq.
Matthew R. Maron, Esq.
Tannenbaum Helpern Syracuse & Hirschtritt LLP
Robert I. Kantowitz, Esq.

This article originally appeared in the January 2015 *NYSBA Journal*.

Zealous Advocacy or Gratuitous Insults?

To the Forum:

I represent one of the defendants in an action brought against a number of parties in an unfair competition case involving various employees who left their employer to work for a competitor. The plaintiff has sued its former employees and their current employer (my client). It is a high-stakes litigation involving huge sums of money, and it has gotten to the boiling point. Plaintiff's counsel and the attorney for one of the employees have been exchanging what I consider to be vulgar and horrifying emails. The level of insults hurled between these two individuals and the language of their exchanges would make schoolyard talk look like dialogue from the Victorian age. One insult by plaintiff's counsel included a reference to the death of opposing counsel's child; another email made a remark about the disabled child of one of the lawyers. I am astounded that two members of the bar would engage in such disgusting behavior or think that their conduct is effective advocacy. Thankfully, none of the attacks have been directed to me. I am trying to represent my client to the best of my ability and have kept out of the fray.

My question for the Forum: How am I supposed to handle this kind of bad behavior?

Sincerely,
Donald Disgusted

Dear Donald Disgusted:

Your question raises issues strikingly similar to those recently confronted by a Florida court. *Craig v. Volkswagen of America, Inc.*, Case No. 07-7823 CI7 (Circuit Court of the Sixth Judicial Circuit, in and for Pinellas County, Florida) proceeded just as many litigations do; after the case was filed and issue was joined, there were motions and court conferences followed by the beginning of discovery. For reasons that are at best unclear, it was discovery that led some of the lawyers to turn to the dark side.

It began with a protracted email exchange among counsel concerning the scheduling of discovery motions. Plaintiff's counsel threw the first stone by insulting defense counsel, his firm and his hearing preparation tactics. In response, defense counsel referred to his adversary as "Junior" and asked him to stop sending "absurd emails," which in turn was answered with an email that called defense counsel an "Old Hack" admonishing him to "[l]earn to litigate professionally." Later, as the parties were attempting to schedule depositions, plaintiff's counsel (who had apparently failed to propose deposition dates) wrote that defense counsel could not "deal with the pressure of litigating…" and that "if [his adversary could not] take the heat then [he should] get out of the kitchen…" The response was quick. Defense counsel's email again called his adversary "Junior" and accused him of being both on "drugs" and a "little punk" whom he then referred to as a "bottom feeding/scum sucking/loser…." who had a "NOTHING life…" and was told to go back to his "single wide trailer…" This obviously did not sit well with plaintiff's counsel whose retort to defense counsel was that "God [had] blessed him with a great life" and that he allowed himself ample time for various hobbies, such as traveling, riding "dirt bikes and atvs" and his "motorcycle." This could have easily been ignored but, no, defense counsel had to have the last word, so this is what he put in an email:

> [T]he fact that you are married means that there is truly someone for everyone even a short/hairless jerk!!! Moreover, the fact that you have pro-created is further proof for the need of forced sterilization!!!

If you think it could not get any worse, guess again. Approximately three months later, plaintiff's counsel wrote an email that characterized opposing counsel as a "lying, dilatory mentally handicapped person" adding in another email that opposing counsel (whom he called "Corky") had a type of "retardism" [sic] resulting from counsel's "closely spaced eyes, dull blank stare, bulbous head, lying and inability to tell fiction from reality…" These statements apparently hit a nerve with defense counsel who then disclosed to his adversary that he had a son with a birth defect but then went on to make various *ad hominem* attacks against plaintiff's counsel's family members and questioned the legitimacy of his adversary's children. If you still think it could not get any worse, it did.

In his response to that email, plaintiff's counsel said the following:

> Three things Corky:

> (1) While I am sorry to hear about your disabled child; that sort of thing is to be expected when a retard reproduces, it is a crap shoot [sic] sometimes retards can produce normal kids, sometimes they produce F***** up kids. Do not hate me, hate your genetics. However, I would look at the bright side at least you definitively know the kid is yours.

> (2) You are confusing realties [sic] again the retard love story you describe taking place in a pinto [sic] and trailer is your story. You remember the other lifetime [sic] movie about your life: "Special Love" the Corky and Marie story; a heartwarming tale of a retard fighting for his love, children, pinto and trailer and hoping to prove to the world that retard can live a normal life (well kinda).

(3) Finally, I am done communicating with you; your language skills, wit and overall skill level is at a level my nine-year old could successfully combat; so for me it is like taking candy from well a retard and I am now bored. So run along and resume your normal activity of attempting to put a square peg into a round hole and come back when science progresses to a level that it can successfully add 50, 75 or 100 points to your I.Q.

When it appears that plaintiff's counsel could not sink any lower, he then writes:

This guy is an absolute a** clown and what he is not going to use his retarded son with 300+ surgeries (must look just like Mooney so they must be all plastic surgeries) to get out of the trial? I can see already your Honor my retarded son is having surgery for the 301st time so there is no way I can try the case I need a continuance. Absolute joke and a** clown. If this is what a 20 year attorney looks like, then I feel sorry for the profession. Yea, that is exactly what I want to do go watch a jester perform at the Court. How pathetic of a life must you have to run around every day talking about how great a trial attorney you are. Especially, when everybody can see you are an a** clown. After all if I am running around to hearings after 20 years lying to courts and using my time to send childish emails to a third year attorney, the last thing I am going to do is run around saying what a great attorney I am. This guy has to go home every night and get absolutely plastered to keep from blowing his huge bulbous head off. Alright, enough about the a** clown. Later.

And finally, the last exchange between these two "professionals" concluded with plaintiff's counsel referring to his adversary once again as an "a** clown" who should be tending to his "retarded son and his 600th surgery…." He concludes by stating that he heard "the little retards [sic] monosyllabic grunts now; Yep I can make [sic] just barely make it out; he is calling for his a** clown. How sweet."

It should be no surprise that both attorneys were brought up on disciplinary charges, including violations of Rules 3-4.3 (commission of any act that is unlawful or contrary to honesty and justice) and 4-8.4(d) (a lawyer shall not engage in conduct in connection with the practice of law that is prejudicial to the administration of justice, including to knowingly, or through callous indifference, disparage, humiliate, or discriminate against litigants, jurors, witnesses, court personnel, or other lawyers on any basis, including, but not limited to, on account of race, ethnicity, gender, religion, national origin, disability, marital status, sexual orientation, age, socioeconomic status, employment, or physical characteristic) of the Rules Regulating the Florida Bar. *See* Complaint, The *Florida Bar v. Mitchell*, TFB No. 2009-10,487(13C), Supreme Court of Florida, and Complaint, *The Florida Bar v. Mooney*, TFB No. 2009-10,745(13C), Supreme Court of Florida.

The result was that plaintiff's counsel was suspended from practice for 10 days, ordered to attend an anger management workshop and pay $2,000 in costs. *See The Florida Bar v. Mitchell*, 46 So. 3d 1003 (Fla. 2010). In addition, plaintiff's counsel was subject to reciprocal discipline in both the District of Columbia and Pennsylvania as a result of the Florida disciplinary decision. *See In re Mitchell*, 21 A.3d 1004 (D.C. App. 2011) and *In re Mitchell*, 2011 Pa. LEXIS 2308 (Pa. 2011). Defense counsel was given a public reprimand as a result of his conduct and had to pay $2,500 in costs. *See The Florida Bar v. Mooney*, 49 So. 3d 748 (Fla. 2010).

Craig makes it easy to answer your question: always take the "high road" and never go "shot for shot" when an adversary tries to drag you into the fray. As officers of the court, we should be civil to each other and must always act in a manner that is consistent our ethical obligations. To that end, you (and more important, the attorneys on your case) should take note of the Standards of Civility (the Standards) (*see* 22 N.Y.C.R.R. § 1200, App. A) in connection with your duties toward other lawyers. Section I of the Standards provides that "[l]awyers should be courteous and civil in all professional dealings with other persons" and further notes, in part,

> A. Lawyers should act in a civil manner regardless of the ill feelings that their clients may have toward others.
>
> B. Lawyers can disagree without being disagreeable. Effective representation does not require antagonistic or acrimonious behavior. Whether orally or in writing, lawyers should avoid vulgar language, disparaging personal remarks or acrimony toward other counsel, parties or witnesses.

See Standards (I).

The Standards have been in place since 1997, and, fortunately, most lawyers follow them. They realize that, totally apart from the risks that bad behavior creates, the practice of law should not be a battlefield that brings out the worst in us. Effective lawyers realize that uncivil conduct is not effective advocacy and does not advance the interests of our clients. It should not be necessary to remind the members of our profession that the rules that govern our conduct apply to emails; lawyers do not get a pass when bad behavior manifests itself in email. Your question and *Craig* tell us that while most lawyers get it, there will always be a few who give in to temptation, especially when using email to communicate. The lawyers in your case fall into this category and appear to have acted in contravention of the recommended behavior under the Standards. Moreover, based on what we have described with regard to the attorneys in *Craig*, they could be subject to disciplinary action under the New York Rules of Professional Conduct (the RPC). As stated in other Forums, while the RPC does not directly address civility, several rules deal with "overly aggressive behavior" by attorneys, including Rule 3.1 (Non-meritorious Claims and Contentions), 3.2 (Delay of Litigation), 3.3 (Conduct Before a Tribunal), 3.4 (Fairness to Opposing Party and Counsel), and 8.4(d) ("engage in conduct that is prejudicial to the administration of justice"). *See* Anthony E. Davis, *Replacing Zealousness With Civility*, N.Y.L.J., Sept. 4, 2012, at 3, col. 1. (*See* Vincent J. Syracuse and Matthew R. Maron, *Attorney Professionalism Forum*, N.Y. St. B.J., Nov./Dec. 2012, Vol. 84. No. 9.) The conduct by both counsel in your action (like the attorneys in *Craig*) could qualify as "overly aggressive behavior."

In addition, the email exchange that you have called to our attention could be viewed as "conduct that is prejudicial to the administration of justice" (*see* Rule. 8.4(d)) and runs contrary to the concept of effective advocacy. Comment [3] states that the Rule "is generally invoked to punish conduct, whether or not it violates another ethics rule, that results in *substantial harm to the justice system comparable to those caused by obstruction of justice*...." and that conduct "must be seriously inconsistent with a lawyer's responsibility as an officer of the court." *See id.* (emphasis added). There can be severe consequences for behavior that runs afoul of these rules. Here in New York, attorneys have been suspended from practice for making offensive remarks to adversaries, clients and even court personnel. *See, e.g., In re Chiofalo*, 78 A.D.3d 9 (1st Dep't 2010) (attorney suspended for two years for using obscene, insulting, sexist, anti-Semitic language, ethnic slurs, and threats in correspondence to his former wife's attorneys and others involved in his matrimonial action. The attorney also filed a meritless federal lawsuit against 29 defendants, including his former wife, her attorneys, judges, and others. The attorney continued to send derogatory and sexist email correspondence to his former wife's attorneys during the pendency of his disciplinary proceeding, indicating a pattern of offensive behavior and a failure to appreciate the seriousness of his actions.); *In re Kahn*, 16 A.D.3d 7 (1st Dep't 2005) (attorney suspended for engaging in a pattern of offensive remarks, including abusive, vulgar and demeaning comments to female adversaries, which included comments about a juvenile client); *In re Brecker*, 309 A.D.2d 77 (2d Dep't 2003) (attorney suspended for two years based on his use of "crude, vulgar and abusive language" in multiple telephone calls and messages to a client and a court examiner over the course of a few hours. The attorney had also been convicted of criminal contempt and had a prior admonition.).

Moreover, there have been instances where attorneys' uncivil conduct has resulted in decisions that had detrimental consequences for their clients in civil litigation. In *Corsini v. U-Haul Int'l*, 212 A.D.2d 288 (1st Dep't 2005), the court found that the attorney's conduct at his own deposition was so lacking in professionalism and civility that the court ordered dismissal of his *pro se* action as "the only appropriate remedy." "Discovery abuse, here in the form of extreme incivility by an attorney, is not to be tolerated....CPLR 3126 provides various sanctions for such misconduct, the most drastic of which is dismissal of the offending party's pleading." *See also Sholes v. Meagher*, 98 N.Y.2d 754 (2002) (the Court denied leave to appeal on procedural grounds for that portion of a case where an attorney was sanctioned and a mistrial granted due to the attorney's lack of decorum by looks of disbelief, sneering, shaking of her head and various expressions designed to indicate to the Court her displeasure); *Heller v. Provenzano*, 257 A.D.2d 378 (1st Dep't 1999) (sanctions awarded against the plaintiff, an attorney, and his counsel because of improper conduct both before and during trial, which included Heller's entering the jury selection room and speaking with jurors without all attorneys present, ignoring the trial judge's warnings not to wander around the courtroom during trial and not to mention another fatal accident which occurred in the same elevator, and referring to the fact that his wife was Hispanic and that he spoke Spanish fluently in an effort to influence Hispanic jury members. Plaintiff's attorney was also sanctioned *because he asked disparaging questions of an expert without a factual basis*); and *Dwyer v. Nicholson et al.*, 193 A.D.2d 70 (2d Dep't 1993), *appeal dismissed*, 220 A.D.2d 555 (2d Dep't 1995), *appeal denied*, 87 N.Y.2d 808, *reargument denied*, 88 N.Y.2d 963 (1996). (A new trial was ordered based, in part, on counsel's "sarcastic, rude, vulgar, pompous, and intemperate utterances on hundreds of pages of the transcript," which were found to be "grossly disrespectful to the court and a violation of accepted and proper courtroom decorum.")

As we have stated both here and previously in this Forum, it is always smart to take the high road when opposing counsel acts inappropriately. Never answer bad behavior with bad (and perhaps worse) behavior.

Sincerely,
The Forum by

Vincent J. Syracuse, Esq.
Matthew R. Maron, Esq.
Tannenbaum Helpern Syracuse & Hirschtritt LLP

This article originally appeared in the July/August 2014 *NYSBA Journal*.

False Information?

To the Forum:

I am an associate at a firm that has maintained a long-standing client relationship with a professional sports league (the League). Recently, the League suspended one of its star players (DD) for two years as a result of an incident where he assaulted his fiancée in a hotel elevator and rendered her unconscious. The player has since filed a legal action against the League in federal court alleging that the League's suspension of him was arbitrary and capricious under the League's personal conduct policy in light of the fact that the League had previously rendered a monetary fine against DD based upon the incident in question which had been documented in a surveillance video showing DD pulling his unconscious fiancée out of the elevator but not the actual assault.

Earlier this year, I participated in a call along with my supervising partner (SP), the League's assistant general counsel (the AGC), the League's General Counsel (the GC) and another League executive. During the call, the GC advised us of the incident and when SP asked if the incident was recorded, the GC quickly responded that it was in possession of the subject video. My first thought upon hearing this information was to find out if other videotapes of the incident existed. I wrote those thoughts on a notepad and showed them to SP who quickly waved me off during the call. After the conclusion of the call, SP chided me and demanded that I never make such inquiry of the client again.

A few weeks later, I ran into the AGC at a client event. He pulled me aside and informed me that although the GC told my firm that only one videotape of the incident existed, the League in fact had another tape in its possession showing the entirety of the incident (including DD physically assaulting his fiancée) but he indicated that he was directed not to ever discuss the existence of the second tape because of the public relations fallout that would almost certainly ensue if the full video ended up in the public realm as well as the potential legal ramifications for the League.

My firm is preparing to defend DD's lawsuit, which will almost certainly include depositions of League executives. I have been told that the plan is to take the position that the only videotape in existence was the one that was disclosed to the public. What if I told you that I know this information to be false? What are my professional responsibilities? Is there a "reporting up" requirement? With regard to how the SP handled his fact gathering, was he obligated to fully probe the League's GC as to his knowledge of the existence of any and all evidence relevant to the incident? Finally, if it is later determined that SP knowingly failed to make the proper inquiries so as to avoid learning damaging information, could my firm be disqualified from representing the League in the lawsuit brought by DD or possibly sanctioned?

Sincerely,
Tim Troubled

Dear Tim Troubled:

Your question first asks us to address the professional obligations that arise when an attorney learns that a client intends to present false information to opposing counsel and/or a tribunal. Rule 4.1 of the New York Rules of Professional Conduct (the RPC) tells us that "[i]n the course of representing a client, a lawyer shall not *knowingly* make a false statement of fact or law to a third person" (emphasis added). Rule 3.4 which requires that attorneys act with fairness and candor when dealing with an opposing party and their counsel is also applicable.

In Rule 3.4, subparagraph (a)(1) states that "a lawyer shall not...suppress any evidence that the lawyer or the client has a legal obligation to reveal or produce."

Subparagraph (a)(4) requires that "a lawyer shall not...*knowingly* use perjured testimony or false evidence" (emphasis added).

Subparagraph (a)(6) requires that "a lawyer shall not *knowingly* engage in other illegal conduct or conduct contrary to these Rules" (emphasis added).

In addition, Rule 3.3 governs your obligations to the court. Rule 3.3(a)(1) states that "[a] lawyer shall not knowingly...make a false statement of fact or law to a tribunal or fail to correct a false statement of material fact or law previously made to the tribunal by the lawyer." In addition, Rule 3.3(a)(3) requires that

> [a] lawyer shall not knowingly...offer or use evidence that the lawyer knows to be false. If a lawyer, the lawyer's client, or a witness called by the lawyer has offered material evidence and the lawyer comes to know of its falsity, the lawyer shall take reasonable remedial measures, including, if necessary, disclosure to the tribunal...

The key words used in the aforementioned sections of the RPC are "know" and "knowingly." Comment [8] to Rule 3.3 states that "[t]he prohibition against offering or using false evidence applies only if the lawyer *knows that the evidence is false*" (emphasis added) and that "[a] lawyer's reasonable belief that evidence is false does not preclude its presentation to the trier of fact."

Generally speaking, lawyers are permitted to rely on a client's recitation of the facts and do not have a duty to second-guess or independently verify what their clients tell them, an issue which we covered in a previous Forum. *See* Vincent J. Syracuse and Matthew R, Maron, *Attorney Professionalism Forum*, New York State Bar Association *Journal*, July/August 2012, Vol. 84, No. 6. In fact, even if a lawyer has doubts about the veracity of a client's version of the relevant facts, so long as a lawyer's investigation of the facts does not conclusively demonstrate that what the client is saying is false or fraudulent, a lawyer is permitted to accept the client's word. Put another way, attorneys are not required to be the judges of their clients' positions. *Id.*; *see also* Lawrence J. Vilardo and Vincent E. Doyle III, *Where Did the Zeal Go?*, Litigation, American Bar Association, Fall 2011, Vol. 38, No. 1.

These principles do not necessarily create a "safe haven" for you. In the circumstances that you have described, the fact that you have apparently become aware that the League has possession of a second video and, nevertheless, wants to take the position that the original video disclosed to the public was the only one in existence, could place you in violation of Rule 4.1 and any one of subsections (1), (4) or (6) of Rule 3.4(a). Moreover, your knowledge of the existence of the second video tape requires full compliance with subsections (1) and (3) of Rule 3.3(a) in order to avoid an ethical violation.

Your next question asks if there is a "reporting up" requirement if you see another lawyer committing an act in violation of the ethical rules.

Rule 8.3(a) states that

> [a] lawyer who knows that another lawyer has committed a violation of the [RPC] that raises a substantial question as to that lawyer's honesty, trustworthiness or fitness as a lawyer shall report such knowledge to a tribunal or other authority empowered to investigate or act upon such violation.

Id.

Whether SP's behavior requires "reporting up" under Rule 8.3(a) cannot be answered without further additional information. Have you told SP what the AGC revealed to you about the existence of a second videotape? If so, how did he react? Did he tell you to ignore what you were told by the AGC? All of these questions must be answered before we can know whether SP should be reported for alleged misconduct. Again, the critical issue is whether SP has *knowledge* of the second video tape, and nevertheless intends to make false representations to opposing counsel and/or the tribunal.

With respect to how SP handled his fact gathering from the client, we note that Rule 1.3(a) provides that "[a] lawyer shall act with reasonable diligence...in representing a client." In addition, SP should also have been guided by competency requirements for attorneys as set forth in Rule 1.1(a), which requires that "[c]ompetent representation requires the legal knowledge, skill, thoroughness and preparation reasonably necessary for the representation." We believe that compliance with both of these ethical obligations would require SP to have conducted a more diligent and thorough fact gathering in his communications with the GC.

SP should not have prevented you from making a proper inquiry as to the relevant events as it could subject him to discipline under Rule 3.4(a) and Rule 4.1. If it is later determined that SP *knowingly* prevented you from making a further inquiry from the client because he was afraid of what the client would say, then he would have likely breached an ethical obligation and should be reported pursuant to Rule 8.3(a).

One thing that should be remembered is that retaliation by law firms against lawyer-employees is not permitted and we call your attention to the decision of the New York Court of Appeals in *Wieder v. Skala*, 80 N.Y.2d 628 (1992), which holds that firing an attorney for reporting misconduct of a fellow attorney employed at the same firm violates public policy. *See* Simon's New York Rules of Professional Conduct Annotated at 1840 (2014 ed.). Indeed, the Court of Appeals took a strong position in *Wieder* by articulating the need to protect those reporting misconduct to the appropriate disciplinary authorities. However, the disciplinary committees should not be the only ones enforcing potential misconduct. At a minimum, we hope that your firm has in place internal policies to handle reporting situations like the one you described involving SP. By having such policies in place, the firm can protect itself from potential exposure resulting from acts of misconduct by its attorneys and, at the same time, provide a mechanism allowing for the firm's attorneys to comply with their ethical obligations.

As to your last inquiry, the consequences stemming from SP's conduct would more likely result in sanctions rather than the disqualification of your firm under Part 130, which we have discussed at length in prior Forums.

If your firm does intend to move forward in the litigation with DD and continues to push the position that only one video exists, this could be deemed frivolous conduct since false, material factual statements are being asserted in the case you have described.

There is no doubt that you are in a precarious situation. It is therefore important to acknowledge that both you and the attorneys at your firm must comply with all ethical obligations, especially when confronted with the scenario discussed here.

Sincerely,
The Forum by

Vincent J. Syracuse, Esq.
Matthew R. Maron, Esq.
Maryann C. Stallone, Esq.
Tannenbaum Helpern Syracuse & Hirschtritt LLP

This article originally appeared in the November/December 2014 *NYSBA Journal*.

Respecting Someone Else's Confidential Information

By James M. Altman

With the proliferation of electronic communications, it is increasingly common for a lawyer (the Receiving Lawyer), during the representation of a client, to gain access to confidential communications between an opposing counsel and the opposing party that neither of them intended the Receiving Lawyer to see. The most common situation is when the Receiving Lawyer comes into possession of confidential information[1] through an inadvertent disclosure.

But, besides that, there are at least three other situations when a Receiving Lawyer may confront confidential information of another lawyer's client. First, the Receiving Lawyer may receive an intentional transmittal of such confidential information from someone without authority to make such transmittal (an "unauthorized disclosure"). Second, the Receiving Lawyer may intentionally search for and uncover such confidential communications embedded in the initially invisible metadata of an electronic document sent by opposing counsel or the opposing party (metadata mining). Third, an organizational client may retrieve from the organization's computer system and deliver to the Receiving Lawyer an employee's electronic communications with personal counsel about a personal legal matter (an "employer disclosure").

When confronting an inadvertent disclosure of confidential information, the ethical obligations of a Receiving Lawyer admitted in New York are prescribed by Rule 4.4(b). The sole ethical duty is to notify the sender promptly of the receipt of the confidential information.[2] The Receiving Lawyer no longer has the obligation to stop examining the information or to follow the sender's instructions as to its disposition.[3] But, what are the Receiving Lawyer's ethical obligations, if any, with respect to the situations of (1) unauthorized disclosure, (2) metadata mining, and (3) employer disclosure? Does Rule 4.4(b) govern those situations as well? And, if not, what is the impact, if any, of Rule 4.4(b) on the ethical obligations prescribed by ethics committees in New York regarding those situations before Rule 4.4(b) became effective on April 1, 2009?

These questions have not yet been answered by the courts or ethics committees in New York. But, unfortunately, the answers provided by the American Bar Association Standing Committee on Ethics and Professional Responsibility (the ABA Committee) to analogous questions regarding the scope and impact of Model Rule 4.4(b) (MR 4.4(b)) have subordinated the importance of preserving someone else's confidential information to other considerations. Over the past six years, that ABA Committee has viewed the adoption of MR 4.4(b) as the basis, in part or in whole, for (1) withdrawing ABA Opinion 94-382, the ABA Committee's prior ethical guidance protecting confidential information in the context of unauthorized disclosure;[4] (2) permitting metadata mining,[5] which both the New York State Bar Association Committee on Professional Ethics (NYSBA Committee) and the New York County Lawyers' Association Committee on Professional Ethics (NYCLA Committee) have viewed as unethical;[6] and (3) allowing a Receiving Lawyer to examine and use confidential communications between an employee and the employee's personal counsel about a personal legal issue that have been recovered from the employer's computer system, without notification to the employee or the employee's personal counsel.[7]

Rule 4.4(b) contains language identical to MR 4.4(b). If, based on an interest in uniformity, the ethics committees in New York reflexively mimic the ABA Committee's recent opinions regarding MR 4.4(b)'s impact in those situations, they will undermine New York's separate tradition of giving great deference to a broad view of the principle of client confidentiality under Rule 8.4(d) and its predecessor, DR 1-102(A)(5).[8] Instead, based upon Rule 8.4(d), the ethics committees in New York should (1) continue to require prompt notice to the opposing party or its counsel when a Receiving Lawyer gains access to confidential information through an unauthorized disclosure, (2) continue to prohibit metadata mining, and (3) require prompt notice to the opposing party or its counsel when a Receiving Lawyer gains access to confidential information through a good-faith review of metadata or an employer disclosure.

Two Different Traditions of Legal Ethics

In order to understand the choice that New York ethics committees face about the scope and impact of Rule 4.4(b), it is fruitful to view the distinct histories of MR 4.4(b) and Rule 4.4(b).

MR 4.4(b)

The history of MR 4.4(b) begins with the problem of the errant fax. Facing what in the late 1980s and early 1990s was a burgeoning problem, the ABA Committee, in Formal Opinion 92-368, opined that the Receiving Lawyer confronting an inadvertently disclosed document that appears on its face to contain confidential information has three ethical obligations: first, to refrain from examining the document after receiving notice or realizing that the document had been inadvertently sent; second, to notify the person who had sent the document (the Sender) of its receipt; and, third, to abide by the instructions of the Sender as to the disposition of the document.[9] Two years later, in Formal Opinion 94-382, that Committee reached a similar conclusion with respect to an unauthorized disclosure of confidential information:

> A lawyer who receives on an unauthorized basis materials of an adverse party that she knows to be privileged

or confidential should, upon recognizing the privileged
or confidential nature of the materials, either refrain
from reviewing such materials or review them only to
the extent required to determine how appropriately to
proceed; she should notify her adversary's lawyer that
she has such materials and should either follow instructions of the adversary's lawyer with respect to the disposition of the materials, or refrain from using the materials until a definitive resolution of the proper disposition
of the materials is obtained from a court.[10]

When the ABA Committee issued both opinions, there was no rule or
statement in the Model Rules directly addressing the situation of either
inadvertent disclosure or unauthorized disclosure. The ABA Committee
based its opinions on a medley of legal and ethics principles, including
recognition that a Receiving Lawyer's ethical duty "to maximize the
advantage his client will gain from careful scrutiny of the missent materials" "pales in comparison to the importance of maintaining confidentiality."[11]

Some commentators and state bar association ethics committees
criticized those opinions because, among other reasons, the ABA Committee was not interpreting a particular Model Rule.[12] Consequently,
in February 2002, the ABA adopted a new rule specifically addressing
inadvertent disclosure—MR 4.4(b).[13] Compared to Opinion 92-368, MR
4.4(b) dramatically reduces the ethical obligations of a Receiving Lawyer
with respect to the protection of confidential information.[14] It requires
the Receiving Lawyer only to "promptly notify the [S]ender."[15] It does
not require the Receiving Lawyer to refrain from examining or using the
document ("to Refrain"), or to return, destroy or sequester the document,
as the Sender might request ("to Return").

New York's Different Ethics Jurisprudence

No ethics committee in New York directly addressed the issue of
inadvertent disclosure until the second half of 2002, after MR 4.4(b) had
been adopted. In 2002 and 2003, the NYCLA Committee and then the Association of the Bar of the City of New York's Committee on Professional
and Judicial Ethics (City Bar Committee) opined, with certain qualifications, that a Receiving Lawyer who receives an inadvertently disclosed
document has the same three ethical obligations prescribed in ABA
Formal Opinion 92-368—to Notify, to Refrain, and to Return.

NYCLA Opinion 730 deals expressly with the conflict between the
principles of client confidentiality and zealous representation posed by
an inadvertent disclosure of confidential information, ultimately concluding, like the ABA Committee in ABA Formal Opinion 92-368, that the
principle of client confidentiality trumps the principle of zealous representation.[16] In reaching that conclusion, the NYCLA Committee articulat-

ed an expansive view of the principle of client confidentiality: "[A]ll lawyers share responsibility for ensuring that the fundamental principle that client confidences be preserved—the most basic tenet of the attorney-client relationship—is respected when privileged information belonging to *a* client [i.e., any client, whether one's own or another lawyer's] is inadvertently disclosed."[17] "[T]he Disciplinary Rule prohibiting lawyers from knowingly revealing the confidences and [secrets] of *their own* clients [i.e., DR 4-101] does incomplete justice to the fundamental principle that client confidences and secrets be preserved," because lawyers have broader ethical obligations to preserve the confidential information of all clients, even those of other lawyers.[18] "Recognizing that lawyers have an ethical obligation upon receipt of inadvertently disclosed privileged information *supplements* and *enhances* the Code's existing requirement that lawyers preserve the confidences and secrets of their own clients."[19] Despite the ABA's adoption of MR 4.4(b), the ethical obligation, in the view of the NYCLA Committee, is to comply with the Receiving Lawyer's three duties recognized in ABA Formal Opinion 92-368.

The NYCLA Committee did not anchor in any particular rule of attorney conduct its view that all lawyers, as part of their professional obligations, share responsibility for preserving confidential information, even confidential information of clients not their own.[20] Indeed, it specifically rejected the need to do so.[21]

But, in Opinion 2003-04, the City Bar Committee "focus[ed] the issues presented by inadvertent disclosure through the lens of DR 1-102(A)(5)," which prohibits "engag[ing] in conduct that is prejudicial to the administration of justice."[22] It concluded that a failure to protect the principle of client confidentiality incumbent on all attorneys in the context of inadvertent disclosure was prejudicial to the administration of justice and, therefore, a violation of DR 1-102(A)(5):

> Obligations of a receiving attorney with respect to a misdirected communication containing confidences or secrets cannot rest squarely on the duties imposed by DR 4-101. After all, the receiving attorney has no attorney-client relationship with the client whose information is exposed. The Code nevertheless recognizes that preservation of client confidences and secrets is crucial to stability of the legal system. As EC 4-1 states, "the proper functioning of the legal system require[s] the preservation by the lawyer of confidences and secrets of one who has employed or sought to employ the lawyer." Failing to notify the sender of an inadvertent disclosure would deprive the sending attorney of the opportunity to seek appropriate protection for the disclosed information and thereby prejudice the administration of justice. Likewise, reading beyond the point where the lawyer knows or

reasonably should know that the communication is an inadvertent disclosure of confidences or secrets undermines the duty incumbent on all attorneys pursuant to DR 1-102(A)(5) to respect the foundations on which our legal system is based.[23]

In relying upon DR 1-102(A)(5), the Committee drew support from other New York ethics opinions construing that provision in similar contexts, as when a Receiving Lawyer has gained access to an opposing party's confidential information without the opposing party's knowledge or intent.[24]

In short, despite certain limited exceptions,[25] NYCLA Opinion 738 and N.Y. City Opinion 2003-04 imposed on New York lawyers the same threefold duty as ABA Formal Opinion 92-368: to Notify, to Refrain, and to Return. In the course of adopting much of the reasoning, and preferring the conclusion of ABA Formal Opinion 92-368 over the more limited approach of MR 4.4(b), the NYCLA Committee and the City Bar Committee distinguished New York's ethics jurisprudence from the ABA's ethics jurisprudence in two important respects:

1. Both Committees agreed that the principle of client confidentiality is broader than the duty to preserve the confidential information of one's own client; that principle protects the confidential information of other lawyers' clients as well, because protection of the principle of client confidentially for all clients is fundamental to the proper functioning of our legal system.

2. Because that protection is so fundamental, the failure to respect and support it, at least in the circumstance of inadvertent disclosure, prejudices the administration of justice and, therefore, violates DR 1-102(A)(5).

In 2005, the NYSBA Committee on Standards of Attorney Conduct (COSAC) commenced the process of revising New York's Code to make it, in both form and substance, more like the ABA's Model Rules. There is no indication, however, that when the NYSBA proposed a new rule specifically addressing inadvertent disclosure or when the Appellate Divisions adopted Rule 4.4(b) that the bar or the bench intended to repudiate either of these two distinguishing features of New York's ethics jurisprudence.[26]

When COSAC proposed Rule 4.4(b) to the House of Delegates, the Reporters' Notes explained that "the provision is needed to guard against breaches of confidentiality and other harms to clients that inevitably arise, even among careful and conscientious lawyers, with the proliferation of email, faxes and other electronic means of communication."[27] There was nothing indicating that Rule 4.4(b) curtailed the previously understood ethical obligations of Receiving Lawyers, except with respect to the particular situation of inadvertent disclosure, and nothing indicating that the principle of client confidentiality was no longer a fundamental element of our legal system or that, except for inadvertent disclosure, the previously understood balance between the principle of client confidentiality and the duty of zealous representation had been altered. Given the ABA Committee's interpretation of MR 4.4(b), it might be asked why the adoption of Rule 4.4(b) does not imply a change in view of the relative importance of the principle of client confidentiality. But, the Reporter's Note that "[a] more detailed rule...would likely be difficult to apply and enforce, and could not possibly anticipate all of the situations"[28] explains that Rule 4.4(b)'s limited notification obligation was due to drafting and enforcement concerns, rather than a changed evaluation about the role or significance of the broadly conceived principle of client confidentiality. Not surprisingly, then, Rule 4.4(b) was not even one of the Rules identified by the courts as marking an important change in New York's ethical jurisprudence.[29]

The Three Other Situations

Given these two different bodies of ethics jurisprudence, what do the recent ABA Committee opinions mean for New York attorneys who confront someone else's confidential information in the three situations other than inadvertent disclosure?

Situation 1: Unauthorized Disclosure

Unauthorized disclosure of confidential information is different from inadvertent disclosure. Unlike inadvertent disclosure, an unauthorized disclosure is not the result of a mistaken transmission of confidential information by an adversary or an opposing party. With an unauthorized disclosure, someone—but *not* the party whose confidential information it is—intends to send or provide the confidential information to the Receiving Lawyer.

Second, because an unauthorized disclosure is not caused by carelessness, there is no justification for allowing the Receiving Lawyer to exploit the disclosure as an incentive to make senders of confidential information more careful, and there is no basis to penalize the party whose confidential information it is, since that party did nothing wrong.

Third, when confidential information is disclosed without authorization, there is no issue of a privilege waiver. Thus, there is no basis for arguing that the Receiving Lawyer may review such confidential information because it is no longer privileged.

Before MR 4.4(b) was adopted, the ABA Committee had opined in Formal Opinion 94-382 that a Receiving Lawyer confronting an opposing party's confidential information that had been disclosed without authorization should (1) Notify; (2) Refrain; and (3) Return, or, in the case of a dispute, refrain from using the information until the court resolves the dispute.[30] In Formal Opinion 06-440, the ABA Committee withdrew that opinion, holding, in essence, that no Model Rule provided a basis for that prescription absent special facts indicating criminal conduct or dishonesty or deceit. Although it viewed MR 4.4(b) as inapplicable to unauthorized (as opposed to inadvertent) disclosure, the ABA Committee pointed out that MR 4.4(b) imposed only a notice requirement, but no requirement limiting examination or use of inadvertently disclosed confidential information and, therefore, those two additional ethical requirements were not supported by MR 4.4(b).[31] In effect, the Model Rules impose no ethical obligations or limitations upon a Receiving Lawyer being offered or gaining access to an unauthorized disclosure of confidential information.

The ABA Committee's withdrawal of ABA Formal Opinion 94-382 in light of MR 4.4(b) indirectly raises a question for New York lawyers: Are the ethics opinions in New York regarding unauthorized disclosure still valid after Rule 4.4(b)? The answer is yes.

In N.Y. City Opinion 1989-01, the City Bar Committee considered, among other things, what a lawyer representing a spouse in a matrimonial action should do when the client provides copies of documents reflecting communications between the other spouse and that spouse's counsel in the lawsuit. Based on DR 1-102(A)(5), the Committee opined that the Receiving Lawyer should notify opposing counsel of receipt of the documents and the circumstances under which they were obtained and return the documents or copies to opposing counsel.

> The inquirer and his client are privy to communications between the opposing party and counsel that are likely to be privileged and that, whether or not privileged, were obtained otherwise than through normal discovery procedures. Having such information gives the inquirer and his client an advantage that, however slight, they are not entitled to have, and to permit them to retain that advantage, of which the opposing party and counsel are unaware, would in the Committee's opinion be prejudicial to the administration of justice and, therefore, ethically impermissible. DR 1-102(A)(5).[32]

However, because the client-spouse's interception and copying of the attorney-client communication constituted a fraud upon the other spouse, the disclosure of which would be embarrassing or detrimental to the client-spouse, the Committee explained that the Receiving Lawyer could not notify opposing counsel about the circumstances of the disclosure without getting the client-spouse's permission; absent that consent, the Receiving Lawyer would have to withdraw from the representation because of the conflicting duties to notify and not to notify opposing counsel.

In NYSBA Opinion 700 (1998), a government lawyer responsible for prosecuting an administrative proceeding received an unsolicited phone call from a former non-lawyer employee of a law firm representing the respondent in the proceeding, who informed the government lawyer that certain documents submitted by the respondent in discovery had been materially altered. Based on DR 1-102(A)(5) and DR 1-102(A)(4), the NYSBA Committee opined that the government lawyer should refrain from seeking further information from opposing counsel's former employee. In support, the Committee relied, among other things, on N.Y. City Opinion 1989-01, ABA Formal Opinions 92-368 and 94-382, and "the strong public policy in favor of confidentiality, which…outweigh heavily the competing principles of zealous representation."[33] The Committee also concluded that the government lawyer should seek judicial guidance regarding the use, if any, that can be made of the information learned from the former law firm employee.

Thus, by the time Rule 4.4(b) was adopted, a Receiving Attorney was ethically obligated to notify opposing counsel of confidential information that is disclosed without authorization and not to use such information prior to such notice. Those ethical requirements conflict with the ABA's current views, which, after Formal Opinion 06-440, do not mandate such notice and place no restrictions on the use of such confidential information.

The adoption of Rule 4.4(b) should not undermine those requirements, because N.Y. City Opinion 1989-01 and NYSBA Opinion 700 were based on DR 1-102(A)(5) and New York's strong public policy in favor of the principle of client confidentiality, even when that principle conflicts with the duty of zealous representation. In April 2009, when New York adopted the new Rules of Professional Conduct, the language of DR 1-102(A)(5) was carried over verbatim in Rule 8.4(d), and there is no indication that either COSAC, which proposed the Rules, or the courts, which adopted them, intended to lessen the importance of the principle of client confidentiality in itself or relative to the duty of zealous representation.[34]

Indeed, if any change in the relative values of the principle of client confidentiality and the duty of zealous representation were intended, it is likely that the relative strength of the principle of client confidentiality was increased, because the Rules eliminated "zealousness" or "zeal" as the standard for ethical representation of a client.[35] Moreover, if the principle of client confidentiality demands prompt notice with respect to an inadvertent disclosure, that principle has even greater weight in the context of an unauthorized disclosure. There, the opposing party and opposing counsel are not responsible for the transmittal of confidential information, so there is no basis for penalizing them for the transmittal (i.e., it's not their mistake) and no justification that allowing the Receiving Lawyer to exploit the unauthorized disclosure will act as a general deterrent against attorney carelessness in handling confidential information.

In short, even though ABA Formal Opinion 94-382 has been withdrawn, the ethical response to an unauthorized disclosure of confidential information under New York's ethical jurisprudence should remain the same under the Rules as it was under the Code. The adoption of Rule 4.4(b), which by its terms concerns only inadvertent disclosure, does not conflict with the reasons supporting a more stringent ethical response to unauthorized disclosure than is required by the Model Rules.

Situation 2: Metadata Mining

"Metadata" is information about other information, often initially invisible, that is embedded in electronic documents.[36] Metadata can be as harmless as information indicating the last date and time that an electronic document was edited, or saved, or printed, but it also can be as consequential as "tracked changes" that can reveal, among other things, the confidential communications between a client and its counsel about an ultimate settlement number or a strategy regarding changes to an agreement being negotiated with opposing counsel.[37] Metadata can just "pop up" when a cursor passes over it or it can be searched for and found using sophisticated forensic tools. A lawyer deliberately searching through metadata with the goal of unearthing someone else's confidential information is engaged in "metadata mining."

Promulgated in 2001, before the ABA adopted MR 4.4(b), NYSBA Opinion 749 was the first ethics opinion anywhere to discuss metadata mining. Even apart from any concerns of illegal conduct under state or federal laws prohibiting the unauthorized interception of electronic communications, NYSBA Opinion 749 prohibits metadata mining because such conduct is dishonest and deceitful and prejudices the administration of justice.

NYSBA Opinion 749 rests upon an analogy between metadata mining and less-technologically-sophisticated means of invading someone else's attorney-client relationship, such as using inadvertent disclosures of confidential information and soliciting and then exploiting disclosure of unauthorized communications. The Committee viewed the relationship between metadata mining and inadvertent disclosure as follows:

> [A]lthough counsel for the other party intends the lawyer to receive the "visible" document, absent an explicit direction to the contrary counsel plainly does not intend the lawyer to receive the "hidden" material or information.... To some extent, therefore, the "inadvertent" and "unauthorized" disclosure cases provide guidance in the present inquiry.[38]

Five years later, when the ABA Committee addressed the issue of metadata mining in Opinion 06-442, the ABA had already adopted MR 4.4(b), and that Rule figured prominently in the ABA Committee's rejection of the conclusion and analysis in NYSBA Opinion 749. The ABA Committee started its analysis with the literalist's observation that the Model Rules "do not contain any specific prohibition against a lawyer's reviewing and using embedded information in electronic documents."[39] The ABA Committee did not take a position on whether the transmittal of metadata was inadvertent or not, viewing that as dependent upon the facts.[40] But it pointed out that even if the transmittal of metadata was considered inadvertent and, therefore, within the scope of MR 4.4(b), that Rule itself "is...silent as to the ethical propriety of a lawyer's review or use of such information."[41] Thus, the ABA Committee said, even if MR 4.4(b) applied, it would not prohibit a lawyer's review or use of confidential information obtained through metadata mining. Moreover, without even an explanation, the ABA Committee expressly rejected NYSBA Opinion 749's conclusion that metadata mining violated the more general ethical requirements that lawyers should not engage in dishonest or deceitful conduct or conduct prejudicial to the administration of justice.[42]

Two years later, in 2008, the NYCLA Committee considered both NYSBA Opinion 749 and ABA Formal Opinion 06-442 and agreed with the former. Based on its own prior opinion regarding inadvertent disclosure and the more general ethical proscriptions against attorney conduct that is dishonest and deceitful or prejudicial to the administration of justice, the NYCLA Committee concluded that a "receiving attorney may not ethically search the metadata in...electronic documents with the intent to find privileged material or if finding privileged material is likely to occur from the search."[43]

Both NYSBA Opinion 749 and NYCLA Opinion 738 predate the adoption of Rule 4.4(b). Did New York's adoption of Rule 4.4(b) undermine the continuing validity of those opinions?

No. Both NYSBA Opinion 749 and NYCLA Opinion 738 concur with the prevailing view in New York's ethics jurisprudence that client confidentiality takes precedence over the duty of competent client representation. The adoption of Rule 4.4(b) did not change that.

Moreover, if that principle holds in the case of unauthorized disclosure, it is even stronger in the situation of metadata mining, because the Receiving Lawyer had no access to that confidential information until he or she deliberately searched the metadata in the electronic document with the intent of uncovering any confidential information therein. Such action is not dissimilar to a lawyer's deliberately questioning an employee of a represented opposing party about that party's confidential information during an informal interview—clearly an unethical act in the eyes of the New York Court of Appeals and the NYSBA Committee.[44] New York's ethics jurisprudence has long recognized that lawyers representing a client sometimes have to restrain their zeal when confronting conflicting ethical principles. Rule 4.4(b) did not change that either.

A related, but different, question concerns a Receiving Lawyer's ethical obligation if, while reviewing "track changes" or some other metadata on the good-faith belief that the Sender intended the Receiving Lawyer to review that metadata, the Receiving Lawyer comes upon the opposing party's confidential information. What should the Receiving Lawyer do?

No New York case or ethics opinion has confronted that question. But, in the more than 10 years since NYSBA Opinion 749, there has been virtual unanimity among ethics committees across the country, including the NYSBA Committee and the NYCLA Committee, that lawyers have an ethical duty to scrub the confidential information out of metadata before they send emails and other electronic documents to non-clients.[45] That unanimity provides the basis for a presumption that if metadata transmitted by opposing counsel contains their client's confidential information, that confidential information was sent by mistake—that is, inadvertently.

That presumption has been expressly adopted by a few bar association ethics committees in other states.[46] If that presumption were recognized in New York—and it should be—then New York lawyers who come upon confidential information when properly reviewing metadata contained in an electronic document sent by opposing counsel or the opposing party would be obligated to comply with Rule 4.4(b)'s direction to notify opposing counsel of the receipt of such information.[47]

Situation 3: Employer Disclosure

As more and more employees make greater use of their employer's computer systems, there have been more cases regarding the legal and ethical issues posed when a lawyer is provided by an organizational client with copies of employees' emails to their personal counsel about personal legal problems. Depending primarily on whether an employee had a reasonable expectation of confidentiality in sending and receiving such email communications, such email communications may be protected by the attorney-client privilege.[48] Regardless of their privileged status, however, what are a lawyer's ethical obligations when provided such emails?

No ethics committee in New York has considered this issue, but the ABA Committee did so in Formal Opinion 11-460. Once again, it concluded that MR 4.4(b) did not address the situation, either expressly or implicitly, because MR 4.4(b) concerns a document that is "inadvertently sent," and the emails between the employee and personal counsel were not "inadvertently sent." "A 'document [is] inadvertently sent' to someone when it is accidentally transmitted to an unintended recipient, as occurs when an email or letter is misaddressed or when a document is accidentally attached to an email or accidentally included among other documents produced in discovery."[49] In the ABA Committee's view, "a document is *not* 'inadvertently sent' when it is retrieved by a third person from a public or private place where it is stored or left."[50]

But Rule 4.4(b) is not so limited in scope. The NYSBA's House of Delegates approved Comments to Rule 4.4 that differ from the ABA's comments to MR 4.4. Unlike Comment 2 to MR 4.4, NYSBA's Comment 2 includes language indicating that the scope of Rule 4.4(b) is not restricted to documents that were mistakenly sent or produced, it also governs documents that were "otherwise made available" by opposing parties or their lawyers.

This language was added because of a proposal made by NYCLA during NYSBA's drafting and approval process regarding Rule 4.4(b). NYCLA believed that Rule 4.4(b) "should include all situations where a lawyer inadvertently comes into possession of a document, not only where a document was mistakenly 'sent' to the lawyer."[51] As examples, NYCLA specifically referred to "documents inadvertently left in court or in a conference room."[52] Thus, when the House of Delegates adopted Rule 4.4(b) with that additional language in Comment 2, it intended Rule 4.4(b) to cover situations when documents are mistakenly made available on an employer's computer or other electronic device.

In sum, despite their identical language, by virtue of their different histories MR 4.4(b) and Rule 4.4(b) provide different answers to the question of a Receiving Lawyer's ethical obligation regarding confidential information made available on an employer's computer system. Under Rule 4.4(b), private communications between an employee and private counsel that reside on the employer's computer systems are inadvertently made available to the employer and its counsel *if* the employee reasonably believed that they were protected from review by the employer and its counsel. Indeed, in at least one New York case—*Forward v. Foschi*[53] in 2010—a court has held that Rule 4.4(b) requires a Receiving Lawyer to notify the employee's personal counsel of receipt of such emails.

Conclusion

For years, New York's ethics jurisprudence has recognized that the principle of client confidentiality is fundamental to the proper functioning of our legal system. There is no evidence that when Rule 4.4(b) was adopted, it was intended to narrow the broad construction of that principle in New York's ethics jurisprudence or diminish that principle's value relative to the duty of competent client representation. Accordingly, Rule 4.4(b) gives no reason to retreat from the greater protection afforded confidential information under New York's existing ethics jurisprudence than under the ABA Committee's recent construction of the Model Rules.

This is no small point. One very significant purpose of enforceable ethical rules is to give voice and support to the fundamental underpinnings of our legal system, such as the principle of client confidentiality.[54] If New York's ethics rules do not sufficiently protect the principle of client confidentiality in situations such as unauthorized disclosure, metadata mining, and employer disclosure, then whenever those conflicts arise, that keystone principle will be sacrificed to the particular, short-term interests of partisan clients.

1. "Confidential information" is defined in Rule 1.6(a) of the New York Rules of Professional Conduct (the Rules), which has been effective since April 1, 2009. In the parlance of the New York Code of Professional Responsibility (the Code), which was effective from January 1, 1970, through March 31, 2009, "confidential information" consists of "confidences"—that is, information protected by the attorney-client privilege—and certain non-privileged information called "secrets." *See* Disciplinary Rule 4-101(A) (DR).

2. Rule 4.4(b) simply states: "A lawyer who receives a document relating to the representation of the lawyer's client and knows or reasonably should know that the document was inadvertently sent shall promptly notify the sender." Because the word "document" in that Rule includes "email and other electronically stored information subject to being read or put into readable form," Rule 4.4(b), Comment 2, covers the errant email as well as the errant fax.

3. *See* James M. Altman, *Inadvertent Disclosure and Rule 4.4(b)'s Erosion of Attorney Professionalism*, N.Y. St. B.J., Nov./Dec. 2010, p. 20 (Altman, *Inadvertent Disclosure*).

4. ABA Formal Op. 06-440 (May 13, 2006).

5. ABA Formal Op. 06-442 (Aug. 5, 2006).

6. NYSBA Comm. on Prof'l Ethics, Op. 749 (2001); NYCLA Comm. on Prof'l Ethics, Op. 738 (2008).

7. ABA Formal Op. 11-460 (Aug. 4, 2011).

8. Already two commentators have argued, based in part on uniformity grounds, that the NYSBA Committee should reconsider its views on metadata mining and adopt the ABA Committee's contrary position. *See* Michael B. de Leeuw & Eric A. Hirsch, *Time to Revisit the Ethics of Metadata*, N.Y.L.J., S4, Mar. 19, 2012. In my view, this argument is misguided for the reasons stated below and in James M. Altman, *Broad Protection of Client Information*, N.Y.L.J., Mar. 28, 2012, p. 6, col. 4.

9. ABA Formal Op. 92-368 (Nov. 10, 1992), withdrawn in ABA Formal Op. 05-437 (Oct. 1, 2005) based upon the adoption of MR 4.4(b).

10. ABA Formal Op. 94-382 (July 5, 1994), withdrawn in ABA Formal Op. 06-440 (May 13, 2006) based upon the adoption of MR 4.4(b).

11. ABA Formal Op. 92-368. The ABA Committee reached its conclusion in ABA Formal Opinion 94-382 "for the reasons outlined in ABA Formal Opinion 92-368," among others. ABA Formal Op. 94-382.

12. *See* James M. Altman, *Model Rule 4.4(b) Should Be Amended*, ABA Center for Prof. Responsibility, The Prof. Lawyer, Vol. 21, No. 1, 16, 18 (2011) (Altman, *Model Rule 4.4(b)*).

13. *See id.*, n.3.

14. According to the ABA Committee, MR 4.4(b) "not only directly addressed the precise issue discussed in Formal Opinion 92-368, but narrowed the obligations of the receiving lawyer." ABA Formal Op. 05-437 (Oct. 1, 2005).

15. *See* note 2, above.

16. NYCLA Op. 730 (2002) (citing ABA Formal Op. 92-368).

17. NYCLA Op. 730 (2002) (emphasis added).

18. *Id.*, n.5 (emphasis added).

19. *Id.* (emphasis added).

20. *Id.*

21. *Id.*

22. Ass'n of the Bar of the City of N.Y., Formal Op. 2003-04 (2003).

23. *Id.*

24. *Id.* (citing N.Y. City Op. 1989-1(1989) (concerning unauthorized disclosure); NYSBA Op. 749 (2001) (concerning metadata mining); NYSBA Op. 700 (1998) (concerning unauthorized disclosure)).

25. In N.Y. City Op. 2003-04, the Committee determined that (i) a Receiving Lawyer may retain an inadvertently disclosed document for the sole purpose of presenting it to a tribunal for in camera review and (ii) a Receiving Lawyer may use confidential information learned from examination of the inadvertently disclosed document before the Receiving Lawyer knew or had reason to know that the document was inadvertently disclosed.

26. Those two elements distinguish New York ethics jurisprudence from the ABA's ethics jurisprudence (*see* ABA Formal Op. 06-442, n.10 (Aug. 5, 2006) (specifically rejecting, among other things, the premise of NYSBA Op. 749 (2001) that a lawyer owes a duty to preserve the confidential information of a client not the lawyer's own and that the failure to do so prejudices the administration of justice)), but not from the ethics jurisprudence applicable in some other states. Ethics committee in other states have recognized, for example, that the principle of client confidentiality, broadly construed, is so fundamental to our adversary system of justice that all attorneys, as part of their professional obligations to help safeguard the key underpinnings of our legal system, share the responsibility for preserving confidential information, even confidential information not of their own clients. *See* Altman, *Model Rule 4.4(b)*, p. 17, nn.13–14 (citing several state ethics opinions).

27. NYSBA, Proposed Rules of Professional Conduct, dated Feb. 1, 2008, at 168.

28. *Id.*

29. Although the Press Release from the New York Uniform Court System identified seven Rules as entailing "significant ethics changes" and identified ten other Rules as "noteworthy developments," Rule 4.4(b) was not mentioned at all. "New Attorney Rules of Professional Conduct Announced," Press Release dated Dec. 16, 2008.

30. *See* note 10, above.

31. The ABA Committee reasoning in Formal Opinion 06-440 is unjustifiably positivistic, since the Committee acknowledges that "the considerations that influenced the Committee in Formal Opinion 92-368, which carried over to Formal Opinion 94-382, are part of the broader perspective that may guide a lawyer's conduct in the situations addressed in those opinions." ABA Formal Op. 06-440. But the Committee did not find those considerations "an appropriate basis for a formal opinion of this Committee, for which we look to the Rules themselves." *Id.* Thus, in Formal Opinion 06-440, the ABA Committee did not discredit the considerations that led to its prescriptions in Formal Opinions 92-368 and 94-382; it just decided that its jurisdiction was limited to interpretation of Model Rules and did not extend to prescriptions based on such a "broader perspective." This self-imposed limitation on the scope of the Committee's role is nowhere stated in the Committee's charter and is inconsistent with the Model Rules themselves, which expressly acknowledge that

"the Rules do not, however, exhaust the moral and ethical considerations that should inform a lawyer." Model Rules, Scope, ¶ 16.

32. N.Y. City Op. 1989-01 (1989).

33. NYSBA Op. 700 (1998).

34. *See* notes 26–27, above, and accompanying text.

35. *See* Lawrence J. Vilardo & Vincent E. Doyle III, *Where Did the Zeal Go?*, ABA J. Section of Litig, Vol. 38, No. 1, 53 (2011).

36. NYSBA Op. 782 (2004).

37. *Id.;* ABA Formal Op. 06-442 (Aug. 5, 2006).

38. NYSBA Op. 749 (2001).

39. ABA Formal Op. 06-442 ((Aug. 5, 2006).

40. *Id.*, n.7.

41. *Id.*

42. *Id.*, n.10.

43. NYCLA Op. 738 (Mar. 24, 2008).

44. *See* Altman, *Inadvertent Disclosure*, p. 27, n.25.

45. *See, e.g.*, ABA Formal Op. 06-442 (Aug. 5, 2006); N.C. 2009-01 (2010); N.H. 2008-2009/4; Colo. 119 (2008); Ariz. 07-03 (2007). *See also* NYSBA Op. 782 (Dec. 8, 2004); NYCLA Op. 738 (Mar. 24, 2008).

46. *See, e.g.*, N.H. 2008-2009/4; Colo. 119 (2008); Ariz. 07-03 (2007).

47. Under Rule 4.4(b), the Receiving Lawyer would have no obligation, however, not to examine the embedded confidential information and not to use it. This illustrates one of the reasons why Rule 4.4(b) is "ethically anemic" and should be amended. *See* Altman, *Inadvertent Disclosure*, p. 26. Rule 4.4(b) offers no protection for confidential information revealed in a transactional setting. *Id.*, pp. 22–23.

48. *See, e.g., Curto v. Med. World Commc'ns, Inc.*, No. 03CV6327 (DRH)(MLO), 2006 WL 1318387 (E.D.N.Y. May 15, 2006); *Forward v. Foschi*, No. 9002/08, 2010 WL 1980838 (Sup. Ct., Westchester Co. May 18, 2010). *But see Scott v. Beth Israel Med. Ctr., Inc.*, 17 Misc. 3d 934 (Sup. Ct., N.Y. Co. 2007) (such emails not privileged); *Long v. Marubeni Am. Corp.*, No. 05-CIV-639 (GEL)(KNF), 2006 WL 2998671 (S.D.N.Y. Oct. 19, 2006) (same). Although these cases arose out of forensic review of the employee's work computer in connection with disputes between the employee and the employer, similar situations may arise following a corporate merger or a takeover by new management when access and control is taken over a computer system previously used by another organization or management team. *E.g., In re Asia Global Crossing, Ltd.*, 322 B.R. 247 (Bankr. S.D.N.Y. 2005).

49. ABA Formal Op. 11-460 (Aug. 4, 2011).

50. *Id.* (emphasis added).

51. NYCLA, Revised Comments on the Proposed New York Rules of Professional Conduct, 16 (undated).

52. *Id.*

53. 2010 WL 1980838.

54. *See* Altman, *Model Rule 4.4(b)*, p. 16.

JAMES M. ALTMAN (jmaltman@bryancave.com), a litigation partner in the New York office of Bryan Cave LLP, is a member and the former chair of the NYSBA Committee on Attorney Professionalism.

This article originally appeared in the May 2012 *NYSBA Journal*.

PATHWAY TO THE PROFESSION: FROM LAW SCHOOL TO LAWYER

TECHNOLOGY AND THE LAW

Embracing Technology in Everyday Practice: Professional and Ethical Obligations

To the Forum:

I am a first-year associate in a large international law firm. Over the first few months of my employment, I have received extensive training concerning the available technological resources (including email, discovery software and document systems) which I will be using in my day-to-day practice. The partners have explained to the first-year associates time and time again that we are ethically obligated to understand how technologies are utilized in connection with a given representation and that we should be intimately familiar in the usage of those technologies.

My uncle, Lou Luddite, has been a solo practitioner for almost his entire legal career spanning nearly 40 years. For the most part, his only office staff has consisted of one secretary and one paralegal. He's never hired an associate (in his words, associates were "utterly useless"). During family holiday gatherings while I was in law school, I would share with him everything I was learning about electronic research tools and applications which I would need to master once I began practicing law. He would always tell me, "Ned, all this technology is hogwash. Real lawyers do not need email, and this whole thing with these hand-held devices, they look like something that Kirk, Spock and McCoy were playing with on *Star Trek*. It's all unnecessary."

Last week, Uncle Lou told me that Ted Techno, an attorney from a firm with whom he was working on a case, was repeatedly using emails and text messages to set up conferences to discuss strategy for an upcoming trial set to occur in three weeks. Uncle Lou boasted that he informed Ted that he doesn't read or write emails and his "policy" was to have his secretary look at his emails "no more than twice a week" and for her alone to "occasionally" reply to emails intended for Lou. Uncle Lou also told me that he had decided to take a vacation in Bali and didn't plan on returning stateside until the evening before the trial. He also said he told Ted Techno that he will be "completely unreachable" while he is away and "not even his secretary would be able to get a hold of him for any reason."

I have been taught that good communication and responsiveness are essential practice skills for all lawyers and that one cannot practice law without using email. I am very fond of my Uncle Lou and think that I should speak with him. I know that I am a novice in our profession especially when compared to my uncle, which is why I would appreciate some guidance from The Forum about whether he is behaving in a professional and ethical manner.

Sincerely,
Concerned Nephew

Dear Concerned Nephew:

A previous Forum reviewed various questions concerning an attorney's obligation to promptly respond to correspondence (including email) from clients and opposing counsel. We also made various suggestions that addressed situations where, for whatever reason, an adversary puts communications on hold and ignores them. *See* Vincent J. Syracuse & Amy S. Beard, Attorney Professionalism Forum, N.Y. St. B.J., Feb. 2012, Vol. 84, No. 2. Your letter raises broader issues, including the question of whether attorneys can choose to ignore electronic communications.

Let's start with that one first. Rule 1.1 of the New York Rules of Professional Conduct (RPC) states the basic ethical obligation of lawyers to provide competent representation. Specifically, in the words of Rule 1.1(a), "[a] lawyer should provide competent representation to a client. Competent representation requires the legal knowledge, skill, thoroughness and preparation reasonably necessary for the representation." In addition, competent representation of clients requires an understanding of how technologies are utilized in connection with the representation of a client. While some may wish that they were practicing law in simpler times, this is not a matter of choice and attorneys must be intimately familiar with the usage of those technologies. The importance of this point was recently underscored in an amendment to Comment [8] to Rule 1.1 of the ABA Model Rules of Professional Conduct (Model Rules) which states that, in maintaining competence, "a lawyer should keep abreast of changes in the law and its practice, *including the benefits and risks associated with relevant technology*, engage in continuing study and education and comply with all continuing legal education requirements to which the lawyer is subject." *Id.* (emphasis added.) At least one jurisdiction is already seeking to enact the amended Comment [8] of the Model Rules. *See The Supreme Judicial Court's Standing Advisory Committee on the Rules of Professional Conduct Invites Comments on Proposed Amendments to the Massachusetts Rules of Professional Conduct*, http://www.mass.gov/courts/sjc/comment-request-rules-professional-conduct.html.

Literally from the first day of law school, future lawyers receive extensive instruction in electronic research tools, and once in practice, they learn first-hand the necessity of utilizing a variety of technological resources in their practice, including electronic discovery programs, document management and other productivity applications. In addition, most attorneys, in law firms of all sizes, utilize mobile devices in their respective practices to communicate (whether by email, text messaging or instant messaging) with clients, adversaries and other attorneys on a particular matter. As previously noted in this Forum, use of mobile devices is just one of many technologies that are integral to today's legal practice. *See* Vincent J. Syracuse & Matthew R. Maron, Attorney Professionalism Forum, N.Y. St. B.J., May 2013, Vol. 85, No. 4.

With all respect to your Uncle Lou, to put it nicely, he is practicing law as if we were in the Stone Age. The disdain for using email not only may be detrimental to the representation of clients but may also violate various ethics rules, specifically, Rule 1.1. Furthermore, Uncle Lou's "policy" of telling others that he doesn't read emails is problematic. Although he may be having his secretary occasionally read and respond to emails, lawyers should not isolate themselves from this basic method of everyday communication. Moreover, the use of a nonlawyer assistant to respond to email could raise issues under Rule 5.3, which governs a lawyer's responsibility for conduct of nonlawyers. Rule 5.3(a) states:

> A law firm shall ensure that the work of nonlawyers who work for the firm is adequately supervised, as appropriate. A lawyer with direct supervisory authority over a nonlawyer shall adequately supervise the work of the nonlawyer, as appropriate. In either case, the degree of supervision required is that which is reasonable under the circumstances, taking into account factors such as the experience of the person whose work is being supervised, the amount of work involved in a particular matter *and the likelihood that ethical problems might arise in the course of working on the matter.*

Id. (emphasis added.)

In addition, Rule 5.3(b) provides:

> A lawyer shall be responsible for conduct of a nonlawyer employed or retained by or associated with the lawyer that would be a violation of these Rules if engaged in by a lawyer, if:
>
> (1) the lawyer orders or directs the specific conduct or, with knowledge of the specific conduct, ratifies it; or
>
> (2) the lawyer is a partner in a law firm or is a lawyer who individually or together with other lawyers possesses comparable managerial responsibility in a law firm in which the nonlawyer is employed or is a lawyer who has supervisory authority over the nonlawyer; and
>
> (i) knows of such conduct at a time when it could be prevented or its consequences avoided or mitigated but fails to take reasonable remedial action; or

(ii) in the exercise of reasonable management or supervisory authority should have known of the conduct so
that reasonable remedial action could have been taken at
a time when the consequences of the conduct could have
been avoided or mitigated.

Id.

Delegation may be a good thing for busy lawyers but trying to turn
back the clock by giving a secretary or personal assistant what is essentially sole responsibility for receiving and responding to email communications directed to the employer creates a multitude of risks that could
lead to violations of Rule 5.3. What if Uncle Lou's secretary is out of the
office on vacation or is out sick for days on end? There is a fairly high
probability that Uncle Lou will not be regularly reachable by email (via
his secretary) under such a scenario; and therefore, he may be in breach
of his diligence obligations pursuant to Rule 1.3, which will be discussed
further below.

Your Uncle Lou's attempt to make himself totally unavailable while
on vacation is also troubling. Although we believe that work/life balance
is essential for everyone, we would not recommend an attorney going
"off the grid" with a trial scheduled to commence almost immediately
upon returning from vacation.

Turning to your other question, while it may be unclear whether the
RPC imposes on lawyers an obligation to promptly communicate with
co-counsel, Rule 1.3(a) requires that lawyers "shall act with reasonable
diligence and promptness in representing a client." Moreover, Rule 1.3(b)
states that lawyers "shall not neglect a legal matter entrusted" to them,
and Rule 3.4(a)(6) provides that lawyers shall not knowingly engage in
conduct contrary to the Rules; together, these rules do suggest that lawyers must communicate with co-counsel in a reasonably prompt fashion.

In our view, it is plainly apparent that ignoring communications
from co-counsel constitutes neglect of a legal matter and is a breach of
the lawyer's duty of diligence, regardless whether the duty is owed to
the client or co-counsel. Furthermore, engaging in conduct contrary to
the Rules—such as neglecting a legal matter—constitutes a breach of
Rule 3.4(a)(6). Apart from ethics, as a matter of basic courtesy, a lawyer
should promptly respond to communications from all counsel, especially
co-counsel.

We suggest you tell Uncle Lou that we recommend the following best practices (which we would strongly suggest that he integrate
into his practice). First, a variety of means of communications should
be utilized when attempting to contact co-counsel, and all attempts to
communicate should be documented. If a voicemail message is ignored,
a follow-up email should be sent; if that email goes unanswered, try
a phone call instead. If your co-counsel has communicated with you

promptly in the past, give him or her the benefit of the doubt, but even if your co-counsel has a history of poor communication, always be civil in your own communications. This is especially critical given the fact that both attorneys share the same client and the client would not look kindly upon hearing that his two attorneys are not communicating regularly as would be expected in this particular representation. Ideally, the best way to resolve communication failures between co-counsel is for attorneys to sit down face-to-face and discuss how to better communicate with each other.

Second, if voicemails and emails alike do not spur a response, send your co-counsel a letter detailing the issue(s) about which you need to communicate and describing your attempts to reach him or her.

Third, and as a last resort, it may be necessary to let the client know that co-counsel has been unresponsive to your inquiries. However, this action carries with it the proverbial double-edged sword. On the one hand, the aggrieved attorney is making the client aware that by his efforts to communicate with co-counsel, he is acting with the utmost diligence in carrying out that client's representation pursuant to his obligations under Rule 1.3. On the other hand, complaining to the client about co-counsel's conduct could result in a deterioration of the relationship between the two attorneys, which could have a detrimental effect on carrying out the representation of their shared client.

Electronic communications have become the primary mechanism of communicating with clients, co-counsel, adversaries and any other relevant persons necessary to carry out a given representation. Although it should go without saying, attorneys cannot ignore the critical importance of using current technologies in their respective practices; technology is here to stay.

Sincerely,
The Forum by

Vincent J. Syracuse, Esq.
Matthew R. Maron, Esq.,
Tannenbaum Helpern Syracuse & Hirschtritt LLP

This article originally appeared in the January 2014 _NYSBA Journal_.

Firm-Wide Data Security Policies

To the Forum:

The news in recent months is full of stories on data security and the risks that must be addressed by businesses to protect their electronic information. As attorneys, I know we all have certain obligations to preserve the confidential information of our clients. I am well aware that much of the electronic information on our firm's networks is made up of confidential information arising from client matters. I am the lucky partner tasked by my colleagues to help implement firm-wide data security policies. What ethical obligations come into play on this issue? Do the attorneys at my firm have an obligation to both advise and coordinate data security policies with our non-attorney staff?

Sincerely,
Richard Risk-Adverse

Dear Richard Risk-Adverse:

As you correctly point out, data security is a frontline issue that has gotten significant attention in the press—both inside and outside of legal circles. Recent data breaches at major corporations and law firms have underscored the need for stronger, more effective mechanisms to protect sensitive and confidential client information.

Prior Forums have focused upon several key provisions of the New York Rules of Professional Conduct (RPC) that give practitioners an ethical blueprint that tells us what attorneys need to know when using various technologies in everyday practice. *See* Vincent J. Syracuse & Matthew R. Maron, Attorney Professionalism Forum, New York State Bar Association *Journal* (N.Y. St. B. J.) May 2013, Vol. 85, No. 4 (mobile devices); Vincent J. Syracuse & Matthew R. Maron, Attorney Professionalism Forum, N.Y. St. B. J., June 2013, Vol. 85, No. 5. (usage of social media to conduct research); Vincent J. Syracuse & Matthew R. Maron, Attorney Professionalism Forum, N.Y. St. B.J., Jan. 2014, Vol. 86, No. 1. (email as a basic method for everyday communication). Your question about data security gives us an opportunity to address what is perhaps one of the most important issues that lawyers face when we have to reconcile the need to use technology with our obligation to protect a client's confidential information.

To answer your question, we begin with Rule 1.1, which recites a lawyer's basic ethical obligation to provide competent representation. Specifically, Rule 1.1(a) states that "[a] lawyer should provide competent representation to a client. Competent representation requires the legal knowledge, skill, thoroughness and preparation reasonably necessary for the representation." This means attorneys must have a basic understanding of how technologies are utilized in connection with the representation of a client. As we have noted on multiple occasions in this Forum, attorneys must be intimately familiar with the usage of those technologies. Although not necessarily applicable in New York, amended Comment [8] to Rule 1.1 of the ABA Model Rules of Professional Conduct states that, in maintaining competence, "a lawyer should keep abreast of changes in the law and its practice, *including the benefits and risks associated with relevant technology….*" *Id.* (emphasis added.) It is foolish for a lawyer to ignore evolving technologies and their impact on the lawyer's practice.

Along with your obligation to provide competent representation, discussed above, establishing the appropriate data security policy for your firm also requires an understanding of Rule 1.6(c) of the RPC which states, in pertinent part, that "[a] lawyer shall exercise reasonable care to prevent the lawyer's employees, associates, and others whose services are utilized by the lawyer from disclosing or using confidential information of a client…."

We assume that, by now, most attorneys are aware of the ethical obligations we have outlined. But what about nonlawyers, and what happens when nonlawyers have access to a client's confidential information? RPC Rule 5.3(a) tells us:

> A law firm shall ensure that the work of nonlawyers who work for the firm is adequately supervised, as appropriate. A lawyer with direct supervisory authority over a nonlawyer shall adequately supervise the work of the nonlawyer, as appropriate. In either case, the degree of supervision required is that which is *reasonable under the circumstances*, taking into account factors such as the experience of the person whose work is being supervised, the amount of work involved in a particular matter and the likelihood that ethical problems might arise in the course of working on the matter.

Id. (emphasis added.)

This may seem relatively straightforward but we must also look at the Comments to this Rule because they point us to other portions of the RPC which discuss an attorney's supervisory obligations. Comment [1] to Rule 5.3 states:

> [Rule 5.3] requires a law firm to ensure that work of nonlawyers is appropriately supervised. In addition, a lawyer with direct supervisory authority over the work of nonlawyers must adequately supervise those nonlawyers. Comments [2] and [3] to Rule 5.1…provide guidance by analogy for the methods and extent of supervising nonlawyers.

Although Rule 5.1 spells out the specific obligations for the supervision of lawyers by those attorneys with management responsibility in a law firm, the Comments to this Rule are applicable in the context of supervising nonlawyer personnel.

Comment [2] to Rule 5.1 states:

> Paragraph (b) [of Rule 5.1] requires lawyers with management authority within a firm or those having direct supervisory authority over other lawyers *to make reasonable efforts to establish internal policies and procedures* designed to provide reasonable assurance that all lawyers in the firm will conform to these Rules....(emphasis added.)

In addition, Comment [3] to Rule 5.1 provides:

> Other measures that may be required to fulfill the responsibility prescribed in paragraph (b) [of Rule 5.1] can depend on the firm's structure and the nature of its practice. In a small firm of experienced lawyers, informal supervision and periodic review of compliance with the required systems ordinarily will suffice. In a large firm, or in practice situations in which difficult ethical problems frequently arise, more elaborate measures may be necessary...the ethical atmosphere of a firm can influence the conduct of all its members and lawyers with management authority may not assume that all lawyers associated with the firm will inevitably conform to the Rules.

The Comments to Rule 5.1 as related to Rule 5.3 are a simple statement of the steps required for proper supervision of nonlawyer personnel in both small- and large-firm environments. However, as is often the case, Comments to the RPC can be subject to varying interpretations as well as numerous questions. For example, what would "reasonable efforts to establish internal policies and procedures" entail, especially in the area of protecting sensitive and confidential client information from improper disclosure or usage? (*See supra* Comment [2] to Rule 5.1.) What level of detail is required when a firm enacts a data security policy to protect client information and how should that policy be updated and communicated to nonlawyer personnel at the firm? Is it proper for a small firm to require only "informal supervision [of nonlawyer personnel] and periodic review of compliance [with supervisory policies]"? (*See supra,* Comment [3] to Rule 5.1.) And is "informal supervision" of nonlawyer personnel (especially when it comes to protecting unauthorized disclosure or use of confidential information) enough so that the supervising attorney is complying with his or her ethical obligations?

In his discussion of Rule 5.3, Professor Roy Simon reminds us that it makes sense to emphasize the importance of confidentiality when supervising nonlawyers even though the RPC is technically inapplicable to nonlawyers. *See* Simon's New York Rules of Professional Conduct Annotated at 1301 (2014 ed.). However, Professor Simon also believes that the law firms and lawyers supervising nonlawyer personnel should give these individuals "specific, formal instruction regarding a lawyer's duty of confidentiality." *Id.*

Comment [2] to Rule 5.3 states:

> With regard to nonlawyers, who are not themselves subject to these Rules, *the purpose of the supervision is to give reasonable assurance that the conduct of all nonlawyers employed by or retained by or associated with the law firm is compatible with the professional obligations of the lawyers and firm.* Lawyers generally employ assistants in their practice, including secretaries, investigators, law student interns and paraprofessionals. Such assistants, whether they are employees or independent contractors, act for the lawyer in rendition of the lawyer's professional services. A law firm must ensure that such assistants are given appropriate instruction and supervision concerning the ethical aspects of their employment, particularly regarding the obligation not to disclose information relating to representation of the client, and should be responsible for their work product. The measures employed in supervising nonlawyers should take account of the fact that they do not have legal training and are not subject to professional discipline. A law firm should make reasonable efforts to establish internal policies and procedures designed to provide reasonable assurance that nonlawyers in the firm will act in a way compatible with these Rules. A lawyer with direct supervisory authority over a nonlawyer has a parallel duty to provide appropriate supervision of the supervised nonlawyer.

Id. (emphasis added.)

If it was not made clear already, Comment [2] to Rule 5.3 suggests that attorneys in supervisory positions must take extra steps to make nonlawyer personnel aware that they must act with the same manner as and in accordance with the ethical obligations of the attorneys who supervise them. That being said, you along with the other attorneys in supervising roles at your office have an obligation to both advise and coordinate data security policies with the nonattorney staff at your firm to prevent the disclosure and usage of confidential information. Rule 5.3 (as discussed above) expressly provides for this supervisory obligation, and although the Comments to Rule 5.3 suggest that nonattorneys are not subject to the RPC, the RPC, as a whole, does define a "type of ethical conduct that the public has a right to expect not only of lawyers but also of their non-professional employees and associates in all matters pertaining to their professional employment." *See* Simon's New York Rules of Professional Conduct Annotated at 1299 (2014 ed.).

To that end, we would recommend the following best practices when implementing a data security policy at your firm.

- A written and regularly updated data security policy which is shared with all firm employees at regular intervals, as well as firm-wide training on such policies. We would recommend circulating and updating such policies quarterly. (These policy recommendations have also been proposed in the context of cloud computing. *See The Cloud and the Small Law Firm: Business, Ethics and Privilege Considerations*, New York City Bar Ass'n, Nov. 2013, at http://www2.nycbar.org/pdf/report/uploads/20072378-TheCloudand theSmallLawFirm.pdf.)

- A near impenetrable encryption system on firm networks and individual computers for accessing confidential and sensitive client information so that the risk of a data breach is significantly reduced.

- A mechanism so that such confidential information remains encrypted if in the event electronic documents are "checked out" from the firm's documents servers or other firm-wide computer servers, so that work on client matters can be conducted outside of the office. We would recommend putting these documents on an encrypted USB flash drive.

- Utilize the Trusted Platform Module standard on all firm-issued laptop computers or tablets to prevent these devices from being improperly accessed if they are ever lost or misplaced. Ideally, laptop computers should contain fingerprint readers.

- Restrict access to certain confidential and sensitive client information to specific firm personnel. At a minimum, your firm's document management and electronic discovery systems should allow for the ability to restrict access to highly sensitive information.

- Use encrypted passwords for hardwire networks and internal wireless Internet systems to prevent unauthorized access and remind all firm employees that passwords should be changed at regular intervals.

- And most important, coordinate all data security policies and protocols with either your internal IT staff or a trusted outside third-party IT vendor.

It is understandable that some may view these data security recommendations as rather extreme in an almost "Big Brother" sort of way. However, it is important to remember that we are in the business of risk management. We are practicing in an environment where client information is almost always kept in electronic form and the risk of unauthorized access is ever-present. Risks have consequences as evidenced by the recent example of a managing clerk of a major international firm who was charged both at the criminal and civil levels with insider trading, based upon information he improperly accessed from his employer's computer system concerning mergers, acquisitions and tender offers involving publicly traded firm clients. *See U.S. v. Metro et al.*, 14-mj-08079 (D.N.J.) and *U.S. v. Eydelman et al.*, 14-cv-01742 (D.N.J).

Indeed, for a lawyer or law firm, it is conceivable that the range of consequences for the failure to preserve and protect confidential information could run the gamut from professional discipline, to a malpractice suit and—taken to its logical extreme—even criminal liability. One former commissioner from the United States Securities and Exchange Commission noted:

> Law firms can be found liable for insider trading by partners or employees under the common law principle of *respondeat superior*, or pursuant to Section 20(a) of the Exchange Act, which imposes liability on controlling persons. *Respondeat superior* liability generally is interpreted to require that the offending act by the employee be within the scope of his or her employment. However, courts have liberally construed this rule to cover conduct that is incidental to, or a foreseeable consequence of, the employee's activities. Under the right circumstances, insider trading by a lawyer or employee with frequent access to material, non-public information might pass the foreseeability test.

See Philip R. Lochner, Jr., *Lawyers and Insider Trading*, Jan. 24, 1991, at http://www.sec.gov/news/speech/1991/012491lochner.pdf.

And, we have also seen recently, a CEO of a prominent national retail store company lose his job because of a massive data breach where the personal financial information for millions of customers was obtained by hackers. *See* Anne D'Innocenzio, *Target's CEO Is Out in Wake of Big Security Breach*, Associated Press, May 5, 2014, http://bigstory.ap.org/article/targets-chairman-and-ceo-out-wake-breach. This is just one of many examples why data security is so important in today's environment. For lawyers, data security is of even greater importance because failure to preserve confidential and sensitive information could put an attorney's career at significant risk.

Sincerely,
The Forum by

Vincent J. Syracuse, Esq.
Matthew R. Maron, Esq.
Tannenbaum Helpern Syracuse & Hirschtritt LLP

This article originally appeared in the June 2014 *NYSBA Journal*.

Mobile Devices, Hotspots and Preserving Attorney-Client Confidentiality

To the Forum:

I just received a tablet device for my birthday. I not only use my tablet for personal reasons (i.e., surfing the Web, accessing my accounts on various social media websites, watching movies, as well as sending and receiving personal emails with family and friends) but I recently found that I can use my tablet for work related to my legal practice. The tablet allows me access to almost all of the same applications I use in the office (email, word processing programs, discovery and legal research software, billing systems, etc.) and I can access these applications (as well as most Internet websites and apps) through either a cellular data network or by way of accessing a wireless Internet hotspot. Most of the wireless hotspots I've accessed allow me to instantly connect to a wireless signal with the click of a few buttons. However, I am never asked to enter a password to access these various hotspots. I have recently read that cyber attacks are increasing at a disturbing rate and such activity oftentimes occurs through hacking over public wireless networks.

I want to act professionally and in a manner consistent with my ethical responsibilities to both my clients and opposing counsel. Are there certain obligations that I must abide by when using a mobile device for work-related purposes, especially with respect to accessing, transmitting and receiving confidential information through the device? How many passwords should I have on my device to make sure it is protected from unauthorized access? Am I obligated to stay informed of technological developments relating to the use of mobile devices? Last, am I required to set forth in the engagement letter with potential clients a stated protocol for the use of electronic communications in connection with a representation?

Sincerely,
Tech Geek

Dear Tech Geek:

At the risk of sounding like a couple of "techies," before we can address the issue of your professional responsibility here and the various ethical obligations associated with the use of mobile devices, it is important to have an understanding of how mobile technology is being utilized as part of current legal practice. Mobile devices and apps have become an integral part of practicing law. They allow you to be away from your physical office even when you need access to various electronic resources. In essence, mobile devices and apps allow your office to almost always be with you. Mobile devices allow us not only to have access to our work emails and voicemails but they have become convenient tools to access most if not all of the computer network applications that you would find on your office system. Examples include: document management systems, productivity applications (such as word processing, spreadsheet and presentation creation programs), discovery database programs, billing software and Internet work voicemail.

The state and federal courts in New York have embraced the use of mobile technology. Indeed, beginning in 2006, the New York State Office of Court Administration began installing free wireless Internet access in a number of New York state courthouses. As for their federal counterparts, in 2010, by Standing Order M10-468, the United States District Court for the Southern District of New York gave attorneys admitted to practice in the Southern District the opportunity to apply for a service pass which would enable them to bring one electronic device with them at a time into any of the courthouses in the district. Previously, all attorneys were required to turn over any and all electronic devices in their possession to security personnel before entering any of the courthouses in the Southern District of New York. However, the service pass program does not authorize attorneys to carry laptops into courtrooms and attorneys with service passes must request permission from individual judges to bring a laptop to court.

Another advantage of mobile technology is that it allows an attorney to conduct legal research and background searches almost instantly. Research database programs can be easily accessed in court from a mobile device either through a mobile web browser or through apps that many of the players in the research database industry have developed for use on both smartphones and tablets. Moreover, one can research prospective jurors while in court as jury selection unfolds. *See* Robert B. Gibson and Jesse D. Capell, *Researching Jurors on the Internet—Ethical Implications*, N.Y. St. B.J., November/December 2012, Vol. 84, No. 9.

So where are the dangers? One of the most prevalent threats faced by those using mobile technology is the chance of physical access by unauthorized users. Almost everyone has either lost or had a device stolen. Lost or stolen devices are easily susceptible to access by a third party depending on what security measures are installed on the device, even though many devices contain a PIN (personal identification number) that if not entered correctly after multiple attempts will lock the device from access for a given period of time. Another threat to mobile device users comes from unauthorized hackers who access data exchanged over unsecured wireless networks. Your mobile device is at risk for unauthorized access if no encryptions are set for either the device or the network that the device is running on. *See* Vincent J. Syracuse and Amy S. Beard, *Attorney Professionalism Forum*, N.Y. St. B.J., February 2012, Vol. 84, No. 2. *See also* State Bar of Calif. Standing Comm. on Prof. Resp. and Conduct

Formal Op. No. 2010-179 (2010) (discusses various factors that attorneys should consider when accessing potentially unsecured wireless networks).

Turning to your first question, there are a number of ethical obligations associated with the use of mobile devices and the duties arising with regard to preserving confidentiality. Rule 1.1 of the New York Rules of Professional Conduct (RPC) establishes our ethical obligation to provide competent representation. This includes understanding how technologies are utilized in connection with a given representation and suggests that attorneys should be intimately familiar with those technologies.

Rule 1.6 of the RPC prohibits disclosure of confidential client information without the client's informed consent. Specifically, Rule 1.6(a) of the RPC states that "[a] lawyer shall not *knowingly* reveal confidential information, as defined in this Rule, or use such information to the disadvantage of a client or for the advantage of the lawyer or a third person...." (emphasis added). As defined by the RPC, confidential information "consists of information gained during or relating to the representation of a client, whatever its source, that is (a) protected by the attorney-client privilege, (b) likely to be embarrassing or detrimental to the client if disclosed, or (c) information that the client has requested be kept confidential" but "does not ordinarily include (i) a lawyer's legal knowledge or legal research or (ii) information that is generally known in the local community or in the trade, field or profession to which the information relates." *Id.* Rule 1.6(c) states that "[a] lawyer shall exercise reasonable care to prevent the lawyer's employees, associates, and others whose services are utilized by the lawyer from disclosing or using confidential information of a client, except that a lawyer may reveal the information permitted to be disclosed by paragraph (b) [of Rule 1.6] through an employee."

The Comments to Rule 1.6 also offer guidance on an attorney's duty to preserve and protect confidential information. Comment [16] to Rule 1.6 of the RPC states:

> Paragraph (c) [of Rule 1.6 of the RPC] requires a lawyer to exercise reasonable care to prevent disclosure of information related to the representation by employees, associates and others whose services are utilized in connection with the representation. *See also* Rules 1.1, 5.1 and 5.3. However, a lawyer may reveal the information permitted to be disclosed by this Rule through an employee.

Furthermore, Comment [17] to Rule 1.6 of the RPC provides:

> When transmitting a communication that includes information relating to the representation of a client, the

lawyer must take reasonable precautions to prevent the information from coming into the hands of unintended recipients. This duty does not require that the lawyer use special security measures if the method of communication affords a reasonable expectation of privacy. Special circumstances, however, may warrant special precautions. Factors to be considered in determining the reasonableness of the lawyer's expectation of confidentiality include the sensitivity of the information and the extent to which the privacy of the communication is protected by law or by a confidentiality agreement. A client may require the lawyer to use a means of communication or security measures not required by this Rule, or may give informed consent (as in an engagement letter or similar document) to the use of means or measures that would otherwise be prohibited by this Rule.

Both Comments [16] and [17] are highly relevant, especially in situations where an attorney supervises those handling confidential and sensitive information on his or her behalf (i.e., document service providers, information technology (IT) staff, electronic discovery consultants, as well as contract or temporary attorneys). In addition, Comment [17] provides guidance as to how an attorney should utilize mobile devices when accessing confidential information. For example, it might not be a good idea for an attorney to check work email or document servers on a mobile device when using an unsecured wireless network. The use of an unsecured wireless network creates an increased risk that confidential information viewed on the device could come into the hands of an unintended recipient by way of hacking or improperly accessing data exchanged over that particular unsecured network. Even prior to the enactment of the RPC, an opinion published by the New York State Bar Association (NYSBA) Committee on Professional Ethics found that "[l]awyers have a duty under DR 4-101 [the former Code of Professional Responsibility] to use reasonable care when transmitting documents by e-mail to prevent the disclosure of metadata containing client confidences or secrets." *See* N.Y. State Bar Op. 782 (2004).

With the constant advances in technology, we would suggest the following best practices for the use of mobile devices in your legal practice. First, if you have an IT staff at your firm, you should get to know them and make them your best friends. Or if you are at a smaller firm, be sure to develop a close working relationship with any third-party IT vendors that may be hired to manage the firm's computer systems. Second, be competent in the areas of mobile technology usage. Last, and in direct response to your question, attorneys must keep pace with the ever-changing technological developments in mobile technology usage, and in particular, data security. *See* N.Y. State Bar Op. 842 (2010).

You should also be cautious when accessing wireless networks with a mobile device because it carries the risk of allowing others unauthorized access to confidential information. Some things to take into consideration include knowing what security measures are in place, the sensitivity of the information, how the potential dissemination of such information would affect the client, and the urgency to have access to a potentially unsecure wireless network based on the circumstances at issue, and client preference with regard to what forms of communication should be used. *See, e.g.*, State Bar of Calif. Formal Op. No. 2010-179. Very often, the potential for hacking or gaining improper access to data is far greater over a public wireless network than through the device's usual operating network (i.e., the 3G or 4G carrier network in which the device is normally operating or a secured and encrypted wireless network).

The factors set forth in the California Ethics Opinion are highly instructive for our modern and often virtual legal workplace, especially since Internet access has become so far-reaching that many airlines now allow passengers the ability to access their offices when in flight. Let's say for example that a lawyer is on a nonstop flight from New York to the Far East, and her client emails her requesting that she include, as part of a previously planned electronic court filing, a number of confidential documents under seal. Before she left for the airport, the lawyer had planned to have a colleague in her office transmit the electronic filing to the court while she was in flight since the filing deadline was to occur sometime when her plane was over the middle of the Pacific Ocean. Because of this request, however, the confidential documents in question must be emailed back and forth between the lawyer, the client and the lawyer's office during the flight. The lawyer did not have to enter any encryption passwords to access the plane's wireless network. An enterprising fellow passenger is somehow able to gain access to the lawyer's confidential communications (which include attachments consisting of the aforementioned confidential documents). Would that lawyer be protected because the urgency of the situation required her to access a potentially unsecured wireless network to meet a court deadline?

The opinion out of California suggests that, under these circumstances, accessing such a network may be permissible since a court filing deadline was imminent. That being said, absent a true emergency, why take the risk? Although many of us often act as if everything can wait until the eleventh hour, our clients deserve better. Attorneys should be forewarned not to leave such sensitive matters to the last minute, especially when their only option is to transmit confidential information over a network with little or no security. In addition, attorneys should be cautioned that unfamiliar wireless networks carry with them the risk that data exchanged on such networks could be breached.

It should be the basic rule of every law office that every mobile device used for work-related purposes contain password-protections, perhaps even utilizing multiple passwords throughout the device in question in order to access any confidential information contained therein. Confidential information may be included not only in email communications but also any documents located on a work server which can be accessed on the device. If you are at a firm and are permitted to use a personal mobile device for work purposes, make sure to follow all policies instituted by your firm as to the use of such device when handling confidential information.

Your last question asks whether you must set forth in the engagement letter with potential clients a stated protocol for the use of electronic communications in connection with a representation. We highly recommend making use of such protocol since email communications with clients have been and are an integral part of the attorney-client relationship. In our view, client engagement letters should include language disclosing the risks and confirming the client's consent to the use of electronic and mobile communications during the representation. Some sample language could include the following:

> In the course of our representation of our clients, we have a duty to preserve the confidentiality of our communications with our clients and other information relating to the representation. We need to recognize that all means of communication are, to some degree, susceptible to misdirection, delay or interception. Email and cellular telephone communications present special risks of inadvertent disclosure. However, because of the countervailing speed, efficiency, and convenience of these methods of communication, we have adopted them as part of the normal course of our operations. Unless instructed in writing to the contrary, we will assume that our clients consent to our use of email and cell phone communications in the course of our engagement.

Mobile device usage has completely altered the way we practice law and communicate with our clients. However, as with any emerging technology, one must always take all necessary precautions, especially when it comes to preventing confidential information from ending up in the hands of unintended recipients.

Sincerely,
The Forum by

Vincent J. Syracuse, Esq.,
and Matthew R. Maron, Esq.
Tannenbaum Helpern Syracuse & Hirschtritt LLP

This article originally appeared in the May 2013 *NYSBA Journal*.

Being Prepared When the Cloud Rolls In

By Natalie Sulimani

With each new technological advance comes at least one new term, if not a whole new language. It seems as if once you get a handle on one term there is yet another one to learn—crowdfunding and crowdsourcing, to name two. And then there is social media, which should not be confused with social networks, of course. All of this is in the spirit of and service to technology and innovation. But none strike more fear in the hearts of attorneys lately than the ubiquitous term "cloud computing." What is the cause of the shudder you just may have felt run through the legal profession? Maybe the discomfort comes from the natural desire in the field of law to control as much of our client's situation as possible, and cloud computing is an environment that we, as attorneys, cannot ultimately control. It is, by its very nature, in the hands of someone else. Hopefully, you have found a trusted IT vendor to manage your part of the cloud.

But, while with technology the players and the terminology may change, what does not and never will change are an attorney's ethical obligations. We have a duty to maintain confidences, a duty to remain conflict-free in our representations and, of particular interest to me lately, a duty to preserve.

The lesson has been taught, and sorely learned, that files must be backed up. Hard drive failures are, unfortunately, a reality. So, you back up to an external hard drive, except the unwritten rule of the cyberverse is, hard drives always fail. Always. Recently, the onslaught of natural disasters, the latest being Hurricane Sandy on the East Coast, has taught some lawyers a very harsh lesson. Redundancy is important. Maintaining files in multiple locations is a must. How many files were lost due to flooding or a server going underwater? How many attorneys were unable to access their files because of these or other similar catastrophes? If it was even one, then it was too many. And worse yet, there is no reason for such things to happen.

Early in my solo career, I had a breakfast networking meeting with an attorney from a midsize firm and the discussion turned to the topic of working from home. Now, technically, I do not have a virtual law firm, but I do consider myself mobile as an attorney. I think most of us do. Technology allows us to do so. Moreover, the amount of work necessitates that we work remotely. Clients expect you to be available on their schedule, and worse yet, clients or opposing counsel may live in a different time zone. Not everyone exists on Eastern Standard Time. So, I casually asked, "How do you manage your work from home?" The answer was, "I email my files to myself." I followed up with, "Okay, to your firm address?" The response that mentally gave me pause was, "No, personal email address." There seemed something wrong about this, but more on that later.

Opinions regarding maintaining confidentiality are numerous and frequent, and as we move forward technologically, the subject keeps returning like a bad penny. We all know that we need to maintain confidentiality, but the challenge as we progress may be to understand new technology so that we are able to use it to be more efficient while at the same time being confident that we are maintaining client confidentiality.

History and the Ethics Trail to Cloud Computing

If you have attended seminars on cloud computing, then you may know that the first iteration of the cloud was voicemail. Answering machines were replaced with voicemail, which meant that your messages were stored on a remote server that required you to use a code to retrieve them. Although this was a shift in where personal and official information was stored, I cannot remember anyone wondering whether this would be an issue of confidentiality or otherwise, and preferred answering machines over voicemail and the convenience of listening to messages anywhere.

The next step in cloud computing came in the form of third-party email providers like Gmail, Yahoo, MSN, Hotmail, AOL, and others. These services stored our communications on remote servers in any number of locations, but most important, all this information resided in the cloud. Again, almost everyone is happy to access his or her email from anywhere without fretting over the fact that all our words and thoughts are floating out there in the cloud.

So how do the courts view this use of the cloud? In 1998, the New York State Bar Association rendered Opinion 709 that a lawyer may use *unencrypted* email to transmit confidential information since it is considered as private as any other form of communication. Unencrypted means that, from point to point, the email could be intercepted and read. The reasoning was that there is a reasonable expectation that email will be as private as other forms of telecommunication. However, the attorney must assess whether there may be a chance that any confidential information could be intercepted. For example, if your client is divorcing his or her spouse, an email that both spouses share, or even an email to which the non-client spouse has access, should not be the method of communication. The attorney must seek alternate methods of communicating.

Gmail did add an extra twist which other email service providers quickly copied. As a "service" to you, email service providers started to scan emails in order to provide you with ad content. They would scan keywords in your email and provide relevant advertising. For instance, if you were discussing shoes in an email, the email service provider would tailor ads when you were in the email inbox and you would now be receiving advertisements for Zappos or any other shoe vendor. After all, nothing is better than a captive audience.

So, the question now becomes whether a lawyer can use an email service that scans emails to provide computer-generated advertisements. The New York State Bar Association opined in Opinion 820 (2/8/08 (32-07)) that, yes, it was okay, since the emails were scanned by machine and not by human eyes. If the emails were read by someone other than sender and recipient, the opinion would certainly have been different.

And now to the topic at hand: storing client files in the cloud. Through services like Dropbox, Box.com, Rackspace, Google Docs, and others, an attorney can add to his or her mobility and efficiency by storing client files online. Although I know there is a lot of debate surrounding this practice, I do not see how it is very different from storing client files off site in a warehouse. In the cyberworld, electronic files are held by a third party on a secure remote server with a guarantee that they will be safe, and only authorized persons will have access. In the brick-and-mortar world, paper files are held by a third party in a warehouse with the same guarantees. Both are equally secure and equally liable to be broken into by nefarious agents bent on getting to the diligently hidden confidential information. Again, the technology might change, but the principles are the same. One should not be more or less afraid of one method of storage over the other.

A number of state bar associations have been grappling with the issue of cloud computing and the ethical issues it raises; these include North Carolina, Massachusetts, Oregon, Florida, as well as our esteemed New York State Bar Association. However, surprisingly, to date only 14 of the 50 states have opined regarding use of cloud computing in the legal profession. One would think more would have joined the fray in giving its lawyers some guidance.

The American Bar Association amended its Model Rules last year, perhaps as a beacon to other bar associations, but certainly as a guide for other states.

Model Rule 1.6 holds:

> A lawyer shall make reasonable efforts to prevent the inadvertent or unauthorized disclosure of, or unauthorized access to, information relating to the representation of a client.

Across the board, opinion is cautious about using cloud computing in the practice of law, but there is nothing about it that could be called unethical. The ethical standard of confidentiality is *reasonable efforts to prevent disclosure.* The question, therefore, lies in what is considered reasonable efforts.

Rule 1.6(a) of the New York Rules of Professional Conduct states that "[a] lawyer shall not knowingly reveal confidential information…" and, at Rule 1.6(c) goes on to say that "[a] lawyer shall exercise reasonable care to prevent the lawyer's employees, associates, and others whose services are utilized by the lawyer from disclosing or using confidential information of a client."

It is safe to assume that Rule 1.6(c) imposes the obligation for lawyers to use reasonable care in choosing their cloud computing and/or IT vendors, but indeed those lawyers may take advantage of the cloud and employ those who provide and manage those services in good conscience.

In fact, in September 2010, the New York State Bar Association issued Ethics Opinion 842 regarding the question of using an outside storage provider to store client information. The question that was asked of the New York State Bar Association was whether a lawyer can use an online storage provider to store confidential material without violating the duty of confidentiality.

So What Exactly Is the Cloud?

To understand what the issue is and why it may pose a problem, it is best to understand what it means to store information in the cloud. A cloud, in its simplest terms, is a third-party server. The server in which the information is stored is neither on the law firm's premises nor owned by the law firm. The law firm's IT person or department does not maintain where the database is stored in any way. It is in the hands of a third party offering a service.

An internal storage system is a closed circuit, meaning there is a direct line from your desktop to the firm's server. Absent hacking, the information is controlled internally. Once removed from this closed system and stored in the cloud, your information may be more vulnerable because you have now created access points in which others may gain access to that data. To illustrate, data will now flow out on the Internet and beyond your control to get to the remote server where it is housed. However, encrypt the data, and you have limited the exposure. As stated above, once encrypted it would take a nefarious and willful mind to be able to read what you are sending into the cloud.

Why Should You Move Your Data to the Cloud?

There are many reasons why you would want to move to the cloud and many reasons why it is prudent to move your storage to the cloud. To begin with, properly using cloud computing in the storage of client information reduces the possibility of human error. Emailing files to yourself, transferring them to a thumb drive, storing client files in off-site warehouses, to name a few, are all steps that introduce and increase the chance for human error. Email to your personal email account runs the risk that your family would access your email at home, thumb drives get lost, people break into warehouses and natural disasters happen that can destroy files. Cloud computing, by contrast, puts your files in the hands of competent IT professionals who will secure your information and provide the necessary redundancy, so if a server goes down your files will live on and be available when you need them from another server. Their major, if not sole, purpose (and the reason you pay them) is to safeguard your files and ensure that you will always have access to them when necessary, so they are highly motivated to do it well and properly. [1]

In December 2010, the Federal Trade Commission (FTC) issued a report titled *Protecting Consumer Privacy in an Era of Rapid Change*.[2] While attorneys may be subject to higher standards in keeping client confidences, I think this is a good guide in understanding the technology and best practices associated with it.

The FTC report recognized that businesses are moving to the cloud because it improves efficiency and is cost effective. However, the overarching concern is privacy. The FTC recommended overall guidelines for technology and consumer data. In particular, there are four recommendations that businesses should follow:

- Scope: Define what information is stored.

- Privacy by Design: Companies should promote privacy in their organizations.

- Simplified Choice: Simplify choice so that the customer is able to choose how information is collected and used in cases where it is not routine, such as order fulfillment.

- Greater Transparency: Companies should be transparent in their data practices.

Using these guidelines, what are best practices for attorneys?

- Consider what client information you will store in the cloud.

- Privacy is easy to ensure; attorney-client privilege should be maintained.

- Determine what information you will share with your clients. For example, will you share their case files with them? You can pick and choose what you share with your clients in the cloud for greater collaboration and reduction of emails going back and forth with attachments. They can upload their data in a secure environment, and you can share information in a secure, password-protected environment where you can ensure that only a specific client or clients have access.

- Choice and transparency go hand in hand. While it is the attorney's best judgment in deciding how to reasonably protect client information, you should make your client aware that you are using these services. Build it into your retainer. If, for any reason, your client objects, you will know and can deal with the reasons why right at the beginning. It may take just a short conversation about the confidentiality, reliability and ease of the cloud to assuage any fears or concerns.

- Finally, have a breach-notification policy in place. This is not just for your corporate clients; any client whose information is in the cloud should be notified of and subject to this policy.

Now that I have you on board with moving your files to the cloud, consider that you need to exercise "reasonable care" in choosing a cloud provider. New York State Bar Association Ethics Opinion 842 offers some guidance:

- Ensure that the online storage provider has an enforceable obligation to preserve confidentiality and security and will notify you of a subpoena.

- Investigate the online storage provider's security measures, policies, recoverability methods and other procedures.

- Ensure that the online storage provider has available technology to guard against breaches.

- Investigate storage provider's ability to wipe data and transfer data to the attorney should you decide to sever the relationship.

Read the Terms of Service and, when you can, negotiate with the cloud vendor. Cloud vendors update their policies and may be willing to change their practices to meet the needs of their (and your) clients. If you have concerns and/or specific needs, contact the vendor, and if it is unwilling to change its practices, go somewhere else. Frankly, there are many online storage providers so be discerning when it comes to client data.

While utilizing an online storage provider, consider its encryption practices. Will your data be encrypted? Will you encrypt the data en route to the online storage? And who has access while it is being stored? Also, if the online storage provides access on mobile devices, just as you would your computer, laptop, tablet and mobile phone, add security by password-protecting the online storage's mobile app. After all, just as in the non-cyber world, a big threat to effective storage is human error. Therefore, it is of utmost importance that you know how to remotely wipe the data if your device is lost or stolen. One aspect of mobile storage to be aware of is that when you download client data to your mobile device, it may be downloaded to your SD card unencrypted. Meaning that while your cloud app would be password protected (because you set it up that way), a file downloaded to your SD card would not be, leaving that file particularly vulnerable to inadvertent or advertent access by other people. Whether you want this is something to consider; take steps to avoid it, if desired. This shows the importance of understanding how the technology works, understanding where problems, such as interception, may occur, and ultimately how to take steps to avoid them. Education is key.

In short, the advantages of cloud computing as outlined in this article make it a perfect complement to an effective and successful law practice. There is little difference in the potential ethical issues or any other such problems that exist in the cloud and in the brick-and-mortar world of physical offsite storage of clients' files. Rather than running away from this new technology, it would be better to embrace it by learning more and making wise decisions that will minimize potential pitfalls down the road, while at the same time increasing the ease and usefulness of client communication and interaction.

1.　　Of course, not everything is appropriate for storage in the cloud.

2.　　http://www.ftc.gov/sites/default/files/documents/reports/federal-trade-commission-report-protecting-consumer-privacy-era-rapid-change-recommendations/120326privacyreport.pdf.

NATALIE SULIMANI (natalie@sulimanilawfirm.com) is the founder and partner of Sulimani & Nahoum, PC. She is engaged in a wide variety of corporate, employment, intellectual property, technology, Internet, arbitration and litigation matters. She counsels both domestic and international clients in an array of industries, including Internet and new media, information technology, entertainment, jewelry, consulting and the arts. Ms. Sulimani earned her LL.B. from the University of Manchester at Kiryat Ono, Israel.

This article originally appeared in the Fall 2013 issue of *Inside,* a publication of the NYSBA's Corporate Counsel Section.

A Tool for Lawyers in Transition: LinkedIn

By Jessica Thaler

LinkedIn can be one of the most powerful tools in your arsenal during a time of career transition. It not only allows you to research people and companies who may ultimately serve as future employers, colleagues, collaborators or clients, but also introduces you to an expanded group of mentors, advisors and sources of relevant information. No matter your current position, having an extensive network is important, and LinkedIn is a great instrument for the maintenance and growth of that invaluable network.

When I speak to people in transition, or those who are thinking about exploring the possibilities, after ensuring they have an up-to-date resume, I inquire if they are on LinkedIn. Too often, the answer is that they are not. People often express concerns about their employer finding out about their LinkedIn profile—thus fearing that they are putting their job at risk—or will make the excuse that there just has not been enough time to set up a profile. "Is it *really* that helpful?," they will ask. Without hesitation or qualification, my answer is "yes." And although the task might seem daunting, LinkedIn makes the profile-creation process easy.

Head Shots

In setting up a profile, it is important to keep in mind that this is a professional venue. I have seen friends post the fun-loving profile shot that they use on Facebook; I have also seen head shots taken with cell phones while the subject was looking into a bathroom mirror. (This makes me shake my head like a disapproving mother.) Make sure your profile picture is of the type you would expect to see on a firm's webpage. Don't have the financial resources to hire a professional photographer? When I was developing my profile, I put on a suit, grabbed my camera and a friend, went to a library, and had her photograph me in front of a wall of books. I (we) felt silly but it was better than the bathroom-mirror shot. Eventually, through alumni and bar association involvement, I participated in professional photo shoots so that those organizations could have photographs of me that they could use in their materials. I asked permission to use several of these photos to update my LinkedIn profile picture, as well as my professional biography.

Work History and Educational Experience

Once your profile picture is chosen and uploaded, complete your work history and educational experience. Some people list only the names of what they think are the relevant entities and the titles of the positions they have held. Others, like me, more or less populate these fields with the extensive information contained in their resumes, and everything in between. In my opinion, the more information the better, so long as that information is germane, as it allows people a complete picture of your qualifications and experience. There is a caveat, however. There is such a thing as "too much" information, especially if the information is irrelevant or can become overwhelming to the reader. Where to draw the line depends on your preferences and those of the intended consumer of the information. The rule I use is if I cannot read it through two or three times without getting distracted or losing interest, it is too long. Also, when I first put up my profile and whenever I make any significant changes, I ask a few trusted friends (a former supervisor and other career professionals I have worked with) to read my profile. As it so often happens, of course, if you ask six people, you will get six opinions. Ultimately, you have to decide what you are comfortable with. You can control how you present yourself and not how you are perceived. Accept the risk that someone may not like your profile and hope that is the exception and not the rule.

Making Connections

When your profile is up, it is time to start making connections. In my first attempt, I made a rookie mistake. LinkedIn will prompt you to allow it to tap into your email address book, wherever it is stored, and retrieve contact information. Once retrieved, it is very easy to click, click, click and send a mass invitation to connect. This sounded like a fantastic, easy and efficient way to get a LinkedIn network together. What I did not realize at the time was that not everyone is on or wants to be on LinkedIn and, once the request goes out, the system will continue to "remind," possibly to the point of annoyance, invitees of the outstanding and yet-to-be-accepted invitation. Then I realized that when LinkedIn pulled my contacts into the system, it marked those who were also on LinkedIn with a little blue box containing the word "in" next to their names. So I focused on pursuing those contacts to be my LinkedIn connections, understanding that they would likely be more likely to accept because they too are using LinkedIn to expand their network.

Once your initial connections are established, LinkedIn will provide you with a list of "people you may know." LinkedIn surprised me with its accuracy. I suspect that the LinkedIn system uses a matrix to compare common connections, common learning institutions, common employers and the like in compiling these suggestions. I continue to look at LinkedIn's suggestions for potential connections. As I meet people through the more traditional methods of networking, I add them to my network, and LinkedIn's suggestions continue to grow.

Another option for enhancing a profile and, therefore, LinkedIn presence, is to join groups. I looked at professional groups, those based on my past employers, school affiliations and associations I was a part of, as well as other affinity groups. There really isn't a downfall to joining many groups outside of the fact that each group may send multiple notices to its members and your inbox may get flooded. (You can change your settings to manage how often emails are received.) Groups often use listserves to share information on trends, current issues, job opportunities and otherwise. Joining a group demonstrates to the LinkedIn community your interest in a particular subject, industry or other issue.

Recommendations

A great feature of LinkedIn is the ability to receive and post recommendations from former clients, employers or colleagues. As wonderful as it may be to have nice things published about you, it is still important that the recommendations are relevant and realistic. If the recommendations are "just too much" or if they appear contrived (i.e., a friend's recommendation is on a personal rather than a professional level), they are probably more detrimental than beneficial. I have sought, and continue to seek, recommendations from people in each stage of my personal and professional career but only after I have had the opportunity to work and collaborate in some real and significant capacity with them. This allows each person to honestly and knowledgably speak to my skills, strengths and otherwise. I provide recommendations to others utilizing a similar "rule." I only offer recommendations for people, focusing on the skills and strengths of those people, with whom I am very familiar.

Research

LinkedIn can also be utilized to obtain relevant information about people and companies. When trying to connect with a company, whether in anticipation of an interview for employment or business development purposes, search for the company on LinkedIn. If the company has a profile, it provides a source of information that can supplement the information available in periodicals or on the company's proprietary website. LinkedIn will also show who you know, directly or indirectly, at that company. The direct connection is easy to identify and understand—someone part of your LinkedIn community is currently, or was previously, at that company. Where I find such a connection, I immediately reach out to that person, ask about the company, the person(s) I am scheduled or trying to meet, the position or project and possibly get the assistance of that person in getting ahead in the process. Even an indirect connection can be just as useful. The indirect connection shows someone in your network who has someone in his or her network who is at or was at that company. When I have this "second degree" connection, I will request that my "first degree" connection make an introduction to that "second degree" connection who can then provide me with the information or "in" I am seeking.

Similarly, before a scheduled meeting, check to see if the person with whom you are meeting is on LinkedIn. If he or she is, you can get information about that person, his or her interests, background and network; that knowledge can aid in your trying to connect. For example, it has allowed me to mention people known-in-common (granted, only after confirming that relationship is a current and amicable one), recognize and reminisce about a common university experience and so on. LinkedIn also allows you to look up someone you do not know and want to connect with, but do not yet have a meeting with. You can see if there is someone in your network who might be willing to make an introduction. Just like with anything else, however, you need to consider how often you ask someone, respect what, if anything, the person is willing to do and the manner in which he or she is willing to do it. And be willing to reciprocate.

I personally have not made great use of the LinkedIn groups feature, although I know many who have, and I have only rarely posted into discussion groups. A danger with becoming too involved with posting is that, in attempting to get your name out, it can be easy to become an annoyance. Every time there is a post into a group's discussion page, the site sends out a notice of a new post to the group's members; so, if a member (who may be just the person someone is trying to impress) has not altered the default email settings, his or her inbox may be loaded with notices about the "serial" poster's latest musing. I have actually heard some colleagues commenting that they have unsubscribed from a group because of serial posts, and their impression of that poster is irreversibly marred.

Should You Get a Subscription?

Finally, do you need to get a paid subscription to get true benefit from using LinkedIn? My opinion is that it is not necessary. I like that the subscription service provides the ability to email people directly even if they are not a connection through the "in-mail" feature, that I can see who has viewed my profile as well as statistics regarding the number of views my profile receives and, when I submit for a job requisition, I am provided with greater information about the position, such as salary information, and can check a box to make my resume a "featured" application. Whether you need or want those or the other additional features that a paid subscription may provide depends on your personal goals and intended usage of the site.

Conclusion

Maintaining a network and a LinkedIn profile needs to be an ongoing endeavor. LinkedIn should be used, in whatever manner and however extensively a person is comfortable with, as a tool for professional networking and development. Most great opportunities come from whom you know, and LinkedIn provides a way to know more people. LinkedIn is also a great marketing tool. It is a personal website, demonstrating experiences and expertise and providing forums in which to share and from which to gather information. Like any other tool, however, you need to use it properly and appropriately not to be injured rather than assisted by it.

JESSICA THALER (jthaleresq@gmail.com), Law Offices of Jessica Thaler Esq., chairs the Committee on Lawyers in Transition of the New York State Bar Association. She received her undergraduate degree, *cum laude*, from UCLA and her law degree from Fordham University.

This article originally appeared in the March/April 2013 *NYSBA Journal*.

Internet Poses New Problems for Lawyers Who Advertise

By Mark Mahoney

The Internet has created a new landscape for legal advertising that challenges traditional lawyer promotional practices and is outpacing changes in established rules of ethical conduct.

Panelists at an Annual Meeting forum, "Internet Advertising—The Traps and Pitfalls," sponsored by the General Practice Section and the Committee on Professional Discipline, said some lawyers follow the standard practice when promoting themselves or their firms.

But other attorneys—often, young lawyers not fully trained in proper etiquette or feeling unbound by tradition—are pushing the envelope as they struggle to compete in a shrinking business market. They are seeking more creative ways to generate business without spending a lot of money, said ethics lawyer Pery D. Krinsky of Krinsky PLLC in New York City.

Eileen J. Shields of New York City (Departmental Disciplinary Committee, Supreme Court Appellate Division, First Department) said some attorneys are following traditional rules while other, more aggressive lawyers, are bending and breaking them. New guidelines would protect attorneys who lose ground by not being as aggressive in pushing the boundaries, she said.

But Krinsky said rules will not solve the problem of irresponsible application of the rules. "It's not just the rules. It's how we teach lawyers to apply the rules," he said.

To demonstrate how an advertising campaign can be interpreted in different ways, Professor Emeritus Roy D. Simon of New York City (Hofstra Law School) cited a case reported in the New York Law Journal that morning.

The case, *Board of Managers of 60 E. 88th St. v. Adam Leitman Bailey, PC*, involved a dispute over legal fees in resolving a dog-barking complaint. The client claimed the fees were exorbitant given the scope of the case, while the attorney claimed the client authorized him to do whatever it took to resolve the matter.

In an attempt to settle on a fair number, the judge in the case took note of the law firm's advertising itself as the firm that "gets results."

"If you hire the firm that 'Gets Results,' you expect hard-nosed attorneys with a practical approach, not gold-plated preparation for a trial that should not have been that complicated, never was imminent, and never occurred," according to the article quoting the judge.

He then found both parties to be responsible for the high fees, the client slightly more so.

Deborah A. Scalise of Scarsdale (Scalise & Hamilton LLP) said the standard is clear: "If it's truthful and accurate ... then what's the problem?"

But Simon disagreed. "I don't think consumers can sort out the crap," he said. "There's a great danger that what people see will reflect their own senses and sensibilities."

Krinsky said the sophistication level of clients in interpreting ads must be considered and asked whether they should be protected.

"We can't assume that clients necessarily get it," he said, adding that rules are needed for situations where there might be misunderstandings.

Be Cautious

Panelists cited examples of proper and improper ads, discussed the rules about applying disclaimers to advertising, examined what constitutes acceptable puffery vs. unacceptable superlatives, and the value of rules prohibiting attorneys from soliciting clients immediately after mass disasters.

The program concluded with a discussion on blogs, which Shields said are often used as thinly disguised advertising vehicles for attorneys.

"Just because you classify it as a blog, it's obviously something that you are doing for non-altruistic purposes," she said. "Much of the time, a blog is written with the purpose of getting you to retain me as an attorney."

There is a thin line between informational and promotional material on a blog, but once you cross it, it triggers the requirements for filing an advertisement, Simon said.

When it comes to Facebook, Twitter and the Internet, the technology and the rules are evolving. Attorneys should use common sense and be extra vigilant in following the rules regarding advertising.

MARK MAHONEY is the former Associate Director of NYSBA's Media Services and Public Affairs Department.

This article originally appeared in the March/April 2014 NYSBA *State Bar News*.

Key Privacy and Information Security Issues Impacting the Practice of Law

By Katherine Suchocki

Your computer and your smartphone have transformed the practice of law.

Have you been in practice long enough to remember when the first fax machines came out? Do you remember when you first started receiving emails from clients? Do you remember designing your firm's first website?

The next generation of lawyers has never worked in a world without email and the Internet. This brings into play a whole host of issues with keeping client information secure and confidential.

I sat down with John R. McCarron, Jr., the co-chair of the Law Practice Management Committee. He recently presented the Law Practice Management Committee-sponsored program, "Safe-Guarding Client Information: Basic Data Security Training for Lawyers," and provided some basic tips on safeguarding client information.

You Need a Written Data Policy

Create a written data policy and start following it. The data policy should apply to computers, laptops and desktops, office and home use, mobile devices, cellphones, smartphones, tablets, eReaders and netbooks. The policy also should apply to network use, including Wifi in the office, at home and public Wifi. A backup policy and use of the cloud also should be outlined.

Password Protection

The best data security in the world can be overcome in seconds by these all-too-common practices: Post-it notes with your passwords on them placed on your monitor, your laptop, under your keyboard or mousepad; not locking your doors; leaving laptops, tablets, cellphones in unsecure places; and letting children use computers or devices that have your secure data on them.

Serious password management should be a bedrock principle in your data security policy. Do not make all of your passwords the same. Even better, do not make them yourself at all.

Utilize a random password generator. Choose long passwords (12+ characters, utilizing upper and lower case letters, numbers and symbols where possible). Password storage programs, such as Keepass and Last-PassRoboform, do a great job of helping create random passwords and managing them. Just make sure your master password is secure—and change it often.

Don't use your web browser's password storage function, its inherently insecure and its security easily defeated once your computer's login security is defeated.

Encryption

Encryption is the conversion of data into a different form (cipher-text), that cannot easily be read or understood by unauthorized individuals.

This sounds much more complicated than it really is. Encryption software will take care of all "heavy lifting." Once employed properly, only the person with the encryption key (password) will be able to access any of the encrypted data.

Do not take this lightly. If you lose your password/key, you will likely lose access to all of your data. There is no "back door" to encryption. Make a backup of the key and keep it safe.

Securing Your Computer

Up-to-date anti-virus protection is relatively inexpensive or free. Be sure your version is the latest. Secure your machine with a strong password and change it often. Keep your operating system up to date. This includes deploying Windows updates in a reasonable time frame. Keep your programs up to date.

Portable Hard Drives/Thumb Drives

A portable hard drive/thumb drive probably can carry a small- to mid-sized law firm's entire client file directory. This should scare you.

What happens when you copy all of these files onto an external drive and it gets lost or stolen? Portable drives should never carry client data without being encrypted. There are external storage products that can be purchased which have built-in encryption mechanisms.

Your Mobile Device

If you have a smartphone (especially if it is synced to your email, contacts, calendar, etc.), be sure to employ a password. This is a minimum "reasonable" step that should be taken to safeguard the data on it. Allowing children to use your phone as a gaming device when it has access to client data is a bad idea.

Track Your Stuff

Employ device tracking technology. If you misplace/lose your phone, most devices now have software built in that allows you to track the phone via GPS, send messages to the phone asking for its safe return, wipe the phone data remotely, or have the phone auto-wipe if the password challenge is not met more than a certain number of times in a row.

Do You Use Wireless in the Office?

Do you use a wireless connection at home? Probably. Make sure, at a minimum, you employ an encryption key so that only people who are given the key have access to your network. Use longer keys and change them regularly. Do not leave the router unsecured. Change default passwords. Hide the SSID (network name) from being broadcast.

Do you use wireless in the office? This used to be frowned upon, but sometimes is a necessary evil. If you must deploy wireless in your office, hire the services of an IT professional who can solidify your wireless (and wired) network.

Only use professional-grade equipment with professional-grade encryption. Consider keeping your wireless access as a separate network with no access to client data. Have a separate wireless network for guest access.

Do You Use Public Wireless Hotspots?

Make sure that you employ good local security on your computer., by using antivirus and firewall software (built-in firewall is more than sufficient, but make sure you have it turned on). Keep your system secure by keeping all of your software up to date.

Allow Windows Update to run automatically so you always have the lastest security patches. Make sure you keep your office suite updated (Microsoft Office updates with Windows Update) as well as utility programs and plug-ins such as Adobe Acrobat, Flash, etc.

Most public hotspots are insecure, so make sure that any data you send over them is through a web browser that is using an encrypted connection. An encrypted connection is indicated by the web URL starting with "https" and the browser displaying a padlock icon within the address bar.

Your Backup Policy

If you don't back up your data every day, you are asking for trouble. Backup is easy, and cheap.

Choose the right methodology for your needs and size. If you back up to external media, encrypt the backup. Most backup software does this automatically. Cloud-based backup is growing in popularity.

The best backup methodology is the one that occurs automatically, daily, and notifies you if there is a problem. Set it and forget it. Periodically, do a "test restore" to see if the backed up data is actually accessible.

The "Cloud"

Choose a reputable cloud-based provider. Read the service agreement. Where is your data being stored physically? What does the provider do in the event of a data subpoena?

Learn about data escrow and copying your data to a third party provider in case there is a problem accessing it through the cloud provider. Consider encrypting your data with your own encryption method while storing it at the cloud provider.

Storing data in the cloud can be more secure than storing it locally (proper due diligence required). Software stays up to date. Your cloud provider has a team of security experts that likely uses the same grade encryption as your online banking.

Things to look for in your cloud provider: profitability, their business model and history; ISO 27001 (Information Security Management Systems Standard); verisign secured; McAfee Secure; or TrustE badges. These show daily security and penetration testing by third party security experts. Look for these icons on the login page.

For more information on data security for lawyers, visit www.nysba.org/LPM.

KATHERINE SUCHOCKI is the NYSBA Director of Law Practice Management.

This article originally appeared in the September/October 2014 NYSBA *State Bar News.*

Hashtag: Social Media and Jury Selection a Courtroom Concern

By Cailin Brown

The social media landscape and its requisite landmines require attorneys to anticipate and engage the wealth of online content that may impact case decisions. That means they should be using Facebook, LinkedIn and other websites to ensure jurors are ready to serve, said two panelists during Annual Meeting.

In the session, "#LegalProbs: Social Media and Its Impact on Jury Selection and Trial," attendees had a birds-eye view of how online traffic yields trial and case evidence.

Claudia Costa of Hackensack, N.J. (Gonzo Law Group) and Robert Gibson of White Plains (Heidell, Pittoni, Murphy & Bach LLP) spoke during a presentation sponsored by the Torts, Insurance and Compensation Law Section and the Trial Lawyers Section.

"As lawyers, we clearly have an obligation to keep up with case studies in the field as well as trends in society," Gibson said. "One of the most explosive trends is the way we communicate using technology."

Gibson said the growth on social media sites such as LinkedIn, Facebook and Twitter has reached hundreds of millions of daily users, statistics that have immediate ramifications in practicing law.

Gibson reviewed the *New York Post*'s coverage of the *U.S. v. Steinberg* insider-trading case and the social media research methods employed in that case to vet jurors.

The Appellate Division in New Jersey held that it was appropriate for both counsel to use readily accessible Wifi Internet access to conduct research.

Therefore, the defense team brought three laptops into the courtroom, allowing it to Google search during jury selection and view social media profiles.

Gibson said that it is ethical for lawyers to research jurors as long as they do not communicate with the prospective jurors.

"You cannot get on a Facebook page and friend them and ask them questions," Gibson said. "Passive research is OK. If you Google a name and get the Facebook, that is OK. If you go on and try to discuss their views, that is completely impermissible."

Internet Knowledge Required

Recent court decisions have shown that Internet searches are practically obligatory now in order for a lawyer to adequately represent a client.

If lawyers validate juror statements, they might learn that a juror has a not-so-objective viewpoint on the case. For instance, in *Apple Inc. v. Samsung Electronics Co.*, the jury foreman previously had been involved in litigation loosely connected with one of the companies.

In the $1 billion patent infringement decision, the judge ruled that attorneys should have discovered the juror's litigation early in the case.

So, one way lawyers can encourage a fair jury, Gibson said, is to learn right away whether a juror has been involved in previous litigation.

"What if the information was out there and you didn't avail yourself of it? Your client might be a little upset," said Gibson. "During the trial you probably want to keep an eye on your jurors. They are not supposed to be posting, blogging. They get an admonition."

Gibson gave several examples from random social media accounts, which illustrated the biases shared so publicly through various outlets.

If a juror is caught reading a plaintiff or defense lawyer's Facebook page, the judge should be notified immediately, he added.

An opinion issued by the New York County Lawyers' Association Committee on Professional Ethics in 2011 states that the burden is on attorneys to track social media in order to advise their clients, said Costa.

"Social media cannot be ignored," she said. "You need to start right away from the beginning of the case. You know what you need to get to trial."

The obligation with social media is the same as it is with a piece of paper, Costa said. Clients cannot destroy evidence.

"You need to educate them and you need to preserve the social media. ...If you do not advise the client to preserve information, you could be subject to sanctions," she said.

Attorneys are obligated to know the policies of sites like LinkedIn and Facebook, and to warn clients to preserve the evidence. In *U.S. Equal Employment Opportunity Commission v. Original Honeybaked Ham, Inc.*, the EEOC was compelled to produce data and was sanctioned for "messing around with electronic discovery," Costa said.

In another instance, both a plaintiff and his lawyer were heavily sanctioned—$180,000 and $542,000—after the lawyer instructed his client to "clean up" his Facebook page.

Costa suggested lawyers discuss the implications of social media with their clients.

Lawyers who know they are going to be on trial, and receive a notice of claim, should get on Google right away, Costa said, and gather information before social media privacy settings are changed. Eventually, attorneys will need to demonstrate a chain of custody to show how any information was gathered, and authenticate that evidence.

Costa noted insurance claims cases where allegedly disabled parties were featured on social media in zumba classes, playing hockey or engaging in another sporting activity.

From now on, Costa said, lawyers may have a professional responsibility to review social media content or face professional liability.

If not now, she said, then in the near future.

CAILIN BROWN is an associate professor of communications at The College of Saint Rose.

This article originally appeared in the March/April 2014 NYSBA *State Bar News*.

TECHLEX
How to Protect Yourself From Hackers Should Be 'Job #1' for Members
By David Adkins

In August, a Russian hacking ring obtained 1.2 billion user name and password combinations and more than 500 million email addresses from more than 420,000 websites.

With that much information, assume you are one of the individuals whose information has been compromised. While exposing this data may not seem as bad as having your credit card information compromised, it could be used to access your Internet accounts. If you use the same user name and password on many sites, you should be even more concerned.

For example, if a site that was compromised disclosed your email address and a password you use for other Internet accounts, those accounts—and your email messages—could be hacked. Attorneys have an obligation to protect client confidentiality, and email communications are one area of potential exposure.

Protection How-To

Your first step when a breach this large is reported is to change your password. More importantly, use different and complex passwords (upper/lowercase, numbers and special characters, non-dictionary words) for your most important accounts. This makes the job of hacking your account harder, and if one account is compromised, it only impacts your accounts that use that password.

It is good practice to change your password at least every six months, but more often is obviously better.

If you have moved your email to the cloud by using services like Microsoft 365 or Google mail, remember that anyone connected to the Internet—anywhere in the world—could compromise your account.

It is easy to figure out your email address. It is on your business card, website, LinkedIn profile, and perhaps, in your social media information. All that's left is to try to guess your password and which service you use. Hackers use automated software to discover hundreds of possible combinations in less than a minute.

Old Is Out

In recent years, we have seen enormous changes in the practice of law produced by the technology resources that attorneys use in their daily practice. Today, no one practicing law can exist without at least an email address and a desk computer/tablet/laptop. We used to fax, now we scan and attach documents, and sometimes they stay in a digital form.

Recently, the State Bar rolled out an online technology community to consider this intersection of technology and the practice of law. We've already begun to post resources, including the Commercial and Federal Litigation Section's Social Media Ethics Guidelines, to help our members use technology. The guidelines also can be found at www.nysba.org/FedSocialMediaGuidelines.

These guidelines cover issues such as:

• Attorney advertising

• Furnishing legal advice through social media

• Review and use of evidence from social media

• Ethically communicating with clients

• Researching social media profiles or posts of prospective and sitting jurors and reporting juror misconduct.

On the technology community webpage, you'll also find links to video tutorials for services, such as Fastcase, our free legal research member benefit.

I encourage you to visit the NYSBA Technology Community and subscribe so you can receive updates as this resource expands.

DAVID ADKINS is NYSBA's chief technology officer.

This article originally appeared in the September/October 2014 NYSBA State Bar News.

Facebook: The New Employment Battleground

By Mary Noe

In June 2010, a New York City fifth-grade teacher at P.S. 203 posted on her Facebook page the following:

"After today, I am thinking the beach sounds like a wonderful idea for my 5th graders! I HATE THEIR GUTS! They are the devils [sic] spawn!" And, "Yes, I wld [sic] not throw a life jacket in for a million!!"[1]

The post was made one day after a student tragically drowned at a local area swimming pool.

Less than two years later, a Paterson, New Jersey, first-grade teacher posted on her Facebook page: "I'm not a teacher—I'm a warden for future criminals!" And, "They had a scared straight program in school—why couldn't [I] bring [first] graders?"[2]

The teachers probably thought only their "friends" would see the postings. But Facebook has over one billion active monthly users and those postings were republished by "friends" to a wider audience and became known to each teacher's school administration. Administrative proceedings charging the teachers with misconduct were commenced. Both teachers were terminated. On appeal, the New Jersey teacher's termination was upheld[3] and the New York teacher's job was reinstated.[4]

In both the public and private sectors, social media postings and text messages have become a battleground in litigation over employee firings. Employees have pushed back and claimed retaliations for exercising their constitutional rights of free speech, privacy and association.

This article will examine recent decisions regarding social media and texting in the employer-employee relationship.

The Public Employment Context

Facebook "Liking" as Speech in Public Sector Employment

Deputy Sheriff Daniel Ray Carter, an employee of the City of Hampton, Virginia, Sheriff's Office for more than 11 years, decided to support his boss's opponent for sheriff by "liking" his election Facebook page. Sheriff Roberts learned of Carter's postings on his opponent's campaign Facebook page and told Carter, "You made your bed, and now you're going to lie in it—after the election, you're gone."[5] In November 2011, Sheriff Roberts was reelected, and it came to pass that Carter and five other deputies were not reappointed.

Carter and others brought an action against Roberts alleging their "firing" was in retaliation for exercising their First Amendment right to free association and free speech, not their job performance. In the 11 years Carter worked for Sheriff Roberts, he had always received performance evaluations of "above average."[6]

In assessing retaliatory actions against governmental employers, courts balance a public employee's right to free speech against the government's interest of creating an efficient workplace environment. A public employee must establish that he or she "was speaking as a citizen upon a matter of public concern," rather than "as an employee about a personal matter of personal interest"; that "the employee's interest in speaking upon the matter of public concern outweighed the government's interest in providing effective and efficient services to the public"; and that "the employee's speech was a substantial factor in the employee's termination decision."[7]

While the trial court did not challenge Carter's assertion that he could establish each of these required elements, it concluded that the act of moving a computer mouse over the Like icon on a Facebook page and clicking on it, without any other accompanying statement, was not speech and was not an expressive activity, and thus did not merit constitutional protection.[8]

The Court of Appeals disagreed. In that court's view, Carter's act of clicking the Like button sent out the announcement on the campaign page of the opposing candidate that Carter approved and endorsed his boss's electoral opponent. The same act of "liking" the opponent also caused that candidate's page to appear on Carter's timeline. The court concluded that Carter's "liking" of the candidate on Facebook was expressive activity and thus is considered speech within the meaning of the First Amendment.[9]

The reasoning of the federal appellate court seems unassailable. The act of "liking" is not materially different than holding up a photograph of a candidate at a campaign rally, wearing a colored arm band, making a rude hand gesture or placing a campaign sign in front of a house, all of which are expressive activities.

Search and Seizure and a Public Employee's Texts on Personal Matters

The city of Ontario, California, purchased text messaging pagers for its police SWAT team to send and receive text messages while on the job, in order to provide immediate communication among the team members during emergencies. The city informed the officers of its right to monitor the messages and notified the officers that they should have no expectation of privacy. Then the city had all team members review and sign the city's policy on the use of pagers, again placing them on notice that they, as individuals, should have no expectation of privacy in messages sent or received.[10] This information was repeated at a meeting and circulated in a memorandum sent to all personnel with pagers, including Jeff Quon, a sergeant on the police SWAT team. The city did from time to time review utilization of text messaging and required officers to reimburse the city for overages. It was not the practice of the city to review the content of messages, even when there was an overage.

Sergeant Quon routinely exceeded his allotted texts and reimbursed the city for the overage fees. The police chief began an audit to determine whether the pagers were being used for "on duty" or "off duty" purposes. Quon's pager was one of two with the highest usage. The chief requested the service provider to submit transcripts of Quon's pager-texts and the provider complied. The transcript revealed messages from Quon's wife and his mistress—some sexually explicit. The chief determined that some of these texts occurred while Quon was "on duty" and forwarded the information to Internal Affairs for further investigation.

Internal Affairs redacted all Quon's texts made when he was "off duty." The Internal Affairs chief stated that the primary purpose of the investigation was to determine if the contract limits with the service provider were appropriate. No action was taken against Quon.

Quon, however, brought an action against the city and the service provider for, among other things, a violation of his Fourth Amendment protection against the unreasonable search and seizure of the content of his messages. Despite the city's notifying the members of the team that they would have no expectation of privacy in their text messages, the trial court determined that Quon had a reasonable expectation of privacy, based on the city's unofficial policy of permitting officers to pay for overages.

As to Quon's claim of a violation of the Fourth Amendment, the court decided that if the purpose of the audit was to determine if there was improper use of the pager while "on duty," then the city violated Quon's Fourth Amendment rights. If, however, the audit's purpose was to determine whether the contract limits for the pagers were appropriate, then no violation occurred. The jury found no violation. There was no liability for the search.

On appeal, the Court of Appeals examined the reasonableness of the search by looking at the totality of the circumstances and "the degree to which it intrudes upon an individual's privacy and...the degree to which it is needed for the promotion of legitimate governmental interests."[11]

The court held that the city's users of text messaging had a reasonable expectation of privacy in the content of their messages. It disagreed, however, with the trial court as to the reasonableness of the search, determining that the search was unreasonable because the information could have been ascertained by less intrusive means.

The U.S. Supreme Court concluded that Quon had a reasonable expectation of privacy.[12] The city's review of the content of the text messages constituted a search within the meaning of the Fourth Amendment. However, the Court concluded that because the search was motivated by a legitimate work-related purpose and was not excessive in scope, the search was reasonable. An employer's right to intrude on an employee "for non-investigatory, work-related purposes, as well as for investigations for work-related misconduct, should be judged by the standard of reasonableness under all the circumstances."[13]

The Court's opinion recognized government employers' and employees' difficulties with social media and provided no bright-line rule but rather signaled that decisions should be made on the totality of circumstances presented in the particular case. The Court opined about the future of the technology and employer and employee relations.

> Rapid changes in the dynamics of communication and information transmission are evident not just in the technology itself but in what society accepts as proper behavior....[T]he Court would have difficulty predicting how employees' privacy expectations will be shaped by those changes or the degree to which society will be prepared to recognize those expectations as reasonable. Cell phone and text message communications are so pervasive that some persons may consider them to be essential means or necessary instruments for self-expression, even self-identification.[14]

The Private Employment Context

The Hot Dog Postings[15]

A car dealership in Lake Bluff, Illinois, planned to roll out the new, redesigned BMW at a grand sales event. The manager told the sales staff that arrangements had been made to offer free hot dogs to visitors. The salespeople voiced their disapproval of the manager's meager offering. The manager responded, in essence, that the event was about selling cars and not about food. Salesperson Robert Becker would later describe his reaction to the manager's plan by comparing a high-end BMW to a fine restaurant but one in which the waiter brings a Happy Meal to the table.

Becker took photos, and five days after the event, he posted them on Facebook under the heading "BMW 2011 5 Series Soiree." He wrote, "I was happy to see that [the manager] went 'All Out' for the most important launch of a new BMW in years....The small 8 oz. bags of chips, and the $2.00 cookie plate...the semi fresh apples and oranges were a nice touch...but to top it all off...the Hot Dog Cart. Where our clients could attain a[n] over cooked wiener and a stale bunn...." Becker posted a picture of a salesperson with a hot dog and pictures of the snack table.

Becker had approximately 95 Facebook "friends," 15 of whom were also BMW employees. By the very next day, the manager had been given copies of Becker's Facebook postings regarding the sales event. When asked about the postings, Becker responded that his Facebook pages and "friends" were "none of your business." The manager claimed he had received calls from other dealers and that Becker had embarrassed management and co-workers. Becker was told to hand in the key to his desk. After the meeting Becker called the manager and apologized. Six days later, Becker was fired. Becker was terminated because he had made negative comments about the company in a public forum.

Salespeople in the BMW dealership were not members of a union. Yet a complaint was filed by the National Labor Relations Board (NLRB) alleging that Becker's termination was an unfair labor practice. The NLRB further asserted that clauses in the dealership's employee handbook violated the National Labor Relations Act (NLRA) by interfering with, restraining, or coercing employees in the exercise of their labor rights.[16]

Here, the NLRB urged that in firing Becker for his Facebook postings, the employer had interfered with "concerted activities" on the part of its employees "for the purpose of collective bargaining or other mutual aid or protection."[17]

The case proceeded before an Administrative Law Judge (ALJ) who found that the dealership did not fire Becker because of his Facebook postings about the BMW sales event but because of another unflattering Facebook posting, which was unrelated to the event.[18] The ALJ noted that he would have found an unfair labor practice to have been proven if the sales event postings had been the cause of the termination. The ALJ suggested that the hot dog postings were really about the impact the manager's perceived poor food choices had on the salespeople's ability to sell cars. Becker was merely communicating his frustration with his employer's actions and the resulting negative impact on sales to Becker's fellow employees. This, the ALJ viewed, as "concerted activity."

The ALJ also reviewed the dealership's employee handbook to determine if it violated the NLRA. The handbook prohibited employees from participating in interviews or answering inquiries from the press concerning the dealerships or its current or former employees. The ALJ found this would reasonably tend to chill employees in the exercise of their Section 7 right to communicate with the media regarding a labor dispute and was therefore unlawful.[19]

Other passages in the handbook were, in the ALJ's view, also in violation of Section 7. Specifically, he took issue with the handbook's statements that "[a] bad attitude creates a difficult working environment and prevents the Dealership from providing quality service to our customers" and "[n]o one should be disrespectful or use profanity or any other language which injures the image or reputation of Dealership."

The dealership rescinded certain paragraphs from the handbook prior to the hearing; however, that did not satisfy the ALJ, who concluded that the employer should have explained to the employees that it would not interfere with their Section 7 rights in the future.

Harassment Through Social Media Postings

Hispanics United of Buffalo, Inc. was a non-union, not-for-profit employer providing social services to the economically disadvantaged. Its employee handbook had a "zero tolerance" policy toward harassment of one employee by another.[20]

One employee texted and spoke to another employee, criticizing the work of five of their co-workers. The first employee told her confidante that she intended to report the five co-workers, whom she had criticized to the executive director. The second employee shared the first employee's emails with the five co-workers. The five offended co-employees chastised the first employee on Facebook. All postings were made on the employees' personal computers. The employer learned of the Facebook postings and fired the five employees because their actions were in violation of the employee harassment policy.

Charged with an unfair labor practice, the employer defended its right to fire these non-union employees because they were not "trying to change their working conditions and…did not communicate their concerns to [the employer]."

The ALJ did not agree and found that the employer violated Section 7 in firing the employees. "Explicit or implicit criticism by a co-worker of the manner in which they are performing their jobs is a subject about which employee discussion is protected by Section 8(a)(1)." After reading the Facebook postings, the ALJ found no harassment of the original employee-critic who set the controversy in motion and no violation of the zero tolerance or discrimination policies.

The ALJ concluded that the Facebook postings by the five who were criticized about their job performance were protected activity. The postings were a concerted activity and hence a firing for the activity was an unfair labor practice. In the words of the ALJ, the five employees "were taking a first step towards taking group action to defend themselves against the accusations they could reasonably believe [the first employee-critic] was going to make to management."

The two ALJ decisions signal a potentially vast expansion of the jurisdiction of the NLRB, premised upon social network postings as the functional equivalent of a gripe session among a group of disgruntled employees endeavoring to decide upon the next step to take collectively. Employers who never dreamed that their non-union businesses fell within the NLRA may find themselves answering charges of unfair labor practices. Employees may find an unexpected ally in employment disputes.[21]

Conclusion

The American Law Institute (ALI) has decided to weigh in on social media postings in the employment arena. The draft Restatement of Laws on Employment Law suggests that courts should recognize a cause of action for the tort of wrongful employer intrusion upon a protected employee privacy interest.

Forty-one states have adopted a common law right to privacy,[22] as well as the tort of intrusion upon seclusion as defined in Section 652B of the Restatement (Second) of Torts (1977).[23] But the confines of privacy in the employment context have been poorly defined and poorly understood. An employer has been thought to have a legitimate interest in the character and fitness of the people it hires. Employers can be civilly liable to others for negligent hiring or supervision of employees who go on to engage in wrongful conduct. The draft Restatement urges that liability be imposed upon an employer for the wrongful intrusion upon an employee's protected privacy interest unless there is a legitimate business interest of the employer.

Chatter around the proverbial office water cooler has been replaced by social media postings chiseled in kilobytes with a semi-permanent life to them. Social media postings may provide employers with information of legitimate interest, such as whether an employee is affirmatively aiding the interests of a competitor, as well as information which is widely viewed as irrelevant to the employer's business, such as an employee's position on controversial social or political issues. Whether an employer is the local sheriff, the principal of a school or a car dealer, all employers have an interest in protecting the goodwill of their establishment and the allegiance of the employee. But employees are entitled to a private life— a zone of privacy into which the employer may not intrude. The stakes are high for both sides, because a single employee can damage a business by defamatory postings viewable by a large population, and an employer can damage an employee's life by an unwarranted termination for nothing more than free expression of ideas on issues of little relevance to the business.

Welcome to the new battleground. This is just the beginning.

---

1. *Dep't of Educ. of the City of N.Y. v. Rubino*, N.Y.S. Educ. Dep't, SED file 17,116 (June 6, 2011), www.parentadvocates.org/nicemedia/documents/Lowitt_second_decision.pdf (June 22, 2012).

2. *O'Brien, Sch. Dist. of the City of Paterson*, OAL Docket. No. edu 05600-11-1, Agency Ref. No. 108-5/11 (Oct. 28, 2011), njlaw.rutgers.edu/collections/oal/html/initial/edu05600-11_1.html.

3.   *O'Brien, School Dist. of the City of Paterson*, 2013 WL 132508 (Passaic Co., N.J. 2013).

4.   *Rubino v. N.Y. City Dep't of Educ.*, 34 Misc. 3d 1220(A), 950 N.Y.S.2d 494 (N.Y. Co., Feb. 1, 2012), *aff'd, Rubino v. City of N.Y.*, 106 A.D.3d 439 (1st Dep't 2013).

5.   *Bland v. Roberts*, 730 F.3d 368, 381 (4th Cir. 2013).

6.   *Id.* at 382.

7.   *Pickering v. Bd. of Educ.*, 391 U.S. 563 (1968).

8.   *Bland v. Roberts*, 857 F. Supp. 2d 599 (E.D. Va. 2012).

9.   *Bland*, 730 F.3d 368.

10.   *Quon v. Arch Wireless*, 445 F. Supp. 2d 1116, 1123 (C.D. Cal. 2006), quoting the city's policy:

> C. Access to all sites on the Internet is recorded and will be periodically reviewed by the City. The City of Ontario reserves the right to monitor and log all network activity including e-mail and Internet use, with or without notice. Users should have no expectation of privacy or confidentiality when using these resources.
>
> D. Access to the Internet and the e-mail system is not confidential; and Information produced either in hard copy or in electronic form is considered City property. As such, these systems should not be used for personal or confidential communications. Deletion of e-mail or other electronic information may not fully delete the information from the system.

11.   *Quon v. Arch Wireless Operating Co., Inc.*, 529 F.3d 892, 903 (9th Cir. 2008) (quoting *U.S. v. Knights*, 534 U.S. 112, 118–19 (2001)).

12.   *City of Ontario v. Quon*, 560 U.S. 746 (2010).

13.   *Id.* at 747.

14.   *Id.* at 759.

15.   NLRB Case No. 13-CA-46452 (2011).

16.   *Id.* at p. 11. The authority of the NLRB in non-union employment settings comes from Section 8(a)(1) of the NLRA which provides that it is an unfair labor practice to interfere with, restrain or coerce employees in the exercise of the rights guaranteed in Section 7, that is, "to engage in other concerted activities for the purpose of collective bargaining or other mutual aid or protection." 29 U.S.C. § 158(a)(1), NLRA § 8(a)(1).

17.   *Id.* at 8.

18.   *Id.* at 9. The manager also owned a Land Rover dealership. A salesperson at the Land Rover dealership allowed a potential customer's 13-year-old son to sit in the driver's seat. The 13-year-old stepped on the gas and drove into a pond. Becker posted a photo of the incident on his Facebook page along with the photos of the hot dog event.

19.   *Id.* at 10 (citing *Lafayette Park Hotel*, 326 NLRB 824, 825 (1978)).

20.   *Hispanics United of Buffalo*, NLRB Case 03-CA-027872 (2012), at 10:

> Hispanics United of Buffalo will not tolerate any form of harassment, joking remarks or other abusive conduct (including verbal, nonverbal, or physical conduct) that demeans or shows hostility toward an individual because of his/her race, color, sex, religion, national origin, age, disability, veteran status or other prohibited basis that creates an intimidating, hostile or offensive work environment, unreasonably interferes with an individual's work performance or otherwise adversely affects an individual's employment opportunity.

21. NLRB Case No. 3-CA-27872.

22. Forty-one states and Washington, D.C., recognize tort. Some states recognize the tort within the employment context: Five states—Hawaii, Massachusetts, Nebraska, Rhode Island and Wisconsin—have not adopted the tort but have constitutional privacy protections that include or mirror the intrusion upon seclusion tort. R. Gen. Law 9-1-28.1(a)(1); Neb. Rev. Stat. 20-203; Wis. Stat. Ann. 995.50(2)(a); Art. I, § 6 of the Hawaii Constitution; Mass. Gen. Laws 214. 1B. Four states—New York, North Dakota, Virginia and Wyoming—have not provided for liability for intrusion upon seclusion. New York has a right to privacy, which protects the right of publicity, rather than privacy (N.Y. Civil Rights Law § 50).

23. "One who intentionally intrudes, physically or otherwise, upon the solitude or seclusion of another or his private affairs or concerns, is subject to liability to the other for invasion of his privacy, if the intrusion would be highly offensive to a reasonable person." Restatement (Second) of Torts § 652B.

MARY NOE (noem@stjohns.edu) is an Associate Professor of Law, Division of Criminal Justice and Legal Studies, St. John's University. She has written articles on the topics of special education and social media for the *New York Law Journal* and the *N.Y. Litigator* (NYSBA). A *magna cum laude* graduate of Brooklyn College, she earned her law degree from St. John's University.

This article originally appeared in the June 2014 *NYSBA Journal*.

Social Media & The Law
Why ABA Opinion on Jurors and Social Media Falls Short
By Mark A. Berman, Ignatius A. Grande & Ronald J. Hedges

We write in response to ABA Formal Opinion 466, "Lawyer Reviewing Jurors' Internet Presence," issued April 24, 2014.[1] It provides in relevant part that it is not an ethically prohibited communication if "a juror or potential juror may become aware that a lawyer is reviewing his Internet presence when a network setting notifies the juror of such."

We suggest that the ABA opinion does not appropriately protect jurors and insulate them from outside influences such as contact by counsel. We believe that the appropriate way to proceed when seeking to investigate jurors is set forth in the *Social Media Ethics Guidelines* issued on March 18, 2014, by the Commercial and Federal Litigation Section of the New York State Bar Association.[2] Guideline 5.B provides: "A lawyer may view the social media…of a prospective juror or sitting juror provided that there is no communication (whether initiated by the lawyer, agent or automatically generated by the social media network) with the juror."

This guideline is based on the well-reasoned New York County Lawyers' Association Formal Opinion No. 743[3] (May 18, 2011) and New York City Bar Association Formal Opinion 2012-02.[4] Specifically, the city bar opinion provides:

> A request or notification transmitted through a social media service may constitute a communication even if it is technically generated by the service rather than the attorney, is not accepted, is ignored, or consists of nothing more than an automated message of which the "sender" was unaware. In each case, at a minimum, the researcher imparted to the person being researched the knowledge that he or she is being investigated.

The ABA opinion, however, does make two recommendations: (1) that lawyers "be aware of these automatic, subscriber-notification procedures," and (2) "lawyers who review juror social media should ensure that their review is purposeful and not crafted to embarrass, delay, or burden the juror or the proceeding." We agree with these recommendations, but believe that they do not go far enough.

The ABA opinion draws the following analogy: an automatic subscriber notification is "akin to a neighbor's recognizing a lawyer's car driving down the juror's street and telling the juror that the lawyer had been seen driving down the street."

The analogy proves the error of the ABA opinion's conclusion. We believe a more apt analogy is this: A lawyer purposefully drives down a juror's street, observes the juror's property (and perhaps the juror herself), and has a sign that says he is a lawyer and is engaged in researching the juror for the pending trial, knowing that a neighbor will see the lawyer and will advise the juror of this drive-by and the signage.

Might that communication or visit infect the juror's thought processes or the proceeding? We think so! Indeed, just last year, a juror in New York complained that an attorney had cyberstalked him on LinkedIn; the court considered declaring a mistrial and admonished counsel after the juror sent a note to the judge complaining "the defense was checking on me on social media."

In this age of limited digital privacy, we believe that social media interactions between jurors and lawyers should not occur and the ABA opinion does not sufficiently seek to ensure that this prohibition is not violated. Receiving multiple notifications indicating that individuals from a law firm or investigative agency are poring over one's social media profile surely would be disconcerting to most jurors, at best, and could result in a mistrial.

The ABA opinion suffers from a second, and perhaps more significant, flaw. It is inconsistent with a lawyer's duty of competence. Comment [8] to ABA Model Rules of Professional Conduct 1.1 provides that, "[t]o maintain the requisite knowledge and skill, a lawyer should keep abreast of changes in the law and its practice, including the benefits and risks associated with relevant technology, engage in continuing study and education and comply with all continuing legal education requirements to which the lawyer is subject."

Granted, the ABA opinion noted that social media technologies change frequently and did acknowledge a lawyer's duty of competence. But, as written, where the opinion provides that such an automatic message is not a prohibited "communication," it encourages lawyers, and their agents, including investigators and jury consultants, not to be diligent in understanding the social media platform they are using.

The opinion leaves attorneys and their agents with no affirmative obligation to minimize their "communications" with jurors, as long as the "communication" is not a "friend" request or connection request, but is just an automated notification that a juror's profile has been viewed.

We believe that lawyers who conduct juror research through social media need to ensure that their research will not come to the attention of a juror or prospective juror. The approach of the *Social Media Ethics Guidelines*, which is elegant in its simplicity, establishes a better standard.

1.   http://www.americanbar.org/content/dam/aba/administrative/professional_responsibility/formal_opinion_466_final_04_23_14.authcheckdam.pdf.

2.   http://www.nysba.org/Sections/Commercial_Federal_Litigation/Com_Fed_PDFs/Social_Media_Ethics_Guidelines.html.

3.   https://www.nycla.org/siteFiles/Publications/Publications1450_0.pdf.

4.   http://www.nycbar.org/ethics/ethics-opinions-local/2012opinions/1479-formal-opinion-2012-02.

MARK A. BERMAN and **IGNATIUS A. GRANDE** are co-chairs of the Social Media Committee of the State Bar Association's Commercial & Federal Litigation Section, which issued the guidelines. **RONALD J. HEDGES** is a member of the committee.

A version of this letter originally appeared in the May 5, 2014, *New York Law Journal.*

This article was originally reprinted in the June 2014 *NYSBA Journal.*

PATHWAY TO THE PROFESSION: FROM LAW SCHOOL TO LAWYER

LAW PRACTICE

The Mobile Law Office—From Lincoln to the Lincoln Lawyer

By Gary Munneke

Mickey Haller runs his practice from the back of a Lincoln Town Car, with the help of an ex-con driver, traversing the freeways and surface roads of L.A. Working from the back of his mobile office, Haller is able to interview clients and witnesses, to make required court appearances and to enjoy the other accoutrements of Angeleno life. Perhaps this is author Michael Connelly's idiom for the fractured life of the 21st century lawyer.

The story of *The Lincoln Lawyer*, however, really starts out with Lincoln, the lawyer. The other Lincoln, who practiced law in the 1830s to the 1850s in central Illinois, before going on to bigger things as an icon of American history, was then and now the quintessential trial attorney. As a boy, I lived in Decatur, the self-proclaimed "Soybean Capital of the World," an agrarian metropolis about halfway between the capital—Springfield—and the campus of the University of Illinois—"Fightin' Illini"—Urbana-Champaign. None of this would be germane to this article but for the small log cabin, which was used as a courthouse, located in Decatur's Fairview Park, where Lincoln, the lawyer, tried several cases as a circuit-riding lawyer.

After learning the law by reading legal commentaries at night, because he couldn't quit his day job, Lincoln was admitted to the Illinois bar on September 9, 1836, after successfully passing an oral, not written, examination, and being certified as possessing good moral character. In the spring of 1837, Lincoln associated himself with J.T. Stuart, in Springfield, and later a partner, Stephen T. Logan, before taking on William Herndon as his junior partner. During this period, Lincoln customarily spent about six months of every year "riding the circuit," trying cases in local communities too small to have permanent courthouses or established local practitioners.

The elegant Greek Revival Lincoln-Herndon Law Offices in Springfield attest to Lincoln's success in the practice of law. The building is fit for a respected barrister and budding politician on the American stage. Lincoln's office would be at once familiar to visitors from our era, who would observe a receiving area, plush offices for the two partners, and back office spaces for files, supplies, and real work. To this day the Lincoln-Herndon model epitomizes law offices throughout the United States.

Lincoln the circuit rider traveled by horse following the courts from county to county in a land where the legal system was still in its infancy.

Lincoln found work by traveling to the work. He built a clientele by representing real people in real disputes. When he returned to a circuit venue, so did his clients, and they recommended him to their friends and neighbors, eventually leading him to bigger clients, like the Illinois Central Railroad, and the good life in the capital. In one sense, Michael Connelly's Mickey Haller is a modern-day paean to the original Lincoln Lawyer.

This leads to the question (with apologies to the Bard): "What's in an office? A workplace by any other address would smell as sweet." What is the purpose of this brick-and-mortar edifice that most of us commute to daily to carry out our work? For many of us, in order to reach this home away from home, we sit in congested traffic or battle the mobs on commuter trains on a daily basis. A lawyer who spends 10 hours in the office, five days a week, 50 weeks each year, will spend 2,500 hours over the course of 250 days in a year at this place—and if we are honest, many of us spend many more hours and many more days than that in the office. For what?

The traditional answer is that we go to a place to do work. For lawyers, the office was the physical location where they went to carry out the multitude of tasks associated with the practice of law. It was a place where they could meet with clients, confront adversaries, conduct negotiations and confer with their partners and associates about cases; it was where the business of delivering legal services took place. The law office was the physical repository of files and records associated with client matters, a storage facility for supplies, and a home for office machines and equipment ancillary to the practice of law. The office was also a workplace for support staff, where lawyers would go to manage and supervise the people who worked for them.

For Lincoln, the office in Springfield was a base of operations from which he launched his circuit practice and political campaigns, but it was also convenient to the two courts in which he appeared most often, the United States District Court for Illinois and the Illinois Supreme Court, where his reputation as an advocate was legendary. With a partner back in Springfield, Lincoln could represent clients on the circuit while still maintaining a visible presence and servicing clients at the home base.

Arguably, electronic communication systems offer an efficient alternative to the traditional model epitomized by the Lincoln-Herndon office. Today, lawyers and staff can work at home (or wherever they might be), access files and other resources via the Internet, and handle all those contacts with clients, other lawyers and third parties without ever going to their law office. Like the movable practice of Mickey Haller and Abe Lincoln before him, the 21st century law office is not anchored to the ground. This mobility presents a number of questions and opportunities.

As a law professor, I find that students (my clients) can reach me easily and instantly 24-7-365. Sometimes it's necessary to arrange a face-to-face appointment, but most contacts are accommodated by email, social media, or the old-fashioned way—by telephone. In fact, students today are much more willing to contact their professors electronically than when they had to actually set up an appointment and go to the professor's office.

Moreover, an increasing number of bar association and law school committee meetings are disposed of by conference calls and listservs. As I travel to and from my office to multiple homes (in multiple states) I ask myself: What is the purpose of an office? Is it just an anachronistic throwback to an era when electronic communication did not exist? If I can handle most of my business online, do I need a physical office at all? Should the Law School simply provide work and conference space on an as-needed basis to faculty members who come in at varying times? The only time we are all on campus at once is when we have faculty meetings—and these could be replaced in short order with video conferencing.

Teaching presents a different set of issues. Assuming that there are certain benefits to live classroom experiences, especially in doctrinal, Socratic courses or live client clinics, we might ask whether other courses might better be offered through distance learning formats. Perhaps legal educators need to recognize that a one-size-fits-all model for law school is not the most effective or efficient way to prepare students for the practice of law.

We all know that the law school will not shutter my office any time soon to make way for an office hotel or get rid of live classes, for that matter. Nor will law offices disappear from the scene. Both legal educators and practitioners have a great deal invested in having an office—if it was good enough for Lincoln, it should be good enough for us. Somewhere in the back of my mind, however, a little voice keeps repeating that the future might not be the same as the past.

Law offices are the product of an era when workers had to go to a central location to do their jobs. Whether they worked in a factory or an insurance company, one had to be there or be square. The Industrial Revolution introduced the concept of aggregating a workforce that could deliver products and services on an exponentially larger scale than the cottage industries that preceded industrialization. The late J. Harris Morgan, the father of modern law practice management, often said that lawyers were like tailors, handling one case at a time, when they should be delivering their services on an assembly line. Whether or not Morgan was right about the need to automate the delivery of legal services, he assumed (in the 1970s and 1980s) that lawyers would provide these services out of a law office. The sea change that now confronts us is the notion that the physical office may be superfluous.

An office, however, provides lawyers more than a desk and chair. An office imbues its occupants with a professional identity—an ephemeral sense that they belong somewhere that they can call their work home: "If you want me, you can find me here." Arguably, this sense of connection between us and our work in a physical space is more important than many people realize. It may also be the case that for lawyers trying to strike a balance between their personal and professional lives, having an office to go to in the morning is as important as having a home to go back to in the evening.

A law office creates a visual identity for the law firm. Whether it is located in an old house on "lawyers' row," a high-rise office tower in Center City, a downtown storefront, a multi-lawyer suite, or a strip mall in the 'burbs, the setting of the office says volumes about its occupants. Inside, the furniture, art, floors and other visuals contribute to the unique identity of each and every firm, reflecting the collective personality of the organization that inhabits this environment. Whether this *je ne sais quoi* reflects an institutional culture or the particular personalities of firm leaders, the law office embodies the lifeblood of the firm. We might fairly ask whether a law firm can exist without the law office to capture its personality and culture. We might also ask whether a law firm can stay together for long if its workers are dispersed to the four winds and they have no core, no hive, to which they can return.

Perhaps the most important aspect of the law office is the human contact among the people who work there and the visitors who pass through. In a workplace, we get to know our fellow workers. We laugh and cry with them; we fight with them; we face mutual challenges with them. We get to know them as individuals, and we share with them the camaraderie of a common enterprise. Sometimes, face time matters. It might be possible to restructure the office to eliminate the extraneous influences, to improve efficiency, and to support flexibility, but these improvements have to be weighed against what is lost, which may be the *esprit de corps* that translates into loyalty to the organization and its leaders. Maybe the physical law office has a value organizationally, which cannot be quantified, which many of us take for granted, but which we dispense with at our peril.

The answer may be that we need our law offices more for our own self-image and professional peace of mind than as a necessary element in the legal service delivery process. To the extent that a law firm develops an institutional identity, the law office might be the glue that holds the firm together. Will employees have the same loyalty to the institution if it does not exist anywhere in the temporal world? Will the next generation of lawyers, raised on computer games and social networking, find the current crop of lawyers' need for face-to-face contact as strange as they would find riding a horse around the circuit to represent their clients? The answers to these questions are less than clear.

There is little doubt that the physical law office is changing. Libraries, which, not too long ago, took up considerable space in most law firms, are ancient history for many firms that do their legal research electronically. File rooms in many firms have shrunk as paper records have been digitized and stored electronically. Secretarial pools have disappeared as the role of legal secretaries has evolved. And if predictions hold true that many firms will be hiring fewer associates in the years ahead, the footprint of the law firm will continue to shrink. Given the facts that law firms spend more on office space than any overhead expense except salaries, and that the cost of office space has risen dramatically in recent years, this is not a bad thing. To the extent that economic considerations drive the way law offices use physical space, it will not be surprising to see firms choose alternatives that cost less money and further reduce the brick-and-mortar workplace.

The story does not end here. Many law firms are experimenting with office alternatives. Given that more than a few law firm dissolutions have been triggered at least in part by rent and other occupancy expenses, there are powerful incentives to build a better mousetrap. Technology provides the tools to innovate change, but the risk of getting it wrong is formidable as well. Will lawyers in the next generation work from home, a Lincoln Town Car, a professional hive, an office hotel, or just practice wherever they happen to be? Will law firms in office buildings and Lincoln-Herndon offices be recognizable to lawyers of the next generation? Will we all be chauffeured around in Lincoln Town Cars to ply our trade? Will lawyers exist only in cyberspace, delivering e-services to clients they never see, assisted by staff they never meet? Will the brick-and-mortar law office survive, and if so, will it need to evolve to do so? Only time will tell.

GARY MUNNEKE (GMunneke@law.pace.edu) is a professor of law at Pace Law School in White Plains, New York, where he teaches Professional Responsibility, Law Practice Management and a Seminar on the Legal Profession. He is Chair of the New York State Bar Association's Law Practice Management Committee and a member of the Board of Editors of the New York State Bar Association *Journal*.

This article originally appeared in the September 2011 *NYSBA Journal*.

How to Fly Not-So Solo
By Cynthia Feathers

Practicing law can be stressful. For a solo practitioner, enduring the challenges alone can be daunting. What's the answer? Giving up the autonomy you covet? Instead, consider greater involvement in bar associations. It could transform your life.

Expand Your Network

Lawyers who are part of a firm or other entity have their own built-in community to sustain them. Solo practitioners can also achieve connectedness—through an active bar life. You may know how vital bar association CLE programs are and may be familiar with NYSBA Law Practice Management and Solo and Small Practice resources. Perhaps you do not know, though, about the value to solo attorneys of actively participating in a committee or section of your legal peers.

You may be amazed at how enjoyable it can be to discuss with colleagues your professional passions. Practitioners with greater expertise than your own may inspire you and be inspired by you. You can keep abreast of—and sometimes help shape—changes in the law. You may have the opportunity to play a leadership role in creating programs that can have a statewide impact. And observing those who are masters at planning and implementing projects, delegating authority, and holding effective and efficient meetings can teach you skills you can apply in other areas of your life.

Do you want appropriate opportunities to talk to judges outside of the courtroom? Through bar life, you can spend time with judges at receptions and other events. You may even have chances to do CLE trainings with judges or to engage in substantive discussions about the law at committee meetings attended by judges. Serving on a Judicial Screening Committee may also be an option.

Do you have a desire to write articles to offer your insights about some aspect of the law? Many of us have no time or desire to write a scholarly piece for a law journal. A bar association publication can offer the perfect vehicle for your contribution, and you may find that some readers send you not only kudos but also referrals.

Broaden Your Views

The next time you need to brainstorm or could use a template to draft a new type of document or want someone to moot court you for an oral argument, you'll know where to turn—to your bar-group friends.

You may be surprised how often your busy colleagues graciously say yes, and you'll return the favor.

The psychic rewards of an active bar life can be just as invaluable as the concrete ones. When you work on bar activities with your frequent opposing counsel, it can elevate your dealings the next time you face that attorney in court. You'll still be a fierce litigator for your client. But you may enjoy a more cooperative and pleasant relationship with the attorney who has perhaps shown an amiable and admirable side you did not know existed. In any event, the collegiality that bar association activities nurture is invaluable.

Another reward is the sense of professional balance bar participation can cultivate. How wonderful to supplant, or at least take the edge off, a gnawing sense of anxiety or an obsession about your latest thorny litigation matter by filling some time and thought with the fascinating issues your bar committee is tackling. It can lighten your mood and broaden your perspective.

Expand Your Practice

Perhaps the most important benefit for lawyers in private practice comes from the contacts they develop with other lawyers who may become the source of cross-referrals; either you do work that they do not, and they send you cases, or you send them cases that you are not able or do not want to take. As you develop relationships with other lawyers, they gain an appreciation for your skill and knowledge as a practitioner, just as you appreciate them. This mutual confidence provides the basis for referrals—and referral fees (see New York Rules of Professional Conduct, Rule 1.5(e)).

Broaden Your Horizons

My own experience has dramatized the power of bar life. It has been like emerging from a cocoon to go from flying very solo in an appellate practice to embracing bar life with gusto. The catalyst for the change was a stint at the State Bar Association as director of pro bono efforts, which gave me a front-row seat to witness how savvy, dedicated members of our profession throughout the state flourish through bar life.

Becoming involved in bar activities has borne unexpected fruit— from becoming an adjunct professor to gaining new business, from serving on boards to finding law clerks, from locating the perfect office suite to learning about pro bono opportunities, from writing better briefs to becoming more sociable. As an appellate attorney for a government agency and a Manhattan criminal appeals office, I was part of teams of attorneys possessing similar talents and missions. Bar life brings different dynamics and joys, as you find yourself among attorneys of different stripes and sensibilities who can expand your horizons.

State Bar and local and specialty bar groups all offer unique ways of enriching your solo practice. Your colleagues there will welcome your involvement in programs that interest you. All you have to do is volunteer your time and talent. The chances are that you will find yourself in very good company that will sustain you on your not-so-solo journey.

Cynthia Feathers (cfeathers@appealsny.com) is an appellate attorney with a law office in Saratoga Springs, NY.

This article originally appeared in the January 2010 *NYSBA Journal*.

Accepting Credit Cards

To the Forum:

I am a partner in a 20-attorney firm that handles litigation and transactional matters. Most, if not all, of our work for our clients is done on a billable hour basis. My fellow partners have given me the task of improving our accounts receivable because we are finding that collecting fees from clients has become more and more difficult as time goes on. One of the suggestions made by the managing partner of my firm is to begin accepting credit card payments from clients both for retainer fees and charges for ongoing services. This sounds like a very practical way to get our fees paid. However, I am concerned about any ethical considerations that may arise if my firm begins accepting credit card payments from clients. What ethical considerations should I be aware of if we begin accepting credit card payments from clients? In addition, if we have a client's credit card number on file, what are the circumstances that would allow our firm to take automatic payment deductions from a client's credit card? And if we do take automatic payment deductions from a credit card, are they considered client funds? Last, what if a dispute over the bill ensues?

Sincerely,
Charlie Cautious

Dear Charlie Cautious:

As all of us know, credit cards are probably one of the most convenient methods of paying for goods and services. However, unlike paying by check or wire transfer, the recipients of credit card payments are in the unique position of being able to retain and potentially access pre-existing credit card information so as to provide a continuous means of compensation for services rendered to the card holder and, more specifically here, the client. Although the New York Rules of Professional Conduct (the RPC) do not directly address credit card payments, there are several ethical rules and ethics opinions that have to be considered when an attorney decides to allow clients to use credit cards when paying for legal services.

Rule 1.15(a) prohibits the commingling and misappropriation of client funds or property. The Rule expressly provides that

> [a] lawyer in possession of any funds or other property belonging to another person, where such possession is incident to his or her practice of law, is a fiduciary, and must not misappropriate such funds or property or commingle such funds or property with his or her own.

Id. In addition, it is important to remember that attorneys have an obligation to protect a client's confidential information (Rule 1.6). A client's credit card information is most likely confidential and must be protected. *Id.* Rule 1.5, which prohibits an attorney from charging or collecting an excessive fee for legal services, is another rule that must be considered. *Id.* Finally, as obvious as this may sound, payment by credit card is not the equivalent of a blank check; when a client's credit card is debited for fees, the firm must always make sure to charge the appropriate fee amount previously billed to the client.

Your question concerning automatic client credit card payments raises a number of issues. First, it all has to start with the engagement letter. We would strongly suggest language in your firm's engagement letter that makes clients aware of the payment arrangements with your firm and, specifically, how credit card payments for legal services rendered are handled by the firm. If you want your client to authorize automatic payment of bills by credit card, the engagement letter should specifically say so.

Second, everyone should understand that retainers and fees paid by credit card will become the property of the law firm and will end up in the firm's operating account. N.Y. State Bar Op. 816 (2007) provides some guidance here. The NYSBA Committee on Professional Ethics (the NYSBA Committee) found that "[i]f the parties agree to treat advance payment of fees as the lawyer's own, the lawyer may not deposit the fee advances in a client trust account, as this would constitute impermissible commingling." *Id.* More recently, the NYSBA Committee found that "advance payment retainers may be treated either as client-owned funds, to be kept in the lawyer's escrow account, or as lawyer-owned funds, subject to the lawyer's obligation to reimburse the client for any portion ultimately not earned in fees." *See* N.Y. State Bar Op. 893 (2013).

On the issue of whether credit card payments may be deemed "client funds," we wish to focus your attention first on the matters arising when such payments are made in connection with a retainer. As we have noted previously in this Forum, attorneys should be highly discouraged from depositing retainer fees into escrow accounts or even client trust accounts. *See* Vincent J. Syracuse, Matthew R. Maron and Peter V. Coffey, *Attorney Professionalism Forum: Rules Governing Escrow Accounts, Retainers, and Communication With Clients Regarding Fees*, N.Y. St. B.J., Vol. 85, No. 1, January 2013. More often than not, when an attorney deposits retainers into an escrow account, the attorney may lose track of what are retainer funds and what are client escrow funds, and before you know it the attorney is dipping into his or her account because the attorney believes these really are his or her retainer funds when in fact they are not. This sort of commingling could be viewed as a misappropriation of client funds. *Id.* Retainers deposited in an escrow account are arguably client funds. They are "off limits" to the lawyer once the client says "no, you cannot pay yourself from the retainer," thus sacrificing the whole idea of having a retainer. *Id.* With regard to subsequent fee payments made by automatic payment deduction from a credit card, as stated above, your engagement letter should clearly specify your firm's procedures for collecting payments by this method.

So what happens if a client gives a lawyer permission to set up automatic bill payment by credit card, and then ends up disputing the bill? The answer is *no*, the lawyer cannot use the client's credit card to pay the bill. This catch-22 was recently addressed by the New York City Bar Association's Committee on Professional Ethics. Its answer to the bar was that "under the [RPC], an attorney may not charge a client's credit card account for any disputed portion of a bill, even if the client has previously given advance authorization to charge the client's credit card account for legal fees." *See* N.Y City Bar Op. 2014-3 (the City Bar Opinion). The City Bar Opinion reminds us of a lawyer's role as the client's fiduciary and extends the fiduciary responsibility of an attorney to matters involving credit card payments for legal services rendered. *Id.*, citing Rule 1.15(a). Furthermore, the City Bar Opinion goes on to state that "[a] lawyer who has been entrusted with a client's credit card information, along with authority to make charges against the credit card account, holds that information as the client's fiduciary" and that "charging the client's credit card account after the client has disputed the fees violates this trust." *Id.* Most important, the City Bar Opinion analogizes such acts as similar to those of a lawyer taking possession of disputed funds being held in escrow for the client's benefit, a practice that is explicitly prohibited under Rule 1.15(b)(4). *Id., see supra.*

In sum, attorneys accepting credit card payments should operate with extreme caution if a fee dispute with a client occurs. As Professor Roy Simon noted, "Rule 1.15 is the longest and most strictly enforced rule in New York's Rules of Professional Conduct." *See* Simon's New York Rules of Professional Conduct Annotated at 786 (2014). As we have explored at length previously in this Forum, any missteps by an attorney in this arena will almost certainly result in disciplinary consequences. *See* Syracuse, Maron and Coffey, *supra*. In essence, credit card payments for disputed fees must be treated with the same care as any other client funds entrusted to an attorney.

Other states have also weighed in on the issues surrounding credit card payments for legal fees. The State Bar of California's Standing Committee on Professional Responsibility and Conduct found that not only may an attorney ethically accept earned fees by credit card, he or she also may ethically accept a deposit for fees not yet earned by credit card but may not ethically accept a deposit made by credit card for advances for costs and expenses. *See* State Bar of Calif. Standing Comm. on Prof'l Resp. and Conduct Formal Op. No. 2007-172 (2007). The District of Columbia Bar also noted the view that credit cards are an acceptable method of paying legal fees on the condition that "the client understands and consents to whatever disclosures to the credit card company are required by the merchant agreement," adding that "the client must also be informed of the actual cost of using the credit card if the lawyer intends to recapture from [the] client" fees intended to be paid to the credit card company. *See* D.C. Bar Ethics Op. 348 (March 2009). This opinion also found that "advance fees and retainers" may be paid by credit card "only if it does not endanger entrusted client funds and only if the lawyer thoroughly understands the merchant agreement and arranges [his or her] affairs so that [he or she] has the ability to meet [his or her] obligation to refund unearned fees." *Id.*

Credit cards obviously make it easier for a lawyer to get paid. But, the catch is that the lawyer must make the extra effort to put in place the appropriate safeguards for acceptance of credit card payments from clients. Although it may require extra time and effort by you, your partners and your firm's accounting staff (or outside bookkeeper), you should establish explicit procedures for handling these sorts of payments to assure compliance with the ethical obligations of both you and your partners.

Sincerely,
The Forum by

Vincent J. Syracuse, Esq.
Matthew R. Maron, Esq.
Tannenbaum Helpern Syracuse & Hirschtritt LLP

This article originally appeared in the October 2014 *NYSBA Journal*.

The Costs of (Inefficient) Legal Services Delivery

By Anastasia Boyko

It seems as if everywhere you turn there is another story about alternative fee arrangements. Clients now expect them, and law firm leaders have conceded that these "new" fee models are here to stay. But this isn't an article about alternative fees; this article is about the core of the fee discussion: What does it cost to deliver the services for which we lawyers charge?

In essence, profits equal revenue less cost. In an alternative fee arrangement, the revenue is predetermined in one way or another, whether as a flat fee or as an incentive tied to performance. This type of arrangement, more so than a traditional hourly billing arrangement, forces us to look to what it costs to deliver the service, because by controlling the cost of delivering the service, we can maximize the profits from these types of fee arrangements. Conversely, if we fail to manage the costs of delivering our services, it is difficult or impossible to sustain profitability. It is only by identifying the inefficiencies in how we deliver legal services and correcting these inefficiencies that attorneys practicing in the current market will be able to compete and stay profitable.

What Goes Into Delivering Legal Services?

What are the intangibles, the inherent costs of delivering legal services that aren't always quantifiable or tied to a line item in the law firm budget? As a practitioner in large New York law firms and as a consultant to firms of all sizes across the country, I have observed a number of ways to practice more efficiently. After speaking to hundreds of firms and thousands of lawyers, I always come back to the same question—Do legal service providers really know how much it costs to deliver their product? The short answer is "sort of," which is not going to help a firm thrive in today's climate.

An Investment in Human Capital

When we start to unbundle what goes into providing legal services—the lease of the office, the copy machines, the electric bill, the water bill, salaries, benefits, legal technology, etc.—the initial costs are easy to identify. But what about the investment in human capital? I became a lawyer in an era that seemed to consider associates a dime a dozen and fairly interchangeable. Our behavior was likened to that of well-compensated mercenaries as we skipped from firm to firm for a better bonus or a better boss (or so we thought). In those pre-2008 days, associates were not investments, we were commodities to be traded and treated on whim. If we didn't get the training we needed to do our jobs, a new crop was around the corner to replace us. If we weren't happy, we could just go to another firm, a different name on a different door. These are the dangerous games firms played in the "good ol' days."

When I talk to law firm partners these days about efficiency and client satisfaction, I start with an introduction of the investment in human capital. Now this would seem to be a simple concept. If you are going to hire associates who—per the current legal economic wisdom—do not begin to cover their overhead until their third year of practice, it would behoove you to make an investment in their training and their careers. This is a good idea for a few reasons. First, you don't want them leaving you while they are still a net loss to you—that is, before that third year. (This is not good for any investment.) Second, they are the future stakeholders of your firm, so they are your *personal* investment, an investment that hopefully will provide you with some retirement income. Third, for a law practice the value of continuity is exponential. When these junior attorneys who have begun to understand your clients—their needs, their business, their plans for the future—walk out the door they take that institutional knowledge with them. Fourth, training a new associate to understand a client's business and needs is expensive and inefficient, and it definitely doesn't make the client very happy. Thus, not investing in your junior talent can cost you current and future income.

Doing It Right From the Start—The Importance of Training

So what goes into this investment in human capital? First, firms need to hire people who possess the skills and background to do the work they will be required to do, not just as associates, but also as senior lawyers in the firm. Although practice skills can be developed over time, it helps to equip hires with the tools they need to grow professionally over time. It is not enough just to hire lawyers with sharp minds or perfect pedigrees, because without a strong set of fundamental lawyering skills, the brightest recruits will fail.

The second element is training, training and more training. If we look back on what our first year of legal practice was like, most of us would agree that those never-ending months were full of worry, anxiety, insecurity and all of those other symptoms of not knowing what we were doing. Who is to blame for that disconnect is well beyond the scope of this article, but I'll venture to guess that no one institution can take the full brunt. Some lawyers got lucky; they had mentors who took the time to explain the components of a merger or a brief—the "why" and "how" that are so priceless. The practice-specific know-how that comes from experience is not often well communicated and can be hard to come by in a busy firm with busy lawyers who have long since forgotten what it was like to be green and not know the ins and outs of a transaction.

The third element is to supplement good training with resources—practical resources from experienced professionals. I have seen many savvy firms use their practical resources or leverage third-party resources for their training programs so that their billing attorneys aren't spending inordinate amounts of time training their junior attorneys. There are so many core principles to most practice areas that trying to re-teach them all internally and maintain those training materials for legislative and marketing updates is both unrealistic and not the best use of senior attorney time. Outsourcing training is often a much better solution.

The Costs of (Not) Training

The costs of inadequate training for junior attorneys are deceptively hidden, but they are massive. It is rare that an associate makes a mistake that can be directly linked to a monetary loss for the client or the firm, although we have all heard of such instances. In most cases, here's what happens: Junior attorneys are left to figure things out on their own, through trial and error. This trial and error, however, can drain hours of a senior attorney's time walking the associate through lengthy documents to explain how and why things should have been drafted. In a less ideal (but probably more common) situation, the senior attorney duplicates the junior's research or drafting, and consequently writes off the junior associate's time, while using his or her more valuable time on junior tasks. The senior attorney would then possibly discount the time it took to duplicate the task. Duplication of work has another nefarious consequence—allocating senior attorney time away from high-value, fully billable tasks to less valuable, discounted tasks. So the cost of providing legal services in this scenario is not only the cost of the junior associate's unbilled, written-off time: factor in the reduced billing of the senior attorney's time, and the lost opportunity of the senior attorney's billing fully on another more valuable matter. Such an environment can handicap a firm in the delivery of legal services, disappoint clients and substantially limit revenue.

Adequate Legal Resources

The second set of resources critical to efficient legal services delivery is an adequate array of legal tools, which includes a combination of legal content and technology. In order for attorneys to be able to address their clients' needs quickly, they need to have the most recent legal resources at their fingertips, and these resources need to be easy to navigate and up-to-date. All of that seems intuitive, but if we realize how recently the Internet entered the realm of legal research—a profession built on precedent and old paper reporters—the idea of on-point legal guidance is a fairly new one. Many attorneys still perform their daily research tasks at the law library, continuing doing business as usual because it may be the cheapest solution available. It should be noted, however, that when the primary good you are selling is your expertise, measured most often by units of time, the time you spend doing legal research in the library that could be done in a fraction of time at your desk can end up being quite expensive. Investing in proper legal research tools, most notably online "efficiency" tools, can help both large- and small-firm lawyers harness more profits through the efficiencies realized.

In a larger sense, legal research should complement and integrate with the organization's internal work product database. For example, if a firm has already conducted research on a particular topic, updating its existing research is less time-consuming than starting the research effort from scratch. To do this, the firm needs to be able to identify and retrieve its prior work in a format that can be effectively re-used and supplemented. Conceptually, the firm owns a substantial knowledge base, or intellectual work product, which it can leverage to the advantage of its clients and ultimately to its own benefit. The more sophisticated this knowledge-management process becomes, the more the firm will be able to reduce delivery costs and at the same time improve the quality of its work.

Outsourcing parts of this knowledge management can be far more efficient than trying to do it all yourself. A recent study that Practical Law Company commissioned with OMC Partners in the UK (where knowledge-management systems and efficiencies are well ahead of those in the U.S.) looked at how law firms use actual legal knowledge as a driver of efficiency. Interviewees included partners, associates and heads of knowledge management in leading UK law firms, which many U.S. firms look to as models of efficiency. The study identified common barriers to efficiency as well as successful best practices to achieve a better, faster and more profitable practice. It concluded that by harnessing a firm's internal knowledge correctly, the cost of delivering legal services could be cut by 25%.

Legal Process Management

Richard Susskind, in *The End of Lawyers? Rethinking the Nature of Legal Services*, repeatedly reminds us that much of legal work is routine work that can be managed by creating a process that consistently delivers the same quality output with the least amount of work. Such a proposition rubs many attorneys the wrong way (not surprisingly). We tend to think of our profession and the corresponding legal work as "unique" and not routine, but the truth is that much of legal work *is* routine. How often do we use the same agreement as the basis for a new transaction or rely on the same brief to begin a new argument? Relying on precedent is at the core of the legal profession, and much of legal work is consequently repeatable.

Accepting this proposition is the first step toward implementing efficiencies in the costs of legal services delivery. Once attorneys acknowledge that they can streamline routine work, for example by relying on and tailoring up-to-date forms, they can begin to reap the benefits of a legal process management system, one which allows them to recreate the routine work in the same matters in the most efficient way possible. Many law firms are thinking about how to re-engineer legal processes to make them more streamlined and efficient. However, this is a topic that warrants an article of its own.

Lessons Learned

As many lawyers already know, the legal landscape in which we currently exist is drastically different than the one in which many of us were trained. This new landscape is fiercely competitive and quickly evolving. The firms and lawyers who will succeed in this new legal frontier will accept these changes as the norm and find ways to harness technology and efficiency to best the competition.

When the commodity we sell is our expertise and our time, looking at how we deliver those legal goods is essential. Profitable legal service delivery depends on efficiently training the future generations of lawyers, providing lawyers with the most cutting-edge and innovative legal research tools, and creating processes for maintaining, managing and leveraging internal knowledge. Clients are savvier and more cost-conscious than ever, and firms that adjust to these market demands by reviewing and improving how they deliver legal services will be the ones that survive and thrive in 2012 and beyond.

ANASTASIA BOYKO (anastasia.v.boyko@gmail.com) works at Practical Law Company, advising firms and companies on issues of legal service efficiency, attorney development and training, knowledge management and business development. She often presents on topics of legal business and project management, alternative fee arrangements, attorney-client business relationships and legal resources. Ms. Boyko is a graduate of Yale Law School and a member of the New York State Bar Association's Committee on Attorney Professionalism.

This article originally appeared in the October 2014 *NYSBA Journal*.

Rules Governing Escrow Accounts, Retainers, and Communication With Clients Regarding Fees

To the Forum:

I recently received a $10,000 retainer to represent a client (Daniel Developer) in a real property development project. I anticipate the project will take about a year to 18 months to complete. I will be billing on an hourly basis every two months. It has been my practice to put these retainers in my escrow account but in discussing the matter with a couple of fellow attorneys, one expressed the opinion that these retainers should not be put into the escrow account and instead should be deposited into our firm's operating account. The other attorney said that the retainer payment belongs to the client and must be put into an escrow account. Which is it?

In addition, could I enter into a "flat fee" or "minimum fee" payment arrangement with Daniel Developer?

With regard to fee amounts, it has been my firm's practice to increase billing rates at the beginning of each calendar year. Am I required to inform Daniel Developer once our new billing rates take effect?

Last, if for some reason I do not use up the retainer given to me by Daniel Developer, am I required to refund the remaining amount to him?

Sincerely,
Andrew Advocate

Dear Andrew Advocate:

As set forth below, the New York Rules of Professional Conduct require that all financial transactions with clients be handled carefully by lawyers and law firms who must keep contemporaneous records. Moreover, be it for fees or other funds received from or on behalf of clients, lawyers and law firms must communicate what services they will provide, or have provided, to the client, as well as funds received from or disbursed on behalf of clients. Having said that, as long as the lawyer or law firm advises the client that the retainer payment will be treated as if it were earned at the time of the payment and that any unearned portion will be refunded to the client, New York allows the fees to be deposited into an operating account.

By far, the proper handling of client funds is one of the most sensitive ethical issues that attorneys face every day. Attorneys are reminded time and time again—from the moment they are admitted to practice—

that there are strict procedures in place governing how an attorney handles money received from a client and, in particular, retainer fees meant to pay for legal services. Although attorneys should be intimately familiar with each and every part of the Rules of Professional Conduct, special attention must be given to Rule 1.15, which deals with, among other things, preserving identity of funds and property of others, fiduciary responsibility, and the prohibition against comingling and misappropriation of client funds or property. To use the words of Professor Roy Simon, "Rule 1.15 is the longest and most strictly enforced rule in New York's Rules of Professional Conduct." *See* Simon's New York Rules of Professional Conduct Annotated 598 (2012).

Rule 1.15(a) prohibits comingling and misappropriation of client funds or property and states that "[a] lawyer in possession of any funds or other property belonging to another person, where such possession is incident to his or her practice of law, is a fiduciary, and must not misappropriate such funds or property or commingle such funds or property with his or her own." The lawyer must maintain separate accounts for funds that are the client's property. *See* Rule 1.15(b). Generally speaking, retainers paid to an attorney are not considered a client's property, which means that retainers should not be deposited into an escrow account. As stated by one commentator, to the contrary New York "*requires* a lawyer to deposit advance retainer fees in the lawyer's own account (or the law firm's operating account) unless the lawyer and client have agreed that the lawyer may deposit them in the lawyer's or law firm's trust account." *See* Simon at 600 (emphasis added); *see also* N.Y. St. Bar Ass'n Op. 816 (2007). Opinion 816 is instructive since the Committee on Professional Ethics found that "[i]f the parties agree to treat advance payment of fees as the lawyer's own, the lawyer may not deposit the fee advances in a client trust account, as this would constitute impermissible comingling." *Id*.

Accordingly, the payment you received from Daniel Developer for his upcoming real estate project appears to be an advance retainer, and therefore belongs to you and no longer to him. The attorney you spoke with who said that the retainer should be placed in your firm's operating account is correct, and you should no longer be depositing retainer payments into your firm's escrow account. Once the retainer is deposited in the operating account, the funds are outside the control of the client and its creditors and are under the control of the lawyer. The obligation to return an unearned part of a retainer is a separate matter (which we will address below). In essence, there is a debtor/creditor relationship between lawyer and client. But, as they say, "the devil is always in the details," so that isn't necessarily the end of our answer.

Perhaps this engenders some controversy, but it has been suggested that lawyers should open a third account dedicated to retainers. While it is important that we emphasize again and again that a third account is not required and that it is perfectly acceptable to deposit retainers in the operating account, a third "retainers only" account may have certain advantages that outweigh any additional bookkeeping burdens it may create. There are always bookkeeping issues when funds are deposited into an escrow account or an operating account. More often than not when an attorney deposits retainers into an escrow account (which should not be done), the attorney may lose track of which are the retainer funds and which are client escrow funds and before you know it the attorney is dipping into his or her account because the attorney believes these really are the retainer funds when in fact they are not. This sort of commingling would also constitute the misappropriation of client funds. The problem of putting retainer funds into the general operating account is, again, a bookkeeping issue. Funds in an operating account usually get spent—particularly by the small firm or single-practitioner firm. These funds get used for taxes, payroll, whatever. Granted attorneys should have the discipline not to do that but, they often lose track of which are the retainer funds and which are not. As seen in the example, if in fact the attorney is "fired" after a couple of weeks, he or she has to return the unused retainer. If the retainer funds have been spent out of the operating account, the attorney may not have the money to return unused retainer fees to the client.

The benefit of the third account is that funds are put in that account and withdrawn only as earned. Furthermore, the client has no control over these funds (as opposed to an escrow account), so if the attorney and client "split up" and the disenchanted client tells the attorney that the attorney cannot pay himself or herself, the attorney would be permitted to retain such funds as payment for services rendered. Retainers deposited in an escrow account are, arguably, client funds. They are "off limits" to the lawyer once the client says no you cannot pay yourself from the retainer, thus sacrificing the whole idea of having a retainer. If the retainer funds are deposited in the third type of account, the funds remain the attorney's and, pursuant to the well-drafted retainer agreement, the attorney may pay himself or herself. And, as opposed to putting retainer funds in a general operating account and perhaps having them dissipated, the balance of funds will be there to return to the client.

Your question mentioned escrow accounts, so it is important to point out the recent decision by the Court of Appeals in *In re Galasso*, 19 N.Y.3d 688 (2012). There various disciplinary charges were upheld against a lawyer who failed to detect the looting of his firm's escrow account by the firm's bookkeeper—who also happened to be his brother. The Court faulted the attorney for breaching his fiduciary duty to pay or deliver escrow funds, failing to supervise a non-lawyer employee, being unjustly enriched by the use of clients' funds for his personal benefit and failing to provide appropriate accounting to his firm's clients. "[A]lthough [the attorney] himself did not steal the money and his conduct was not venal, his acts in setting in place the firm's procedures, as well as his ensuing omissions, permitted his [brother] to do so"; and "[he] ceded an unacceptable level of control over the firm accounts to his brother, thereby creating the opportunity for the misuse of client funds." *Id*. In light of *Galasso*, we cannot stress enough the need for attorneys to implement and maintain strict financial controls and consistently maintaining those controls through regular supervision of the firm's staff, especially in matters involving the financial affairs of both the law firm and the clients it represents.

Your remaining questions provide us with an opportunity to discuss Rule 1.5, which governs fees and division of fees. Rule 1.5(a) states:

> (a) A lawyer shall not make an agreement for, charge, or collect an excessive or illegal fee or expense. A fee is excessive when, after a review of the facts, a reasonable lawyer would be left with a definite and firm conviction that the fee is excessive. The factors to be considered in determining whether a fee is excessive may include the following:
>
>> (1) the time and labor required, the novelty and difficulty of the questions involved, and the skill requisite to perform the legal service properly;
>>
>> (2) the likelihood, if apparent or made known to the client, that the acceptance of the particular employment will preclude other employment by the lawyer;
>>
>> (3) the fee customarily charged in the locality for similar legal services;
>>
>> (4) the amount involved and the results obtained;
>>
>> (5) the time limitations imposed by the client or by circumstances;
>>
>> (6) the nature and length of the professional relationship with the client;
>>
>> (7) the experience, reputation and ability of the lawyer or lawyers performing the services; and
>>
>> (8) whether the fee is fixed or contingent.

Furthermore, Rule 1.5(d)(4) provides:

> (d) A lawyer shall not enter into an arrangement for, charge or collect:
>
>> (4) a nonrefundable retainer fee; provided that a lawyer may enter into a retainer agreement with a client containing a reasonable minimum fee clause if

> it defines in plain language and sets forth the circum-
> stances under which such fee may be incurred and
> how it will be calculated…

We should first turn to your questions whether it is appropriate to
enter into a "minimum fee" payment arrangement with Daniel Developer and whether you are required to return to him the unused portions
of the fee received from him. Rule 1.5(d)(4) incorporates, amongst other
things, the finding by the Court of Appeals in *In re Cooperman*, 83 N.Y.2d
465 (1994) which essentially put an end to nonrefundable fees in New
York holding that they generally violate a lawyer's obligation to return
any unearned fee upon withdrawal. Although nonrefundable retainers
are not permitted, *Cooperman* allows lawyers to charge a minimum fee
"as long as the minimum fee is refunded if the work is not completed."
Id.

The $10,000 payment you have received from Daniel Developer for
his real estate project would be reasonable depending on the scope of the
project and how much time it will take you to complete the tasks necessary to fulfill the objectives of your representation. If it is reasonable to
expect that the legal services required to achieve your client's objectives
would cost $10,000, then qualifying the $10,000 payment as a minimum
fee would be reasonable under these circumstances. The factors outlined
above as per Rule 1.5(a) are instructive in the determination of what
would qualify as a reasonable fee. However, if for some reason Daniel
Developer terminated your representation or you decided to withdraw
from the representation before completing the project or triggering payment of the minimum fee, then you must refund whatever part of the
minimum fee has not been earned, because nonrefundable retainer fees
are prohibited.

Your letter mentions that it is your firm's practice to increase billing
rates at the beginning of each calendar year (like many firms) and asks if
you are required to inform Daniel Developer of any fee increases by your
firm. Rule 1.5(b) states:

> (b) A lawyer shall communicate to a client the scope of
> the representation and the basis or rate of the fee and
> expenses for which the client will be responsible. This
> information shall be communicated to the client before
> or within a reasonable time after commencement of the
> representation and shall be in writing where required by
> statute or court rule. This provision shall not apply when
> the lawyer will charge a regularly represented client on
> the same basis or rate and perform services that are of
> the same general kind as previously rendered to and
> paid for by the client. Any changes in the scope of the
> representation or the basis or rate of the fee or expenses
> shall also be communicated to the client.

Comment [2] to Rule 1.5 provides:

> When the lawyer has regularly represented a client,
> they ordinarily will have evolved an understanding
> concerning the basis or rate of the fee and the expenses
> for which the client will be responsible. In a new client-
> lawyer relationship, however, an understanding as to
> fees and expenses must be promptly established. Court
> rules regarding engagement letters require that such an
> understanding be memorialized in writing in certain cas-
> es. See 22 N.Y.C.R.R. Part 1215. Even where not required,
> it is desirable to furnish the client with at least a simple
> memorandum or copy of the lawyer's customary fee
> arrangements that states the general nature of the legal
> services to be provided, the basis, rate or total amount
> of the fee, and whether and to what extent the client will
> be responsible for any costs, expenses or disbursements
> in the course of the representation. A written statement
> concerning the terms of the engagement reduces the pos-
> sibility of misunderstanding.

As Comment [2] suggests, the length of time of the relationship
between the lawyer and client is a primary factor in determining the
required level of understanding between the lawyer and client as to what
fees and expenses will be incurred in connection with a given representation. If Daniel Developer happened to be a longtime client of your firm,
then there should be a regular understanding between him and your
firm as to the scope of the representation and the basis or rate of the fee
and expenses for which he will ultimately be responsible. If, however,
Daniel Developer is a new client, you must almost immediately establish
a written understanding as to fees and expenses, which may be done by
way of the required letter of engagement prescribed in 22 N.Y.C.R.R. part
1215.

In any case, when firms have a practice of annually increasing rates
during the course of a representation, the firm should give advance
notice to the client in the retainer agreement or engagement letter sent to
the client at the outset of the representation by using language such as
the following:

> We review our rates from time to time and may adjust
> them periodically, without notice to our client, based
> upon our determination of the value of each individual's
> services in the legal marketplace in which we serve our
> clients.

This puts the client on notice of your firm's practice and opens the
door to a negotiation for a different arrangement if the client objects to
the practice. Since you anticipate that Daniel Developer's project will

take a year to 18 months to complete, we believe that your firm's practice of raising rates annually must be disclosed in the engagement letter or retainer agreement sent to Daniel Developer.

Sincerely,
The Forum by

Vincent J. Syracuse, Esq.,
Matthew R. Maron, Esq.,
Tannenbaum Helpern Syracuse & Hirschtritt LLP, and

Peter V. Coffey, Esq.,
Englert, Coffey, McHugh & Fantauzzi, LLP

This article originally appeared in the January 2013 *NYSBA Journal*.

Unauthorized Practice of Law

To the Forum:

My firm represents Blackacre, a real estate investment trust (REIT) with real estate holdings located throughout many portions of the United States, and has represented the company in almost all of its real estate transactions. A wholly owned subsidiary of Blackacre owns a luxury ski resort development in Utah, and the principals of Blackacre have located a second resort property in Utah that they hope to purchase and add to the company's ever-growing real estate portfolio. My firm only has an office in New York and does not employ any attorneys who are admitted to practice in Utah. Would this transaction require Blackacre to hire local counsel in Utah to assist my firm in the deal? I have heard that if I do not retain local counsel, then I would potentially be engaging in the unauthorized practice of law. Is this true? What are the consequences for engaging in the unauthorized practice of law?

Sincerely,
I. Need Help

Dear I. Need Help:

The unauthorized practice of law is a complicated question, one which at times has been met with fiercely diverging viewpoints. Those who run afoul of unauthorized practice regulations, however, can be subjected to a variety of penalties including disgorgement of legal fees, disciplinary action, and possible criminal sanctions.

Lawyers are often asked by their clients to handle matters that may take them outside their home territory. For example, in the litigation realm, an attorney admitted in New York could be handling the representation of a client in a New York state court action which may require the attorney to conduct discovery in other jurisdictions in connection with the case, even though that attorney may not be admitted in those states. Corporate, real estate and other transactional attorneys admitted in New York may also be asked to represent their New York-based clients in mergers and acquisitions where the transaction at issue involves a purchaser or seller in another state.

Rule 5.5(a) of the New York Rules of Professional Conduct (the RPC) gives attorneys the rules of the road (at least from the New York perspective) when their practices take them to other jurisdictions. The Rule provides that "[a] lawyer shall not practice law in a jurisdiction in violation of the regulation of the legal profession in that jurisdiction."

Comment [1] to Rule 5.5 states:

A lawyer may practice law only in a jurisdiction in which the lawyer is authorized to practice. A lawyer may be admitted to practice law in a jurisdiction on a regular basis or may be authorized by court rule or order or by law to practice for a limited purpose or on a restricted basis. Paragraph (a) applies to unauthorized practice of law in another jurisdiction by a lawyer through the lawyer's direct action, and paragraph (b) prohibits a lawyer from aiding a nonlawyer in the unauthorized practice of law.

New York may not always be the friendliest place for out-of-state attorneys who venture into our jurisdiction (even on a temporary basis) as part of their representation of a client. In the words of Professor Roy Simon, "Rule 5.5 is one of the great disappointments in the New York Rules of Professional Conduct." Simon's New York Rules of Professional Conduct Annotated at 1340 (2014 ed.). New York Judiciary Law §§ 478 and 484 make it a crime for a person to practice law in New York when not admitted to practice in this state, and the statutes do not distinguish "between nonlawyers who have never been admitted anywhere and lawyers who have been admitted elsewhere but not in New York." Simon's at 1340. Although enforcement of these statutes may be inconsistent, the message being sent by both the Legislature and the courts is that out-of-state attorneys should engage New York-admitted counsel in connection with their matters in New York.

When the RPC was enacted in April 2009, New York did not incorporate many of the "safe harbor" provisions in Rule 5.5 of the American Bar Association's Model Rules of Professional Conduct (the Model Rules) that permit lawyers to do work outside the jurisdiction where they are admitted. Specifically, Rule 5.5(c) of the Model Rules tells our profession:

A lawyer admitted in another United States jurisdiction, and not disbarred or suspended from practice in any jurisdiction, may provide legal services on a temporary basis in this jurisdiction that:

(1) are undertaken in association with a lawyer who is admitted to practice in this jurisdiction and who actively participates in the matter;

(2) are in or reasonably related to a pending or potential proceeding before a tribunal in this or another jurisdiction, if the lawyer, or a person the lawyer is assisting, is authorized by law or order to appear in such proceeding or reasonably expects to be so authorized;

(3) are in or reasonably related to a pending or potential arbitration, mediation, or other alternative

dispute resolution proceeding in this or another jurisdiction, if the services arise out of or are reasonably
related to the lawyer's practice in a jurisdiction in
which the lawyer is admitted to practice and are not
services for which the forum requires pro hac vice
admission; or

(4) are not within paragraphs (c)(2) or (c)(3) and arise
out of or are reasonably related to the lawyer's practice in a jurisdiction in which the lawyer is admitted
to practice.

Perhaps addressing the needs of a broader audience, the ABA made
several comments to Rule 5.5(c) that assist lawyers with multijurisdictional practices. Comment [10] to Rule 5.5 of the Model Rules states:

Paragraph (c)(2) also provides that a lawyer rendering services in this jurisdiction on a temporary basis
does not violate this Rule when the lawyer engages in
conduct in anticipation of a proceeding or hearing in a
jurisdiction in which the lawyer is authorized to practice law or in which the lawyer reasonably expects to be
admitted pro hac vice. Examples of such conduct include
meetings with the client, interviews of potential witnesses, and the review of documents. Similarly, a lawyer
admitted only in another jurisdiction may engage in
conduct temporarily in this jurisdiction in connection
with pending litigation in another jurisdiction in which
the lawyer is or reasonably expects to be authorized to
appear, including taking depositions in this jurisdiction.

In addition, Comment [13] to Rule 5.5 of the Model Rules provides:

Paragraph (c)(4) permits a lawyer admitted in another
jurisdiction to provide certain legal services on a temporary basis in this jurisdiction that arise out of or are
reasonably related to the lawyer's practice in a jurisdiction in which the lawyer is admitted but are not within
paragraphs (c)(2) or (c)(3). These services include both
legal services and services that nonlawyers may perform
but that are considered the practice of law when performed by lawyers.

Paragraphs (c)(2) and (c)(3) to Rule 5.5 of the Model Rules clearly
were meant to lower the hurdles for attorneys to engage in multijurisdictional practice in both the litigation and alternative dispute resolution
(ADR) forums, respectively. Moreover, Paragraph (c)(4) can be interpreted as permitting out-of-state attorneys to engage in the representation of
a client in the transactional context in jurisdictions which have adopted
this specific provision of the Model Rules. Indeed, one of our neighbors

in the tri-state area (Connecticut) adopted these sections of Rule 5.5 of the Model Rules nearly verbatim so as to allow Connecticut to be more hospitable to multijurisdictional practitioners. Taking an even more enlightened approach to embracing out-of-state attorneys, our neighbors in the Garden State have adopted a version of Rule 5.5 which sets forth a number of varying situations where out-of-state attorneys could practice in New Jersey on either an occasional or temporary basis in connection with matters in their respective home states. The relevant provisions of Rule 5.5 of the New Jersey Rules of Professional Conduct provide:

> (b) A lawyer not admitted to the Bar of [New Jersey] who is admitted to practice law before the highest court of any other state, territory of the United States, Puerto Rico, or the District of Columbia (hereinafter a United States jurisdiction) may engage in the lawful practice of law in New Jersey only if:
>
>> (1) the lawyer is admitted to practice pro hac vice pursuant to R. 1:21-2 [of the Rules Governing the Courts of the State of New Jersey (the New Jersey Rules)] or is preparing for a proceeding in which the lawyer reasonably expects to be so admitted and is associated in that preparation with a lawyer admitted to practice in this jurisdiction; or
>>
>> * * *
>>
>> (3) under any of the following circumstances:
>>
>>> (i) *the lawyer engages in the negotiation of the terms of a transaction in furtherance of the lawyer's representation on behalf of an existing client* in a jurisdiction in which the lawyer is admitted to practice and the transaction originates in or is otherwise related to a jurisdiction in which the lawyer is admitted to practice;
>>>
>>> (ii) *the lawyer engages in representation of a party to a dispute by participating in arbitration, mediation or other alternate or complementary dispute resolution program and the services arise out of or are reasonably related to the lawyer's practice* in a jurisdiction in which the lawyer is admitted to practice and are not services for which pro hac vice admission pursuant to R. 1:21-2 [of the New Jersey Rules] is required;
>>>
>>> (iii) the lawyer investigates, engages in discovery, interviews witnesses or deposes witnesses in this jurisdiction for a proceeding pending or antici-

pated to be instituted in a jurisdiction in which the lawyer is admitted to practice;

(iv) the out-of-state lawyer's practice in this jurisdiction is occasional and the lawyer associates in the matter with, and designates and discloses to all parties in interest, a lawyer admitted to the Bar of [New Jersey] who shall be held responsible for the conduct of the out-of-State lawyer in the matter; or

(v) the lawyer practices under circumstances other than (i) through (iv) above, with respect to a matter where the practice activity arises directly out of the lawyer's representation on behalf of an existing client in a jurisdiction in which the lawyer is admitted to practice, *provided that such practice in this jurisdiction is occasional and is undertaken only when the lawyer's disengagement would result in substantial inefficiency, impracticality or detriment to the client* (emphasis added).

As demonstrated above, it appears that our neighbors in the tri-state area are more than happy to allow New York attorneys on their turf. However, the feeling may not be mutual, and it is uncertain whether New York is likely to change its rules anytime soon.

With that in mind, we turn to your question. Obviously, in addition to being well-versed in the RPC, you should also make yourself familiar with the rules applicable to the jurisdiction where your client's matter may take you; in this case it would be the Utah Rules of Professional Conduct (the Utah Rules). The good news is that Rule 5.5 of the Utah Rules tracks the language of Rule 5.5(c) of the Model Rules and its respective comments.

The Utah Rules appear to have adopted the ABA Model Rules in order to embrace the concept of multijurisdictional practice. Being that your representation of Blackacre in connection with its real property purchase in Utah could be "reasonably related" to your ongoing representation of Blackacre as its New York counsel in its other real estate ventures, your representation of Blackacre under these circumstances would not be considered an unauthorized practice of law and would be permissible under Rule 5.5(c)(4) of the Utah Rules.

That being said, we believe that it is smart for you to engage local counsel in Utah to assist with Blackacre's resort purchase. While local counsel may not be an absolute necessity, we are guided by the competency requirements outlined in Rule 1.1 of the RPC. Rule 1.1 provides:

(a) A lawyer should provide competent representation to a client. Competent representation requires the legal knowledge, skill, thoroughness and preparation reasonably necessary for the representation.

(b) A lawyer shall not handle a legal matter that the lawyer knows or should know that the lawyer is not competent to handle, without associating with a lawyer who is competent to handle it.

Attorneys often feel the need to handle everything on their own for a particular client. Nevertheless, you should not close your eyes to the fact that local counsel would most likely be more familiar with local procedures and requirements relating to this potential purchase by your client. With more and more clients involved in matters in other states and even overseas, the decision to engage local counsel under the circumstances you have described is clearly in line with your obligations under Rule 1.1.

Lawyers, like sailors, often find themselves navigating through the shoals of foreign waters. We have learned to heed the wisdom of an old racing adage: "A sailor knows when you enter a race away from home that local knowledge is always critical and can often determine the outcome of the race."

Sincerely,
The Forum by

Vincent J. Syracuse, Esq.
Matthew R. Maron, Esq.
Tannenbaum Helpern Syracuse & Hirschtritt LLP

This article originally appeared in the March/April 2014 *NYSBA Journal*.

Engagement Letters, Don't Let the Client Leave Without One and What Happens When You Do

To the Forum:

Jonathan Entrepreneur ("Jonathan") had been a long time client of my firm. Back in 2011, he decided that he wanted to set up a hedge fund with his friend, Paul Partner ("Paul"). At Jonathan's request, my firm did the work that resulted in the creation of Hedge Fund GP, in which Jonathan and Paul became equal partners. My firm also prepared the papers for Hedge Fund GP to become the general partner of Hedge Fund Partners, an onshore fund my firm organized. Because of my firm's long-standing relationship with Jonathan, we did not issue an engagement letter for this work. In addition, Jonathan asked that our firm also represent Paul in the formation of the fund entities, and we were happy to grant his request.

My firm generated a bill each month for legal services rendered to Hedge Fund GP, to Hedge Fund Partners, to Jonathan, and to Paul and addressed the bills only to Hedge Fund GP.

Hedge Fund GP was always behind on paying its bills. However, earlier this year, Hedge Fund GP ran into trouble and completely stopped paying our firm's bills.

We want to commence an action against Hedge Fund GP, Hedge Fund Partners, Jonathan and Paul to collect the fees that are owed. I have heard different views from several people on whether we were required to issue engagement letters to Hedge Fund GP, Hedge Fund Partners, Jonathan and Paul if they were all to be responsible for our fees, but I have been unable to get a definitive answer. What are the rules on engagement letters and is the absence of an engagement letter fatal to my firm's claim for unpaid legal fees?

Sincerely,
I.N. Confusion

Dear I.N. Confusion:

Attorneys should be familiar with the rules requiring written engagement letters. 22 N.Y.C.R.R. Part 1215 (Part 1215) contains several rules that no lawyer can or should overlook:

§ 1215.1. Requirements

(a) Effective March 4, 2002, an attorney who undertakes to represent a client and enters into an arrangement for, charges or collects any fee from a client shall provide to the client a written letter of engagement before commencing the representation, or within a reasonable time thereafter

(1) if otherwise impracticable or

(2) if the scope of services to be provided cannot be determined at the time of the commencement of representation. For purposes of this rule, where an entity (such as an insurance carrier) engages an attorney to represent a third party, the term *client* shall mean the entity that engages the attorney. Where there is a significant change in the scope of services or the fee to be charged, an updated letter of engagement shall be provided to the client.

(b) The letter of engagement shall address the following matters:

(1) Explanation of the scope of the legal services to be provided;

(2) Explanation of attorney's fees to be charged, expenses and billing practices; and, where applicable, shall provide that the client may have a right to arbitrate fee disputes under Part 137 of the Rules of the Chief Administrator.

(c) Instead of providing the client with a written letter of engagement, an attorney may comply with the provisions of subdivision (a) by entering into a signed written retainer agreement with the client, before or within a reasonable time after commencing the representation, provided that the agreement addresses the matters set forth in subdivision (b).

§ 1215.2. Exceptions

This section shall not apply to:

(a) representation of a client where the fee to be charged is expected to be less than $3,000,

(b) representation where the attorney's services are of the same general kind as previously rendered to and paid for by the client, or

(c) representation in domestic relations matters subject to Part 1400 of the Joint Rules of the Appellate Division (22 N.Y.C.R.R.), or

(d) representation where the attorney is admitted to
practice in another jurisdiction and maintains no office
in the State of New York, or where no material portion of
the services are to be rendered in New York.

As originally enacted, the requirement that attorneys issue written
engagement letters was a court rule and not a matter of professional
responsibility or legal ethics. That changed in April 2009 when New York
adopted the Rules of Professional Conduct (RPC). Rule 1.5(b), which
essentially incorporated Part 1215, makes written engagement letters an
ethical obligation:

A lawyer shall communicate to a client the scope of
the representation and the basis or rate of the fee and
expenses for which the client will be responsible. This
information shall be communicated to the client before
or within a reasonable time after commencement of the
representation and shall be in writing where required by
statute or court rule. This provision shall not apply when
the lawyer will charge a regularly represented client on
the same basis or rate and perform services that are of
the same general kind as previously rendered to and
paid for by the client. Any changes in the scope of the
representation or the basis or rate of the fee or expenses
shall also be communicated to the client.

Prior to 2009, the penalty for not having a written engagement letter
was arguably, at best, the loss of a breach of contract claim in an action to
collect fees. *See Brown Rudnick Berlack Israels LLP v. Zelmanovitch*, 11 Misc.
3d 1090(A), 2006 N.Y. Slip Op. 50800(U) (Sup. Ct., Kings Co. Mar. 14,
2006). Rule 1.5(b) takes the engagement letter rule beyond the realm of
fee collection matters and can potentially expose an attorney to disciplinary action. Although this is uncharted territory, there is a risk that cases
interpreting Part 1215 in the fee collection context (which we discuss
below) will be applied in the disciplinary forum.

Many lawyers believe that there is a safe harbor which makes
engagement letters unnecessary when they get new work from existing
clients. So the question is, what would be considered new work? And,
which existing clients would fall within the scope of the exception? It is
true that Rule 1.5(b) says that engagement letters are not necessary for "a
regularly represented client" where there is no change in the fee arrangement and the engagement is for "services that are of the same general
kind as previously rendered." *Id.* The problem is that there is no definition of "regularly represented client," and there may be a difference in
the two rules because Part 1215 does not use the words "regularly represented client" or even the words "existing client." Comment [2] to Rule
1.5 reminds all of us that it is best to always issue an engagement letter
and avoid the risks associated with not having one.

When the lawyer has regularly represented a client,
they ordinarily will have evolved an understanding
concerning the basis or rate of the fee and the expenses
for which the client will be responsible. In a new client-
lawyer relationship, however, an understanding as to
fees and expenses must be promptly established. Court
rules regarding engagement letters require that such an
understanding be memorialized in writing in certain cases. *See* 22 N.Y.C.R.R. Part 1215. Even where not required,
it is desirable to furnish the client with at least a simple
memorandum or copy of the lawyer's customary fee
arrangements that states the general nature of the legal
services to be provided, the basis, rate or total amount
of the fee, and whether and to what extent the client will
be responsible for any costs, expenses or disbursements
in the course of the representation. A written statement
concerning the terms of the engagement reduces the possibility of misunderstanding.

Another issue that is worth avoiding is whether a new engagement
involves "services that are of the same general kind" as the services that
the firm has been providing. In the words of one commentator, "if it's a
close call as to whether the new services are the 'same general kind' as
prior matters, it will take less time to send a written engagement letter
than to analyze Rule 1.5(b)." *See* Simon's New York Rules of Professional
Conduct Annotated at 171 (2014 ed.).

You don't have an engagement letter and want to recover your fees,
so what can you do about your non-paying client? Since the enactment
of Part 1215, although the absence of a written engagement letter may be
fatal to a breach of contract claim, several courts have ruled that a law
firm's failure to comply with the written engagement letter rule "does
not preclude it from suing to recover legal fees for the services it provided." *See Miller v. Nadler*, 60 A.D.3d 499, 500 (1st Dep't 2009) (citing *Seth
Rubenstein, P.C. v. Ganea*, 41 A.D.3d 54, 63–64 (2d Dep't 2007)). One court
has also held that

the caselaw does not distinguish between the recovery
of fees under a theory of *quantum meruit* or an account
stated. Instead, this Court has held that [22 N.Y.C.R.R.
§ 1215.1] contains no provision stating that failure to
comply with its requirements *bars a fee collection action.*
Indeed, the regulation is silent as to what penalty, if any,
should be assessed against an attorney who fails to abide
by the rule.

Constantine Cannon LLP v. Parnes, 2010 N.Y. Slip Op. 31956(U), 15 (Sup.
Ct., N.Y. Co. July 22, 2010) (emphasis in original) (internal citations omitted.)

The fact that you did not issue an engagement letter to Jonathan and thereafter sent invoices exclusively to Hedge Fund GP does not in our view prevent you from pursuing a legal fee claim against either Jonathan or Paul, or their related entities. But, as suggested in one case, this may not be an easy road and you may face certain obstacles in your attempt to collect fees. *See Davidoff Malito & Hutcher, LLP v. Scheiner*, 38 Misc. 3d 1201(A), 966 N.Y.S.2d 345 (Sup. Ct., Queens Co. Dec. 11, 2012) (law firm's motion for summary judgment on its *quantum meruit* and account stated claims denied where issues of fact existed arising from the law firm's failure to enter into a written fee agreement with its client).

The better practice would have been to issue an engagement letter to all individuals and entities involved in connection with the formation of Hedge Fund GP and Hedge Fund Partners. Furthermore, because your firm appeared to represent both Jonathan and Paul in connection with this matter, one way your firm could have drafted the engagement letter was to set forth clear language about the potential for conflicts of interest. Sample language could state:

> While we do not currently see a conflict between your interests, whenever a firm represents multiple parties in a single matter, there is always the possibility that a conflict may develop. In the event such a conflict arises, we may be required to cease representing one of you in connection with this matter. We will make the decision with respect to our representation if and when such circumstances arise. Lastly, you understand that if we continue to represent one or more of you, we will be able to use any information we obtained during the joint representation in the continuing representation.

A word to the wise is that strict compliance with Part 1215 is a critical part of professional responsibility. The importance of this was underscored by the court in *Seth Rubenstein, P.C.*, 41 A.D.3d 54:

> Attorneys who fail to heed rule 1215.1 place themselves at a marked disadvantage, as the recovery of fees becomes dependent upon factors that attorneys do not necessarily control, such as meeting the burden of proving the terms of the retainer and establishing that the terms were fair, understood, and agreed upon. There is never any guarantee that an arbitrator or court will find this burden met or that the fact-finder will determine the reasonable value of services under quantum meruit to be equal to the compensation that would have been earned under a clearly written retainer agreement or letter of engagement.

Id. at 64.

We hope that this gives you an understanding of the rules, their potential impact on fee collection cases, and the possible issues that may arise when law firms fail to issue engagement letters. It should come as no surprise that we believe that lawyers should err on the side of caution when it comes to engagement letters. Borrowing from Professor Simon, if you need to spend time thinking about whether an engagement letter is required, it's probably a good idea to simply send one.

Sincerely,
The Forum by

Vincent J. Syracuse, Esq.
Matthew R. Maron, Esq.,
Tannenbaum Helpern Syracuse & Hirschtritt LLP

This article originally appeared in the February 2014 *NYSBA Journal*.

How to Lose a Client in 10 Steps
By Richard B. Friedman and Carla M. Miller

Many litigators in law firms devote a great deal of time and energy to developing new relationships and winning new corporate clients. Once the client has signed on and a case is under way, however, too often outside counsel concentrates so much upon the matter at hand that they neglect the client relationship. While outside counsel may be unaware of this inadvertent lack of attention, the client will certainly notice. This failure to communicate properly can easily turn a promising long-term relationship into a one-off representation, no matter how favorable the outcome of the matter. Maintaining a good working relationship with in-house counsel is the key to keeping that client.

In our careers as outside counsel with extensive experience in litigation and arbitration matters and as in-house litigation counsel for several major corporations, we have seen how a lack of communication, as well as failing to meet in-house counsel's expectations and ignoring the client's corporate dynamics, can quickly ruin the relationship between outside and in-house counsel. Whether through oversight, overwork or lack of attention, these 10 common missteps will help to make sure that the client does not come back.

1. Don't Learn About the Client's Industry, Business Lines and Internal Dynamics

While the facts of any given case may be plain enough for outside counsel within the framework of the law, the context of the matter is often more important for the corporate client. The only way to assess the relative importance of a given matter for a corporation is to understand how it fits in with the client's industry, business lines and internal dynamics. For instance, while the matter may involve a relatively small revenue stream, the business unit at issue could be a rapidly growing, high-profit line that senior company personnel view as crucial to a strategic shift from older, low-margin lines. By neglecting to develop an understanding of the client, outside counsel cannot properly prioritize and will be unable to provide the value-added advice and counsel that keeps a client coming back.

2. Don't Discuss Projected Fees

Outside counsel will, of course, want to achieve the best possible result for the client on any given matter. While focusing on winning a case, however, counsel may lose sight of the overall context of the matter for the client. Corporate executives assess most corporate-related projects in terms of revenues, costs, margins and income. Litigation is an added, if unavoidable, cost that corporate clients want to keep as low as possible. They may seek a fee cap; they may want to be notified when fees for a given matter hit a certain level; or they may want to take advantage of, or initiate, early settlement possibilities. Outside counsel may be confident that they are performing excellent work for the client, but the price of such services may simply be too high. Surprising the client with a higher-than-expected bill is a surefire way to strain, if not end, what might seem to be a thriving business relationship.

3. Ignore the Client's Billing Guidelines

Use of outside legal services, such as in a takeover contest, almost always represents a cost center for corporations that reduces the money available for more profitable endeavors (the most notable exceptions being when a corporation sues to gain advantage in a business dispute or to recover a substantial amount of damages). While litigation is not a cost that can be unilaterally reduced, an overwhelming number of large corporations still seek to manage litigation costs to the extent possible through the implementation of billing guidelines. Outside counsel have the duty to adhere to those guidelines. If a case demands an exemption from certain guidelines, counsel should seek client approval for such exemption for a matter in its entirety or for a particular period of time; they also should be able to provide a compelling argument as to why those guidelines would be counterproductive in the pending matter. Clients hate surprises, particularly costly ones. Failing to pay attention to billing guidelines will present clients with the kind of surprise they will not wish to repeat.

4. Ignore the Client's Staffing Preferences for Outside Counsel

Like any other corporate department, the legal department has to live within its budget, or the head of the department must be able to explain why it could not. To make it easier to estimate legal costs and to keep fees manageable, many companies have gone to a great deal of trouble to develop staffing guidelines for outside counsel. For instance, the guidelines may specify that no more than two attorneys can attend a deposition or conference absent explicit client approval. If outside counsel believe that the staffing guidelines are unreasonable in a given case, they need to seek permission from the client before departing from those guidelines so that in-house counsel can make the case to their own management. Budgeting for litigation is difficult enough for in-house counsel. Making that job even harder is one way to quickly alienate a corporate client.

5. Change Key Personnel Without Telling the Client

The relationship between in-house and outside counsel is built upon the interaction between people. The better the communication between the client and outside counsel, the stronger the relationship will be. A key part of that communication involves staffing. If outside counsel is contemplating staffing changes, counsel should communicate them to in-house counsel. The client may have strong preferences as to which attorneys are involved in certain aspects of a given matter. In addition, the client may work very well with particular support staff and an unexplained personnel change may cause a serious disruption to the relationship. Clients often like the certainty gained by dealing with people they know. Changing personnel with little or no notice adds unnecessary uncertainty for the client and potential strain to the relationship with outside counsel.

6. Don't Answer Client Queries Promptly

One of the most important practices within the legal profession is being responsive to clients. It is, after all, their money, their time and perhaps their business that is at stake in the matter. While it is not always possible to respond to a client query right away due to various circumstances, outside counsel should make it their practice to respond in as timely a manner as possible. When the lead partner in the matter is unavailable, another lawyer should be able to answer the client query or find someone who can do so. If the client does not hear back in a timely manner, he or she may assume that outside counsel is not actively working on the matter, even if that is decidedly untrue. A failure to communicate is one of the fastest ways to jeopardize a client relationship.

7. Don't Explore Settlement Possibilities

Everyone likes to win, but for corporations the definition of winning generally comes down to the bottom line. Viewed through that lens, an expensive win may be far less desirable for a corporation than a less expensive loss or settlement. Accordingly, outside counsel should not only be focused on winning the case. When the final costs are tallied, that success may be too expensive in the corporate context. Besides the cost in money, corporations also must account for the cost in time and disruption to day-to-day business. Reaching an early settlement on the most favorable terms may not be as gratifying to outside counsel as winning a difficult case in court, but winning at all costs is not a winning strategy for keeping corporate clients.

8. Engage in Unduly Aggressive Tactics

No one wants a lawyer who is not going to aggressively represent his or her interests. As U.S. Supreme Court Justice Antonin Scalia said in a case involving the right to choose defense counsel, "I don't want a 'competent' lawyer....I want to win."[1] No court, however, wants to have to deal with overly aggressive counsel or to wade through pages of gratuitously nasty correspondence. While it may seem like an easy way to demonstrate a winning attitude for clients, unduly aggressive tactics and offensive communications rarely, if ever, serve a client's best interests in any particular matter. Such behavior by outside counsel only alienates judges and results in unnecessary costs, which will eventually alienate the client.

9. Don't Communicate Key Dates

In-house counsel need to be able to properly oversee litigation. To do that they may want to attend certain depositions and/or hearings to observe the interaction between outside counsel, on the one hand, and adverse counsel and the judge, on the other hand. Outside counsel should make it a practice to always alert in-house counsel to key events ahead of time so that the client can choose whether to attend. Indeed, in-house counsel should be considered not only as clients but as partners in the litigation and should be kept abreast of all upcoming key dates. It is demeaning to the client if in-house counsel are not given the opportunity to participate meaningfully in the client's own case.

10. Send Working Drafts and Submit Briefs for Review at the Last Minute

Unless they have specifically said otherwise, clients do not want to see working drafts that are not ready to be filed. In addition, in-house counsel have a host of non-litigation responsibilities which may make it impossible to review briefs on very short notice. While briefs must sometimes be turned around very quickly, outside counsel should strive to give the client sufficient time to review all draft papers. Outside counsel should also devote the same care to invoices, which may be the only work product the client sees for weeks. Failing to ensure that work product is of the highest quality will not engender respect or consideration for future matters.

Conclusion

While it is easy enough to lose a client through these 10 steps, the key to keeping the client happy is, simply, communication. Communication is the key to any good relationship. Where potential issues arise, communication enables both parties to address these issues and resolve them in a timely fashion. By making sure to develop and maintain open lines of communication with in-house counsel, outside counsel improve their chances of achieving the best possible result for the client in the matter at hand and heighten their prospects for future business.

---

1.   Linda Greenhouse, *Justices Hear Case on Right to Choose Defense Counsel*, N.Y. Times, Apr. 19, 2006.

RICHARD B. FRIEDMAN (rfriedman@dreierllp.com) and **CARLA M. MILLER** (carla.miller@umusic.com) are co-chairs of the NYSBA's Corporate Litigation Counsel Committee of the Commercial & Federal Litigation Section. Mr. Friedman is a partner in the Litigation Department at Dreier LLP. Ms. Miller is the Senior Director-Litigation Counsel, Business & Legal Affairs, Universal Music Group.

This article originally appeared in the July/August 2008 *NYSBA Journal*.

When Declining a Case, What Obligations Do Attorneys Owe to the Prospective Clients and How to Address Confidential Information Acquired During the Initial Meeting?

To the Forum:

I am a partner in a 10-person law firm and I regularly see prospective clients for initial consultations, which I provide at no charge. We do not take every case presented to us. When we decline a representation, do we have a duty to provide a non-engagement letter or to warn the person about statutes of limitations that may apply to his or her case? What is our risk of malpractice exposure, if we decline a representation although the person did have a viable claim and, if the person later pursues it on his/her own, finds that the claim is time-barred? Finally, if a prospective client provides me or one of my partners with confidential information during that initial consultation and I do not take the case, am I obligated to keep the person's confidential information confidential, and can information acquired that way create a conflict that would prohibit me from taking some future litigation? Recently, we had a situation where one of my partners met someone at a Friday evening cocktail party who talked with her about a potential litigation. By coincidence, I had met the opposing party and had set up a meeting in our office to take the case. We ended up deciding not to take on the matter which we thought was the only possible decision that we could make. Were we correct?

Sincerely,
W.E. Declined

Dear W.E. Declined:

Every attorney faces, at one time or another, the situation you describe. It is important to know that attorneys owe certain duties to prospective clients under the Rules of Professional Conduct and they should also be aware of any issues which may arise concerning the receipt of confidential information from a prospective client as well as the potential for imputation of conflicts of interests that almost certainly will come up in connection with such a representation.

Rules 1.18(a) defines a prospective client as "[a] person who discusses with a lawyer the possibility of forming a client lawyer relationship with respect to a matter…." Under the Rules, there is no specific duty to provide a non-engagement letter to a prospective client that does not retain an attorney, however, best practice suggests that the issuance of a non-engagement letter to the prospective client which you describe (who we'll refer to as "AA") is an appropriate way of confirming that an attorney-client relationship has not been created. In addition, the non-engagement letter should spell out any potential statute of limitations issues arising from AA's potential claim.

With regard to confidential information that the prospective client has communicated to the attorney, Rule 1.18(b) states: "Even when no client-lawyer relationship ensues, a lawyer who has had discussions with a prospective client shall not use or reveal information learned in the consultation, except as Rule 1.9 would permit with respect to information of a former client." Although Rule 1.9 does not expressly set forth duties owed to prospective clients, pursuant to Rule 1.9(a), "[a] lawyer who has formerly represented a client in a matter shall not thereafter represent another person in the same or a substantially related matter in which that person's interests are materially adverse to the interests of the former client unless the former client gives informed consent, confirmed in writing." In essence, the duties owed to a prospective client under the Rules concerning information learned from the prospective client are treated similarly as those duties that would be owed by attorneys who receive information from a former client.

Furthermore, Rule 1.6(a) requires that "[a] lawyer shall not knowingly reveal confidential information, as defined in this Rule, or use such information to the disadvantage of a client or for the advantage of the lawyer or a third person" except under certain specific circumstances as defined in Rule 1.6. Moreover, Rule 1.6(a) defines confidential information as "information gained during or relating to the representation of a client, whatever its source, that is (a) protected by the attorney-client privilege, (b) likely to be embarrassing or detrimental to the client if disclosed, or (c) information that the client has requested be kept confidential." Whether or not an individual or entity retains an attorney, the duties owed by an attorney to preserve confidential information are of tremendous importance.

It is also stated in Rule 1.18(c) that

> [a] lawyer subject to paragraph (b) [of Rule 1.18] shall not represent a client with interests materially adverse to those of a prospective client in the same or a substantially related matter if the lawyer received information from the prospective client that could be significantly harmful to that person in the matter, except as provided in paragraph (d) [of Rule 1.18]. If a lawyer is disqualified from representation under this paragraph, no lawyer in a firm with which that lawyer is associated may knowingly

undertake or continue representation in such a matter, except as provided in paragraph (d) [of Rule 1.18].

Moreover, Rule 1.18(d) provides that

[w]hen the lawyer has received disqualifying information as defined in paragraph (c) [of Rule 1.18], representation is permissible if: (1) both the affected client and the prospective client have given informed consent, confirmed in writing; or (2) the lawyer who received the information took reasonable measures to avoid exposure to more disqualifying information than was reasonably necessary to determine whether to represent the prospective client; and (i) the firm acts promptly and reasonably to notify, as appropriate, lawyers and non-lawyer personnel within the firm that the personally disqualified lawyer is prohibited from participating in the representation of the current client; (ii) the firm implements effective screening procedures to prevent the flow of information about the matter between the disqualified lawyer and the others in the firm; (iii) the disqualified lawyer is apportioned no part of the fee therefrom; and (iv) written notice is promptly given to the prospective client; and (3) a reasonable lawyer would conclude that the law firm will be able to provide competent and diligent representation in the matter.

It was entirely proper for your firm to pass on representing the opposing party that your partner had met at the cocktail party (we'll refer to the opposing party as "BB"). Rule 1.10(e) requires all lawyers to maintain "a written record of its engagements." With respect to prospective clients, the Rule states that "lawyers shall implement and maintain a system by which proposed engagements are checked against current and previous engagements when: (1) the firm agrees to represent a new client; (2) the firm agrees to represent an existing client in a new matter; (3) the firm hires or associates with another lawyer; or (4) an additional party is named or appears in a pending matter." Although Rule 1.10(e) uses the words "proposed engagements" in contrast to Rule 1.18's use of the words "prospective client," it would seem that the best practice in the situation you describe would be to implement a system at your firm which records all such contacts in your firm's records to deal with a conflict as soon as possible and allow for screening.

Since you are part of a relatively smaller firm, setting up screening mechanisms to deal with potential conflicts of interest requires greater vigilance since information within a smaller firm environment could easily be communicated to all attorneys and staff of the firm. Comments [7B] and [7C] to Rule 1.18 contain an extensive discussion on the establishment of appropriate screening mechanisms, with a particular emphasis on establishing screening mechanisms in a small firm environment. One of the factors in determining if disqualification would be appropriate under Rule 1.18(c) is if the information learned from the prospective client would be "significantly harmful" to that prospective client. Although Rule 1.18(d) could potentially allow a firm to represent BB even if the information previously received from AA was significantly harmful to AA's interest, the fact that you are at a smaller firm would suggest that unless you established very clear and detailed screening mechanisms, it would be significantly more difficult to screen out any attorney who receives information from someone in AA's position who does not retain your firm.

Sincerely,
The Forum by

Vincent J. Syracuse, Esq., and
Mathew R. Maron, Esq.,
Tannenbaum Helpern Syracuse & Hirschtritt LLP

This article originally appeared in the October 2014 *NYSBA Journal*.

File Retention Update: How Long Should I Keep Closed Files?

By Katherine Suchocki

Law practice management resources are available to all members. Our department educates lawyers about practice management, marketing and client development, legal technology and finance. In addition to providing CLE programs on practice management topics, the department serves as a resource center and fields calls daily from members.

One of the most frequent inquiries we receive is about file retention and closed files.

There are tens of thousands of boxes of closed client files sitting around in warehouses, storage buildings, spare offices and, believe it or not, probably garages. Some firms spend thousands of dollars on closed file storage.

While many firms are moving toward paperless office environments, many attorneys are asking about what to do with their banker boxes full of closed files. "How long do I have to keep my closed files?" is one of the most frequent questions sent to the "Ask LPM" email box.

Stating the "Rules"

The New York Rules of Professional Conduct specify kinds of records that must be maintained and uses a seven-year retention period. Rule 1.15(d) states:

(d) Required Bookkeeping Records.

(1) A lawyer shall maintain for seven years after the events that they record:

(i) the records of all deposits in and withdrawals from the accounts specified in Rule 1.15(b) and of any other bank account that concerns or affects the lawyer's practice of law; these records shall specifically identify the date, source and description of each item deposited, as well as the date, payee and purpose of each withdrawal or disbursement;

(ii) a record for special accounts, showing the source of all funds deposited in such accounts, the names of all persons for whom the funds are or were held, the amount of such funds, the description and amounts, and the names of all persons to whom such funds were disbursed;

(iii) copies of all retainer and compensation agreements with clients;

(iv) copies of all statements to clients or other persons showing the disbursement of funds to them or on their behalf;

(v) copies of all bills rendered to clients;

(vi) copies of all records showing payments to lawyers, investigators or other persons, not in the lawyer's regular employ, for services rendered or performed;

(vii) copies of all retainer and closing statements filed with the Office of Court Administration; and

(viii) all checkbooks and check stubs, bank statements, prenumbered canceled checks and duplicate deposit slips.

We refer attorneys to Ethics Opinion 460—Preservation of Closed Files, which describes the circumstances under which lawyers may dispose of closed files.

To quote from the opinion: "What is required of lawyers must for the most part be determined in the light of common sense and certain general principles of considerably broader application."

The final paragraph of the opinion states, "Whenever possible, the client should be consulted concerning the disposition of his files and encouraged to preserve them on his own. Lawyers are advocates and advisors. They are not warehousemen or perpetual repositories for the files of their clients. A good lawyer need not retain his clients by holding on to their files and a poor one will soon learn that such tactics avail him nothing but additional expense."

Ethics Opinion 623 should be reviewed when dissolving a law firm and procedures for disposing of closed files.

Ethics Opinion 641 discusses disposition procedures and compliance with recycling regulations. In many communities, there are recycling regulations. "A lawyer who is subject to a recycling law must ensure that compliance with that law does not entail violation of the lawyer's obligation to maintain the confidentiality of client information."

In disposing of client files, it is important to remember the need to preserve client confidences and secrets. If you use a recycling or shredding company to dispose of paper, take extra care to ensure that disposed documents are not reviewed by third parties.

Similar steps also should be taken when donating, recycling, or disposing of firm computers. Deleting an electronic file from a hard drive does not mean that a record is destroyed in the same way that paper can be destroyed. "Scrubbing" software should be used.

File Retention Policies

Your firm should have a file retention policy in place. A file retention policy provides a step-by-step outline of the processes and procedures on how firm files should be closed, retained and destroyed. Links to sample file retention policies and resources on document management are available at www.nysba.org/LPM under the Document Management Tab.

Tell Your Clients

Tell your clients about your file retention and destruction policy when you are retained. Include your policy in your retainer agreement or engagement letter to set expectations at the outset and clearly indicate that file destruction is anticipated a certain number of years after the representation.

This keeps everyone on the same page as to what happens with the contents of the file while the matter is pending and after the file is closed. For example, your retainer can include the following language: "The firm retains closed files for at least seven years after they are closed."

You also should include a reminder that copies of all pleadings, correspondence and other documents will be provided to the client during representation. The client is free to maintain a copy of the file and keep it forever.

For those firms striving to go paperless, retainers sometimes note that most original documents will be scanned and forwarded to clients as they arrive at the office, and that the firm will keep only an electronic record of that document.

After Seven Years

Always evaluate the statutes of limitation for legal malpractice cases. Retain these files for at least as long as anyone could conceivably make a claim in connection with your work.

Original wills, client files involving minors or those under a disability, select real estate files, family law matters—for instance those involving matters relating to future college or school tuition and expenses—should be kept for more than seven years.

Disposing of closed client files requires good judgment and common sense.

For more information, visit the Document Management section of the Law Practice Management website at www.nysba.org/LPM. Review the New York Rules of Professional Conduct and Ethics Opinions 460, 623 and 641.

Connect with LPM

I encourage you to connect with LPM. If you have questions, visit our website, call me at 518-487-5590 or use the email link on the LPM website.

KATHERINE SUCHOCKI is the NYSBA Director of Law Practice Management.

This article originally appeared in the July/August 2014 NYSBA *State Bar News.*

Tips on Being a Better Manager
By Katherine Suchocki

A great boss can inspire and motivate you. A great boss can shape your career and the type of manager you become. A positive relationship with a manager or boss directly influences an employee's job satisfaction.

Whether you manage one person or a staff of 500, mastering management skills is crucial to your firm or business. Many people become managers without getting proper training to manage. The Law Practice Management Committee will host several programs on management this fall.

I asked colleagues to share tips about the best bosses they've ever had, what they learned from leaders and advice on various management styles. Following is a summary of responses.

Hire the Right People; Value Your Employees

Everything starts with hiring the right employees and staff, and fostering their growth. A firm is only as good as the people who work there.

You have to build from the ground up. Be sure your employees know their purpose. If you know what your employees do and how they do it, you are better able to identify obstacles when they arise.

It is your job as a manager to remove those obstacles. You have to value your employees. If there are issues with firm management and high employee turnover, you have to work on those issues first.

Be a Leader, Manager and Motivator

Leaders and managers are not one and the same. Leaders are not working alone; they are working with others and help to instill a vision.

As a leader you have to value those working for you. If you don't, it shows. The key is to keep lines of communication open, set expectations and have the flexibility to know when you should go in another direction.

Communicate Clear Expectations

Provide direction. Say what you mean and mean what you say. Your employees should know what your expectations are so they can meet or exceed them.

Be specific; don't leave details up to their imaginations. Being vague just increases the chances for misunderstandings and mistakes.

Empowerment and Engagement Leads to Success

People support a world they help create. Employee engagement is key to retention and productivity. To get buy-in from others, you need to make staff feel empowered in the process, so they feel personally vested in the project or initiative.

When someone feels that he or she is personally having an impact on something, they will work to see it through.

Trust Your Employees to Do Their Work

You set up your staff; trust they can do the work. Let them take vacation time and allow flexible work environments. Trust them to manage their time effectively and efficiently.

Nothing else matters if the work is getting done and getting done well. Employees in trust environments perform better and innovate more. Hold employees accountable for results.

Invite Others to Solve Problems

Feedback is the answer to most management challenges. The higher you are in management, the less likely that you will be in touch with reality.

People tend to tell managers what they want to hear. Branch out for information and ask for input. As a manager you are leading and steering, but your employees who do the work have control over the process.

Many of the best improvement ideas routinely come from employees in the trenches, as they are the ones closest to the actual work. When you implement their ideas, they are committed to success because of their personal involvement.

The Power of a Thank You

Praise the hard work of your staff. Acknowledge good performance and your appreciation. Genuine and meaningful praise goes a long way. You would be amazed at how people go out of their way for you because they know you appreciate them and value their work.

Be An Agent for Change

Think about the big picture; be flexible and adaptable. Recognize the effect your actions have on current and future efforts. Understand where you want to go and how you will get there.

William Pollard once warned, "The arrogance of success is to think that what you did yesterday will be sufficient for tomorrow."

Advances in technology have significantly changed the practice of law and workflow, not only for law firms, but for businesses in general. One of the mistakes managers tend to make is failing to embrace new developments. The other is relying too much on technology to solve all problems.

Be a "Can-Do" Person

View problems as challenges and do everything you can to find ways to overcome them. Taking issues head on and resolving them immediately can prevent an issue from getting worse.

Open lines of communication, employee appreciation and long-range planning are key to firm culture. Well-chosen words can inspire staff. Your firm culture is only as strong as you make it.

We want to help you be a better law firm manager. This fall, the Law Practice Management Committee will sponsor a mini-MBA series of programs covering topics including finance, human resources, marketing and technology. Learn more at www.nysba.org/LPM.

Law Practice Management resources provide lawyers, law firm managers and legal professionals with information on practice management trends, marketing, client development, legal technology and finance. Whether you are a solo practitioner or a managing partner at a national law firm, you will find law practice management resources to meet your day-to-day practice needs. Checklists, best practices, publications and continuing legal education programs provide up-to-date information and practical tips to help you better manage your law practice.

KATHERINE SUCHOCKI is the NYSBA Director of Law Practice Management.

This article originally appeared in the July/August 2014 NYSBA *State Bar News.*

PATHWAY TO THE PROFESSION: FROM LAW SCHOOL TO LAWYER

LEGAL WRITING

Appellate Brief Writing: What Not to Do

By Tamala Boyd

The author Isabel Allende said, "Write what should not be forgotten." Of course, she was speaking about writing fiction, but the quote also fits perfectly within the realm of legal writing—especially when you are writing for a court like New York's Appellate Division, First Department, quite easily one of the busiest courts in the country. The First Department handles approximately 3,000 appeals, 6,000 motions and 1,000 interim applications each year. Unlike many other intermediate appellate courts, the First Department has broad powers to review questions of both law and fact, and to make new findings of fact. With few exceptions, appeals to the Court of Appeals are by permission only; the First Department, along with the other three Appellate Departments, is the court of last resort in the majority of its cases.

Until recently, I was a principal appellate court attorney in the First Department's Law Department. The Law Department includes the chief and deputy court attorneys, a group of supervisors, attorneys who primarily do motions and applications, and a team of court attorneys with varying degrees of experience and expertise. Court attorney titles range from "appellate" at the junior level to "principal," the most senior. While, generally speaking, all court attorneys research and analyze legal issues and questions for the court, and perform other related duties as assigned, such as motions and applications, more senior court attorneys tend to work on more complex legal issues with little to no direct supervision.

In my time as a principal appellate court attorney, I worked on hundreds of appeals, read close to a thousand briefs, and pored over a mind-boggling number of records. Significantly, while court attorneys are not the first people to look at your briefs (that would be the wonderful people in the clerk's office), they are the first to truly scrutinize your submissions, parse the various sections, and evaluate your arguments. Moreover, as one of the people charged with producing detailed, often lengthy, reports based upon a review of your materials and the court attorney's own independent legal research, I feel confident in saying that court attorneys probably care the most about the quality of your work product.

With that background, you understand that when I borrow from Ms. Allende and say to you, "Write only what you want us to remember," I know from whence I speak. And while I do not presume to speak for every court attorney working in the First Department, much of the advice given below finds support among those with whom I have spoken.[1]

Because there is a rich variety of offerings available covering what you should do when drafting an appellate brief, I thought it might be most useful to tell you, from a court attorney's perspective, what not to do. What are the things that made my heart skip a beat with despair; lay my head down on my desk and cry; scroll back to the cover page to see who submitted the brief; run for the nearest window, shredder or fire pit and—well, you get the point. So, appellate brief, section by section, here is my list of what not to do.

Preliminary Statement

A preliminary statement should, ideally, not

1. take up any significant portion of your page count;

2. contain any facts or argument.

The purpose of a preliminary statement is to give the reader a concise rendering of the case. It should identify the party, the order being appealed from, why the appeal was taken and the result sought. It is helpful to include the order entry date and the judge who rendered the decision. While it is perfectly fine to include a short preview of your case (think of a 30-second advertisement), it is not okay for this to be part and parcel of your factual recitation or argument.

Now, you are perfectly welcome to submit a preliminary statement that goes on for five or more pages. Just do so with the knowledge that you may have set the tone for the reception of the remainder of your brief.

Question Presented

For reasons I fail to understand, some parties seem to believe that the more questions they can present, the better their chances on appeal. Allow me to disabuse you of that notion. Try the following exercise. Close your eyes and imagine the following scenario: I have just put the finishing touches on a 50-page report. Your appeal is the second of the week, and there is a third waiting. I open your brief, flip to the questions presented, and find 12 of them. What do you suppose I am feeling? If your answer is "impressed by my ingenuity," you're wrong.

Questions presented should not

1. contain numerous subparts;

2. contain argument;

3. disparage the lower court; or

4. be contrived, or otherwise lacking in any bases in the law.

While there is no magic number for how many questions presented are appropriate, rarely did I encounter a situation where more than five or six questions, stated in one or two pages, proved insufficient. If you find your questions presented section running longer than that, consider examining whether you have sufficiently parsed your case and understood your viable legal issues. Go over your questions presented to be certain that you are not using them as an opportunity to make factual arguments or answer legal questions. Bottom line: resist the urge to overstate the complexity of your case, because doing so adds nothing.

Statement of Facts

The statement of facts should be just that—a statement of facts—not an attorney's characterization of those facts. Moreover, a statement of facts should not:

1. Be in a personal relationship with adjectives, italics, underlining or exclamation points.

2. Obscure facts, especially in criminal cases. If I sensed that counsel was obscuring facts, that person's arguments would begin to lose credibility.

3. Underutilize correct citations to the record. Nothing would send me to your adversary's brief faster than a statement of facts with no citations to the record or with citations that were mostly incorrect. I once received an opening brief where every citation in the first 13 pages was wrong. And not just a little off, but completely wrong. Although I muddled through, I also counted the errors and dropped a footnote to the judges about the unreliability of that party's papers. Suffice it to say, my initial understanding of the case came not from the brief of the party who had instituted the appeal but from the better-drafted and error-free respondent's brief.

4. Cite to portions of the record that do not actually support the statement for which it was cited. Or, worse still, cite to portions of the record that contradict the statement. Do that and not only do you lose credibility, but if you win, you do so only in spite of yourself.

5. Characterize the facts. Example of a factual statement: "Witnesses at the scene identified the car as a green Mercedes Benz." Example of a characterization: "The speeding car that plastered plaintiff all over the sidewalk was a flashy green luxury vehicle." You get the point.

6. Pull "facts" exclusively from an attorney's affirmation. More specifically, on a motion to dismiss, facts should come almost exclusively from the complaint. On a motion to dismiss on the documents, facts should come from those documents. On summary judgment, facts can come from the record generally, but

you should take care that your facts are not contradicted by other record evidence because, I assure you, most court attorneys check. And, dare I say it again? When the record contradicts your characterizations, you lose credibility.

7. List every single fact there is to know about every single aspect of your case. Although it is called a "statement of facts," you should think of it more as a "statement of relevant facts." This is not an invitation to obscure those facts that go against you. This is merely to say that if you are appealing only certain aspects of an order, you need include only those facts that are relevant to what is being appealed. Example: forcing me to read a long recitation of your client's injuries when the threshold issue was one of liability did not make me feel sorry for your client. It just made me tired.

In short, "show, don't tell." Show the reader where in the record your facts originated and where they are supported. Be brutal in both your brevity and clarity. But don't fret. Remember, you have an entire section in which to let the reader know exactly what you think of those facts. Which brings me to…

Argument

I have always considered the argument section to be the meat and potatoes of the entire appeal. This is where you get to be the super lawyer. This is where your case comes to thrive or to die a slow, painful death. Here are some of the things that can help it along its path to the grave:

1. *Not knowing, or simply not considering, the procedural posture of your case.* It matters whether an appeal is taken from a motion to dismiss, summary judgment or a trial on the merits. And nothing made me want to bang my head against the wall more than an attorney who wanted to wax nostalgic about failures of proof and material issues of fact when the appeal was taken from the denial of a motion to dismiss.

2. *Not knowing the standard of review for the issues on appeal.* This is especially true where an appeal is taken from an arbitration award, or from an Article 78 proceeding.

3. *Refusing to acknowledge that "motion to dismiss" is not the equivalent of "free-for-all."* Yes, you get the benefit of the doubt, but no, the reader is not obliged to abandon his or her common sense. To wit, the sky does not become green because it says so in the complaint, and if you try to tell the court that it does, you begin to lose credibility.

4. *Failing to cite authority from the Appellate Department presiding over your matter.* The First Department is not bound by the decisions of her sister Departments, and it is not uncommon to find wildly divergent views. It made my job more difficult if a brief had citations only to, or primarily to, cases from other Appellate Departments, especially if I knew from previous experience, or discovered from my own independent research, that there was ample First Department authority on the issue. Citations to cases from other Appellate Departments is even more off-putting when the First Department authority an attorney fails to cite contradicts the authority cited.

   Note also that the Appellate Departments are not bound by federal court decisions or by federal law, even if the federal court at issue sits in New York State. Be especially careful that the federal cases you cite are actually interpreting New York state law (keeping in mind that the Second Circuit covers more than just New York). And, if the only case you can find to support your argument is from the middle district of east-west Arkansas, perhaps you should rethink your argument.

   This is not to say you should never cite cases from the other Departments or jurisdictions. For example, if there is no precedent in the First Department, or you would like to argue that another court's resolution of an issue is more persuasive, by all means do so. But in so doing, do not ignore the First Department (or other appropriate Appellate Department) cases that do exist.

5. *Forcing the reader to guess your argument or the legal basis of your claim.* While stating an argument seems so basic, it is astounding how many briefs fail to do so—probably because the attorney has lived with the issues for so long, they just seem obvious. Although most court attorneys will eventually figure it out, it will help if your argument is stated clearly and succinctly at the beginning of the appropriate section, along with the point of law upon which the argument is premised.

6. *Ignoring contrary authority.* Do not ignore it; distinguish it. If you cannot distinguish it, rethink your argument. In all cases, however, you should at least acknowledge it.

7. *Ignoring your adversary's arguments and counterarguments.* The respondent should address each of the appellant's arguments, no matter how unworthy those arguments might seem. Think of it this way: appellant's arguments are what brought you to the court, and it is a colossal waste of everyone's time for those arguments to be ignored, especially since the court attorney must address them, whether or not you do. You don't want that. Con-

versely, the appellant should address each of the respondent's counterarguments because, again, the court attorney will.

8. *Using exaggeration and extreme hyperbole.* Keep underlining, exclamation points, bold and italics to a bare minimum.[2] If you need those things to make your point, you probably haven't got much of one.

9. *Insulting the lower court.* I will not soon forget reading in a brief that a lower court decision "lacked intellectual rigor." Hmmm. What was that party saying about the First Department panel considering the case, should it agree with the decision being appealed? And yes, the panel did agree. You should probably resist the urge to insult the lower court and, thereby, risk insulting the panel deciding your appeal.

10. *Engaging in ad hominem attacks on opposing counsel or the opposing party.* I did not care how much you disliked your adversary; I cared only whether you had a viable claim or defense. In most instances, excess emotion and hyperbole were correlated negatively to facts and good advocacy.

11. *Employing a "kitchen sink" theory on appeal.* You should think long and hard about including anything but relevant, viable issues in your brief. Generally speaking, if you cannot come up with a legal reason why the court below failed you, you probably have no viable issues on appeal. Similarly, if your brief presses only extraneous legal theories—i.e., implied covenant of good faith and fair dealing; multiple equitable contractual theories, especially where there is an express contract; unjust enrichment; or conversion—perhaps some rethinking is in order.

12. *Citing cases for propositions of law that are not actually supported by those cases.* Read the cases you cite. Understand the cases you cite. When I reviewed a case cited in a brief only to discover that it either: (a) did not support the argument for which it was cited, or worse (b) supported the opposite argument, that party lost credibility.

13. *Making citation errors.* I had a very short amount of time in which to produce a lot of work. I was not going to spend that time trying to figure out what you meant to type. Check your citations and use a format that includes all relevant information, i.e., the decision year. New York cases should be cited from the official reports, if reported, and should include the court and the year. So, for example, I liked to see this: (*Kasachkoff v. New York*, 107 AD2d 130 [1st Dept 1985]); but not this: (*Kasachkoff v. New York*, 107 A.D.2d 130, 485 N.Y.S.2d 992).[3]

14. *Making up quotations or misusing quotation marks.* I once encountered a quotation that was a case winner. It perfectly stated a point of law, was from this court, and was from a decision published the previous year. I pulled up the opinion, which turned out to be only two paragraphs long. One of those paragraphs was the decretal. Uh-oh….The second paragraph bore no relation to the quoted language. Curious, I performed a full database search, hoping to find the paragraph somewhere, anywhere—even in a law review article. The quote did not exist. Please don't do that.

15. *Submitting records containing illegible copies of important documents,* i.e., the decision for review and notice of appeal. If I could not read it, it was of no use to me.

Some other things that, while not necessarily sufficient to put your brief on life support, should be avoided to the extent possible:

1. *Putting citations in footnotes.* You are not journal writing, and it was both annoying and inconvenient to have to search through footnotes to find a citation that should have been placed after the proposition for which it was cited. It was especially annoying when footnotes began to contain nothing but *"id.s," "supras"* and *"infras."*

2. *Overutilizing footnotes.* Footnotes should be used to deliver information that, while not directly relevant, is still notable. To that end, footnotes should generally not drone on for multiple paragraphs across multiple pages.

3. *String citing cases for general points of law,* i.e., the summary judgment standard. Believe me when I tell you that there is not a person in the courthouse who does not know the summary judgment standard. If you feel compelled to state it, one or two case citations will take you farther than six. Any more than that and the only thing you accomplish is padding your table of authorities.

4. *String citing cases without using pin cites or parentheticals.* You should avoid string citing at all, to the extent possible. But if you must do so, please tell the reader why he or she should care.

5. *Attaching exhibits to your brief.* Most of the court attorneys I knew used PDF versions of your documents and attachments are not scanned with your briefs. So you should put your exhibits in the record, where they belong.

6. *Including excessive volumes of records.* Ask yourself whether 22 volumes of records are actually necessary. For example, if the only issue on your appeal is whether the lower court used the proper standard of review, you do not need to include the transcripts of every deposition taken in the case. Conversely, if your entire ar-

gument hinges on the court's misconstruing of facts, you should offer more than your client's affidavit. In most cases, you should include the complaint. It helps if your files are all searchable.

7. *Submitting sloppy, non-paginated records.*

8. *Using reply briefs for information dumps* or regurgitation of arguments already made in the opening brief. Doing so is a missed opportunity and, frankly, a waste of your time.

9. *Failing to proofread your work product.* I have seen it all. Too much punctuation; no punctuation at all; sentences that drop off midthought; pasted-in sections wherein the attorney forgot to change the client's name....All of these things could be avoided with one careful proofread. It is folly not to do so.

10. *Submitting a 70-page brief or requesting an enlargement to submit an 80-page brief.* In my experience, it is rare that a 70-page brief proves either necessary or useful. Even in the most complex commercial appeals (which was primarily what I handled), 50 pages was sufficient, with 60 being an upper limit. If your brief is running longer than that, perhaps it can be streamlined by instituting a few of the suggestions listed above.

In closing, I leave you with one final thought by a master of words, Dr. Seuss: "[T]he writer who breeds more words than he needs is making a chore for the reader who reads."

Here's wishing you happy writing, but bountiful editing!

---

1. I feel compelled to reiterate that I do not speak for the court, any other court attorney or the justices. This article contains my advice, based upon my own experiences and observations after three years as a principal appellate court attorney with the First Department.

2. For formatting rules, see the Appellate Division, First Department Rules, Section 600.10, titled "Format and Content of Records, Appendices and Briefs."

3. See the New York Official Reports Style Manual.

TAMALA BOYD (ttb1368@gmail.com) is an associate general counsel with the New York City Department of Consumer Affairs. She began her legal career in private practice with the New York City law firm Simpson Thacher & Bartlett, LLP, as a general litigation associate. She then spent three years as a principal appellate court attorney with the Appellate Division, First Department. Ms. Boyd earned her law degree from Duke Law School.

This article originally appeared in the February 2014 *NYSBA Journal*.

The Legal Writer
Drafting New York Civil-Litigation Documents: Part XIII—Motion Practice Overview
By Gerald Lebovits

The *Legal Writer* continues its series on civil litigation.

In the last issue, the *Legal Writer* discussed responding to interrogatories. In this issue, the *Legal Writer* offers an overview of motions and their essential components. In the following issues, the *Legal Writer* will emphasize motions to dismiss under CPLR 3211 and summary-judgment motions under CPLR 3212, two weapons in a litigator's arsenal. The *Legal Writer* will also discuss cross-motions and replies.

To draft effective motion papers, litigators must be familiar with the Uniform Rules for New York trial courts and the parameters of motion practice found in CPLR 2211 through 2222. Because of New York's Individual Assignment System (IAS), in which a case assigned to a judge might remain with that judge up to and including the trial,[1] litigators must also know what each judge requires in a motion, including motions in the commercial parts. Judges in one county will have rules and preferences different from judges in the same or different counties. The lack of uniformity among judges causes confusion.

General Information About Motions

A motion is a request for an order from a court.[2] Some motions are made in writing; others, orally. Motions are powerful litigation tools. A successful motion might help you resolve key substantive issues or even dispose of an entire case. A motion might also help you learn critical information for your client. The common practice is for a party to initiate and move the court for some type of relief, although the court might grant an order it has made on its own motion, or sua sponte. Most motions are on notice to the opposing side. Those motions not on notice to the opposing side are called ex parte motions. Courts generally disfavor ex parte motions. Ex parte motions are permissible only when a statute or rule explicitly authorizes them.[3]

Preliminary Motions

Moving for preliminary relief "protect[s] the movant by maintaining the status quo while the [court determines the] legal and factual issues of the case."[4] Preliminary injunctive relief is an extraordinary remedy a court grants in its discretion. CPLR 6301 and 6313 explain preliminary injunctions and temporary restraining orders.

Request a stay of the proceedings or a temporary restraining order if a risk of imminent harm exists before the court hears the motion on its merits. If you're seeking a temporary restraining order, a court may require you to give notice to the opposing side and give an undertaking.

To obtain a temporary restraining order without notice, you must show that "immediate and irreparable injury, loss or damages will result unless the defendant is restrained before a hearing can be held."[5] Once a court grants a temporary restraining order, the court sets, or schedules, the hearing for the preliminary injunction.[6] If sought ex parte, a temporary restraining order might be easier to obtain than a preliminary injunction.

Emergency Motions

A moving party may bring a motion by order to show cause in an emergency. Bringing a motion by order to show cause is an expedited way to move the court for relief when little or no time exists to move on notice. Bringing a motion by order to show cause allows shorter notice than the minimum eight days' notice provided under CPLR 2214(b) for bringing a motion on notice. An order to show cause is obtained ex parte, although a court in its discretion may allow the other side to see it and oppose it before the court signs or declines to sign it. Like a motion on notice, an order to show cause must provide the return date (the date the court will hear the order to show), the time, the place, and the relief you seek. The court sets the day and time when it will hear your order to show cause; leave the day and time blank.

Ex Parte Motions

Ex parte motions are made to a judge without notice to your adversary. The CPLR authorizes ex parte motions in limited situations: attachment (CPLR 6211); temporary restraining orders (CPLR 6313); and orders specifying the manner of effecting service of process (CPLR 308(5)). CPLR 2217(b) requires you to accompany an ex parte motion with an affidavit or affirmation stating whether you've moved before for similar relief and the result of that motion. Specify the new facts, if any, on which you base the new motion, if you've asked for similar relief before. When moving ex parte, a court might require you as the moving party to post an undertaking.[7] Under the IAS system, submit your ex parte motion to the assigned judge.

Stay of Proceedings

Under CPLR 2201, you may move a court in which an action or proceeding is pending to grant a stay of the case. A stay suspends the case. Make your application for a stay in the court in which the matter is pending. You may move for a stay by notice of motion or by order to show cause. Seeking a stay isn't the same as seeking injunctive relief.[8] When a court grants an injunction, it directs a party to do or not do something. The rules about injunctive relief are set forth in CPLR article 63. A court may grant injunctive relief only if it has the jurisdiction to grant an injunction.

Motions to Correct Pleadings

Before filing a responsive pleading, you may move under CPLR 3024(a), 3024(b), or 3014 to correct pleadings. Under CPLR 3024(b), you may move for a more definite statement if you can't respond to a pleading because the pleading is vague. Under 3024(b), you may move to strike any scandalous or prejudicial material in a pleading. If you can't respond to a pleading because your adversary hasn't separately numbered the allegations or causes of action in the pleading, you may move under 3014 to require your adversary to number its pleading separately.[9]

Disclosure Motions

They're motions in which you seek relief from the court regarding disclosure, called "discovery" in federal court. The reason you'll move for disclosure might be that the other side has failed to disclose information that you sought and you're asking the court to compel the other side to turn it over to you.[10] You might also be asking the court to penalize the other side because it failed to disclose to you information you sought.

Under CPLR 3124, move to compel your adversary to comply or respond to "any request, notice, interrogatory, demand, question or order." Under CPLR 3126, move for penalties against another party. Under CPLR 3126, a court may strike all or part of your adversary's pleadings, dismiss the case, enter a default judgment against your adversary, preclude your adversary from offering information into evidence at trial, stay the proceedings until your adversary complies, or conditionally order your adversary to comply.

A court, sua sponte or on notice by motion, might also grant a protective order to "prevent unreasonable annoyance, expense, embarrassment, disadvantage, or other prejudice."[11]

Pre-Trial Motions

A pre-trial motion is a motion in which you seek relief from the court before the trial begins. A pre-trial motion must be on notice to the other parties and in writing.[12] You may move for pre-trial relief (1) by notice of motion with supporting papers[13] or (2) by order to show cause with supporting papers.[14] Motions to dismiss under CPLR 3211 and motions for summary judgment under 3212 are pre-trial motions. Moving to dismiss under 3211 is a quick way to dispose of a case. Under 3212, you may move for summary judgment or partial summary judgment. The *Legal Writer* will discuss more on motions to dismiss and summary-judgment motions in the upcoming issues.

You may file an in limine motion before trial to preclude the other side from offering evidence at trial. You may also file an in limine motion before trial to get an advance ruling to assure that your evidence will be admitted at trial.

Trial and Post-Trial Motions

Trial and post-trial motions are motions in which you seek relief from the court during trial (or a hearing) or when the trial has concluded. Depending on the individual judge's rules, trial and post-trial motions may be made orally.

Under CPLR 4401 and 4404, you may move for judgment during and after trial. CPLR 4402 allows you during the trial to move for a continuance or new trial. CPLR 4404(a) allows you to move post-trial for a judgment notwithstanding a verdict. CPLR 4404(a) also allows you to move for a new trial in jury cases.[15]

After a Judge Has Ruled: Motions to Renew or Reargue

After a judge has decided a motion against you, you must decide whether to move to renew, to reargue, or to renew and reargue. You'll have to make this motion before the judge who decided against you the first time you made the motion.[16] Identify whether you're moving for renewal, reargument, or both. If you're unclear what you're moving for (renewal, reargument, or both), don't expect the court to figure it out for you.

In a motion for renewal, you must show that you have new facts you didn't offer on the earlier motion that would change the court's determination had it known about the facts initially and that you have a justifiable reason why you didn't offer those facts before.[17] As the moving party, you have the burden to show that the facts didn't exist before or were unknown. You must also show that even with reasonable diligence, you couldn't have discovered the facts to offer them on the original motion.

In a motion for reargument, you're informing the court that it overlooked or misapprehended relevant law or fact.[18] Explain how the court misapplied or misconstrued a statute, rule, or case. Explain the applicable law. But don't repeat your earlier arguments. And don't advance new or additional arguments from your original motion.

Form and Content of Motions: General Overview

- Motions and orders to show cause must comply with CPLR 2101: All papers must be typed or printed in black on 8 1/2 by 11-inch white paper in at least 10-point type.[19]

- Each motion paper must have a caption containing the court's name and venue, the action's title, and the index number.

- Each motion must state whether the document is a notice of motion or an order to show cause.[20]

- Double-space the text but single-space the caption, title, footnotes, and quotations.[21]

- If counsel represents you, the motion must be endorsed with the attorney's name, address, and telephone number. If you're unrepresented, and thus proceeding pro se, endorse the motion with your name and give your address and telephone number.[22]

- If an attorney represents you, your attorney must sign every written motion. The attorney's signature certifies that its contents aren't frivolous.[23]

The Essential Components of a Notice of Motion

A notice of motion, usually one or two pages long, specifies the preliminary information that appears before your motion. The notice of motion gives your adversary essential information about the motion. In your notice of motion, include the following:

- The date,[24] time, court location (address of court and part), and department, if applicable.

- The nature of the order you're seeking.

- The evidence on which you're basing your motion. For example, any affidavits, exhibits, or other evidence on which you're basing your motion.

- The caption of the case, including the venue for the motion.

- The assigned judge's name if the case has been assigned to a judge.

- The index number.

- The name and address of the attorney on the motion.

- Whether you're seeking oral argument. Some judges require oral argument on all types of motions; other judges require argument in limited circumstances. In most New York courts, oral argument is the requirement, not the exception.

Affidavits and Exhibits

Affidavits are the "principal means" to submit evidence to a court in a motion.[25] No evidentiary rules dictate the contents of New York affidavits. But beware attacks from your adversary when you submit affidavits not based on personal knowledge or on documentary evidence: A court will give no probative value to affidavits not premised on personal knowledge or on documentary evidence.[26] If you're relying on pleadings, attach them to your motion in the form of exhibits. How you choose to put together your exhibits (binding them professionally or with clips or staples or hole punches, including a cover and exhibit tabs) is up to you. But make sure you make it easy for the court to find and read your exhibits.

Affidavit(s) accompany a motion. If necessary to your motion, attach documentary exhibits. Affidavits and exhibits help the court rule for you. Affidavits must be sworn before a notary public. An attorney, physician, osteopath, or dentist may swear to information in an affirmation instead of an affidavit.

In an attachment to an affidavit, give the court information or documents obtained during disclosure. Describe in the affidavit the document and why it's important to your motion. In an attachment to an affidavit, you may also give the court testimony from an examination before trial (EBT)—called a deposition in federal court—relevant to your motion. Include the cover page of the transcription and the relevant text.

Your summary-judgment motion must include the pleadings as attachments.[27]

Your motion to dismiss must attach a copy of the complaint.[28]

Brief or Memorandum of Law in Support of Your Motion

You're not required to submit a brief, sometimes called a memorandum of law, to support a motion. But better attorneys do so in important cases. It's not just the facts of your case that will persuade the court to rule for you. It's also how the facts of your case apply to the law. Some attorneys put their legal arguments in their affirmations. But that's the inferior practice: You should save your legal points for your memorandum of law, a document separate from your affirmation. In affirmations, attorneys affirm to the truth of factual statements. Attorneys may not swear to the truth of legal arguments.[29] And judges sometimes can't recall what you've said during oral argument. Submitting a separate memorandum of law lets the judge hear your arguments again. Sometimes judges ask their law clerks to write their decisions, and the law clerks will not hear your brilliant oral argument. It's thus best to submit a separate memorandum of law with your legal arguments.

For more information on writing briefs, consult the *Legal Writer*'s column "Writing Bad Briefs: How to Lose a Case in 100 Pages or More."[30] You'll find useful techniques on concision, precision, organization, citation, writing your facts, offering legal argument, and treating the judge and your adversary respectfully. And you'll also learn to avoid legalese, boilerplate, clichés, metadiscourse, negatives, and the passive voice.

In the next issue, the *Legal Writer* will continue with specifics on motions to dismiss.

---

1.   David D. Siegel, New York Practice § 245, at 413 (4th ed. 2005).

2.   CPLR 2211.

3.   Siegel, *supra* note 1, at § 247, at 420.

4.   Jane Chuang, *The "How To" of Successful Motion Practice: Program Outline*, N.Y. City Bar Ctr. for CLE 1, 4 (May 18, 2011).

5. CPLR 6301 & 6313.

6. Chuang, *supra* note 4, at 5.

7. CPLR 6313(c).

8. 1 Michael Barr, Myriam J. Altman, Burton N. Lipshie & Sharon S. Gerstman, New York Civil Practice Before Trial at § 16:270, at 16-32 (2006; Dec. 2009 Supp.).

9. In the Second Department, a motion separately to state and number under CPLR 3014 is distinct from a corrective motion under CPLR 3024. *See Consolidated Airborne Sys. v. Silverman*, 23 A.D.2d 695, 257 N.Y.S.2d 827, 828 (2d Dep't 1965). The First and Third Departments authorize corrective motions under CPLR 3024, not CPLR 3014. *See Alexander v. Kiviranna*, 52 A.D.2d 982, 982, 383 N.Y.S.2d 122, 123 (3d Dep't 1976); *Weicker v. Weicker*, 26 A.D.2d 39, 40, 270 N.Y.S.2d 640, 641 (1st Dep't 1996).

10. For more information, review the earlier issues of the *Legal Writer* in this series on drafting civil-litigation documents: Gerald Lebovits, *The Legal Writer, Drafting New York Civil-Litigation Documents: Part XI—Interrogatories*, 83 N.Y. St. B.J. 64 (Nov./Dec. 2011); Gerald Lebovits, *The Legal Writer, Drafting New York Civil-Litigation Documents: Part X—Bill of Particulars*, 83 N.Y. St. B.J. 64 (Oct. 2011).

11. Chuang, *supra* note 4, at 9 (citing CPLR 3103).

12. CPLR 2211.

13. CPLR 2214(a).

14. CPLR 2214(d).

15. Chuang, *supra* note 4, at 29.

16. Exceptions: when the original motion was ex parte; granted on default; or when court "so ordered" a stipulation. CPLR 2221(a).

17. CPLR 2221(e)(2)–(3).

18. CPLR 2221(d).

19. A summons must be printed in at least 12-point type. CPLR 2101(a).

20. CPLR 2101(c).

21. 22 N.Y.C.R.R. § 202.5(a).

22. CPLR 2101(d).

23. 22 N.Y.C.R.R. § 130-1.1(b).

24. CPLR 2214(b) specifies the minimum time period for noticing a motion, except when moving by order to show cause. Some judges will hear certain motions on certain days of the week. Make sure to check with the court and the judge's individual rules.

25. Barr et al., *supra* note 8, at § 16:62, at 16-13.

26. *Id.* at § 16:65, at 16-13.

27. CPLR 3212(b).

28. Barr et al., *supra* note 8, at § 16:60, at 16-65 (citing *Dupuy v. Carrier Corp.*, 204 A.D.2d 977, 977, 614 N.Y.S.2d 950, 960 (4th Dep't 1994)).

29. *Id.* at § 16:670 at 16-14.

30. Gerald Lebovits, *The Legal Writer, Writing Bad Briefs: How to Lose a Case in 100 Pages or More*, 82 N.Y. St. B.J. 64 (May 2010).

GERALD LEBOVITS, a Civil Court judge in the Bronx, New York, teaches part time at Columbia, Fordham, and St. John's law schools. He thanks court attorney Alexandra Standish for researching this column. Judge Lebovits's email address is GLebovits@aol.com.

This article originally appeared in the February 2012 *NYSBA Journal*.

The Legal Writer
Drafting New York Civil-Litigation Documents: Part XIV—Motion Practice Overview Continued
By Gerald Lebovits

In the last issue, the *Legal Writer* discussed the motions that litigators have in their civil-practice arsenal. The *Legal Writer* briefly discussed the form and content of motions. It also discussed a motion's component parts: the notice of motion;[1] the supporting affirmations, affidavits, and exhibits; and the brief, or memorandum of law, in support of the motion. In this issue, the *Legal Writer* continues with more on motion practice.

Motion Practice Overview

The documents in motion practice are your motion papers, also known as your moving papers. This includes your notice of motion along with supporting affirmations, affidavits, and exhibits and your brief, also called a memorandum of law. Your adversary might want to answer your motion. Your adversary's papers are known as the opposition, or opposition papers. You might then want to respond to your adversary's opposition. Your response is called a reply.

You must prepare, serve, and file the notice of motion along with supporting affirmations, affidavits, and exhibits to have a court clerk calendar your motion before a judge. Also serve and file your brief, or memorandum of law, if you write one. A brief is helpful but not required.

Attach as exhibits to your motion copies of the pleadings if your motion puts the pleadings in issue. Attach them even if they're in the court file. If you're seeking to add or amend pleadings, moving to intervene, cross-claiming, or adding a party, include copies of the older pleadings and your proposed pleadings.[2] If you don't attach a copy of the pleadings, or the old and proposed pleadings, a court might deny your motion.[3]

Many of the rules discussed below apply to actions and special proceedings in New York, although this column is directed toward actions. Special proceedings sometimes have their own rules and unique procedures. So does Federal Court. Determine what kind of case you have and which court will hear it before consulting the rules below.

Serving Motions

Serve all copies of your motion and any supporting papers on all the parties appearing in the action.[4] You must also serve all parties in the action irrespective of the number of motions you make, and even if you're opposing or replying to a motion.[5]

You don't need to serve a party who has failed to appear.

When you're moving to join additional parties, you needn't serve the prospective parties with copies of your motion, but you may do so as a courtesy.[6]

Serve your motion papers the same way you'd serve other papers. The CPLR provides that "papers may be served by any person not a party of the age of eighteen years or over."[7] Follow the CPLR 2103 requirements for serving motion papers.

If an attorney represents a party, you must serve the party's attorney. If the same attorney represents more than one party, serve only one copy of your motion papers on that attorney.[8]

Serve the party's attorney by any of the methods outlined in CPLR 2103(b)(1)–(7). Under CPLR 2103(b)(1), you may deliver the motion personally on the attorney, inhand. Or, under CPLR 2103(b)(2), you may mail the papers to the attorney at the address the attorney designated; use the address on the attorney's notice of appearance. If the attorney has not designated an address, mail the motion to the attorney's last known address. Or, under CPLR 2103(b)(3), you may leave the motion papers at the attorney's office with a person in charge. If no one's in charge, you may leave the papers in a conspicuous place. If the office is closed, you may drop the papers in the letter drop or box at the attorney's office. Or, under CPLR 2103(b)(4), if you can't serve the papers at the attorney's office, leave the papers at the attorney's New York residence with a person of suitable age or discretion. Or, under CPLR 2103(b)(5), you may transmit the papers to the attorney by facsimile. Or, under CPLR 2103(b)(6), you may serve the papers by overnight mail at the address the attorney designated; if no address is designated, serve the attorney's last known address. Or, under CPLR 2103(b)(7), you may serve the papers electronically (email) if the chief administrator of the court has authorized this method of service and if the party has consented to this method of service. Most practitioners who serve by email do so because the case is part of an electronic filing (e-filing) program through the New York state courts and the court rules allow for service by email.[9]

The CPLR explains that if a party to the action is pro se or you can't serve the party's attorney, you must serve the pro se party as outlined in CPLR 2103(b)(1), (2), (4), (5), or (6).[10]

If you serve your motion papers or opposition papers by facsimile, use facsimile only when your adversary designates a facsimile number for service of papers. CPLR 2103(b)(5) provides that

> [t]he designation of a facsimile telephone number in the address block subscribed on a paper served or filed in the course of an action or proceeding shall constitute consent to service by facsimile transmission in accordance with this subdivision. An attorney may change or rescind a facsimile telephone number by serving a notice on the other parties.

Serve the motion and supporting papers at least eight days before the return date—the date the motion is scheduled for the judge to hear it in court. If you're opposing a motion, serve your opposition papers at least two days before the return date.[11] The moving party might not always receive the opposition papers in time for the return date. If you're the moving party, give your opposing party enough time to oppose your motion. For example, file your moving papers at least 16 days before the return date. Your adversary will have to serve its opposition papers at least seven days before the return date. If you need to reply to those papers, do so at least one day before the return date. See below for more information on replies.

In the last issue, the *Legal Writer* discussed bringing motions by order to show cause. You may not bring a notice of motion earlier than the eighth day after you've served the motion papers;[12] therefore, if you want the motion heard faster, you'll have to bring your motion by order to show cause. If you move by order to show cause, it's up to the court to determine the return date, the method of service, and the service date for the order to show cause and any opposition papers.[13] Practitioners usually leave blanks on their orders to show cause for the court to choose the dates.

When you serve your motion papers by mail, add five days to the return date.[14] For example, on an eight-day notice of motion, the return date will be 13 days after mailing (eight days' notice plus five days for mail equal 13). On a 16-day notice of motion, the return date will be 21 days after mailing (16 days plus five days for mailing equal 21 days).[15] A court might deny your motion even if your adversary doesn't appear on the return date if you didn't account for the five days it takes for mailing and for your adversary to respond on time.

If you use a facsimile to serve your papers, no additional time need be added to the CPLR service period. CPLR defines "facsimile transmission" as "any method of transmission of documents to a facsimile machine at a remote location which can automatically produce a tangible copy of such documents."[16] Facsimile is almost instantaneous; your adversary receives your motion almost as soon as you send it. If you use an overnight-delivery service to serve the motion, add one day to the prescribed CPLR time periods.[17] The CPLR defines "overnight delivery service" as "any delivery service which regularly accepts items for overnight delivery to any address in the state.[18] On an eight-day notice of motion, for example, the return date will be nine days after mailing (eight days' notice plus one day for overnight mail equal nine).

You may always ask your adversary for more time to oppose a motion or to reply or to postpone the return date of the motion; if your adversary doesn't consent, you may ask the court for more time on the return date.[19]

Filing Motions

You must give the court all the motion papers you've served. File your papers by the return date, at the latest, with the clerk's office or motion support office.[20]

When you file your papers, attach an affidavit of service to the motion papers. Provide in the affidavit of service (or affirmation of service, if an attorney effectuates service) the date of and the method of service.[21]

If a judge hasn't yet been assigned to the case, accompany your motion with a Request for Judicial Intervention (RJI). File your RJI along with your motion and serve it on all the parties. Otherwise, the court clerk won't accept your motion papers.[22]

Check for specific filing rules with the motion support office or the clerk's office in the county where you're filing your motion papers. You'll have to pay a fee when filing your motion.[23] The clerk of the commercial part or other specialized court parts might have different filing rules and fees. Check CPLR Article 80 for an explanation of court fees.

Local rules and the assigned judge's rules often discuss requirements pertaining to motions. Some judges require practitioners to deliver their motion papers directly to the judge's chambers even after the practitioner filed the motion. Some judges like courtesy copies. Others hate them.

Opposing the Motion

If you've been served with a motion, you must decide whether to oppose it.[24]

If you don't oppose the motion, some courts will determine whether the law supports the motion. But many will grant the motion on default, without thinking about it too much. You should therefore oppose your adversary's motion even if you think the motion is meritless.

Also, most courts won't allow attorneys who haven't opposed a motion in writing to oppose the motion orally. The failure to submit written opposition results in a default.[25]

Sometimes you might not need or want to oppose a motion. Your client might not want to spend the money to oppose the motion. Sometimes filing opposition papers will unnecessarily delay your client's case. Sometimes your adversary's motion is inconsequential: Your adversary may, for example, move to extend your adversary's time to do something in the case or move to correct a technical problem. And sometimes you'll know that the judge will grant the motion despite your opposition. Consider the possibility of consenting to the motion in these circumstances.

If you draft opposition to the motion, label your opposition. Example: "Plaintiff's Opposition to Defendant's Motion to Dismiss." Name the exact motion you're opposing. If you're opposing more than one motion, draft a separate affidavit (or affirmation) for each motion.

You may also serve and file a brief or memorandum of law if you have a legal basis for opposing the motion. If you have only a factual basis to oppose the motion, affirmations, affidavits, and exhibits might suffice to explain to the court why you're opposing the motion.

You must serve your opposition papers on all parties.[26]

Cross-Motions

A party seeking relief against the moving party may do so by moving in a separate motion or by cross-moving. If you cross-move, the same court or judge will hear the motion and the cross-motion at the same time. Under CPLR 2215, a cross-motion is a demand for relief by someone other than the moving party. In your cross-motion, you may demand relief that doesn't respond to the relief the moving party sought. You may demand several different types of relief or relief in the alternative.[27]

A cross-motion is as effective as a motion on notice. It seeks affirmative relief, just like a regular motion.

If you seek affirmative relief from the court but you put in opposition papers instead of cross-moving, it would be error for the court to grant you the relief you seek.[28]

Any party served with a motion may cross-move.

You must serve your cross-motion on the moving party.[29]

If you're seeking relief from a nonmoving party, don't cross-move. File a separate motion.

If you're cross-moving, serve and file a notice of cross-motion.[30] You'll have to pay a court fee when you file your notice of cross-motion.[31]

May you cross-move if you've been served with a motion but the motion doesn't directly affect you? CPLR 2215 suggests that you may cross-move if you're seeking affirmative relief. When in doubt about cross-moving, move in a separate motion, and file your notice of motion and supporting affidavits.

You may oppose your adversary's motion and cross-move at the same time. All the papers you'd need to serve and file are in your opposition and a notice of cross-motion. Your notice of cross-motion is all you need to alert the court and your adversary that you're seeking affirmative relief.[32] And your opposition papers might contain all the evidence the court needs to decide your cross-motion. CPLR 2215 provides that "a party may serve upon the moving party a notice of cross-motion demanding relief, with or without supporting papers" provided you comply with CPLR 2215(a) and (b). If you need to give the court additional information—information not in your opposition papers—to support the affirmative relief you're seeking, you may submit in your cross-motion any affidavits, exhibits, and brief or memorandum of law.

The amount of time you have to serve your cross-motion depends on the amount of notice in the original motion. Serve a notice of cross-motion at least three days before the return date.[33] If you serve by mail, add three days; therefore, you'd need six days' notice before the return date (three days' notice plus three days for mailing). If you use overnight delivery you'll need one day's notice. Therefore, you'd need four days' notice before the return date (three days' notice plus one day for overnight mail).

If the original motion gave you at least 16 days' notice and demanded that you respond to the motion at least seven days in advance of the return date, you must serve your cross-motion at least seven days in advance of the return date. If you mail your cross-motion, you must give at least 10 days' notice (seven days' notice plus three days for mailing). If you use overnight mail, you'll need to give one day's notice. Therefore, you'll need eight days' notice before the return date (seven days' notice plus one day for overnight mail).

You may, but you're not required to, accompany your cross-motion with supporting papers to substantiate your cross-motion.[34] A court may decide the cross-motion on the papers in the original motion.

Moving Party's Reply

You may want to reply to your adversary's opposition papers. If you reply, don't repeat the arguments you made in your original motion, and don't assert new arguments. Only if your adversary raised new legal arguments in the opposition papers should you address those arguments in a reply.[35]

If you raise new arguments in your reply, your adversary won't have the opportunity to respond in a sur-reply. The CPLR doesn't mention a sur-reply. If your adversary submits a sur-reply, a court will not consider it. In its discretion, though, a court may sua sponte ask for a sur-reply. A lawyer must offer a good reason to explain to the court why a sur-reply is appropriate.

If you gave your adversary eight days' notice on the original motion, you probably won't have any time to reply to the opposition papers. If you gave your adversary 16 days' notice on the original motion, your adversary will have seven days to oppose the motion, and you'll have one day before the return date to reply.

You must file all papers with the court no later than the return date.[36] Because of time constraints, some practitioners bring their reply papers to court on the return date. If you do that, file your reply and bring a courtesy copy for the court and, possibly, your adversary.

Appearance on the Return Date and Oral Argument

In some New York counties, you'll need to request oral argument formally on a motion. To request oral argument formally, writing "oral argument requested" on the notice of motion, order to show cause, opposition paper, or notice of cross-motion will be sufficient.

In other New York counties, and depending on the judge, a court might require oral argument on a motion. Appear on the return date and be prepared for oral argument.

In other counties, and depending on the judge, you might have to request to submit your motion without oral argument.

Judges have the discretion to allow, limit, forbid, or require oral argument on a motion.[37] Some judges require oral argument on some motions but not on others. Some judges require oral argument on the return date; other judges will schedule the argument or a motion conference for a later date.

Follow the court procedures in your county and the individual judge's rules.

Don't risk defaulting for failing to appear on the return date for oral argument in a court that requires a personal appearance.[38] If your adversary fails to oppose your motion or to appear in person (if required), the court will grant your motion on default if you made out a prima facie case for the relief you're seeking in your motion. If your adversary defaults, your adversary may move to vacate the default under CPLR 5015(a)(1) if your adversary demonstrates an excusable default and a meritorious defense or claim.[39]

If you and your adversary agree, you may adjourn the motion. If the court or judge's rules permit, prepare a stipulation of adjournment and submit it to the court clerk or judge. You may not adjourn a motion by stipulation more than three times (no more than 60 total days) unless the judge's rules permit longer or frequent adjournments.[40]

In the next issue, the *Legal Writer* will discuss motions to dismiss and some nuances to CPLR 3211(a) and (b).

---

1. *See* CPLR 2214(a) ("A notice of motion shall specify the time and place of the hearing on the motion, the supporting papers upon which the motion is based, the relief demanded and the grounds therefor.").

2. 1 Michael Barr, Myriam J. Altman, Burton N. Lipshie & Sharon S. Gerstman, New York Civil Practice Before Trial at § 16:101, at 16-16 (2006; Dec. 2009 Supp.)

3. *See, e.g., In re Curcio v. Kelly*, 193 A.D.2d 738, 739, 597 N.Y.S.2d 731, 733 (2d Dep't 1993) ("The court further properly denied the appellants' request for leave to interpose a cross claim nunc pro tunc, since their motion papers failed to annex a copy of the proposed cross claim."); *but see, e.g., Anderson Props., Inc. v. Sawhill Tubular Div., Cyclops Corp.*, 149 A.D.2d 950, 950-51, 540 N.Y.S.2d 82, 83 (4th Dep't 1989) (granting plaintiff leave to serve amended complaint asserting additional causes of action; plaintiff had failed to serve cross-motion requesting this relief and did not give court proposed amended pleading or affidavit showing that proposed amendment had merit.).

4. Barr et al., *supra* note 2, at § 16:101, at 16-16.

5. CPLR 2103(e).

6. Barr et al., *supra* note 2, at § 16:1-4, at 16-16.

7. CPLR 2103(a).

8. CPLR 2103(b).

9. *See generally* Gerald Lebovits, The Legal Writer, *E-Filing: Mastering the Tech-Rhetoric*, 83 N.Y. St. B.J. 64 (May 2011).

10. CPLR 2103(c).

11. CPLR 2214(b).

12. *Id.*

13. Most courts prohibit parties from serving replies on orders to show cause. *See, e.g.,* N.Y. County Justices' R. 13(b); *Forward v. Foschi*, 2010 N.Y. Slip Op. 52397(U), 31 Misc. 3d 1210(A), 929 N.Y.S.2d 199, 2010 WL 6490253, at *9, 2010 N.Y. Misc. LEXIS 6625, at *29 (Sup. Ct., Westchester Co. 2010) (Scheinkman, J.) ("This Court's rules and practice guide specifically advise counsel that replies are not accepted on motions pursued by orders to show cause. The submission of replies delays the disposition of motions and, thus, it would defeat the purpose of the order to show cause procedure to invite replies."). But reply papers are allowed in the New York City Civil Court's plenary part. According to the Unified Court System, "If you have received opposition papers prior to the hearing date of the Order to Show Cause, you may have time to prepare an affidavit in reply….You must serve a copy of the reply affidavit on the other side and bring extra copies and the original, along with proof of service, to the courtroom on the date the Order to Show Cause is to be heard. If you did not have time to prepare reply papers and feel that it is necessary, you can ask the court for an adjournment for time to prepare papers. The judge may or may not grant your request." http://www.nycourts.gov/courts/nyc/civil/osc.shtml (last visited Feb. 23, 2012). The rule is nearly verbatim for Housing Court. *See* http://www.nycourts.gov/courts/nyc/housing/osc.shtml#reply (last visited Feb. 23, 2012).

14. CPLR 2103(b).

15. Barr et al., *supra* note 2, at § 16:107, at 16-17.

16. CPLR 2103(f)(3).

17. CPLR 2103(b)(6).

18. *Id.*

19. CPLR 2104.

20. CPLR 2214(c).

21. *See* 22 N.Y.C.R.R. 202.8(b) (uniform rules for Supreme and County Courts); *see generally* CPLR 2214(b).

22. 22 N.Y.C.R.R. 202.6.

23. CPLR 8020(a).

24. Barr et al., *supra* note 2, at § 16:130, at 16-19.

25. *See, e.g., Kohn v. Kohn*, 86 A.D.3d 630, 630, 928 N.Y.S.2d 55, 56 (2d Dep't 2011).

26. *See* CPLR 2214(c), 2103(e).

27. CPLR 2215(b).

28. Barr et al., *supra* note 2, at § 16:145, at 16-20.1, 16-21.

29. CPLR 2215.

30. *Id.*

31. CPLR 8020(a).

32. CPLR 2215; *see Palmieri v. Salsimo Realty Co.*, 202 Misc. 251, 252, 115 N.Y.2d 88, 90 (Sup. Ct., Bronx Co. 1952).

33. CPLR 2215.

34. *Id.*

35. For more on reply papers, see Gerald Lebovits, The Legal Writer, *Or Forever Hold Your Peace: Reply Briefs*, 82 N.Y. St. B.J. 64 (June 2010).

36. 22 N.Y.C.R.R 202.8(a); *see* CPLR 2214(c).

37. 22 N.Y.C.R.R. 202.8(d).

38. *McGoldrick v. 2100 Park Assoc.*, 279 A.D.2d 287, 288 (1st Dep't 2001); *Brosnan v. Behette*, 186 A.D.2d 165, 166 (2d Dep't 1992).

39. Barr et al., *supra* note 2, at § 16:172, at 16-22, 16-23.

40. 22 N.Y.C.R.R. 202.8(e)(1).

GERALD LEBOVITS, a Bronx County Civil Court judge, teaches part time at Columbia, Fordham, and St. John's law schools. He thanks court attorney Alexandra Standish for researching this column. Judge Lebovits's email address is GLebovits@aol.com.

This article originally appeared in the March/April 2012 *NYSBA Journal.*

The Legal Writer
E-Mail Netiquette for Lawyers
By Gerald Lebovits

Electronic mail, called "e-mail" and often spelled "email," has electrified the practice of law. E-mail is invaluable. It's "cheaper and faster than a letter, less intrusive than a phone call, [and] less hassle than a fax."[1] It eliminates location and time-zone obstacles.[2]

E-mail isn't perfect. Attorneys are besieged by the volume of e-mails. It's hard to sort through the mix of solicitations, SPAM, correspondence, and critical, time-sensitive information. One result: "people are either annoyed by the intrusion [of e-mail] or are overwhelmed by the sheer number of e-mails they receive each day."[3] E-mail also leads to misunderstandings.[4]

Despite its problems, e-mail is an essential tool. Attorneys must make the most of it—so long as the attorney follows this good advice: "Think. Pause. Think again. Then send."[5] This column reviews e-mail etiquette, e-mail tips, and e-mail's implications for the legal profession. Good protocol makes e-mail fit to print.

Etiquette

Lawyers must consider the e-mail's recipient to determine how formal or informal etiquette should be. E-mails among colleagues sent in a series of quick responses are different from e-mails to a potential client. The varied purposes of e-mails and the diversity of recipients lead to conflicting etiquette rules. Many equate e-mail with traditional correspondence. Others see it as a new and different way to write. Some authorities argue that old-fashioned "snail mail" letters are better when interacting with adversaries, clients, and courts.[6] Others criticize the informal and sloppy writing common in e-mails. To them, "the e-mail culture is transforming us into a nation of hurried, careless note makers."[7]

The following etiquette rules outline general concepts and apply to all forms of electronic mail, regardless of the recipient.

Don't hide behind the electronic curtain. Easy access to e-mail leads to the common but poor practice of relying on e-mail's impersonal characteristics to deal with things better done in person. The mantra must be "Never do anything electronically that you would want others to do to you in person."[8] E-mail writers must ask themselves: "Would I say this in person?"[9] Asking this question reduces the potential to use e-mail for an exchange best suited for oral communication.

End confrontations. If communication leads to confrontation, end the dialogue and, if appropriate, agree to speak by telephone or in person.[10] E-mail is an imperfect way to resolve differences. Unlike oral communication, e-mail provides no tone or inflection. The reader must assign character to the communication. Angry, or "flame," mail[11] escalates disputes.[12]

Cut the back-and-forth. Stop e-mailing when an exchange, called a "thread," turns into a long back-and-forth discussion.[13] It's better to discuss on the telephone or in person any matter requiring more than three replies. Long threads lead to confusion when the discussion strays from the original subject. Sending e-mails also gives senders a sense of absolved responsibility when nothing has been accomplished. Just click the "send" button and it's the other guy's responsibility. Clarifying tasks by telephone or in person avoids this trap.

Interpret generously. Just as e-mail writers must consider the tone recipients might assign to the text, so must recipients generously interpret the writer's text.[14] Recipients should assume the best of the writer to avoid overreacting to a text that might be brief, hostile, or unclear. Avoid misunderstandings by giving e-mail writers leeway when deciphering meaning.

Always edit. Avoid confusion through editing. Reading what you've written will let you see how an intended recipient might misinterpret your writing. An example of this is an e-mail that reads "I resent your message" when the writer meant to say, "I re-sent your message."[15]

Editing includes more than reading for meaning. It means checking spelling and grammar. Informality like making typos or using only lowercase letters is fine between friends. It has no place in professional correspondence. To ensure credibility and respect, avoid grammar and spelling errors. Use your e-mail program's spell-check function. Editing is necessary because "[c]lients often can't tell whether your legal advice is sound, but they can certainly tell if you made careless typos."[16]

Be concise. Given the volume of e-mail and the limited time to read and respond, make e-mail readable. Write so that readers can read and comprehend quickly. Compose short sentences, short paragraphs,[17] and short e-mails. To make the reader's job easier, condense brief, casual e-mails into one paragraph.

This doesn't mean that e-mail writers should abandon all formalities of correspondence for brevity. Maintain a professional tone through proper capitalization and word choice. Many traditional-correspondence rules apply to e-mail.[18]

Front load and summarize questions and answers. If you're asking a question in your e-mail, ask it before you say why you're asking. If you ask the question up front, you're more likely to get an answer;

the reader is less likely to stop reading before getting to your question.[19] Another technique when you reply is to summarize the question you were asked—and only then answer the question.[20] That'll let your reader know you're both on the same e-mail page.

Use the subject line to its full potential. Attorneys are inundated by e-mail. They must decide what to read and take care of first. An e-mail's subject line often determines the decision a recipient makes about when, or whether, to deal with it. Use the subject line to inform recipients of the e-mail's subject and purpose.[21]

A recipient will be frustrated by false or insufficient information in the subject line. Include key information to let recipients evaluate quickly whether they've time to deal with your e-mail at that moment. Don't make your subject line too short or too long.[22] Use initial capitals for subject-line messages, but don't capitalize short articles or prepositions. Don't end subject-line messages with a period.

Occasionally you can fit your entire message in the subject line. This works when the message is extremely brief and when asked to reply to a short, simple question. Use the abbreviation "EOM" at the end of the subject line-message.[23] EOM means "end of message." It tells the recipient that the subject line is the complete message and that they needn't waste time opening the message.

Format replies for clarity. Answer at the top of an e-mail so that readers need not search through text.[24] To answer multiple questions or make various points, organize replies with numbers or letters. If you're interlacing your answer between paragraphs of the original e-mail, use a different color, size, or font to set your writing apart from the sender's.[25]

Don't overuse abbreviations. LOL! To be brief and to type quickly, it's tempting to use lots of abbreviations. This isn't as time-saving as it might seem. Abbreviations waste time if your e-mail, filled with ambiguous abbreviations, requires the recipient to reply seeking clarification. The solution is to use them sparingly.[26] Stick with familiar abbreviations that express your meaning.

Use contractions. Although contractions are inappropriate in formal letters, contractions, which enable readers to understand text quickly, are encouraged in e-mails. Not using contractions sounds awkward and fussy and makes readers feel scolded.[27] Using the uncontracted form in the directive "Do not make extra copies of the report," for instance, suggests that dire consequences will follow for doing so.[28] Reserve the uncontracted form for special emphasis.[29]

Be sensitive when e-mailing to and from telephones. Smartphones like Blackberrys and iPhones are increasingly prevalent. Their small screens and cramped keyboards make writing concisely and using the subject line to its full potential even more important. In your quest for concision, never use, in a professional context, SMS (Short Message Service) language, or "textese," like substituting "c u l8r" for "see you later."[30] This extreme form of abbreviation is like writing in another language.

☹ **Emoticons are inappropriate.** Emoticons are small faces made by combining colons, semi-colons, parentheses, and other symbols. The authorities have different opinions about emoticons, but the consensus is that they don't convey meaning in a professional setting.[31]

Correspondence littered with smiley and frowny faces looks juvenile. It reveals the writer's inability to find good words, phrases, and sentences. Readers find emoticons annoying[32] and disruptive.

All capitals are ineffective. All capitals equals SHOUTING. Never use them, regardless of the context.[33]

Exclamation points liven up e-mails! Because e-mail has no affect, "exclamation points can instantly infuse electronic communication with human warmth."[34] They show enthusiasm. Writing "Congratulations!" is more expressive than writing "Congratulations," which sounds apathetic or sarcastic. Don't use multiple exclamation points. Also, don't use exclamation points to convey negative emotion. It means you're throwing a tantrum.[35]

Avoid format embellishments. Many e-mail programs offer options to personalize e-mail. These options include different fonts and background "wall paper" featuring pictures and clip art. Personalize with content, not format embellishments. Stick to a plain font, like Times New Roman or Arial in black type,[36] and 10- to 12-point type size on a plain background.

Project respect. Appropriate salutations and closings express respect. Writers should use salutations and closings in most professional settings. Sometimes official salutations and closings are unwarranted, as in a string of replies between peers or colleagues or among friends.[37]

If you're unsure how to address your recipients, mirror the earlier correspondence.[38] When there's no correspondence, the following are helpful salutations and closings. Use last names and titles until you're told otherwise. For an individual, "Dear Mr./Ms. [*last name*]:" is always appropriate. If you're unsure whether your relationship is familiar enough to allow first names, "Dear [*first name*] (if I may),"[39] allows informality and addresses whether first names are appropriate.

These closings aren't comprehensive, but they're a start to your finding the appropriate ending to correspondence: "All best," "All the best," "Best," "Best regards," "Best wishes," "Cordially," "Regards," "Respectfully," "Sincerely," "Sincerely yours," and "Yours."[40]

Sign your e-mail. An e-mail exchange might be your only correspondence with a recipient. Signatures tell recipients how you like to be addressed and signal that the e-mail is complete. The context of your e-mail determines the appropriate signature. Not every e-mail requires a full signature. Quick responses between co-workers and friends about simple issues dispense with e-mail formalities, including signatures. Alternatively, consider correspondence between opposing counsel at the start of litigation. Signatures with full names and titles are informative. Make the most of this line to tell recipients whether you wish to be addressed by your first name, your last name, or a title.

Start smart. Don't both begin and end an e-mail with your name and who you are. A formal, polite way to write is to introduce yourself up front but to sign your name only at the end. Thus: "I represent Mr. Y, the defendant in X v. Y. Please telephone me tomorrow. Sincerely, John Smith." Not: "My name is John Smith. I represent Mr. Y, the defendant in X v. Y. Please telephone me tomorrow. Sincerely, John Smith."

Tell recipients how they can contact you. Include contact information below your signature. It sets the right business tone and shows your desire to be available to recipients. Include your full name, title, organization name, telephone number, e-mail address, mailing address, Web site, fax number, and other relevant information.[41] Save time with your e-mail program's automatic signature-line feature.

Announce prolonged absences. Tell correspondents when you'll be away from your e-mail for more than a day or two. If you don't, they might e-mail expecting quick action and grow frustrated when you don't reply. Use your e-mail software's "Out of Office" function to send an automatic reply announcing your absence. Or set your program to forward mail to an account you'll monitor while you're away.

Limit urgent e-mail. E-mail programs contain an option to flag or highlight messages as "urgent" or "important." This option helps senders and recipients supplement information in the subject line, but only if the "urgent" or "important" designation is accurate. Using flags to entice recipients to read e-mail that doesn't qualify for a flag harms the flag's purpose and your credibility.[42] Use "urgent" and "important" sparingly.

Never forward without permission, but always assume that recipients will forward without permission. E-mail makes it easy to reply with the click of a button. Forwarding and carbon copying e-mail is just as simple. The ease with which you can pass along e-mail makes it tempting to do so. But etiquette dictates that you not forward any e-mail unless you have the original sender's permission. Also, when carbon copying (CC) or blind carbon copying (BCC) someone unfamiliar to your reader, state the reason for copying.

Your commitment to following the rules of etiquette doesn't guarantee that others will do the same. Assume that any e-mail you write will be forwarded, copied, and blind copied to others without your permission.[43] Protect your wish that your mail remain with your recipient by placing that request in the subject line and in your e-mail's body. These precautions don't guarantee compliance. E-mail isn't confidential. Don't assume it is.[44]

Don't abuse e-mail. Sending unsolicited advertisements to a mass list of recipients (SPAM) is like clogging up your friends' and colleagues' inboxes with unwanted jokes and chain mail. Don't be a spammer.

Note e-mail policies. Most large employers have e-mail policies. Follow them.

Beware of using business e-mail for personal use. Most large companies can access their employees' e-mail and hard drives. If in doubt, never e-mail anything you wouldn't want to see in tomorrow's newspaper.[45] Never send inappropriate mail, let alone to or from your office e-mail address.[46]

Your company might require a disclaimer at the end of your e-mail to specify the level of privacy assigned to e-mail communications and a warning that the e-mail shouldn't be used outside its stated context.

The New York State Bar Association provides a sample e-mail policy in its resources for small and solo practice firms.[47] The sample includes a list of risks and liabilities, legal requirements to use company e-mail, and suggested format for company e-mail. The policy is helpful if you're setting up an e-mail system.

E-Mail Tips

Here are some tips to make writing, sending, and receiving e-mail efficient and hassle-free.

Fill in the address box only when you're ready to send. The ease of sending out mass e-mail, purposely or inadvertently, means that you must take care when addressing your message. To avoid sending an e-mail before you're ready, write your entire e-mail, do all your edits, and proofread before you fill in the address box.[48]

Make managing e-mail part of your daily tasks. If the constant inflow of mail becomes overwhelming, set up a schedule to read e-mail just as you would an appointment.[49] Otherwise, read e-mail as received.

Start by answering e-mails that require a response. If you can't give the e-mail full attention, send a quick response to let the sender know that you received the message and that a more complete response awaits.

Set up a filing system. Most e-mail programs allow multiple folders you can add to manually or automatically based on your criteria. Consider a pending folder for e-mail you must deal with later, a monthly or weekly review folder for follow-up exchanges, a permanent folder for mail you must never delete, and folders for clients or personal matters. Don't clog up your inbox. Deal with your mail and then discard it or place it in a folder.

Take the time to respond appropriately. The immediacy of e-mail leads people to send messages before they've fully thought through their ideas. Combined with the constant access to e-mail, instantaneous e-mail correspondence leads to situations in which senders often wish they could take their message back. This is wishful thinking: "No one will remember that you responded instantaneously. Everyone will remember if you respond inappropriately."[50]

Some people are always online. When they press the "send" button, their computer immediately sends the e-mail. Most e-mail programs allow an intermediate step between sending e-mail and its actual delivery: the outbox feature. An outbox works like your home mailbox. You place the letter in the box, but it isn't sent until the letter carrier picks it up.[51] Set your program to send all e-mails in the outbox at a particular time or only when you manually empty the outbox. In the meantime, the e-mail is in the outbox and available to edit or delete.

This feature also helps those who e-mail outside business hours. Setting your outbox to deliver all messages at 9:00 a.m. will hide that you were awake at 4:00 a.m. when you wrote it.

Watch out for Reply All. The "Reply All" feature is convenient to exchange responses with a large group. The feature can turn disastrous if used in error. The horror stories are well known, but the mistakes continue.

Use CC and BCC properly. Several options let senders address messages. The "To" box should include all those to whom the message is directed. The "CC" box is reserved for those who should receive the message for informational purposes but from whom no response or action is required. The "BCC" box works the same way as the "CC" box but preserves recipients' anonymity.[52]

Check and explain attachments. Correspondents can instantly share documents by attaching them to e-mails. This useful feature requires careful attention. First, consider whether to send a document by e-mail. Sending large files (anything over two or three megabytes) causes problems. Many servers block large e-mails. Or an e-mail that goes through might exceed the memory capacity of the recipient's inbox, causing it to crash. Next, remember to attach a document when you state in your e-mail that you're attaching it. Also, explain early in the e-mail message what you've attached, in what form, and why. Finally, attach the correct document, especially when dealing with sensitive materials.

Use your address book wisely. Most e-mail programs offer options to store contacts in an address book. This allows you to maintain a database of e-mail addresses to send e-mails without searching for addresses. Ready access to your contact list might lead to costly mistakes. Confusing your intended recipient is embarrassing. Although it's impractical to maintain separate address books for each contact, maintain separate address books for media,[53] professional, and personal contacts.

Save time: Set up group e-mails. When you're collaborating on a project or regularly exchange e-mail with a set of recipients, set up a group e-mail list. This assures completeness and saves time.

Request an acknowledgment of receipt. If you're concerned that your recipient might not receive an e-mail with time-sensitive or other important information, request an acknowledgment of receipt. Most e-mail programs have an option to do this, but you can also request an acknowledgment in the body of your e-mail. Not all e-mail communications require acknowledgment. Give yourself peace of mind, but don't burden recipients.

Rely on timestamps cautiously. Each e-mail message sent or received is stamped with date and time information. This information is good for documentation, but it's not 100% accurate.[54] Glitches in computer software and other electronic anomalies result in inaccurate timestamps.

Be careful with interoffice e-mail. Interoffice e-mail systems offer options and features different from personal e-mail programs. Some interoffice systems allow access to the "Properties" of e-mail exchanges to permit senders to check when their recipients read a message, how long the recipient looked at a message, whether the recipient deleted a message, and whether the recipient forwarded a message. Each system is unique. Be aware of these possibilities.

Save your recipient's time with "No reply needed." In an age when so many e-mails are exchanged daily, include a notation in e-mails sent only for informational purposes that no reply is needed.[55]

E-Mail and the Law

E-mail etiquette is important for attorneys because "[e]mail leaves a written, time stamped, and traceable record of your lazy habits, and flip email replies can come back to haunt you."[56]

Not all e-mail between attorneys and clients is privileged: "[E]mail communications in which legal advice is neither sought nor given are not necessarily privileged and could be discoverable."[57] Avoid off-topic banter when corresponding with clients.

You're responsible for your mail. The costs of misdirecting e-mail containing confidential information are incalculable. Check and double check the accuracy of a recipient's address. Attorneys are charged with a standard of care that includes "carefully checking the addresses prior to sending an e-mail and ensuring that privileged information is not inadvertently sent to a third party."[58]

Consider the impact and repercussions each e-mail might have. Arthur Andersen's fall can be attributed to an Anderson in-house attorney's e-mail directing staff to follow its document retention policy—a direction to shred documents.[59] Because electronically stored data, including e-mail, is generally discoverable in lawsuits,[60] consider the legal implications of what you write.

Conclusion

Corresponding with the click of a button instead of dropping an envelope into a mailbox doesn't give you license to become complacent. When attorneys correspond in their professional capacity, it reflects on their capacity as professionals.

---

1. Kaitlin Duck Sherwood, *A Beginner's Guide to Effective Email*, http://webfoot.com/advice/email.top.php (last visited Oct. 14, 2009).

2. *Id.*

3. Thomas E. Kane, Letters for Lawyers: Essential Communications for Clients, Prospects, and Others ix (2d ed. 2004).

4. Janice Mac Avoy et al., *Think Twice Before You Hit the Send Button! Practical Considerations in the Use of Email*, 54 Prac. Law. 45, 45 (Dec. 2008).

5. Wayne Schiess, *Email Advice Part 2*, Austin Law. 6 (June 2009).

6. Kane, *supra* note 3, at ix.

7. Tom Goldstein & Jethro Lieberman, The Lawyer's Guide to Writing Well 62 (2d ed. 2002).

8. David Shipley & Will Schwalbe, Send: Why People Email So Badly and How To Do It Better 53 (2d ed. 2008).

9. Deborah Bouchoux, Aspen Handbook for Legal Writers 141 (2005).

10. *Id.*

11. Monte Enbysk, Microsoft.com Small Business Center, *Email Etiquette at Work*, http://tech.msn.com/howto/article.aspx?cp-documentid=812126 (last visited Oct. 14, 2009) (defining "flame" mail as e-mail that's terse, critical, or venomous).

12. Shipley & Schwalbe, *supra* note 8, at 11–13.

13. Enbysk, *supra* note 11.

14. Bouchoux, *supra* note 9, at 141.

15. *Id.* at 140.

16. Joshua Stein, *How to Prevent Email Embarrassments, Control the Email Deluge, and Get People to Read the Email You Send*, 19 Prac. Real Est. Law. 7, 9 (Jan. 2003).

17. Shipley & Schwalbe, *supra* note 8, at 132.

18. *See generally* Kane, *supra* note 3 (containing sample letters and examples of legal correspondence).

19. Wayne Schiess, *E-Mail Like a Lawyer*, Student Law. 22, 25 (May 2007).

20. *Id.* at 26.

21. Laura Stack, *12 Tips for Better E-mail Etiquette*, http://office.microsoft.com/en-us/outlook/HA012054101033.aspx (last visited Oct. 14, 2009).

22.   Mark Grossman, *Email Etiquette is Important*, http://www.ecomputerlaw.com/articles/show_article.php?article=2008_email_etiquette_is_important (last visited Oct. 14, 2009).

23.   Shipley & Schwalbe, *supra* note 8, at 88.

24.   *Id.* at 158.

25.   *Id.*

26.   Bouchoux, *supra* note 9, at 141.

27.   Shipley & Schwalbe, *supra* note 8 at 132.

28.   *Id.* at 133.

29.   *Id.*

30.   Wikipedia, SMS Language, http://en.wikipedia.org/wiki/SMS_language (last visited Oct. 14, 2009).

31.   Bouchoux, *supra* note 9, at 141.

32.   Mac Avoy et al., *supra* note 4, at 51.

33.   Grossman, *supra* note 22; Mac Avoy et al., *supra* note 4, at 51.

34.   Shipley & Schwalbe, *supra* note 8, at 137.

35.   *Id.* at 138.

36.   *Id.* at 97–98.

37.   *Id.* at 107.

38.   *Id.* at 110.

39.   *Id.* at 105.

40.   *Id.* at 108.

41.   *Id.* at 114–15; Stack, *supra* note 21.

42.   Shipley & Schwalbe, *supra* note 8, at 95–96.

43.   Stein, *supra* note 16, at 10.

44.   Bouchoux, *supra* note 9, at 141.

45.   Mac Avoy et al., *supra* note 4, at 51; Shipley & Schwalbe, *supra* note 8, at 61 ("Never send anything to a business email address that the recipient would be embarrassed to have the entire company read.").

46.   Bouchoux, *supra* note 9, at 141.

47.   New York State Bar Association Solo and Small Firm Resource Center, http://www.nysba.org/AM/Template.cfm?Section=For_Attorneys&TEMPLATE=/CM/ContentDisplay.cfm&CONTENTID=14569 (last visited Oct. 14, 2009).

48.   Mac Avoy et al., *supra* note 4, at 49.

49.   *See* Dennis M. Kennedy & Tom L. Mighell, The Lawyer's Guide to Collaboration Tools and Technologies: Smart Ways to Work Together 127 (2008) (advising readers to use "triage" on their inbox by identifying which e-mails must be dealt with immediately, which require action but can wait for a response, and which can be deleted immediately because they are of no future use.)

50.   Mac Avoy et al., *supra* note 4, at 50.

51.   Jonathan Soll, *Managing Electronic Data Risks Through an Email Retention Policy*, 18 Am. Corp. Counsel Ass'n Docket 18, 25 (Apr. 2000).

52.   Shipley & Schwalbe, *supra* note 8, at 59–60.

53.   Mac Avoy et al., *supra* note 4, at 50.

54. Shipley & Schwalbe, *supra* note 8, at 50–51.

55. *Id.* at 54.

56. Kennedy & Mighell, *supra* note 49, at 125.

57. Christopher Wesser, *Ethical Considerations and the Use of Email*, 49 For the Def. 68, 71 (Feb. 2007).

58. Mac Avoy et al., *supra* note 4, at 48.

59. Veda Charrow et al., Clear and Effective Legal Writing 16-17 (4th ed. 2007).

60. Soll, *supra* note 51, at 19.

GERALD LEBOVITS, a Bronx County Civil Court judge, teaches part time at Columbia, Fordham, and St. John's law schools. He thanks court attorney Alexandra Standish for researching this column. Judge Lebovits's email address is GLebovits@aol.com.

This article originally appeared in the November/December 2009 *NYSBA Journal*.

Proofreading, the Evil Corollary*
By Peter Siviglia

"What a boring subject! I can't believe anyone would write an essay on this topic—no less read it. C'mon, let's find something better to do."

Wait a minute; wait a minute. Just give me a chance. Read a bit further. Trust me.

Death and taxes; the two certainties in life. Well, it's time to add a third: mistakes. Errors are part of the human condition. They are unavoidable. Even God is not immune. Just look around.

I worked for a lawyer who once told me: "Peter, you can't help making mistakes. Just pray that they're small." He was half-right: prayer is not the answer. Checking your work—quality control!—is: not once; not twice; but several times. Even then there will be mistakes, but by then they should be small.

An article by David Margolick, which appeared in the October 4, 1991 edition of *The New York Times*, provides a perfect study.

In the 1980s an insurance company and a finance company lent substantial sums of money to a shipping company. The loans were secured by mortgages on the borrower's fleet—the insurance company having first priority. Later, when the financing was restructured and the new mortgage for the insurance company prepared, three digits were omitted from a crucial figure. Instead of stating that the mortgage secured a debt of $XX,XXX,XXX, the mortgage stated that it secured a debt of $XX,XXX—not an insubstantial difference. According to the article, the error was repeated on numerous documents; but the error was never discovered until after the mortgage had been recorded and the shipping company had gone into bankruptcy. The error had not been detected by the insurance company's in-house counsel, nor had it been detected by the insurance company's out-house counsel. It was not detected by the lawyers for the shipping company, and it was not detected by the lawyers for the other lender, the finance company. The article reports that the insurance company "reckoned that the typo cost it at least $31 million."

"Didn't they proofread?!" you exclaim. Of course they proofread. Each draft was proofread. What happened is a lawyer's nightmare. And what happened probably occurred because of the one or two most common mistakes in proofreading—the most boring of endeavors: (1) lack of concentration, (2) the eyes tend to see and the ears tend to hear *what they expect rather than what is.*

But the point of this essay is not to explore the techniques of proofreading. The point of this essay is the impression *The New York Times* article gives of who was to blame: the secretary who typed the mortgage. The article closes with a statement by one of the members of the firm at which she worked: "the firm knew the name of the erring secretary. He described her as contrite. He also said her current whereabouts were unknown."

To blame a secretary for this mistake is to blame the manufacturer of the knife used by Jack the Ripper. For the lawyers to hide behind a secretary's typographical error is not only absurd but despicable. A secretary types thousands upon thousands of characters a day—nay, an hour. Mistakes must inevitably occur. At the secretary's stage of production, there is no difference between dropping the last three digits of a number and dropping a three-letter word ("the") from a sentence. No one knows where or how serious the errors will be, but "as sure as God made little green apples," the errors will be there. And the only person responsible for the quality of the document is the lawyer, not the secretary.

I tell the lawyers in our firm: the secretary's responsibility for accuracy in the final document begins and ends with the address on the letter and the envelope. The attorney is responsible for everything else. If a secretary makes too many mistakes, get a new secretary; but when that final version leaves the office, there is no such thing as a "typo." There are proofreading errors and "lawyeros," but not typos. And it does not matter that paralegals or others do the proofreading. The lawyer is accountable. And the lawyer who does not adhere to this principle will ultimately bat $000.

*Section 1.3, *Commercial Agreements—A Lawyer's Guide to Drafting and Negotiating*, by Peter Siviglia (Rochester: Lawyers Cooperative Publishing, 1993) pages 7-9.

This article originally appeared in the January 1994 *NYSBA Journal*.

PATHWAY TO THE PROFESSION: FROM LAW SCHOOL TO LAWYER

CONTRACTS

Contract Law
Options
By Peter Siviglia

The task of transactional attorneys is to place commercial litigators on the endangered species list by preparing well-thought-out, well-written contracts. That mandate generated this article, because the option—certainly one of the most, if not the most, important and valuable of commercial instruments—is frequently not given the attention it requires in private transactions. This neglect may well be due to the fact that in private transactions the option, like the right to buy leased equipment or a right of first refusal, is often a sideshow to the main event: the primary, underlying deal.

Unlike a contract written to address a negotiated transaction about to take place for which the terms have been agreed, the option addresses a transaction that *might* occur sometime in the future. Nevertheless, the attorney must, with the client, anticipate all aspects of that possible future transaction and deal with all of those aspects in the option agreement as if the subject of the option were a transaction about to take place.

Options to Buy or Lease a Physical Asset

Thus, for example, if the option is to buy equipment, the option must contain the entire contract to purchase that equipment: specifications for the equipment, delivery terms, price, payment terms, warranties, and every other term of the purchase all the way to governing law. If the contract includes deferred payment terms with the seller taking a security interest in the equipment, then the entire text of the security agreement must be included as an exhibit to the option agreement. And if the buyer is to issue its promissory note to evidence the debt and the payment terms, that note must also be added as an exhibit to the option agreement.

If any blank spaces, such as dates, must be completed when the option is exercised, the option agreement must specify how to complete those blank spaces. Their completion must be purely mechanical. Nothing must be left to discussion.

The same rules apply to a lease: the entire lease agreement must be attached as an exhibit to the option agreement, with any blank spaces to be completed mechanically as specified in the option agreement.

Failure to adhere to this mandate by leaving terms of the underlying transaction incomplete can create an arena of dispute and litigation, all to the benefit of none other than commercial litigators. For example, witness the allegations in a complaint filed in the New York State Supreme

Court involving an option to purchase real estate in Manhattan. The option in question was written by two well-known New York law firms. The complaint stated:

> Pursuant to the Agreement, if [Plaintiff] exercised the option on or before January 31, 1995, then [Plaintiff] and [Defendant] were to enter into a definitive Contract of Sale of the Premises…for the sum of $18,000,000… [with] a deposit in the sum of $1,800,000. The Agreement expressly provided that *the Contract of Sale was to be "reasonably satisfactory to [Plaintiff] and its counsel."*(emphasis supplied)

> Prior to January 1, 1995, [Plaintiff] attempted to exercise the option under the Agreement and advised defendant that it was ready, willing and able to enter into a contract of sale and make the required deposit.

> *[Defendant], in response to [Plaintiff's] exercise of its option, proposed a contract of sale that contained terms that were not reasonably satisfactory to [Plaintiff] and its counsel. Among other things, [Defendant's] proposed contract (i) would have required…*(emphasis supplied)

…and straight on 'til morning. (Apart from containing the entire contract of sale, the option should have required that the notice of exercise be accompanied by the down payment.)

To state just the basic terms of the underlying transaction and how and when an option may be exercised is to design a playground of litigation. The option must not leave to future negotiation any term of the sale, lease, or other transaction. The option must contain the entire contract for the sale, for the lease, or for the other transaction.

Rights of First Refusal

This mandate of comprehensive specificity applies equally to rights of first refusal, but, because of the nature of those rights, certain adjustments are necessary. Too often contracts only state that a party will have "a right of first refusal," nothing more.

Alone, the term right of first refusal means little, if anything. As the allegations in the complaint cited above bear painful witness, the term "right of first refusal," by itself, is an invitation to dispute and to litigation.

To operate properly, a right of first refusal must be written along the lines set forth below. It is not even necessary to use the term right of first refusal:

1. Before the Seller may sell an item, the Seller must first offer the option holder the right to purchase the item on specified terms, all as set forth in a proposed contract of sale.

2. The option holder then has a stated period to elect to buy the item on those terms.

3. If the option holder elects not to buy the item, then the Seller may sell the item elsewhere on those same terms within a specified period.

4. If the terms are changed within that specified period, the Seller must then offer the option holder the right to purchase the item on the new terms under the foregoing procedures.

5. If the Seller does not sell the item within the allotted time on the required terms, then the Seller may not sell the item without first offering it again to the option holder on specified terms (old or new) under the foregoing procedures.

One additional comment on the right of first refusal: When restrictions on the sale or transfer of an asset require a bona fide offer, it is essential that the offer meet certain requirements so that it does not frustrate a right of first refusal with features that the optionee cannot match.

A bona fide offer to purchase should require an all-cash purchase price payable within a short, specified period without any collateral securing payment of that purchase price. These requirements eliminate types of payment (such as shares in a company or some other asset) and types of collateral to which the optionee might not have access.

That's right: Rights of first refusal can be a pain in an area located about midway between the heel and the back of the head. Clients like to receive them but beware of giving them because the very procedures required to make a right of first refusal work properly can frustrate a sale or a marketing effort. And the fact that a first-refusal right-holder can commandeer the transaction may well discourage a prospective buyer from playing the game.

Shareholder Arrangements: The Non-Agreement Option

A common feature of privately held corporations is the right of first refusal. This right has a dual personality in the corporate context: (1) preemptive rights in favor of the shareholders when the corporation, itself, issues additional shares; and (2) rights of first refusal in favor of the other shareholders when one of the shareholders wishes to sell all or some of its shares.

Preemptive rights generally reside in the state's corporation law or in the articles or certificate of incorporation. New York's corporation law provides that shareholders do not have preemptive rights "except as otherwise expressly provided in the certificate of incorporation."[1] Thus, in New York, preemptive rights should never be recorded in a shareholder agreement lest they run the risk of being declared invalid. They must reside in the certificate of incorporation.

On the other hand, rights of first refusal pertaining to the sale of shares by a shareholder—together with provisions dealing with voting rights pertaining to matters such as representation on the board, shareholder approvals, and control—are commonly housed in shareholder agreements. The danger, though, with a shareholder agreement is that its provisions are subject to challenge because of an alleged default. Therefore, as an alternative, attorneys should borrow a page from the preemptive-rights mandate of New York's corporation law and consider a different home for these shareholder arrangements—not an agreement, but, instead, the company's constitution: its certificate of incorporation.

Placing these provisions in the company's certificate of incorporation eliminates the risk of challenge based on default. Under this solution, the delineation of voting rights and control are handled by different classes of stock. Each class would have its own right to elect members to the board. And matters requiring director and shareholder approval would be determined in accordance with the wishes of the parties—in some cases by class vote at each level, and in other cases, without regard to a class vote.

Both preemptive rights and rights of first refusal pertaining to these shares must respect the sanctity of each class. So, for example:

1. In the case of preemptive rights and rights of first refusal, holders of the shares of the class being offered would have first priority. Only if none of the shareholders of that class exercise options would shareholders of the other class or classes have a right to purchase the offered shares.

2. In the case of rights of first refusal, the corporation as well as the other shareholders would have the right to purchase. Only if the corporation does not or cannot exercise its option[2] would shareholders have the right to purchase the offered shares. And, then, as in item (1) above, only if none of the shareholders of the offered class exercise options would shareholders of the other class or classes have a right to purchase the shares.

3. Shareholders would be required to exercise their options only with respect to *all*—not some—of the offered shares; and if more than one eligible shareholder exercise options, then (a) in the case of shareholders of the offered class, the shares would be allocated among the purchasers in proportion to their respective shareholdings of that class; and (b) in the case of shareholders of other classes exercising their rights to purchase, the offered shares

would be allocated among them in proportion to their respective shareholdings in the company.

As observed at the opening of this article, the option is one of the most—if not the most—important and valuable commercial instruments. Even as an adjunct to another transaction, the option requires careful, diligent attention lest that value be lost in a jungle of litigation.[3]

---

1. N.Y. Business Corporation Law § 622(b)(2) (BCL).

2. A corporation may not purchase its own shares "if the corporation is then insolvent or would thereby be made insolvent." BCL § 513(a).

3. For forms on the types of options treated in this article as well as others, see Chapters 8, 8B and 12 of *Commercial Agreements: A Lawyer's Guide to Drafting and Negotiating,* West 2014.

Peter Siviglia is an attorney in Tarrytown, NY. He is the author of *Commercial Agreements: A Lawyer's Guide to Drafting and Negotiating,* West 2014 (supplemented annually), and *Writing Contracts: A Distinct Discipline,* Carolina Academic Press.

This article originally appeared in the January 2015 *NYSBA Journal.*

Writing Contracts: Suggestions for Law Schools and Young Attorneys

By Peter Siviglia

Preface

My wife, the English teacher, once said, "In this world, Peter, there are two forms of writing: Creative, such as novels, plays and poetry; and Expository such as treatises, letters, memoranda and briefs." This author has tried both, but prefers a third: Contracts, which do not entertain, do not convey information or ideas, and do not try to persuade.

The English teacher now agrees that there are, indeed, three forms of writing. And that the third, Contracts, is a distinct discipline.

Unfortunately, the writing of contracts has been sorely neglected by law schools, perhaps, in part, because teaching writing is a labor-intensive exercise; and perhaps, in part, because a course in this discipline would best be taught by lawyers practicing in the commercial, transactional field. Consequently, the criticisms of this neglect are numerous, and the consequences are significant. For example:

> It should not be surprising to practicing lawyers that new associates come to work without the slightest idea about how to draft a contract....[I]f you assign them a contract to draft, they will freeze like a deer in your headlights.[1]

> * * *

> ....have been shocked by the number of times in litigation that I have asked more senior lawyers—including some fairly good lawyers—to explain the meaning of some provision in a document they prepared and found out they had no idea what it meant. Indeed, I have just finished litigating one such case. The litigation did no one any good and would not have happened but for some sloppy drafting.[2]

> * * *

> Muddied prose can have real costs. In one of the few attempts to calculate the impact, a Harvard Law School study years ago suggested that a quarter of all contract disputes arose because of poor drafting.[3]

The balance of the article from which this last piece is taken goes on to suggest content that could comprise the body of one or more courses on contract writing. It also contains suggestions that young practicing attorneys might find useful.

What Is a Contract?

In the beginning, to write a proper contract, the student must first understand intellectually and then appreciate viscerally what a contract really is. "An agreement between or among two or more persons" provides but a bare hint. Precisely, a contract is simply a set of instructions for a transaction (the purchase of real estate), or for a relationship (a partnership), or for a combination of the two (a partnership to purchase and develop real estate). It is no different from the plans and specifications to build a bridge. And if there is a flaw in those plans or specifications, problems will arise—in the case of a contract, a table set for the litigators, as the letter from Mr. Jenkins and *The Wall Street Journal* article observed.

Contract Formation

Any course or group of courses that teach contract writing must include a study of those laws and principles that bear on contract formation, for a contract is nothing if it is not enforceable. An awareness of these rules is fundamental, lest the draftsman sink piles into sand. A former partner—yes, a partner—closed a secured financing in the erroneous belief that a Uniform Commercial Code financing statement also constituted the security agreement required by the Code.

However, a detailed knowledge of these legal considerations is not necessary. This would be in the nature of a survey—or perhaps, to some extent, a recapitulation of lessons learned in other courses—in order to establish an alertness to those requirements of the law to which the contract must conform in order to assure its enforceability. The course should instill a knowledge of the basics and a sensitivity to know when they are applicable to the job at hand.

"Consideration," the quid pro quo, the basic element in the universe of contracts, is the place to start: What constitutes proper consideration and, perhaps more important, what does not; and what contracts do not require consideration.[4]

Next explore the "Statute of Frauds," beginning, perhaps, with § 2-201 and § 2A-201 of the UCC, and then move on to other statutory provisions such as Titles 7 and 11 of Article 5 and Title 3 of Article 15 in the General Obligations Law, which deal with various requirements bearing on the enforceability of a contract.

Then, make several other stops along the UCC: Articles 2 (Sales) and 2A (Leases), which emphasize the warranty and disclaimer of warranty requirements; Article 3, which focuses on the requirements for negotiable instruments; and Article 9 and its requirements for a proper security agreement. If time allows, make a brief stop at Article 5 (Letters of Credit) and the ICC Uniform Customs and Practice for Documentary Credits and its rules for Standby Credits.

In the discussion of UCC Article 9, emphasize the need to understand each transaction and its collateral before carefully examining the Code to determine what must be done to perfect the security interest. Avoid the details of perfection, for Article 9 of the Uniform Commercial Code rivals the Internal Revenue Code in complexity. It is a conundrum that must be solved transaction by transaction.

Of course, other legal requirements apply to contract formation such as employment law, corporate law, tax considerations, real estate law,… and straight on 'til morning. So students must be made aware that, when they find themselves outside their area of expertise, they must consult with colleagues who have expertise in those areas. For example, a client called one day and said, "We have a problem, Peter. When we bought Fiddley Dee Company [at that time my client was represented by another attorney], we gave the sellers rights to buy shares in Fiddley Dee; and we also gave them the right to sell those shares back to Fiddley Dee simultaneously with the purchase. The sellers have exercised both options, the buy and the put, but it will cripple Fiddley Dee to buy back the shares."

The fact was that Fiddley Dee had lost money for many years, but was now quite profitable. The formula to determine the buy-back price was based on those recent earnings. Fiddley Dee still had an accumulated deficit.

Well, under applicable corporate law, the company could not buy back its shares. It was illegal. The company could only buy its shares from surplus.

The lawyer for the shareholders agreed. However, if he had done his research or asked an expert during the original transaction, he would have focused on the legal requirement that redemptions be made only from surplus, and he might have insisted on a guarantee from the parent company, that is, the buyer of Fiddley Dee; or he might have arranged the put to the parent company rather than to Fiddley Dee. (For those curious of the outcome, the issue was resolved amicably by an alternate, deferred compensation arrangement.)

In Contracts, Know Your Limitations

As Dirty Harry observed in *Magnum Force*: "A man's got to know his limitations." This is important in commercial practice. Law students must be made aware that when working on a transaction in a foreign state or other foreign jurisdiction, counsel in that state or other jurisdiction must be consulted. The transaction involved in *IRB-Brasil Resseguros, S.A. v. Inepar Investments, S.A.*,[5] addressed by the New York Court of Appeals in a 2012 decision, provides an excellent study of this too-often overlooked mandate.

IRB-Brasil Resseguros, S.A. involved a conflict of laws issue to which the court applied § 5-1401 of the General Obligations Law. That section permits parties to a contract involving at least $250,000 to select New York as the governing law. The plaintiff had brought suit to enforce payment under a guarantee issued by a Brazilian guarantor. The guarantee contained a New York choice of law clause. An agency agreement that applied to both the guarantee and the guaranteed debt stated that both "shall be governed by, and construed in accordance with, the laws of the State of New York," without regard to conflict of laws principles.

Under Brazilian law, the guarantee was "void" because it was not authorized by the guarantor's board of directors. New York law does not contain that requirement. Of course, the guarantor argued that Brazilian law governed the guarantee. The plaintiff-beneficiary argued that New York law governed. The Court of Appeals held that "New York substantive law" governed and, accordingly, that the guarantee was enforceable. So, what's the point? That the choice of law clause prevailed? Well, there are at least two other points.

First: Though the plaintiff prevailed, the plaintiff's lawyer could have easily avoided the lawsuit at far less cost to the client by consulting with Brazilian counsel regarding the enforceability of the guarantee and requiring proper authorization by the board. Failure to consult with local counsel could well constitute malpractice.

Second: Assume that the winning plaintiff has to enforce the guarantee in Brazil because that is where the assets of the guarantor reside. Will the Brazilian courts honor the New York ruling or will they find, instead, that enforcing an instrument "void" under Brazilian law is against public policy, and, therefore, deny collection? For example, just reverse the situation:

Section 505 of the New York Business Corporation Law requires, with certain exceptions, that the board of directors of a corporation fix the consideration, terms and conditions of any option to acquire shares of that corporation. Thus, it is the stated policy of New York that an option issued in violation of that requirement is unenforceable. Would the New York courts, then, enforce a foreign judgement declaring enforceable an option on which the board of directors had been required to act and had not acted? That is a risk no attorney should take.

Elements of Basic Contracts

Following their education in the legal considerations in drafting contracts, introduce the students to the considerations involved in certain basic contracts such as a promissory note, a guarantee, security agreements, employment contracts, shareholder arrangements, the sale and purchase of goods, acquisitions, leases, licenses and options.

Boilerplate

The term "boilerplate" refers to clauses commonly and variously included in most contracts. But the use of that term is misleading and dangerous because it carries with it a prejudice that these clauses need little or no scrutiny when added to a contract. Not a clause or a form exists, however, that can or should be added to a contract without critical examination to determine whether any changes are needed; virtually always, changes are needed in order to adapt the provision to fit properly to the deal. Below is a list of some of these clauses.

1.1.1   Termination

1.1.2   Assignment

1.1.3   Governing Law

1.1.4   Arbitration

1.1.5   Notice

1.1.6   Amendment

1.1.7   Waiver

1.1.8   Warranties

1.1.9   Indemnities

1.1.10   Remedies

By way of example, below are a few simple variations on assignment clauses; but, as noted above, any one of these variations is subject to modification based on the particulars of the transaction being addressed.

- Neither party may transfer or assign any of its rights or obligations under this agreement without the written consent of the other, and any transfer or assignment without such consent will be null and void.

- Neither party may transfer or assign any of its rights or obligations under this agreement without the written consent of the other. A merger or consolidation, regardless of which participant therein is the surviving entity, will constitute a transfer. Any transfer or assignment in violation of the requirements of this paragraph will be null and void.

- Neither party may transfer or assign any of its rights or obligations under this agreement without the written consent of the other except that either party may, without the consent of the other, transfer its rights and obligations hereunder to a successor to all or substantially all of its business and assets. Any transfer or assignment in violation of the requirements of this paragraph will be null and void.

- Licensee may not transfer or assign any of its rights under this agreement without Licensor's written consent.

- Licensor may not transfer or assign any of its rights under this agreement without Licensee's written consent except that Licensor may transfer and assign its rights and obligations under this agreement to any transferee of the intellectual property licensed hereunder, and licensor may assign its rights to the royalties under this agreement. Notwithstanding any such permitted transfer or assignment, Licensor will remain liable for its obligations under this agreement.

- Any transfer or assignment in violation of the requirements of this section will be null and void.

Drafting Exercises

Finally, we get to drafting—what this course is all about. And an understanding of the basics discussed above provides the foundation to the writing phase.

Again: A contract is no more than a set of instructions. The prime directive in writing any contract is "accuracy stated as simply as possible." Accuracy, though, must be the controlling feature, for sometimes the concepts are so complex—not due to the lawyer, but due to the deal concocted by the client—that simplicity in the purest sense is not possible.

Because teaching the writing segment of the course is so labor intensive, a procedure that might prove helpful and productive is for two or three students to work together on assignments, especially the longer and more complex ones. Their collaboration should add perspective, which is essential to the drafting process, helping to produce a better product and, more important, helping to develop and improve technique and skills more quickly.

A variation on this approach is to have the teams prepare different assignments which would be presented at different times during the course. Copies of completed assignments would be distributed to the other students for comment during class sessions. The object of this critique is not to attack and defend. The goal is to determine whether the agreement adequately and comfortably houses the transaction and whether the construction work (i.e., the drafting) is sound, and then to decide how best to correct any deficiencies. Guidance by the teacher in these discussions will be essential to focus attention on critical issues and to avoid digressions into minutiae. My wife has sucessfully used a similar technique in her writing classes. She has observed that meaningful comments from peers often carry greater weight with students than those from teachers.

In contracts, there is either good writing or bad writing. And if the writer properly executes the prime directive—that is, accuracy stated as simply as possible—the writing will be good. But if the writer fails to execute the prime directive, that writer will be setting the stage for litigation.

Ethical Considerations

Even the discipline of contract preparation engenders ethical considerations.

One of these is the mandate that the draftsman prepare a fair agreement. The reasons are simple:

- a one-sided contract—especially when the bargaining positions are relatively equal—will invariably be negotiated back to the middle;

- an even-handed contract will result in minimal, non-confrontational negotiation and a quick conclusion of the deal;

- an even-handed contract, raising few issues, will result in less cost to the client in terms of legal fees.

That's right, lower legal costs. And yes, that's good; and it's also right. The lawyer is a fiduciary and, as a fiduciary, the lawyer owes a duty to the client to keep those legal fees on a diet. Those lawyers with high IQs ("I" for Integrity and "Q" for Quality of Performance) will not have to panhandle for lunch. The Clint Eastwood character in the movie *In the Line of Fire*, a Secret Service agent assigned to protect the President, teaches us this lesson: The client comes first.

A second ethical principle is, There is no shame in helping the other guy. Commercial transactions should not be adversarial proceedings. The goal is not to win; the goal is to create. The goal is to do a deal that conforms to the intent of the parties. Thus, while attorneys must at all times represent the interests of their clients, attorneys must not seek to gain an advantage contrary to the terms of the deal because of a mistake by the other lawyer. An obvious example—and surely one that begs correction—is the inadvertent omission of a word: "The Company will pay the following expenses…" vs. "The Company will not pay the following expenses…" Do unto the other lawyer as you would have that lawyer do unto you.

In the context of a commercial transaction, I doubt there is a better application of the Golden Rule than this: correct the drafting errors of the other attorney. In fact, because the object of a contract is to reflect accurately the intent of all parties, this principle is the ethical equivalent of the "given" in geometry. Allowing errors that one detects to remain uncorrected serves a perverse desire to gain an improper advantage and opens the door to possible litigation. The client is ill-represented by that type of practice.

A Final Thought

Ezra Pound once observed that the English language is the best language in which to write.

Though we, here, may have the best verbal means of communication on the planet, that facility is of little benefit unless we writers have the ability to apply it properly. Between expository writing, like this article, and a contract, the objective is the same: "accuracy stated as simply as possible." To achieve that objective, the writer must have a command of the language. While the responsibility for teaching students a command of the language should not be the job of the law school—it is the responsibility of the primary and secondary schools and, to a lesser extent, the responsibility of the colleges—if those formative institutions did not succeed, law schools and the other institutions of higher learning must.

---

1. Lewis, *Turning the Firm into a School*, Business L. Today, Vol. 15, No. 3 (Jan./Feb. 2006) (American Bar Association). Mr. Lewis is a law school teacher.

2. Letter from Stephen E. Jenkins to the author, September 13, 1993. Mr. Jenkins is a trial lawyer with Ashby & Geddes in Wilmington, Delaware.

3. Richard B. Schmitt, Lawyers and Clients, *Law Schools, Firms Sending a Message: Polish Your Prose*, Wall St. J., Aug. 28, 1995, p. B3.

4. *See, e.g.*, N.Y. Uniform Commercial Code, § 2-205 (UCC); N.Y. General Obligations Law, §§ 5-1101–1115.

5. 20 N.Y.3d 310 (2012).

Peter Siviglia is an attorney in Tarrytown, NY. He is the author of *Commercial Agreements: A Lawyer's Guide to Drafting and Negotiating*, West 2014 (supplemented annually), and *Writing Contracts: A Distinct Discipline*, Carolina Academic Press.

This article originally appeared in the January 2015 *NYSBA Journal*.

PATHWAY TO THE PROFESSION: FROM LAW SCHOOL TO LAWYER

EVIDENCE

Burden of Proof
Sweat the Small Stuff
By David Paul Horowitz

Introduction

I like to think of myself as a "big picture" kind of guy, never lost in the trees, always able to see the forest. I also like to think of myself as highly evolved, aided in this evolution by heavy doses of self-help palaver. A personal favorite: "Don't sweat the small stuff."

While this combination of qualities helps make me a thoughtful, easygoing fellow (just ask my sons), the combination can have dangerous repercussions in my professional life. Danger lurks behind many of those trees, and the small stuff can be deadly. Reading the Court of Appeals decision in *Galetta v. Galetta*,[1] it is clear that the lawyer's touchstone should be: "Sweat the small stuff."

In *Galetta*, a prospective bride and groom executed a prenuptial agreement shortly before their wedding. Each signed the agreement, and each signature was notarized. In the litigation that ensued after the husband filed for divorce, the wife sought to set aside the prenuptial agreement. It was undisputed that both parties' signatures on the document were authentic, and that the agreement, prepared by the husband's attorney (the wife elected not to be represented by counsel), was not procured by fraud or duress.[2] What possible basis could there be for setting the agreement aside?

Oops!

While the signatures on the prenuptial agreement were on a single page, the parties had executed the agreement at different times, before different notaries, and neither was present when the other executed the document.[3] Up to this point, the execution was not subject to attack. The Court of Appeals zeroed in on the certificates of acknowledgement that accompanied each signature:

> The certificates appear to have been typed at the same time, with spaces left blank for dates and signatures that were to be filled in by hand. The certificate of acknowledgment relating to [the wife's] signature contains the boilerplate language typical of the time. However, in the acknowledgment relating to [the husband's] signature, a key phrase was omitted and, as a result, the certificate fails to indicate that the notary public confirmed the identity of the person executing the document or that the person was the individual described in the document.

The record does not reveal how this error occurred and apparently no one noticed the omission until the issue was raised in this litigation.[4]

Domestic Relations Law § 236(B)(3)[5] (DRL) requires that prenuptial agreements be executed with the same formality as a recorded deed,[6] and the certificate of acknowledgment accompanying the husband's signature did not comply with the requirements of the Real Property Law (RPL).[7] It was upon this error that the wife sought a declaration that the agreement was unenforceable.

The husband argued that the agreement was enforceable because "the acknowledgment substantially complied with the Real Property Law":[8]

> [The husband] submitted an affidavit from the notary public who had witnessed his signature in 1997 and executed the certificate of acknowledgment. The notary, an employee of a local bank where the husband then did business, averred that it was his custom and practice, prior to acknowledging a signature, to confirm the identity of the signer and assure that the signer was the person named in the document. He stated in the affidavit that he presumed he had followed that practice before acknowledging the husband's signature.[9]

The trial court denied the wife's motion for summary judgment, finding that the "acknowledgment of the husband's signature substantially complied with the requirements of the Real Property Law."[10] On appeal, three justices of the Fourth Department affirmed, but upon a different rationale, holding "that the certificate of acknowledgment was defective but…that the deficiency could be cured after the fact and that the notary public affidavit raised a triable question of fact as to whether the prenuptial agreement had been properly acknowledged when it was signed in 1997."[11]

The two dissenters, believing first that the husband's argument was unpreserved, would have granted summary judgment to the wife, "declaring the prenuptial agreement to be invalid because the acknowledgment was fatally defective."[12]

No Cure From the Court of Appeals

A unanimous Court of Appeals[13] reversed, determining that the wife "was entitled to summary judgment declaring the prenuptial agreement to be unenforceable."[14] The Court first examined the language of DRL § 236(B)(3) and reviewed its 1997 decision in *Matisoff v. Dobi*,[15] where the Court held that an unacknowledged prenuptial agreement was invalid.

The Court next examined the acknowledgement procedure set forth in RPL § 291, the procedure DRL § 236(B)(3) requires for proper execution:

> Real Property Law § 291, governing the recording of deeds, states that "[a] conveyance of real property…on being duly acknowledged by the person executing the same, or proved as required by this chapter,…may be recorded in the office of the clerk of the county where such real property is situated." Thus, a deed may be recorded if it is either "duly acknowledged" or "proved" by use of a subscribing witness. Because this case involves an attempt to use the acknowledgment procedure, we focus on that methodology.

The Court explained that the acknowledgment procedure achieves two goals. First, to prove the identity of the person whose name and signature appears on the document and, second, "[to impose] on the signer a measure of deliberation in the act of executing the document."[16]

The Court turned to the specific issues at bar, to wit, "whether the certificate of acknowledgment accompanying defendant husband's signature was defective"[17] and, if the certificate was defective, "whether such a deficiency can be cured and, if so, whether the affidavit of the notary public prepared in the course of litigation was sufficient to raise a question of fact precluding summary judgment in the wife's favor."[18]

The Court noted that three provisions of the RPL "must be read together to discern the requisites of a proper acknowledgment,"[19] that is §§ 292, 303, and 306, and discussed the prevailing practice in 1997, when the document was executed, for certificates of acknowledgement:

> At the time the parties here signed the prenuptial agreement in 1997, proper certificates of acknowledgment typically contained boilerplate language substantially the same as that included in the certificate accompanying the wife's signature: "before me came (name of signer) to me known and known to me to be the person described in and who executed the foregoing instrument and duly acknowledged to me that s/he executed the same." The "to me known and known to me to be the person described in the document" phrase satisfied the requirement that the official indicate that he or she knew or had ascertained that the signer was the person described in the document. The clause beginning with the words "and duly acknowledged…" established that the signer had made the requisite oral declaration.[20]

This language was omitted in the certificate accompanying the husband's signature:

In the certificate of acknowledgment relating to the
husband's signature, the "to me known and known to
me" phrase was inexplicably omitted, leaving only the
following statement: "On the 8 [sic] day of July, 1997,
before me came Gary Galetta described in and who executed the foregoing instrument and duly acknowledged
to me that he executed the same." Absent the omitted
language, the certificate does not indicate either that
the notary public knew the husband or had ascertained
through some form of proof that he was the person described in the prenuptial agreement.[21]

Determining that the acknowledgement did not conform to the statutory requirements, the Court next considered whether the defect could
be cured, and whether the notary public's affidavit submitted to the trial
court created a question of fact precluding summary judgment.[22] The
Court distinguished *Galetta* from *Matisoff*, the earlier case where there
was no acknowledgement,[23] because in *Galetta* "there was an attempt
to secure an acknowledged document but there was an omission in the
requisite language of the certificate of acknowledgment."[24] The Court
acknowledged that

[a] compelling argument can be made that the door
should be left open to curing a deficiency like the one
that occurred here where the signatures on the prenuptial agreement are authentic, there are no claims of fraud
or duress, and the parties believed their signatures were
being duly acknowledged but, due to no fault of their
own, the certificate of acknowledgment was defective or
incomplete. Although neither party submitted evidence
concerning how the error occurred, we can infer from
the fact that the signatures and certificates of acknowledgment are contained on a single page of the document
in the same typeface that the certificates were typed or
printed by the same person at the same time. Since one
acknowledgment included all the requisite language
and the other did not, it seems likely that the omission
resulted from a typographical error. Thus, the deficiency
may not have arisen from the failure of the notary public
to engage in the formalities required when witnessing
and acknowledging a signature. To the contrary, it may
well be that the prerequisites of an acknowledgment
occurred but the certificate simply failed to reflect that
fact. Thus, the husband makes a strong case for a rule
permitting evidence to be submitted after the fact to cure
a defect in a certificate of acknowledgment when that
evidence consists of proof that the acknowledgment was
properly made in the first instance—that at the time the

document was signed the notary or other official did everything he or she was supposed to do, other than include the proper language in the certificate. By considering this type of evidence, courts would not be allowing a new acknowledgment to occur for a signature that was not properly acknowledged in the first instance; instead, parties who properly signed and acknowledged the document years before would merely be permitted to conform the certificate to reflect that fact.[25]

Unfortunately for the husband, the Court never arrived at considering whether a cure was possible.

[S]imilar to what occurred in *Matisoff*, the proof submitted here was insufficient. In his affidavit, the notary public did not state that he actually recalled having acknowledged the husband's signature, nor did he indicate that he knew the husband prior to acknowledging his signature. The notary averred only that he recognized his own signature on the certificate and that he had been employed at a particular bank at that time (corroborating the husband's statement concerning the circumstances under which he executed the document). As for the procedures followed, the notary had no independent recollection but maintained that it was his custom and practice "to ask and confirm that the person signing the document was the same person named in the document" and he was "confident" he had done so when witnessing the husband's signature.[26]

The Court concluded:

[E]ven assuming a defect in a certificate of acknowledgment could be cured under Domestic Relations Law § 236(B)(3), defendant's submission was insufficient to raise a triable question of fact as to the propriety of the original acknowledgment procedure. Plaintiff was therefore entitled to summary judgment declaring that the prenuptial agreement was unenforceable.[27]

"Be Afraid, Be Very Afraid"

For the small subset of practitioners engaged in the practice of drafting prenuptial agreements and overseeing their execution, the implications of *Galetta* are clear.

Does *Galetta* have any lessons for the rest of us?

Certainly, affidavits are a part of every litigator's (and many a non-litigator's) professional life. They are, I suspect, the most common litigation document, and their ubiquity means they rarely rate a second thought.

Affidavits must be in admissible form, and that requires proper execution. An attorney who routinely spends hours agonizing over the text of a 10-line affidavit often will not even glance at what appears above or below the body of the affidavit.[28] If familiarity breeds contempt, contempt can breed mistakes, sometimes fatal.

Accordingly, practitioners should heed *Galetta's* strict application of the rules governing execution of documents in all situations, not just those involving DRL § 236(B)(3). For example, CPLR 2309(c) requires that an affidavit that is executed outside New York State be accompanied by a Certificate of Conformity:

> § 2309. Oaths and affirmations
>
> (c) Oaths and affirmations taken without the state. An oath or affirmation taken without the state shall be treated as if taken within the state if it is accompanied by such certificate or certificates as would be required to entitle a deed acknowledged without the state to be recorded within the state if such deed had been acknowledged before the officer who administered the oath or affirmation.

A number of courts have held that the absence of a certificate of conformity, absent effort to remedy the defect, is a fatal defect.[29] However, most courts that have considered the issue have held the absence of a certificate of conformity is not a fatal defect, but a "mere irregularity" subject to the generous standard of relief set forth in CPLR 2001.

In a recent decision (noting the agreement of the First and Third Departments), the Second Department, in *Fredette v. Town of Southampton*,[30] held that a trial court

> improvidently exercised its discretion in excluding from consideration the affidavits of Ken Glaser and Kris Kubly on the ground that the affidavits, while notarized, were not accompanied by a certificate of conformity required by CPLR 2309(c). This Court has previously held that the absence of a certificate of conformity for an out-of-state affidavit is not a fatal defect, a view shared by the Appellate Division, First and Third Departments as well.[31]

Whether the rule from this line of cases survives *Galetta* is a question, to paraphrase Professor David Siegel, better left to be determined in someone else's case.

Conclusion

On the one hand, *Galetta* can be regarded as a paean to form over substance. After all, the husband and wife both signed the prenuptial agreement, before notaries, and there was no fraud or duress. While the notary acknowledging the husband's signature may not have ascertained the husband's identity before witnessing his signature, it was, in fact, the husband's name and signature that were endorsed on the agreement. As for the goal of imposing "on the signer a measure of deliberation in the act of executing the document," that requisite language was present in the acknowledgment for the husband's signature, and there was no proof that any error on the part of the notary detracted from the husband's "deliberation" in executing the agreement.

On the other hand, the procedures set forth in RPL § 291 have a purpose and reflect societal goals. Unlike *Galetta*, there are many cases where parties executing a document are not available, or able, to offer testimony concerning the circumstances surrounding the execution of a document when a dispute later arises. And, let's not forget that the Court left open the possibility that a defect in a certificate of acknowledgement could be cured upon a proper evidentiary showing.

Regardless of how you view the *Galetta* decision, the Court's message is clear: "Sweat the small stuff."

---

1. *Galetta v. Galetta*, 2013 N.Y. Slip Op. 03871 (2013).

2. No issue as to capacity of either party was raised.

3. *Galetta*, 2013 N.Y. Slip Op. 03871.

4. *Id.* at *2.

5. DRL § 236(B)(3) provides, in pertinent part:

    Agreement of the parties. An agreement by the parties, made before or during the marriage, shall be valid and enforceable in a matrimonial action if such agreement is in writing, subscribed by the parties, and acknowledged or proven in the manner required to entitle a deed to be recorded.

6. *Galetta*, 2013 N.Y. Slip Op. 03871.

7. *Id.*

8. *Id.*

9. *Id.* at *2.

10. *Id.*

11. *Id.* at *3

12. *Id.*

13. Judge Abdus-Salaam took no part in the case.

14. *Galetta*, 2013 N.Y. Slip Op. 2831.

15. 90 N.Y.2d 127 (1997).

16. *Galetta*, 2013 N.Y. Slip Op. 2831.

17. *Id.*

18. *Id.*

19. *Id.* at *4.

20. *Id.* at *4–5 (footnote omitted).

21. *Id.* at *5.

22. *Id.* The Court rejected the wife's argument that the issue was not preserved.

23. The Court explained: "When there is no acknowledgment at all, it is evident that one of the purposes of the acknowledgment requirement—to impose a measure of deliberation and impress upon the signer the significance of the document—has not been fulfilled. Thus, a rule precluding a party from attempting to cure the absence of an acknowledgment through subsequent submissions appears to be sound." *Id.* at *8.

24. *Id.*

25. *Id.* at *8.

26. *Id.* The Court discussed in detail the deficiencies in proof, and how those defects might have been overcome.

27. *Id.* at *9.

28. An earlier *Burden of Proof* column, *We All Do It*, N.Y. St. B.J. (Mar./Apr. 2010), p. 20, addressed an item appearing above the body of the affidavit.

29. *PRA III v. Gonzalez*, 54 A.D.3d 917 (2d Dep't 2008) (Summary judgment for plaintiff was reversed where, inter alia, the affidavits in support of the motion did not have certificates of conformity: "We further note that the affidavits provided by the plaintiff were both signed and notarized outside of the State of New York, and were not accompanied by the required certificates of conformity, and the plaintiff made no attempt to rectify this defect" (citation omitted)).

30. 95 A.D.3d 940 (2d Dep't 2012).

31. *Id.* (citations omitted).

David Paul Horowitz (david@newyorkpractice.org) has represented plaintiffs in personal injury cases for over 24 years and is "of counsel" to Ressler & Ressler in New York City. He is the author of *New York Civil Disclosure* and *Bender's New York Evidence* (both by LexisNexis), as well as the 2008 and 2012 Supplements to *Fisch on New York Evidence* (Lond Publications). Mr. Horowitz teaches New York Practice, Professional Responsibility and Electronic Evidence & Disclosure at Brooklyn Law School. He serves on the Office of Court Administration's CPLR Advisory Committee, as Associate Reporter to the New York Pattern Jury Instruction (P.J.I.) Committee, and is a frequent lecturer and writer on these subjects.

This article originally appeared in the July/August 2013 *NYSBA Journal*.

Burden of Proof
"You Gotta Have Faith"
By David Paul Horowitz

Specifically, "good faith." In litigation, the concept of possessing a "good faith basis" for, *inter alia*, commencing an action, seeking disclosure, and posing questions to a witness, is an essential, albeit often neglected, requirement. In two recent decisions, trial court judges have reminded the particular attorneys appearing before them, as well as the bar as a whole, of this fundamental foundation requirement.

Before reviewing these and other cases, an examination of a "good faith basis" familiar to most litigators, contained in Uniform Rule 202.7, provides a useful backdrop for the requirement in other situations.

Uniform Rule 202.7

Uniform Rule 202.7 of the Uniform Rules for the New York State Trial Courts, which has several procedural rules regarding motions, contains a good faith requirement

> with respect to a motion relating to disclosure or to a bill of particulars, an affirmation that counsel has conferred with counsel for the opposing party in a good faith effort to resolve the issues raised by the motion.[1]

The First Department has held that a motion relating to disclosure must contain an affidavit of good faith, and that the failure to furnish such an affidavit requires denial of the motion.[2] The same rule, of course, applies to motions directed to bills of particulars, inasmuch as 22 N.Y.C.R.R. § 202.7(c)'s requirement of a good faith affidavit applies to motions seeking bills of particulars and to motions seeking disclosure.

The failure to confer with counsel cannot constitute good faith and requires denial of the motion:

> Furthermore, the court did not err in summarily denying the appellant's motion to strike the complaint since counsel for the appellant failed to confer with counsel for the plaintiffs in a good faith effort to resolve the issues raised by the motion.[3]

Similarly, the failure to set forth the good faith efforts requires denial of the motion:

> The affirmation submitted by the plaintiff's attorney was deficient in that it did not set forth any good faith effort to resolve the issue of the defendants' failure to appear for examinations before trial.[4]

An early trial-level decision, *Eaton v. Chahal*,[5] held "a 'good faith' effort to mean more than an exchange of computer generated letters or cursory telephone conversations."[6] *Eaton* has been cited by the First,[7] Second,[8] and Third[9] Departments. Denial of a motion for disclosure was required where the trial court improperly considered an affirmation of good faith "since it failed to discuss the notice for discovery and inspection which was the subject of the plaintiff's motion to compel."[10]

Of course, when drafting an affirmation of good faith, counsel must bear in mind one of the mandates of Rule 130-1.1(c)(3), which defines "frivolous conduct" to include asserting "material factual statements that are false."[11]

Pleadings

In *Palmieri v. The Piano Exchange, Inc.*,[12] the plaintiff's counsel moved for a sanction pursuant to CPLR 3126, based upon the defendant's failure to appear for examination before trial. The court's decision must have come as a bit of a surprise to the plaintiff's counsel. The court first summarized the transaction at issue and the plaintiff's claims in the complaint:

> Palmieri purchased a rebuilt and refinished piano for the sum of Nine Thousand Dollars ($9,000.00).
>
> * * *
>
> In connection with this transaction of March 1996, involving Nine Thousand Dollars ($9,000.00) in exchange for a piano, on or about March 21, 2011, Plaintiff filed a Verified Complaint alleging a breach of contract seeking damages in the sum Two Hundred Fifty Thousand Dollars ($250,000.00); alleging deceit claiming damages of Five Hundred Thousand Dollars ($500,000.00); alleging breach of the covenant of good faith and fair dealing and seeking damages of Three Hundred and Fifty Thousand Dollars ($350,000.00); alleging tortious interference with a contract seeking damages of One Hundred and Fifty Thousand Dollars ($150,000.00) and lastly, alleging unjust enrichment seeking Nine Thousand Dollars ($9,000.00). In short, Plaintiff alleges One Million Two Hundred Fifty Nine Thousand Dollars ($1,259.000.00) as damages stemming from a contract made seventeen (17) years ago involving a used piano in exchange for Nine Thousand Dollars ($9,000.00).[13]

After citing Rule 130-1.1, the court both posed and answered two questions:

Is it a reasonable application of the privilege to practice law to serve a complaint upon a person, in these circumstances, and stun the recipient-defendant with damage claims beyond the universe of those which logically follow the alleged breach? The Court thinks not...

Does the administration of Justice include a responsibility to shield litigants from conduct that may cause stress, anxiety and fear of pecuniary ruination far beyond the bounds of reasonable foreseeability? The Court thinks it does.[14]

The court then made the following direction concerning the plaintiff's pleading:

The Court is mindful of CPLR §3017(a) which includes that a complaint, "shall contain a demand for the relief to which the pleader deems himself entitled." As the above captioned matter will appear on the court's compliance calendar on March 27, 2013, the Court expects Plaintiff's counsel to articulate some good faith basis supporting prayers for relief in excess of One Million Two Hundred Fifty Nine Thousand Dollars ($1,259,000.00) (not including a prayer for relief seeking punitive damages) in an action involving the sale of a used piano some seventeen years ago at a cost of Nine Thousand Dollars ($9,000.00). *Additionally, counsel shall offer argument as to why such conduct, in the absence of good faith, is not sanctionable.*[15]

And, what about the defendant's examinations before trial? The court denied the plaintiff's motion pursuant to CPLR 3126, provided the defendant appeared for the examination on or before a date set by the court in its order.[16]

Disclosure

In *Fawcett v. Altieri*,[17] defense counsel moved to compel the disclosure of social media matter posted by the plaintiff. After an overview of this hot-button topic, the court zeroed in on the foundation requirement for obtaining non-public social media matter protected by an individual's privacy setting:

In order to obtain a closed or private social media account by a court order for the subscriber to execute an authorization for their release, the adversary must show with some credible facts that the adversary subscriber has posted information or photographs that are relevant to the facts of the case at hand. The courts should not accommodate blanket searches for any kind of information or photos to impeach a person's character, which may be embarrassing, but are irrelevant to the facts of the case at hand.

> *The party requesting the discovery of an adversary's restricted*
> *social media accounts should first demonstrate a good faith*
> *basis to make the request.*[18]

The requirement that a foundation be established in order to obtain non-public social media matter has received uniform appellate approval.[19]

Questioning a Witness

Although no recent decision stands out for the proposition, a long line of cases make clear that counsel must have a good faith basis for posing a question to a witness. A leading Court of Appeals case, *People v. Kass*,[20] confronted the requirement where a prosecutor sought to question the defendant about a prior act of misappropriation:

> Defendant argues that the Trial Judge improperly permitted the prosecutor to ask defendant if he had "misappropriated two diamonds worth about $4,000 from a jeweler in New York City?" It is well established that a defendant who testifies may be cross-examined concerning any immoral, vicious, or criminal acts which have a bearing on his credibility as a witness. "The offenses inquired into on cross-examination to impeach credibility need not be similar to the crime charged, and questions are not rendered improper * * * *provided they have some basis in fact and are asked in good faith.*" Here, the inquiry into defendant's misappropriation of the diamonds is relevant to his credibility as a witness. *The question was proper, therefore, if made by the prosecutor in good faith and had some basis in fact.*[21]

People v. Kass applies in civil cases. In *McNeill v. LaSalle Partners*,[22] the trial court properly permitted defense counsel to question the plaintiff in a personal injury case, where the plaintiff was the only witness to the accident, concerning the reason the plaintiff had been terminated from a prior job:

> Such dishonest conduct (assuming plaintiff engaged in it) plainly falls within the category of prior immoral, vicious or criminal acts having a direct bearing on the witness's credibility, inasmuch as "it demonstrates an untruthful bent or significantly reveals a willingness or disposition…voluntarily to place the advancement of his individual self-interest ahead of principle or of the interests of society." Moreover, appellants sought to question plaintiff about this matter in good faith, and with a reasonable basis in fact.[23]

Conclusion

A good faith basis is a necessary foundation requirement, and counsel must be prepared to explain the good faith basis if put to the task. So, before drafting a pleading, serving a disclosure request, or posing a question to a witness, "you gotta have faith."

1.   22 N.Y.C.R.R. § 202.7(a)(2).

2.   *Molyneaux v. City of N.Y.*, 64 A.D.3d 406, 406–407 (1st Dep't 2009).

3.   *Gonzalez v. I.B.M.*, 236 A.D.2d 363 (1st Dep't 1997) (citations omitted).

4.   *Tine v. Courtview Owners Court*, 40 A.D.3d 966 (1st Dep't 2007).

5.   *Eaton v. Chahal*, 146 Misc. 2d 977 (Sup. Ct., Rensselaer Co. 1990).

6.   *Id.* at 983.

7.   *Barber v. Ford Motor Co.*, 250 A.D.2d 552 (1st Dep't 1998).

8.   *Romero v. Korn*, 236 A.D.2d 65 (2d Dep't 1997).

9.   *Koelbl v. Harvey*, 176 A.D.2d 1040 (3d Dep't 1991).

10.   *Barnes v. NYNEX, Inc.*, 274 A.D.2d 368 (1st Dep't 2000).

11.   22 N.Y.C.R.R. § 130-1.1(c)(3).

12.   N.Y.L.J., Mar. 12, 2013 (Sup. Ct. Suffolk Co.) (Jerry Garguilo, J.S.C.).

13.   *Id.*

14.   *Id.*

15.   *Id.* (emphasis added).

16.   *Id.*

17.   38 Misc. 3d 1022 (Sup. Ct., Richmond Co. 2013) (Joseph J. Maltese, J.S.C.).

18.   *Id.* at 1027–28 (emphasis added).

19.   *See, e.g., Tapp v. N.Y. State Urban Dev. Corp.*, 102 A.D.3d 620 (1st Dep't 2013); *Abrams v. Pecile*, 83 A.D.3d 527 (1st Dep't 2011); *McCann v. Harleysville Ins. Co. of N.Y.*, 78 A.D.3d 1524 (4th Dep't 2010).

20.   25 N.Y.2d 123 (1969).

21.   *Id.* at 125–26 (citation omitted; emphasis added).

22.   52 A.D.3d 407 (1st Dep't 2008).

23.   *Id.* (citations and parenthetical omitted).

DAVID PAUL HOROWITZ (david@newyorkpractice.org) has represented plaintiffs in personal injury cases for over 25 years and is of counsel to Ressler & Ressler in New York City. He is the author of New York Civil Disclosure and Bender's New York Evidence (both by LexisNexis), as well as the 2008 and 2013 Supplements (to be issued June 2013) to Fisch on New York Evidence (Lond Publications). Mr. Horowitz teaches New York Practice at Columbia Law School, and Professional Responsibility and Electronic Evidence & Disclosure at Brooklyn Law School. In addition to presenting NYSBA's Annual CPLR Update Program statewide, he serves on the Office of Court Administration's CPLR Advisory Committee, as Associate Reporter to the New York Pattern Jury Instruction (P.J.I.) Committee, and is a frequent lecturer and writer on these subjects.

This article originally appeared in the June 2013 *NYSBA Journal*.

The Duty to Preserve and the Risks of Spoliation
How Organizations Can Preemptively Limit the Costs of Electronic Discovery
By Jamie Weissglass and Rossana Parrotta

Introduction

The best defense against spoliation sanctions is preserving evidence. However, in the era of Big Data, organizations often face a Goldilocks dilemma: preserve too much electronically stored information (ESI) and discovery becomes unwieldy and expensive; preserve too little and face sanctions, which can range from shifting the costs of discovery to adverse inference instructions to dismissal.[1] Moreover, the more data an organization has, the more difficult it is to find needed information; delays in response can lead to noncompliance with court and government agency rules and result in penalties. Consequently, saving everything is risky and not economically feasible. On the other hand, it is clear that failing to retain the right information is equally, if not more, risky. Fortunately, there is a solution that is "just right": developing an information governance and management program that provides for routine, defensible destruction of data pursuant to well-researched and documented retention schedules. Under Rule 37(e) of the Federal Rules of Civil Procedure, federal courts cannot impose sanctions for data lost "as a result of the routine, good-faith operation of an electronic information system." In other words, routine, automatic deletions of electronic records that have met their retention requirements and are not subject to a duty to preserve should not be penalized. The best defense against discovery sanctions, therefore, starts with comprehensive information governance and litigation readiness programs that begin well before litigation is on the horizon.

Litigation Readiness

Litigation readiness begins with an organization focusing on managing information responsibly. The core of this responsibility is consistently following an information governance and management program that addresses the entire life cycle of information, from creation or receipt to disposition.

Establish a Litigation Readiness Team

First, the organization should establish a team to create and oversee its litigation readiness program. In implementing the program, the team will be responsible for working with the records and information management group (RIM) to confirm that there is a defensible records retention policy, establishing procedures relating to preservation of information when there is a duty to preserve, creating and monitoring litigation holds to ensure preservation, and training employees on the program. The team should consist of representatives from the Legal, RIM, IT, and Compliance departments, as well as representation from the business units. The team may also include outside partners, such as e-discovery specialists and third-party vendors that the organization will rely upon in the event of litigation.

Assess the Information Landscape

The next task is to identify likely locations of information typically sought in litigation. Many organizations find it helpful to create a data map that memorializes the locations and types of the organization's most commonly requested forms of ESI. In creating the map, the team should not overlook legacy data or emerging forms of information, such as voicemail, social media, and text messages. It should also account for any data stored in the Cloud or on mobile devices. If the team cannot determine what is stored in a particular repository, sometimes sampling or cataloging the data may be of some help. As important as creating the data map is maintaining it in what is a very dynamic and constantly changing information management landscape. Data maps can quickly become stale without this vigilance.

Create a Defensible Disposal Program

The organization's information governance program should define records retention periods and provide for routine destruction of records, including ESI, whose retention requirements have expired and are not subject to a preservation hold order. The records and information management team typically develops the retention schedule by working with the business unit representatives to identify their information and related systems, as well as the business needs for the records—their purposes and useful life. The records and information management team will then conduct the legal research into the applicable recordkeeping regulations, validated and approved by the team's legal experts. The legal and operational needs for the records are then used to determine the appropriate retention period, and the sensitivity classification of the information determines the method of disposal. It is particularly important to work with IT to understand the disposal of ESI, because often those processes can be automatic. (For example, many organizations have systems that automatically delete emails after a certain period.)

A key procedure to develop is one that addresses records and information of departing employees to ensure responsibilities for on-going retention are defined, and to ensure information is available and accessible. Otherwise, the information may be lost. For example, data can be lost if the former employee's computer is wiped and given to another employee, if a mailbox or the Exchange server is shut down, or if a file share that belonged to the former employee is deleted.

Note that the information governance program and records retention policy is regarded as "best practice" and is not something to institute in anticipation of litigation. Instituting a program or changing its rules after learning of a potential dispute may give rise to an inference that the party enacted its policy to facilitate the destruction of evidence.[2]

Determine When the Duty to Preserve May Be Triggered

Once the information governance program is in place, it can be helpful for the team to anticipate scenarios when the duty to preserve will be triggered. Pre-planning can mitigate the risk of *ad hoc* decisions that could prove inefficient and inconsistent.

Unfortunately, there is no bright-line test to determine when the duty is triggered. Under New York federal and state law, the duty to preserve arises when litigation is "reasonably anticipated."[3] Obviously, initiating litigation, retaining counsel or receiving a complaint, subpoena, or notice of government inquiry puts a party on notice. But New York courts have established that the duty to preserve can arise well before a party receives notice of a claim.[4] Consider the following common, thought-provoking scenarios.

Does a triggering dispute exist? The "mere existence of a dispute between two parties does not necessarily mean that a party should reasonably have anticipated litigation and taken steps to preserve evidence."[5] Some courts have excused parties from the duty to preserve where they show that claims similar to those in the lawsuit usually do not lead to litigation;[6] other courts disagree.[7]

Who knows about the dispute? Key personnel must be aware that litigation is likely.[8] If only a few employees in a firm or municipality are aware that litigation may be imminent, it will not necessarily trigger the duty. However, if a lawyer receives notice, a higher standard may apply: in one case, receiving a letter terminating an attorney's representation "for some reasons not yet fully defined" established the duty.[9]

Is litigation foreseeable for other purposes? At least one court has found that designating documents as protected work product prepared "in anticipation of litigation" triggers the duty to preserve.[10] The court ruled that if "litigation was reasonably foreseeable for one purpose...it was reasonably foreseeable for all purposes."[11]

What is the regulatory environment? New York courts have found regulations requiring the retention of records sufficient to warn an organization to preserve documents, even if litigation involving those records is not reasonably foreseeable.[12] Similarly, a duty to preserve can arise as early as the inception of a relationship between regulated parties.[13] For example, one court relied on the rules of professional responsibility and ethics opinions in finding the obligation to preserve documents arose when lawyers began to represent a party.[14]

When does the duty end? At some point, the duty to preserve will end and organizations can resume programmatic destruction. Settlement talks do not "vitiate the duty to preserve"; such a standard "ignores the practical reality that parties often engage in settlement discussions before and during litigation....[A contrary] argument would allow parties to freely shred documents and purge e-mails, simply by faking a willingness to engage in settlement negotiations."[15]

Given the range of circumstances that can create reasonable anticipation, when in doubt, parties should err on the side of presuming the duty exists.

Determine the Scope of the Litigation Hold

Once the duty to preserve is triggered, the next step is to figure out what data to save. A party must preserve "what it knows, or reasonably should know, is relevant in the action, is reasonably calculated to lead to the discovery of admissible evidence, is reasonably likely to be requested during discovery, and/or is the subject of a pending discovery request."[16] This does not mean parties must preserve "every shred of paper, every e-mail or electronic document, and every backup tape."[17] Instead, they must preserve ESI that is relevant and unique; it is unnecessary to retain multiple copies.

The NYSBA's E-Discovery Committee suggests using the following criteria to determine what to preserve: "the facts upon which the triggering event is based and the subject matter of the triggering event; whether the ESI is relevant to that event; the expense and burden incurred in preserving the ESI; and whether the loss of the ESI would be prejudicial to an opposing party."[18]

Some courts outside New York have directed parties to *The Sedona Conference Commentary on Proportionality*, which suggests weighing the burden of preservation against the data's potential value and uniqueness, in setting the scope.[19] Some federal courts also tend toward considerations of proportionality, and a proposed amendment to Fed. R. Civ. P. 26(b) would limit the scope of discovery to information "proportional to the needs of the case." However, New York courts have not been receptive to this concept. One judge explained that the proportionality "standard may prove too amorphous to provide much comfort to a party deciding what files it may delete or backup tapes it may recycle."[20]

As with other aspects of preservation, a conservative approach is best. In consultation with key stakeholders counsel can identify issues likely to arise; they can then pinpoint the types of documents likely to be relevant and the probable key custodians. Before deeming ESI inaccessible because of undue burden, counsel should consider whether the data is available elsewhere; if it is not, courts can override considerations of undue burden where the "requesting party shows good cause."[21]

One of the best ways to limit the scope of preservation and manage costs is to reach an agreement with opposing counsel regarding the scope of discovery. For example, agreement can be reached on issues such as the identity of key custodians, types of information sought, etc. The "meet and confer" process in federal court and in New York Commercial Division cases provides structured venues for discussions with opposing counsel, but counsel can also reach agreements without formally required meetings.

Stop the Destruction of Data to Be Preserved

Satisfying the duty to preserve requires organizations to suspend their routine destruction mechanisms.[22] A litigation hold is the communication mechanism typically used to document and inform employees of the need to suspend destruction. It has been held that the "utter failure to establish any form of litigation hold at the outset of litigation is grossly negligent."[23] However, the proper form of litigation holds is an open question: must they be in writing, or will oral holds suffice? There is arguably a mix of opinions on the subject.

While at least one federal court held that the failure to issue a written litigation hold constituted gross negligence,[24] the Second Circuit rejected that position.[25] New York state courts have also declined to follow that stance. For example, one court found "the functional equivalent of a litigation hold" where a company's policy was "to retain all information relevant to the claims and litigation."[26] Furthermore, it ruled "a directive to refrain from purging documents is unnecessary and unwarranted... [and] would risk confusion regarding the policy and practice to preserve all documents in all formats for all files."[27]

At least one New York court has supported tailoring a litigation hold's form to the organization's size.[28] The court noted that in smaller organizations, "issuing a written litigation hold may not only be unnecessary, but it could be counterproductive, since such a hold would likely be more general and less tailored to individual records custodians than oral directives could be."[29]

Even so, the best practice is to issue a clearly written litigation hold, to provide tangible evidence of a party's good-faith attempt to meet its discovery obligations.[30] Litigation holds should describe the subject matter and relevant date ranges, instruct recipients to preserve ESI until notified otherwise, and provide a contact person in case of questions.[31]

In preserving ESI, it is important for the legal department to collaborate with IT in stopping automatic destruction and in issuing the legal hold. Discussions should cover the types of data that may be implicated and the names of key custodians. If any of these types of data are subject to automatic destruction, IT should halt that process for those categories of data. Some organizations find it useful to adopt a "triage" approach—immediately addressing data for the most critical custodians while continuing to identify additional relevant information. In addition to stopping automatic destruction and issuing a legal hold, counsel can consider whether there is the need for IT to collect any data immediately; for example, if certain employees may not follow the directive to preserve data.

Identifying the sources of data early can also help determine whether collecting that data may place an undue burden on the organization, necessitating discussions with opposing counsel or motions to the court for protection.

Ensure Compliance With the Litigation Hold

Issuing a litigation hold is not the final word in meeting the duty to preserve. Organizations should take affirmative steps to ensure compliance throughout the organization; leaving preservation up to lay employees without adequate guidance is asking for trouble. Counsel too, should work to ensure compliance.[32]

Some organizations require employees to sign an acknowledgment that they have read, understood, and agree to the terms of the litigation hold. Tracking the distribution of the holds as well as any employee acknowledgements is important in demonstrating the organization's efforts to ensure preservation.

In addition, organizations should reissue and update litigation holds periodically to ensure their effectiveness.[33] It is also counsel's responsibility to remind custodians of their duty to preserve, communicating directly with key players.[34] Again, keep in mind that documentation of these reminders may be important in establishing the company's good faith effort to preserve evidence.

In fact, it is a best practice to record every step of the litigation hold process to ensure defensibility, including the reasoning for determining when the duty to preserve was triggered and decisions for what data to preserve. If the scope of the litigation shifts, not only should the litigation hold be updated to reflect new claims, date ranges, and custodians, but the reasoning for doing so should be memorialized. It is also important to record critical dates, including when the initial hold and reminders are issued. Although litigation holds are typically privileged, courts have required their production when spoliation has occurred.[35]

To help ensure consistency in following litigation hold procedures, the team may want to consider litigation hold software, which can build in rules consistent with a retention policy and document employees' receipt and acknowledgement of the hold and reminders.

Educate Employees and Monitor Compliance

A litigation readiness program is only as good as the degree to which its policies and processes are adhered to. Because employees are on the front lines, they may be the first to become aware of circumstances giving rise to potential litigation. Therefore, they should be coached to approach management or legal counsel as soon as they learn of any risk. The litigation readiness team can establish a training program that simply explains the company's discovery process, legal hold policies, and document retention protocol. To reinforce the training, the team may want to share examples of the negative ramifications of failing to follow policy.

Conclusion

A proactive litigation readiness program can move an organization from a reactive to a proactive stance. When controlled in a systematic, consistent fashion, the disposal of ESI in compliance with the organization's retention policy can enhance defensibility, reduce the likelihood of spoliation claims and sanctions, and save significant expense. Furthermore, better information management leads to more efficient searches for information, faster decision making, and better compliance with record-keeping rules. In sum, litigation readiness programs that incorporate strong information governance will lead to controlled discovery costs and minimize the risks of unwelcome budget surprises.

1. *Fitzpatrick v. Am. Int'l Grp., Inc.,* 10 Civ. 142 (MHD) (S.D.N.Y. May 29, 2013) (footnotes and citation omitted); *QK Healthcare, Inc. v. Forest Labs., Inc.,* No. 117407/09 (Sup. Ct, N.Y. Co. May 13, 2013).

2. *See, e.g., Rimkus Consulting Grp., Inc. v. Cammarata,* 688 F. Supp. 2d 598, 642 (S.D. Tex. 2010) (where one former employee claimed emails were destroyed pursuant to an email destruction policy at the new competing entity; the court held that, even if that was true, because any such policy was selectively implemented, the Rule 37 safe harbor would not apply).

3. *Zubulake v. UBS Warburg LLC,* 220 F.RD. 212, 216 (S.D.N.Y. 2003) (*Zubulake IV*); *Voom HD Holdings LLC v. EchoStar Satellite L.L.C.,* 93A.D.3d 33, 36 (1st Dep't 2012).

4. *Voom HD Holdings,* 93 A.D.3d at 40 (citation omitted).

5. *Treppel v. Biovail Corp.,* 233 F.RD. 363, 371 (S.D.N.Y. 2006).

6. *See, e.g., Star Direct Telecom, Inc. v. Global Crossing Bandwidth, Inc.,* No. 05-CV-6734T (W.D.N.Y. Mar. 22, 2012) (finding it unreasonable to anticipate litigation where data showed that "out of approximately 3,800 billing disputes filed during 2005 and 2006, only three customers (including the plaintiffs) commenced litigation").

7. *Field Day, LLC v. Cnty. of Suffolk,* No. 04-2202 (S.D.N.Y. Mar. 25, 2010) (rejecting the argument that a defendant's duty to preserve was triggered only when it received notice of a claim because "it receives thousands of claims a year while the percentage of notices that result in actual lawsuits is small").

8. *Toussie v. Cnty. of Suffolk,* No. CV 01-6716 OS) (ARL) (E.D.N.Y. Dec. 21, 2007) (citing *Zubulake IV,* 220 F.RD. 212, 217 (S.D.N.Y. 2003)).

9. *DiStefano v. Law Offices of Barbara H. Katsos, PC,* CV 11-2893 (JS) (AKT) (E.D.N.Y. Mar. 29, 2013) (citation omitted).

10. *Siani v. State Univ. of N.Y. at Farmingdale,* No. CV09-407 (JFB) (WDW) (E.D.N.Y. Aug. 10, 2010).

11. *Id.*

12. *Byrnie v. Town of Cromwell,* 243 F.3d 93, 109 (2d Cir. 2001).

13. *FDIC v. Malik,* 09-CV-4805 (KAM) (JMA) (E.D.N.Y. Mar. 26, 2012).

14. *Id.* (noting that the defendants failed to contest this assertion).

15. *Voom HD Holdings LLC v. EchoStar Satellite L.L.C.,* 93A.D.3d 33, 40 (1st Dep't 2012).

16. *Zubulake IV*, 220 F.R.D. 212, 217 (S.D.N.Y. 2003).

17. *Id.*

18. NYSBA E-Discovery Comm., Best Practices in E-Discovery in New York State and Federal Courts (2011), http://www.nysba.org/AM/Template.cfm?Section=Home&Template=/CM/ContentDisplay.cfm&ContentID=58331(NYSBA Best Practices).

19. The Sedona Conference, The Sedona Conference Commentary on Proportionality (2013), https://thesedonaconference.org/publication/The%20Sedona%20Conference%20Commentary"/%20 on%20Proportionality.

20. *Orbit One Commc'ns, Inc. v. Numerex Corp.*, 271 F.RD. 429, 436 (S.D.N.Y. 2010) (citation omitted).

21. Fed. R. Civ. P. 26(b)(2)(B).

22. *915 Broadway Assocs. LLC v. Paul, Hastings, Janofsky & Walker, LLP*, No. 403124/08 (Sup. Ct., N.Y. Co. Feb. 16, 2012); see also Kravtsov v. Town of Greenburgh, No. 10-CV-3142 (CS) (S.D.N.Y. July 9, 2012) (finding the failure to suspend the automatic deletion of video recordings at least grossly negligent).

23. *Heng Chan v. Triple 8 Palace, Inc.*, No. 03 Civ. 6048 (GEL) (JCF) (S.D.N.Y. Aug. 11, 2005); *Einstein v. 357 LLC*, No. 604199/07 (Sup. Ct., N.Y. Co. Nov. 12, 2009).

24. *Pension Comm. of Univ. of Montreal Pension Plan v. Banc of Am. Secs.*, 685 F. Supp. 2d 456, 471, 476–77 (S.D.N.Y. 2010).

25. *Chin v. Port Auth. of N.Y. & N.J.*, 685 F.3d 135, 162 (2d Cir. 2012).

26. *Estee Lauder Inc. v. One Beacon Ins. Grp., LLC*, No. 602379/05 (Sup. Ct., N.Y. Co. Apr. 15, 2013).

27. *Id.*

28. *Orbit One Commc'ns, Inc. v. Numerex Corp.*, 271 F.RD. 429, 441 (S.D.N.Y. 2010).

29. *Id.; see also Steuben Foods, Inc. v. Country Gourmet Foods, LLC*, No. 08-CV-561S(F) (W.D.N.Y. Apr. 21, 2011) (finding "series of oral communications" from counsel to senior staff in a company of 400 employees sufficient to avoid sanctions).

30. NYSBA Best Practices.

31. *Id.*

32. *915 Broadway Assocs. LLC v. Paul, Hastings, Janofsky & Walker, LLP*, No. 403124/08 (Sup. Ct., N.Y. Co. Feb. 16, 2012) ("Counsel must oversee compliance with the litigation hold.").

33. *Zubulake v. UBS Warburg LLC*, 229 F.RD. 422, 433–34 (S.D.N.Y. 2004).

34. *Id.*

35. *See, e.g., Tracy v. NVR, Inc.*, No. 04-CV-6541L (W.D.N.Y. Mar. 26, 2012).

JAMIE WEISSGLASS has a B.A. and M.S. from the University of Pennsylvania and received her J.D. from Fordham University School of Law. Jamie currently works as a Manager of Business Development at Huron Legal. In this capacity, she works with many Fortune 500 corporations and AmLaw 200 firms to create customized legal solutions for a variety of complex needs including litigation readiness protocols, eDiscovery and managed review services, operational restructuring, and cost-efficiency modeling.

ROSSANA PARROTTA is a head of Strategic Sales, East Coast, at Huron Legal, based in New York City. She has 10 years of experience in litigation discovery, managed review, database and repository management, and trial support. She has a B.A. from Fordham University and a J.D. from CUNY School of Law. This article first appeared, in a slightly different format, in the Fall 2013 issue of *Inside*, a publication of the NYSBA's Corporate Counsel Section.

This article originally appeared in the September 2014 *NYSBA Journal*.

PATHWAY TO THE PROFESSION: FROM LAW SCHOOL TO LAWYER

TRIAL PRACTICE

Opening, Motion Argument, and Summation
A Walk in a Park or a Minefield?
By Hon. John J. Brunetti

T rial lawyers are often told that what they say in court is not evidence. After hearing the rule stated over and over in preliminary and final jury instructions, in civil[1] and criminal[2] cases, some lawyers may be lulled into a false sense of security, thinking they can say almost anything in court without consequence—a walk in the park, metaphorically speaking. Case law shows that nothing could be further from the truth. In fact, case law shows that an appellate court may classify what a lawyer says in court as "ruinous" and "fatal" to the client's case.[3] With that backdrop, we discuss the minefield that awaits the unwary trial lawyer.

Openings

First, there is the danger of opening the door to ruination in the opening statement. For example, the Court of Appeals upheld a trial court's ruling that the lawyer for a county jail inmate, charged with assault on a deputy during his incarceration, had opened the door to proof of the inmate's record, which had been precluded *in limine*. In the Court's view, counsel "converted the shield of the preclusion order into a sword."[4] The client suffered the consequence.

In a Third Department case, a victory on a statement suppression motion was lost by a defense lawyer who, on opening, claimed "there was no proof" connecting the defendant to the drug at issue.[5] This opened the door to the use of the suppressed statement. Perhaps a more cautious lawyer would have said that the jury "will not hear" any proof, rather than "there was no proof."

Admissions—Formal and Informal

Another mistake made in opening statements is making an admission as the agent of the client. Such an admission by counsel may be classified as either formal or informal. A formal judicial admission is conclusive and dispenses with the need for evidence of the fact admitted.[6] An informal judicial admission, on the other hand, is simply evidence of the fact admitted therein.[7]

In 2013, both the First and Second Departments left no doubt that "a factual assertion made by an attorney during an opening statement is a judicial admission."[8] The fact that the admissions in these two civil cases were classified as informal was likely of little solace to the lawyers who made them.

The Second Department case was a divorce action where the status of real property as marital property was in issue. Counsel's concession in the opening statement that the husband acquired title during the marriage, albeit partially with money from a non-marital source, was ruled an informal admission.[9]

"Ruinous" and "fatal" were the adjectives used by the First Department to describe the consequences of a lawyer admitting the client's negligence in the opening statement, resulting in a directed verdict in the plaintiff's favor on the claim of negligent maintenance of steps where the plaintiff had fallen.[10]

As for admissions by criminal defense counsel in openings, a Fourth Department case has addressed the issue. There, the defendant was convicted of possession of a dangerous instrument, consisting of sneakers.[11] Defense counsel admitted in opening statement that the defendant was wearing sneakers. On appeal, the People conceded that there was no explicit proof offered at trial indicating that the defendant was wearing sneakers at the time of the crime. The Appellate Division rejected the People's attempt to advance defense counsel's admission so as to relieve them of their burden to prove an essential element of the crime, and so the conviction was reversed for insufficient evidence. The court did not address whether things would have been different had the People ordered a transcript of the defense opening and offered it into evidence before they rested.

When it comes to other stages of a criminal case, informal judicial admissions by counsel may be committed where defense counsel expressly names the client as the source of the proffered information, or it may be fairly inferred that the client was its source. That was the ruling of the Court of Appeals in *People v. Rivera*.[12] There, defense counsel averred in an affidavit in support of a motion that the defendant possessed "buy money" in a drug sale case because he had made change for the true seller. The trial court ruled the affidavit to be admissible as an informal admission when the defendant testified that he never possessed the buy money. The Appellate Division ruled that the affidavit was a conclusive judicial admission.[13] The Court of Appeals affirmed on the Appellate Division opinion with the proviso that the admission was informal.

Prior Inconsistent Statements

Akin to admissions by counsel are prior inconsistent statements by counsel with which the client may be impeached. See, for example, the Court of Appeals ruling in *People v. Brown*.[14] At trial, defense counsel moved *in limine* for a ruling that, if the client testified that he was present at the scene to buy drugs, not to sell drugs, with money earned from legitimate employment, he would not be deemed to have opened the door to specified prejudicial information. After the defendant testified at trial in a manner inconsistent with his former counsel's statements, the prosecutor sought to use counsel's statements to impeach the defendant. The Court of Appeals found that, since the defendant was the "only source of the information" for counsel's statements concerning the defendant's proposed testimony and that counsel was acting as the defendant's authorized agent in making those statements, counsel's statement was properly used to impeach the client.

Prior inconsistent statements by counsel made at arraignments[15] and bail hearings[16] are also admissible to impeach the client. For example, the Second Department has ruled that a defendant may be impeached with his counsel's statement at arraignment that "[my client] defendant tells me that the complaining witness…came towards him in a very threatening manner and he thought he was going to be attacked" if the client's trial testimony is inconsistent with that assertion.[17]

A review of the impeachment-by-counsel's-statement cases indicates that, when confronted with the attorney's prior statement, the client conceded the attorney's prior inconsistent statement during cross-examination, thereby rendering extrinsic proof of it unnecessary. No appellate court has ever been forced to address two issues: What if the client denies being the source of counsel's statement? And, what if the client denies that the lawyer made the statement?

The answer to the second question is easy. The cross-examiner need not call the attorney who made the statement to prove the statement. Since the attorney speaks for the client, all the cross-examiner need do is to call any witness who heard the attorney make the statement[18]—usually a court reporter.

A denial by the client that the client was the source of counsel's statement presents a more difficult issue. If the lawyer who made the statement is the lawyer trying the case, that lawyer would likely be precluded from testifying by the advocate-witness rule[19] found in the New York Rules of Professional Conduct.[20] But what of former counsel? Does the attorney-client privilege apply? On the issue of whether the admissibility of an affidavit of counsel presents an attorney-client privilege issue, the First Department said "no" in *Brown* before review by the Court of Appeals, saying, "The objection that receipt of the evidence violates the attorney-client privilege of confidentiality is patently invalid. There can be no confidentiality about an affidavit filed in open court."[21] That ruling would appear to allow testimony by a former counsel as to what a former client had said. The only exception would be if the court were to rule that the client's denial implicating the prior counsel in a misrepresentation to the court was not a sufficient allegation of misconduct so as to result in a waiver of the privilege.[22]

In criminal cases, a notice of alibi is required to be served upon the prosecution if the defendant plans to introduce alibi evidence, and thus has the potential to become an admission or prior inconsistent statement. However, if the notice is withdrawn well in advance of trial, it may not be used as an admission or a prior inconsistent statement because it is required so early in the case that it is more a procedural device and should not force the defendant to form a fixed defense so early in the litigation.[23] However, absent a timely withdrawal of an alibi notice, the notice may be used as an informal judicial admission and/or to impeach the defendant if he testifies[24] and/or to impeach a defense witness who is named in the notice.[25]

Closing Arguments

Closing arguments present another fertile ground for a lawyer to speak with negative consequences. Case law shows that even though what a lawyer says in summation is not evidence,[26] a lawyer may not make statements in summation with impunity. A lawyer who operates under the assumption that the proof is closed may be in for a rude awakening because there is still the opportunity for counsel to make admissions and open the door during summation.

The Third Department has recognized the possibility that a lawyer may commit an informal judicial admission in summation, though the court found in that case that what the lawyer said did not measure up to an admission.[27] In *Wheeler*, the plaintiff had sued GTE for gender discrimination in the form of discharge. In order to prevail, she had the burden to prove that the discharge occurred under circumstances giving rise to an inference of gender discrimination. The defense took the position that there was no discharge, but rather a resignation. The jury found that the plaintiff was fired, but for misconduct. The trial court set aside that verdict as against the weight of the evidence, but rejected the plaintiff's claims that defense counsel's statements in summation were admissions. Those statements included: (1) "The issues we had with Ms. Wheeler…didn't warrant her discharge and no one was going to discharge her"; and (2) "You're going to hear that somehow [GTE] terminated the plaintiff for misconduct. I'm not quite sure how we did that. The fact is that—is that she quit."[28] The Appellate Division reinstated the verdict, observing that while the trial court was wrong in setting aside the verdict, the trial court correctly recognized defense counsel's statements as arguments, and not as judicial admissions, because none was a concession of a fact.[29]

The First Department and the Court of Appeals have ruled that criminal defense counsel may open the door to additional proof in summation. In the First Department case, defense counsel was found to have opened the door during summation to proof of a photographic identification procedure that would otherwise have been inadmissible,[30] because counsel had "created an unfair impression" about the witness's identification of the defendant. In the Court of Appeals case, *People v. Thompson*, decided in 2014, defense counsel was found to have opened the door during summation to evidence (a glove) that had been ordered suppressed. The Court affirmed the trial court's order permitting the People to re-open their proof to introduce the suppressed evidence before returning to summations.[31]

The *Thompson* case makes re-examination of a case decided by the Court of Appeals 10 years earlier well worthwhile. In *People v. Massie*,[32] the Court took particular note that in summation defense counsel asserted a proposition that defense lawyers sometimes advance during jury selection, in opening and in closing: "Look at the setting. We're here in a courtroom. I'm the defense attorney. I'm asking the questions. [The defendant] is sitting next to me. Who else are [the witnesses] going to identify in this courtroom?"

In *Massie*, there were a total of three identifications by a single witness: (1) a photo identification that, absent an exception, is inadmissible on the People's case in chief;[33] (2) a line-up identification that had been ruled inadmissible on right to counsel grounds;[34] and (3) an in-court identification. When defense counsel elicited evidence about the photo identification, the trial court ruled that the door was opened to the use of the suppressed line-up identification. In the wake of *Thompson*, the "who else are the witnesses going to identify in this courtroom" argument may very well be viewed by a court as an attempt to create a misimpression that the witness had not identified the defendant or his or her picture as the perpetrator until the witness came into the courtroom. Under today's case law, that is the kind of misimpression that may very well open the door to the re-opening of proof, to allow the People to prove the prior identification.

Conclusion

The foregoing tour of the minefield that awaits the unwary lawyer who speaks in court would not be complete without mention of a Court of Appeals case where a lawyer opened the door by failing to speak. That case is *People v. Bolden*,[35] where defense counsel on cross-examination asked a question that called for a "yes" or "no" answer. Did you ever say that you "did not get a good look at the perpetrator"? The witness's non-responsive answer was that "she had been shown a number of photographs at the time she made that statement." The Court of Appeals upheld the trial court's ruling that "[b]y failing to move to strike that unresponsive answer, defendant's attorney opened the door to an explanation by the People concerning the circumstances under which she had seen the photographs."[36]

---

1.   The pattern jury preliminary instruction for civil cases contains the following assertion: "What is said [by counsel] in opening statements is not evidence." PJI 1:3.

The pattern final PLJ instruction states: "[A]rguments, remarks, and summation of attorneys are not evidence." PJI 1:25.

2. The pattern jury preliminary instruction for criminal cases contains the following assertion: "What the lawyers say in an opening statement or at any time thereafter is not evidence." CJI 2nd. The pattern final instruction for criminal cases states: "Remember, nothing the lawyers say at any time is evidence." CJI 2nd.

3. *Echavarria v. Cromwell Assocs.*, 232 A.D.2d 347 (1st Dep't 1996).

4. *People v. Rojas*, 97 N.Y.2d 32 (2001) ("In its opening statement, the defense strongly suggested, if not argued, that the jury should acquit defendant because, having done nothing wrong, he was abused and mistreated, culminating in a scuffle with guards who surrounded him in his cell....Having argued that defendant's confinement was unjustified, the defense converted the shield of the preclusion order into a sword by arguing that the People should not be allowed to supply that justification.").

5. *People v. Everett*, 96 A.D.3d 1105 (3d Dep't 2012) ("County Court did, in fact, grant his motion to suppress most of his statements. The court permitted the People to introduce those suppressed statements at trial, however, after defense counsel stated during his opening remarks that there was no proof to connect defendant with the cocaine or the sneakers. The court did not abuse its discretion when it held that these comments created a misleading impression, thereby opening the door to the admission of defendant's statements.").

6. *See* Richardson 8-215.

7. *See* Richardson 8-219.

8. *Kosturek v. Kosturek*, 107 A.D.3d 762 (2d Dep't 2013); *Tullett Prebon Fin. Servs. v. BGC Fin., L.P.*, 111 A.D.3d 480 (1st Dep't 2013).

9. *Kosturek*, 107 A.D.3d 762 ("This unequivocal, factual assertion made during opening statements constituted a judicial admission.").

10. *Echavarria*, 232 A.D.2d 347.

11. *People v. Johnson*, 241 A.D.2d 954, 955 (4th Dep't 1997) ("The People concede that there was no explicit proof offered at trial indicating that defendant was wearing sneakers. The admission by defendant's attorney in his opening statement does not constitute evidence, nor does it relieve the People of their burden of proof.").

12. *People v. Rivera*, 45 N.Y.2d 989 (1978).

13. *People v. Rivera*, 58 A.D.2d 147, 149 (1977).

14. *People v. Brown*, 98 N.Y.2d 226 (2002).

15. *People v. Gary*, 44 A.D.3d 416 (1st Dep't), *lv. denied*, 9 N.Y.3d 1006 (2007) ("The court properly permitted the prosecutor to impeach defendant by way of statements his attorney made at arraignment (citations omitted). It was a reasonable inference that these statements were attributable to defendant, and they significantly contradicted his trial testimony."); *People v. Moye*, 11 A.D.3d 212 (1st Dep't 2004), *lv. denied*, 4 N.Y.3d 766 (2005) ("On cross-examination of defendant Moye, the court properly received statements that defendant Moye's original counsel had made at arraignment as prior inconsistent statements by Moye affecting his credibility. Moye was concededly the source of the information and counsel, attorney of record at the time, was acting as Moye's agent (*see People v. Brown*, 98 NY2d 226, 232–33 (2002)). An attorney's statement at arraignment, relaying information supplied by the defendant and offered for the purpose of obtaining favorable rulings on matters such as bail, clearly falls within Brown's ambit.").

16. *People v. Mahone*, 206 A.D.2d 263 (1st Dep't), *lv. denied*, 84 N.Y.3d 869 (1994) ("Further, it was not improper for the prosecutor to use for impeachment purposes a statement

made by defendant's attorney at a bail application which was made in defendant's presence and with his active participation (citation omitted).").

People v. Johnson, 46 A.D.3d 276 (1st Dep't 2007), *lv. denied*, 10 N.Y.3d 865 (2008) ("[T]rial court properly permitted the prosecutor to impeach defendant by way of statements made by her attorney at the bail hearing as it is a reasonable inference that such statements were attributable to defendant, and they significantly contradicted her trial testimony.").

17. *People v. Killiebrew*, 280 A.D.2d 684 (2d Dep't), *lv. denied*, 96 N.Y.2d 802 (2001).

18. *Rivera*, 58 A.D.2d at 149 ["The fact that the attorney was not called to testify is not a valid objection to the admissibility of the affidavit. Almost the whole point to the vicarious admission rule is that someone other than the agent testifies to the fact that the agent has made an admission out of court."].

19. *See People v. Paperno*, 54 N.Y.2d 294 (1981).

20. N.Y. Rules of Prof'l Conduct, Rule 3.7.

21. *Rivera*, 58 A.D.2d at 149.

22. *See., e.g., Gen. Realty Assocs. v. Walters*, 136 Misc. 2d 1027, 1029 (N.Y. City Civ. Ct. 1987) ("DR 4–101(C)(4) permits the attorney to testify in defense of the charge, even if the testimony breaches the confidentiality rule. Nor need the charge be formal or precise: Where the fair implication of the client's assertion tends to jeopardize the attorney's position, the right of self-defense attaches.").

23. *People v. Burgos-Santos*, 98 N.Y.2d 226, 235 (2002).

24. *People v. Harvey*, 309 A.D.2d 713 (1st Dep't), *lv. denied*, 1 N.Y.3d 573 (2003) ("Defendant failed to preserve his argument that, since he had withdrawn or disavowed the notice, it was error for the court to admit his false notice of alibi as an informal judicial admission.…Unlike the situation in *People v Burgos-Santos* (98 NY2d 226, 233–35 [2002]), defendant first attempted to disavow the alibi notice late in the trial. In any event, were we to find any error in this regard, we would find it to be harmless.").

25. *People v. Byfield*, 15 A.D.3d 262 (1st Dep't), *lv. denied*, 4 N.Y.3d 884 (2005) ("The court properly exercised its discretion in permitting the People to cross-examine a defense witness as to whether she was the source of certain information contained in defendant's alibi notice, as well as in receiving the alibi notice as an informal judicial admission that was contrary to defendant's position at trial.")

26. *People v. Roche*, 98 N.Y.2d 70, 78 (2002) ("[W]e note that the People's closing argument does not provide an evidentiary basis for [the requested charge]. As cogently stated by the dissenting Justice at the Appellate Division, statements in a summation are not evidence and may not supply proof supporting a charge request.").

27. *Wheeler v. Citizens Telecomm. Co. of N.Y., Inc.*, 18 A.D.3d 1002 (3d Dep't 2005) ("Supreme Court correctly recognized defense counsel's statements as arguments, and not as judicial admissions. Formal judicial admissions take the place of evidence and are concessions, for the purposes of the litigation, of the truth of a fact alleged by an adversary (*see* Prince, Richardson on Evidence § 8–215 [Farrell 11th ed.]). Informal judicial admissions are facts incidentally admitted during the trial. These are not conclusive, being merely evidence of the fact or facts admitted (*see* Prince, Richardson on Evidence § 8–219 (Farrell 11th ed.)). A review of the statements made by defendant's counsel during argument reveals that none are formal or informal concessions of a fact alleged by plaintiff.").

28. Drawn from the Plaintiff's brief on appeal reproduced in Westlaw as follows: 2005 WL 5746264 (Appellate Brief) Plaintiff-Respondent's Brief (Jan. 18, 2005).

29. *See Ferrante v. Am. Lung Ass'n*, 90 N.Y.2d 623, 629 (1997) ("To support a prima facie case of age discrimination under the Human Rights Law, plaintiff must demonstrate (1) that he is a member of the class protected by the statute; (2) that he was actively

or constructively discharged; (3) that he was qualified to hold the position from which he was terminated; and (4) that the discharge occurred under circumstances giving rise to an inference of age discrimination (citations omitted). The burden then shifts to the employer 'to rebut the presumption of discrimination by clearly setting forth, through the introduction of admissible evidence, legitimate, independent, and nondiscriminatory reasons to support its employment decision' (citations omitted).").

30. *People v. De Los Angeles*, 270 A.D.2d 196 (1st Dep't), *lv. denied*, 95 N.Y.2d 889 (2000).

31. *People v. Thompson*, 81 A.D.3d 670 (2d Dep't 2011), *aff'd*, 22 N.Y.3d 687 (2014).

32. *People v. Massie*, 2 N.Y.3d 179, 182 (2004).

33. *People v. Caserta*, 19 N.Y.2d 18 (1966).

34. *People v. Massie*, 305 A.D.2d 116, 117 (1st Dep't 2003).

35. *People v. Bolden*, 58 N.Y.2d 741, 741–42 (1982).

36. *Id.* at 742.

The Honorable Judge **JOHN J. BRUNETTI** is a justice of the Onondaga County Supreme Court in the 5th Judicial District of New York.

This article originally appeared in the November/December 2014 *NYSBA Journal*.

What to Do When Opposing Counsels Do Not Engage in or Comply With Good Faith Discovery Efforts?

To the Forum:

I am an attorney at a law firm with a large litigation practice. Obviously, this entails the exchange of numerous discovery demands between parties, including demands for a bill of particulars or interrogatories, and demands for discovery and inspection. In addition, my cases involve the scheduling of numerous depositions.

Because of the demands of a busy practice, opposing attorneys do not always respond timely to discovery requests issued by my firm. In addition, disputes arise between parties regarding what is discoverable and whether certain documents have to be produced. Parties also struggle with scheduling depositions when written discovery requests have not been honored. I have sometimes encountered attorneys who refuse to respond to requests for their client's availability for deposition.

It is my understanding that attorneys are required to engage in good faith efforts prior to filing motions to compel discovery responses. However, I have received motions to compel from adversaries who have made little to no effort to confer with my office prior to filing their discovery motions. I have even received motions which include the obligatory affirmation of good faith efforts when no effort has been made by that party to speak with me about the allegedly outstanding discovery. In addition, I have often been in the position of making several attempts to contact opposing counsel with respect to outstanding discovery demands or a refusal to cooperate in deposition scheduling, without receiving any response. Phone calls and letters have gone unanswered.

Can the Forum please shed some light on what is required in order to fulfill the good faith efforts requirement prior to filing a discovery motion, including a motion to compel? What efforts are required prior to filing the motion by the party demanding compliance? How long must I wait before filing a motion to compel where opposing counsel is nonresponsive to my efforts to communicate on this issue? Do lawyers have an ethical obligation to cooperate with each other during discovery?

Sincerely,
Undiscovered

Dear Undiscovered:

Unfortunately, we all have at least one case where counsel for the opposing party is non-responsive to discovery and refuses to return phone calls or respond to correspondence seeking compliance. Obviously, dealing with such an adversary can be quite frustrating. But in addition to frustration, such behavior also violates the Rules of Professional Conduct, including Rules 1.1, 1.3, 3.1 and 3.2.

Rule 1.1(c) provides that an attorney "shall not intentionally: (1) fail to seek the objectives of the client through reasonably available means permitted by law and these Rules; or (2) prejudice or damage the client during the course of the representation except as permitted or required by these Rules." When an attorney fails to comply with discovery, whether by failing to respond to written discovery requests or requests to schedule depositions, the attorney exposes his or her client to a possible discovery motion, including sanctions and fees. Even if fees are not awarded to the party making the discovery motion, the non-responsive attorney will have prejudiced his or her client by incurring the legal fees for having to defend against a discovery motion which should have been unnecessary had the attorney merely responded to the opposing party's good faith efforts to resolve the issue. Moreover, a failure to comply with discovery can also cause the attorney and his or her client to lose goodwill with the court.

Rule 1.3(a) requires an attorney to "act with reasonable diligence and promptness in representing a client." While attorneys generally think of this rule in terms of responding to client communications, an attorney's failure to respond to correspondence, discovery requests and inquiries from opposing counsel demonstrates a lack of diligence in the representation and therefore implicates this rule.

Rule 3.1 deals with frivolous conduct, which includes conduct which is undertaken "to delay or prolong the resolution of litigation." Similarly, Rule 3.2 provides: "In representing a client, a lawyer shall not use means that have no substantial purpose other than to delay or prolong the proceeding or to cause needless expense." An attorney's deliberate refusal to cooperate during discovery, thereby delaying the resolution of the proceeding, violates both rules. Unfortunately, it is not always possible to determine whether an attorney is deliberately failing to respond.

When faced with unresponsive opposing counsel, it is important to document all efforts to obtain compliance, both by phone and in writing, so that you can demonstrate that you made good faith efforts to obtain opposing counsel's compliance. Correspondence with opposing counsel should detail the issues; it should also advise the adversary that you intend to seek court intervention based on continued non-compliance.

Opposing counsel may not respond to good faith efforts to obtain compliance, thereby necessitating a motion to compel discovery responses or for other relief, such as preclusion or striking pleadings. In the event you must seek court intervention, you must demonstrate that you engaged in good faith efforts to secure the opposing party's compliance prior to submitting the motion. Pursuant to 22 N.Y.C.R.R. § 202.7(a), any motion "relating to disclosure or to a bill of particulars" must include an affirmation by counsel noting "that counsel has conferred with counsel for the opposing party in a good faith effort to resolve the issues raised by the motion." Section 202.7(c) requires that the affirmation "indicate the time, place and nature of the consultation and the issues discussed and any resolutions, or shall indicate good cause why no such conferral with counsel for opposing parties was held." Courts strictly construe this requirement, and have routinely held that discovery motions which did not include the requisite good faith affirmation must be denied. *148 Magnolia, LLC v. Merrimack Mut. Fire Ins. Co.*, 62 A.D.3d 486 (1st Dep't 2009); *Molyneux v. City of New York*, 64 A.D.3d 406 (1st Dep't 2009); *Cerreta v. New Jersey Transit Corp.*, 251 A.D.2d 190 (1st Dep't 1998); *Barnes v. Nynex, Inc.*, 274 A.D.2d 368; 711 N.Y.S.2d 893 (2d Dep't 2000).

Courts have also held that it is not enough simply to state that counsel engaged in good faith efforts to secure an adversary's compliance. The First Department has held that a motion for sanctions based on an opposing party's lack of compliance with discovery was properly denied where the affirmation of good faith "failed to detail the good faith effort to resolve the discovery disputes." *Reyes v. Riverside Park Community (Stage I), Inc.*, 47 A.D.3d 599 (1st Dep't 2008). In this regard, an affirmation of good faith is considered deficient where it fails to comply with 22 N.Y.C.R.R. § 202.7(c). *148 Magnolia*, 62 A.D.3d at 487 (quoting *Amherst Synagogue v. Schueule Paint Co.*, 30 A.D.3d 1055, 1057 (4th Dep't 2006). Courts generally require a showing that a diligent effort was made to resolve the dispute prior to seeking court intervention. *See Baez v. Sugrue*, 300 A.D.2d 519 (2d Dep't 2002). This effort includes actual communication between the parties. *Natoli v. Milazzo*, 65 A.D.3d 1309 (2d Dep't 2009).

While there is no fixed time frame before the party seeking compliance can make a discovery motion, a good faith effort to obtain compliance should require more than simply one letter or phone call. It is important that opposing counsel be afforded a reasonable opportunity to respond before any discovery motion is filed. Your communication with opposing counsel should also set forth a date by which you expect a response or compliance.

In our experience, discovery motions can be avoided if attorneys have the courtesy to respond to voicemail messages and correspondence seeking compliance. A continued refusal to respond to the opposing party's efforts to resolve an issue, whether deliberate or inadvertent, may cause unnecessary rancor between the parties which could have been avoided. Attorneys routinely encounter situations where, due to the demands of a busy practice, they cannot always provide meaningful responses to correspondence or messages as quickly as they would like. When this occurs, the best practice is for counsel to acknowledge receipt of the communication by a quick email or voicemail message to the party seeking compliance. This acknowledgement should state that counsel is otherwise engaged and unable to respond fully at this time and should set forth a time by which he or she will provide a meaningful response. Even a voicemail from a secretary or another attorney at the firm notifying opposing counsel that you have received the message but are out of the office or on trial, can go a long way toward preventing an unnecessary motion to compel and preserving a cordial relationship between the parties. Moreover, in the event that opposing counsel pursues a motion to compel despite diligent efforts, you can then argue that he or she failed to engage in the requisite good faith efforts to resolve the issue.

An attorney's failure to respond to efforts to secure compliance with discovery not only violates several rules of professional conduct, it can lead to unnecessary costs and fees for motion practice on an issue which should be resolved. On the other hand, counsel seeking compliance also has an obligation to engage in diligent good faith efforts to resolve discovery issues prior to seeking court intervention.

Sincerely,
The Forum by

Jennifer Lewkowski, Esq.,
Traub Lieberman Straus & Shrewsberry LLP

Vincent J. Syracuse, Esq.,
Tannenbaum Helpern Syracuse & Hirschtritt LLP

This article originally appeared in the May 2012 *NYSBA Journal*.

Summary Judgment Do's and Don'ts

By John R. Higgitt

Summary judgment is serious business. It's the procedural equivalent of trial that, when granted, results in judgment as a matter of law in favor of one or more parties. But the opportunity to obtain (or defeat) that coveted remedy is often lost, sometimes irretrievably, because of a misstep in preparation of the motion papers. This article offers 10 tips—5 do's, 5 don'ts—to avoid frequently recurring missteps in accelerated judgment practice.

Do Calculate the Deadline for Seeking Summary Judgment in a Given Case

CPLR 3212(a) provides that a summary-judgment motion must be made within 120 days of the filing of the note of issue unless the court sets a different deadline. If the deadline is missed, a party still can make a summary-judgment motion if, and only if, the party can demonstrate "good cause." Good cause here means a reasonable excuse for the untimely motion; neither the merits of the motion nor the lack of prejudice to the other parties is relevant in gauging good cause.[1] Thus, the good cause standard is not easily satisfied.

Because a movant's failure to make a timely summary-judgment motion may preclude the court from considering the merits of the motion, counsel should calculate accurately the deadline for making the motion. To do this, counsel must (1) ascertain the period of time the parties are afforded to make summary-judgment motions (e.g., the 120-day default period of CPLR 3212(a), a shorter period set by the court in a court order or part rule), and (2) determine the date on which the note of issue was filed. Running the relevant period of time from the filing date of the note of issue yields the deadline.

If seeking summary judgment, make the motion[2] before the deadline (or demonstrate in the underlying motion papers that you have a reasonable excuse for the untimely motion). If opposing the motion, review whether it was made timely and, if it was not, insist that the movant demonstrate good cause before the court considers the merits.[3]

Don't Omit the Pleadings if You Are Moving for Summary Judgment

CPLR 3212(b) requires the movant to submit with the summary-judgment motion a complete set of the pleadings in the case. This straightforward requirement is often overlooked. While some courts will forgive a movant's failure to submit the pleadings (especially if they were supplied by another party or by the movant belatedly),[4] others will not, and denials of summary judgment motions that do not contain the pleadings are common.[5] The movant must therefore ensure that a complete set of the pleadings accompanies the underlying motion papers. A party opposing summary-judgment should check the motion papers for the pleadings and may argue for denial of the motion if any of the pleadings are absent.

Don't Ignore the Burden Imposed on the Party Seeking Summary Judgment

A party seeking summary judgment must demonstrate the absence of any triable issues of fact.[6] It does this by *affirmatively* showing, through evidence in admissible form, the merits of its cause of action or defense.[7] Merely pointing to gaps in the evidence produced in the discovery process is insufficient to satisfy the moving party's burden.[8]

A different rule applies in federal court. There, on an issue on which the non-moving party bears the burden of proof at trial (e.g., where the defendant seeks summary judgment dismissing the plaintiff's complaint), the burden on the moving party may be satisfied by showing (i.e., pointing out to the court) that there is an absence of evidence to support the non-moving party's cause of action or defense.[9] In such a situation, the moving party is not required to negate with evidence the non-moving party's claim.[10]

Do Avoid Boilerplate Language Regarding General Summary-Judgment Principles in Your Affirmation in Support of or Opposition to the Motion

The attention of a court is a precious commodity. Don't waste it by reciting chapter and verse the often-echoed general rules of decision underlying summary judgment.[11] The court is already aware of these principles, and larding up an affirmation in support of or opposition to a motion may lead the court to skim the affirmation and miss the substance of counsel's argument.[12] Sparing reference to general principles may be useful to highlight or reinforce why summary judgment is appropriate (or inappropriate) in a given case. Such references should be supported by a single citation to a recent Court of Appeals decision; uncontroversial, well-established summary-judgment principles need not be evidenced by anything more.

Do Ensure That Your Evidence Is in Admissible Form

We've made this point before,[13] but it's worth repeating: counsel for the movant should review each piece of evidence that will be included with the motion and ensure that it is in admissible form.[14] Start with the affidavits. Is each signed by the witness and properly notarized? And, if acknowledged outside of New York, is each affidavit accompanied by the appropriate certification "flag" demonstrating the authority of the oathtaker, that the oath was taken in accordance with the laws of the state or country in which it occurred, or both?[15]

Next, check the deposition transcripts. Is each transcript certified by the court reporter and signed by the deponent? A transcript that has not been signed by the deponent may still be admissible, but counsel must demonstrate that (1) execution of the transcript is unnecessary because it was forwarded to the deponent, but he or she did not sign and return it within 60 days,[16] or (2) the unsigned deposition is being used against a party-deponent as an admission.[17]

A foundation should be laid for each record relied on in the motion, especially business and medical records,[18] which are so frequently utilized in motion practice. And any statement in the evidence that is hearsay should, if possible, be qualified for the court's consideration under an exception to the hearsay rule.[19]

Don't Ignore the Flexibility of the Evidence-in-Admissible-Form Requirement With Respect to Evidence Submitted by the Party Opposing the Motion

The rigidity of the rule requiring the movant to tender evidence in admissible form should be contrasted with the principle that, under certain circumstances, a party opposing summary judgment may rely on evidence that is not in admissible form. "The rule with respect to defeating a motion for summary judgment…is more flexible, [because] the opposing party…may be permitted to demonstrate [an] acceptable excuse for [the] failure to meet the strict requirement of tender in admissible form."[20] Thus, a party opposing summary judgment may defeat the motion if the party can provide the court with a *reasonable* excuse for the failure to submit evidence in admissible form.[21]

Additionally, a party opposing summary judgment may rely on hearsay, provided it is not the only evidence submitted by the party.[22] And the benefit of the doubt as to the admissibility at trial of a particular item of evidence submitted by a party opposing summary judgment is resolved in favor of that party: if the admissibility of the non-movant's evidence is arguable, the motion should be denied.[23]

Don't Forget That Unpleaded Causes of Action and Defenses Can Be Considered on the Motion

Unpleaded causes of action or defenses may be considered on a motion for summary judgment. So held the Court of Appeals in *Alvord & Swift v. Stewart M. Muller Construction Co., Inc.*, in which the Court stated that "[m]odern principles of procedure do not permit an unconditional grant of summary judgment against a plaintiff who, despite defects in pleading, has in [it]s submissions made out a cause of action."[24] The Court also observed that, "[w]ith the advent of the modern principles underlying the CPLR, application of the archaic rule [allowing a court to grant summary judgment for a defendant when a plaintiff's submissions, but not its pleadings, made out a cause of action] is no longer merited."[25] Therefore, a party opposing summary judgment may attempt to defeat the motion by asserting an unpleaded cause of action or defense, provided the claim finds evidentiary support in the party's papers.[26] Moreover, a party may seek summary judgment on an unpleaded cause of action or defense if the party's evidence establishes its entitlement to judgment as a matter of law on the unpleaded claim, and the party opposing the motion will not be surprised or prejudiced by the assertion of the unpleaded claim.[27]

Do Remember to Demonstrate That Your Expert Is Qualified to Render an Opinion

Expert evidence plays a critical role in summary-judgment practice. Expert affidavits (or, where appropriate, affirmations)[28] are used to support or defeat summary judgment in myriad types of cases. The party offering expert evidence must establish that the putative expert is qualified to render an opinion on the relevant subject matter. While the issue of the qualification of a witness to render an expert opinion customarily arises at trial, the requirement that a witness be so qualified applies with equal force to a witness offering an opinion in connection with a motion. Therefore, if counsel is submitting an expert's affidavit on a summary-judgment motion, counsel must ensure the expert demonstrates that he or she possesses sufficient skill, training, education, knowledge, or experience from which it may reasonably be inferred that the information the expert imparts and any opinion that the expert states is reliable.[29] The expert's affidavit should contain detailed information regarding the expert's background in the subject matter on which he or she is offering an opinion, and that information should evince that the expert is qualified to render the proffered opinion.[30]

Do Consider Disclosing Your Expert Prior to the Filing of the Note of Issue

Much ink has been spilled on the issue of *when* a party must disclose its expert.[31] We focus on the matter as it relates to the use of experts on a summary judgment motion. A line of cases from the Second Department held or indicated that a party's failure to disclose its expert in accordance with CPLR 3101(d)(1)(i)[32] prior to the filing of the note of issue should result in the party being precluded from offering the expert's opinions on a summary-judgment motion, unless the party can demonstrate good cause for belated disclosure.[33] The First Department signaled that it may agree with that approach.[34] However, the majority of one panel of the Second Department has sought to clarify that court's jurisprudence on the timing-of-expert-disclosure issue, holding that

> the fact that the disclosure of an expert pursuant to CPLR 3101(d)(1)(i) takes place after the filing of the note of issue and certificate of readiness does not, by itself, render the disclosure untimely. Rather, the fact that pre-trial disclosure of an expert pursuant to CPLR 3101(d)(1)(i) has been made after the filing of the note of issue and certificate of readiness is but one factor in determining whether disclosure is untimely. If a court finds that the disclosure is untimely after considering all of the relevant circumstances in a particular case, it still may, in its discretion, consider an affidavit or affirmation from that expert submitted in the context of a motion for summary judgment, or it may impose an appropriate sanction.[35]

The foregoing suggests that the issues of whether a party must disclose its expert prior to the filing of the note of issue and, if it fails to do so, the extent of a trial court's discretion to forgive that failure, are not settled concretely.[36]

To avoid a finding that a party's expert disclosure is untimely and preclusion of the use of the expert on a motion, the party can disclose its expert before the filing of the note of issue. A safe play, but the party may not want to do that. Maybe the party is trying to resolve the case before retaining (and paying) an expert, a course of action that spares the client a potentially significant expense. If post-note disclosure is counsel's preferred route, he or she should address the timeliness issue in the affirmation in support of or opposition to a summary-judgment motion. Counsel should, if possible, attempt to demonstrate that the disclosure, although occurring after the filing of the note of issue, was timely.[37] Counsel should also argue in the alternative that, assuming the disclosure was untimely, the court should exercise its discretion to consider the expert's affidavit.[38]

Don't Misuse the Reply

A reply serves valuable functions: it allows the movant to answer points made by the party opposing the motion and to reiterate central points made by the movant in its underlying motion papers. It cannot be used to introduce new arguments, new grounds or new evidence in support of the motion.[39] The rule serves to prevent a movant from remedying in reply basic deficiencies in its prima facie showing of entitlement to judgment as a matter of law.[40] So, counsel for the movant should ensure that all arguments in favor of the motion and all evidence necessary to support them are included in the underlying motion papers. Note, too, that the practice of using "supplemental submissions," that is, papers that parties attempt to submit beyond reply, has fallen into disrepute.[41] Counsel should therefore lay bare the client's proof at the appropriate time (for the movant, in the underlying motion papers; for the party opposing the motion, in opposition papers) and not count on any additional chance to submit evidence in connection with the motion.[42]

---

1. *See Brill v. City of N.Y.*, 2 N.Y.3d 648 (2004).

2. Generally, service of the motion—not its filing—will determine when the motion was "made" and whether it was timely. *See* CPLR 2211; *cf. Corchado v. City of N.Y.*, 64 A.D.3d 429 (1st Dep't 2009) (where so-ordered stipulation stated that filing of motion was act that had to occur by deadline, court required motion to be filed not served before deadline).

3. For a thorough charting of the various issues associated with calculating the deadline, as well as a detailed discussion of the good cause requirement, see Patrick M. Connors, *CPLR 3212(a)'s Timing Requirement for Summary Judgment Motions*, 71 Brook. L. Rev. 1529 (2006).

4. *See Avalon Gardens Rehabilitation & Health Care Ctr., LLC v. Morsello*, 97 A.D.3d 611 (2d Dep't 2012); *Crossett v. Wing Farm, Inc.*, 79 A.D.3d 1334 (3d Dep't 2010).

5. *See, e.g., Weinstein v. Gindi*, 92 A.D.3d 526 (1st Dep't 2012); *Ahern v. Shepherd*, 89 A.D.3d 1046 (2d Dep't 2011); *Riddell v. Brown*, 32 A.D.3d 1212 (4th Dep't 2006).

6. *See Vega v. Restani Constr. Corp.*, 18 N.Y.3d 499 (2012).

7. *Velasquez v. Gomez*, 44 A.D.3d 649 (2d Dep't 2007); *George Larkin Trucking Co. v. Lisbon Tire Mart, Inc.*, 185 A.D.2d 614 (4th Dep't 1992); *see Chow v. Reckitt & Coleman, Inc.*, 17 N.Y.3d 29 (2011); *Smalls v. AJI Indus., Inc.*, 10 N.Y.3d 733 (2008); *Sosa v. 46th St. Dev. LLC*, 101 A.D.3d 490 (1st Dep't 2012).

8. *See River Ridge Living Ctr., LLC v. ADL Data Sys., Inc.*, 98 A.D.3d 724 (2d Dep't 2012); *Lane v. Texas Roadhouse Holdings, LLC*, 96 A.D.3d 1364 (4th Dep't 2012); *Alvarez v. 21st Century Renovations Ltd.*, 66 A.D.3d 524 (1st Dep't 2009).

9. *Celotex Corp. v. Catrett*, 477 U.S. 317, 323 (1986); *see Chow*, 17 N.Y.3d at 36 (Smith, J., concurring).

10. *Celotex Corp.*, 477 U.S. at 323.

11. Here are some examples of first principles of summary-judgment motion practice:

    - summary judgment is a drastic remedy;
    - issue finding, rather than issue-determination, is the key to the summary-judgment procedure;
    - matters of credibility cannot be resolved on a summary-judgment motion;
    - the facts must be viewed in the light most favorable to the non-moving party;
    - the moving party's failure to make a prima facie showing of entitlement to summary judgment requires a denial of the motion, regardless of the sufficiency of the opposing papers.

    See generally Siegel, N.Y. Practice § 278 (5th ed.).

12. *See generally* Gerald Lebovits, *Do's, Don'ts and Maybes: Legal Writing Don'ts—Part I*, N.Y. St. B.J. 64 (July/Aug. 2007).

13. John R. Higgitt, *Ten Tips to Improve Your Motion Practice*, N.Y.L.J., Apr. 3, 2012, p. 4.

14. *See Friends of Animals, Inc. v. Associated Fur Mfrs., Inc.*, 46 N.Y.2d 1065, 1067 (1979).

15. *See* Connors, McKinney's Practice Commentary, CPLR 2309 (2013).

16. *See* Connors, McKinney's Practice Commentary, CPLR 3116 (2008).

17. *See Morchik v. Trinity Sch.*, 257 A.D.2d 534 (1st Dep't 1999); *see also Delishi v. Prop. Owner (USA) LLC*, 31 Misc. 3d 661 (Sup. Ct., Kings Co. 2011).

18. *See* CPLR 4518.

19. *See JP Morgan Chase Bank, N.A. v. RADS Grp., Inc.*, 88 A.D.3d 766 (2d Dep't 2011); *Whitfield v. City of N.Y.*, 48 A.D.3d 798 (2d Dep't 2008). The following are commonly invoked hearsay exceptions:

    * an admission by a party;
    * a present sense impression;
    * an excited utterance;
    * a statement reflecting the declarant's state of mind or physical condition;
    * a statement made for the purpose of medical diagnosis or treatment.

    See generally Barker and Alexander, Evidence in New York State and Federal Courts, §§ 8:15-8:22, 8:29-8:33 (5A West's N.Y. Prac. Series 2012).

20. *Friends of Animals, Inc.*, 46 N.Y.2d at 1068.

21. *See Zuckerman v. City of N.Y.*, 49 N.Y.2d 557 (1980); *Phillips v. Joseph Kantor & Co.*, 31 N.Y.2d 307 (1972) (party can defeat summary judgment by submitting affidavit setting forth names of witnesses, the substance of their testimony, how it was known what their testimony would be, and how the witnesses acquired their knowledge). Furthermore, CPLR 3212(f) provides that, "[s]hould it appear from affidavits submitted in opposition to the motion that facts essential to justify opposition may exist but cannot then be stated, the court may deny the motion or may order a continuance to permit affidavits to be obtained or disclosure to be had...." *See* John R. Higgitt, *Opposing Summary Judgment Motions Under CPLR 3212(f)*, N.Y.L.J., Oct. 17, 2005, pp. 4, 8.

22. *See Sumitomo Mitsui Banking Corp. v. Credit Suisse*, 89 A.D.3d 561 (1st Dep't 2011); *see also* Vincent C. Alexander, *Opposing Summary Judgment With Hearsay*, N.Y.L.J., Mar. 15, 2004, pp. 4, 8.

23. *See* Siegel, N.Y. Practice § 281.

24. *Alvord & Swift v. Stewart M. Muller Constr. Co., Inc.*, 46 N.Y.2d 276, 279 (1978).

25. *Id.* at 281; *see Perry v. Edwards*, 79 A.D.3d 1629 (4th Dep't 2010); *but see, e.g., Ostrov v. Rozbruch*, 91 A.D.3d 147, 154 (1st Dep't 2012) ("'A court should not consider the merits of a new theory of recovery, raised for the first time in opposition to a motion for summary judgment, that was not pleaded in the complaint'" (quoting *Mezger v. Wyndham Homes, Inc.*, 81 A.D.3d 795, 796 (2d Dep't 2011))).

26. *See Nassau Trust Co. v. Montrose Concrete Prods. Corp.*, 56 N.Y.2d 175 (1982); *Preferred Capital, Inc. v. PBK, Inc.*, 309 A.D.2d 1168 (4th Dep't 2003); *see also* Siegel, Practice Commentaries, *supra*, CPLR 3212, C3212:10.

27. *See Herbert F. Darling, Inc. v. City of Niagara Falls*, 69 A.D.2d 989 (4th Dep't 1979), aff'd, 49 N.Y.2d 855 (1980); *Rosario v. City of N.Y.*, 261 A.D.2d 380 (2d Dep't 1999); *Weinstock v. Handler*, 254 A.D.2d 165, 679 N.Y.S.2d 48 (1st Dep't 1998); *see also* Siegel, Practice Commentaries, *supra*, CPLR 3212, C3212:11. If the client is relying on an unpleaded cause of action or defense in support of or opposition to a summary judgment motion, counsel should, in his or her affirmation, highlight the new claim and, if possible, explain why the claim was not asserted sooner. *Cf., e.g., Comsewogue Union Free Sch. Dist. v. Allied-Trent Roofing Sys., Inc.*, 15 A.D.3d 523 (2d Dep't 2005). Also, counsel in his or her affirmation should quote the operative language from *Alvord*

permitting the use of unpleaded claims. This strategy may help counsel deal with case law suggesting that reliance on unpleaded claims is prohibited. *See, e.g., Ostrov*, 91 A.D.3d 147; *Mezger*, 81 A.D.3d 795; *Abalola v. Flower Hosp.*, 44 A.D.3d 522 (1st Dep't 2007).

28.   An expert may be allowed to submit a sworn statement in an affirmation instead of an affidavit (which obviates the need for a notary public or other similar official), but only certain expressly listed professionals are authorized to use an affirmation (*see* CPLR 2106). Care must therefore be taken in utilizing an affirmation. *See generally* Alexander, Practice Commentaries, *supra*, CPLR 2106).

29.   *Matott v. Ward*, 48 N.Y.2d 455, 459 (1979); *see Price v. N.Y. City Hous. Auth.*, 92 N.Y.2d 553, 562 (1998) (neither formal training nor attainment of academic degree is a precondition to witness being deemed qualified; qualification may be demonstrated by showing practical experience in relevant field).

30.   *See Stever v. HSBC Bank USA, NA*, 82 A.D.3d 1680 (4th Dep't 2011); *Shank v. Mehling*, 84 A.D.3d 776 (2d Dep't 2011); *Schechter v. 3320 Holding LLC*, 64 A.D.3d 446, 883 N.Y.S.2d 193 (1st Dep't 2009). In his or her affidavit, the witness need only make a prima facie showing that he or she is qualified to render an expert opinion (*see Breese v. Hertz Corp.*, 25 A.D.2d 621, 267 N.Y.S.2d 703 [1st Dep't 1966]; *see also Lack v. E.P. Lawson Co.*, 16 N.Y.2d 942, 264 N.Y.S.2d 926 [1965]), a point counsel should stress in his or her affirmation. Once that showing has been made, any challenge to the scope or caliber of the witness' qualifications relates to weight the opinion will be afforded by the trier of fact. *See Miele v. Am. Tobacco Co.*, 2 A.D.3d 799 (2d Dep't 2003).

31.   *See, e.g.*, Connors, Practice Commentaries, CPLR 3101, C3101:29A; David Paul Horowitz, *If a [Singletree] Falls...*, 84 N.Y. St. B.J. 16 (Nov./Dec. 2012); David Paul Horowitz, *A [Single]tree Grows in Manhattan*, N.Y. St. B.J. 22 (Oct. 2012); Patrick M. Connors, *Case Law on CPLR 3101(d)(1)(i), Expert Disclosure, Is in Shambles*, N.Y.L.J., Jan. 20, 2009, pp. 3, 6.

32.   CPLR 3101(d)(1)(i) provides, in relevant part, that

> [u]pon request, each party shall identify each person whom the party expects to call as an expert witness at trial and shall disclose in reasonable detail the subject matter on which each expert is expected to testify, the substance of the facts and opinions on which each expert is expected to testify, the qualifications of each expert witness and a summary of the grounds for each expert's opinion. However, where a party for good cause shown retains an expert an insufficient period of time before the commencement of trial to give appropriate notice thereof, the party shall not thereupon be precluded from introducing the expert's testimony at the trial solely on grounds of noncompliance with this paragraph. In that instance, upon motion of any party, made before or at trial, or on its own initiative, the court may make whatever order may be just.

33.   *See, e.g., Stolarski v. DeSimone*, 83 A.D.3d 1042 (2d Dep't 2011); *Gerardi v. Verizon N.Y., Inc.*, 66 A.D.3d 960 (2d Dep't 2009); *Constr. by Singletree, Inc. v. Lowe*, 55 A.D.3d 861 (2d Dep't 2008).

34.   *See Garcia v. City of N.Y.*, 98 A.D.3d 857 (1st Dep't 2012).

35.   *Rivers v. Birnbaum*, 102 A.D.3d 26 (2d Dep't 2012); *see Jacobs v. Nussbaum*, 100 A.D.3d 702 (2d Dep't 2012).

36.   The court in *Rivers* stated that a trial court can impose a specific deadline (e.g., prior to the filing of the note of issue) for the disclosure of experts. Such deadlines can appear in an order, a judge's part rules or the rules of a court or judicial district. When the court has set a specific deadline, the issue of whether a given disclosure is timely should be clear-cut. Additionally, the parties should be free to enter into a so-ordered stipulation in the nature of a scheduling order to set the deadlines for expert disclosure. These so-ordered stipulations may be particularly useful in commercial

actions, since many members of the commercial bar are accustomed to stipulating to engage in expert disclosure within designated timeframes (*see* Haig, Commercial Litigation in New York State Courts, § 11:16 (2 West's N.Y. Prac. Series 3d ed.) ("[I]n New York's Commercial Division, parties often stipulate to expert disclosure similar in breadth to that required in federal court. Indeed, some commercial division form pretrial orders anticipate expert depositions. In many such cases, counsel on both sides prefer the ability to take such discovery.")).

37. *Rivers*, 102 A.D.3d at 27 ("[T]he fact that the disclosure of an expert pursuant to CPLR 3101(d)(1)(i) takes place after the filing of the note of issue and certificate of readiness does not, by itself, render the disclosure untimely. Rather, the fact that pretrial disclosure of an expert pursuant to CPLR 3101(d)(1)(i) has been made after the filing of the note of issue and certificate of readiness is but one factor in determining whether disclosure is untimely.").

38. *Id.* at 27 ("[I]f a court finds that the disclosure is untimely after considering all of the relevant circumstances in a particular case, it still may, in its discretion, consider an affidavit or affirmation from that expert submitted in the context of a motion for summary judgment, or it may impose an appropriate sanction."). In determining whether to exercise its discretion to consider the affidavit of an expert who was not disclosed timely, a court may give particular weight to whether the party proffering the expert offers a reasonable excuse for the failure to disclose timely the expert, whether that party intentionally or willfully failed to disclosure timely the expert and whether the opposing party was prejudiced (*see, e.g., Kozlowski v. Oana*, 102 A.D.3d 751 (2d Dep't 2013); *LeMaire v. Kuncham*, 102 A.D.3d 659 (2d Dep't 2013)).

39. *Dannasch v. Bifulco*, 184 A.D.2d 415 (1st Dep't 1992).

40. *Kennelly v. Mobius Realty Holdings LLC*, 33 A.D.3d 380 (1st Dep't 2006).

41. *See Ostrov*, 91 A.D.3d at 155 (trial court has inherent discretion to consider supplemental submissions, but they "should be sparingly used to clarify limited issues, and should not be utilized…to correct deficiencies in a party's moving or answering papers").

42. *See* Patrick M. Connors, *Just One More Thing: Supplemental Submissions on Summary Judgment*, N.Y.L.J., Sept. 17, 2012, pp. 4, 8.

JOHN R. HIGGITT (jhiggitt@courts.state.ny.us) is a principal court attorney to the Administrative Judge for Civil and Criminal Matters of the Twelfth Judicial District (Hon. Douglas E. McKeon), a member of the Advisory Committee on Civil Practice to the Chief Administrative Judge of the Courts of the State of New York, and a reporter to the Committee on the New York Pattern Jury Instructions, Civil. Sophia Rackman, Esq., a law clerk to Justice McKeon, assisted in the editing of this article. The views expressed here are the author's own.

This article originally appeared in the March/April 2013 *NYSBA Journal*.

Burden of Proof
"How Much Is That Witness in the Window?"
By David Paul Horowitz

Introduction

Jokes about witnesses (especially expert witnesses) being paid for their testimony are legion.[1] A recent example:

> Q: "Doctor, you are being paid $750 an hour for your testimony in court today, correct?"
>
> A: "No, counselor, I am not paid for my testimony, I am paid for my time."
>
> Q: "Doctor, isn't that sort of like a call girl saying she is paid for her time, not for the sex?"
>
> "OBJECTION!"
>
> "SUSTAINED!"

Jokes notwithstanding, it is permitted and, in some circumstances, required, to pay certain fees to witnesses. These include statutory witness fees, reimbursement for certain expenses, and compensation for time lost from work.

CPLR Statutory Witness Fees

While parties to an action, together with their agents, servants, employees, family, friends, and others aligned with their interests, will generally appear willingly in court to give testimony, those without a connection to the parties are apt to be reluctant to appear in court. Witnesses subpoenaed to testify at trial are entitled to be paid statutory fees for appearing in court, and witnesses may request compensation for, *inter alia*, time lost from work as a result of their appearances in court.

CPLR 8001(a) governs the payment of witness fees:

> § 8001. Persons subpoenaed; examination before trial; transcripts of records
>
> Persons subpoenaed. Any person whose attendance is compelled by a subpoena, whether or not actual testimony is taken, shall receive for each day's attendance fifteen dollars for attendance fees and twenty-three cents as travel expenses for each mile to the place of attendance from the place where he or she was served, and return. There shall be no mileage fee for travel wholly within a city.

The sums, while not princely, are extravagant in comparison to the statutory fees available prior to the most recent amendment in 1988, when the daily attendance fee was $2, and the mileage reimbursement fee was set at eight cents.[2]

The subject of witness fees has not, until recently, been a fertile ground for case law. A number of cases have addressed ministerial issues; for example, CPLR 2303(a) requires that "[a]ny person subpoenaed shall be paid or tendered in advance authorized traveling expenses and one day's witness fee." A trial court determined that the tender of witness and mileage fees at the time the subpoena was served was best practice; it was sufficient if the payment was made prior to the return date of the subpoena.[3] In another proceeding, to hold a witness in contempt, the Second Department held the contempt application had to be denied because where the subpoena was unaccompanied by payment of the statutory witness fee: "Witness fees must be tendered when the subpoena is served or within a reasonable time before it is returnable."[4]

In another action, a trial court had to determine who bore the cost of transporting a prisoner to appear at a correction officer's disciplinary hearing. The trial court determined that there was no statutory exception permitting the Department of Corrections to be paid an amount greater than the statutory rate, concluding "that the Department should be required to produce the inmate at the Otisville facility hearing solely upon the payment of $2 witness fee and 8 cents per mile."[5]

Payment for a Witness's Testimony

What fees may be paid to a witness, in excess of the statutory fees, was addressed 100 years ago in a case where the Court of Appeals affirmed the disbarment of an attorney for, *inter alia*, improper payments to witnesses.[6] The Court of Appeals affirmed a decision by the First Department,[7] which described in detail the conduct at issue:

> A considerable number of these vouchers represented disbursements to or with the defendant's witnesses by these investigators or detectives, and there seem to be many cases where sums of money were paid far in excess of any proper compensation to witnesses for the time lost in attending court. Thus on October 20, 1909, there was paid in the Nowak case three hundred and thirty-five dollars to different witnesses, the amount paid to each ranging from sixty-five dollars to ten dollars. In another case one hundred dollars was paid to a witness for time lost and expenses attending court, and payments of twenty-five dollars and ten dollars to witnesses were quite numerous. These, standing alone, might not justify action, but they tend to sustain the conclusion that the payments were made in these cases out

of all proportion to the proper allowance to a witness for lost time or expenses in attending court.[8]

The First Department explained what may, and may not, be paid to witnesses:

> To procure the testimony of witnesses it is often necessary to pay the actual expenses of a witness in attending court and a reasonable compensation for the time lost. It is often necessary to pay a reasonable fee to an expert in preparing to testify for a party in an action. And there are many incidental expenses in relation to the prosecution or defense of an action at law which can with propriety be paid by a party to the action. But on the other hand, the payment of a sum of money to a witness to testify in a particular way; the payment of money to prevent a witness' attendance at a trial; the payment of money to a witness to make him "sympathetic" with the party expecting to call him; these are all payments which are absolutely indefensible and which are really included in the general definition of subornation of perjury. The payment of a sum of money to a witness to "tell the truth" is as clearly subversive of the proper administration of justice as to pay him to testify to what is not true. The prevalence of perjury is a serious menace to the administration of justice, to prevent which no means have as yet been satisfactorily devised. But there certainly can be no greater incentive to perjury than to allow a party to make payments to its opponent's witnesses under any guise or on any excuse, and at least attorneys who are officers of the court to aid it in the administration of justice must keep themselves clear of any connection which in the slightest degree tends to induce witnesses to testify in favor of their clients. The action of the respondent in controlling and managing a system which had a direct tendency to accomplish that purpose is one that we cannot too severely condemn. Attorneys, whether representing corporations or individuals, must clearly understand that any conduct which tends to participate in or approve the payment of money to witnesses or public officials to influence the administration of justice will be most severely condemned and considered a case for disbarment.[9]

Nearly a century later, the Second Department, in *Caldwell v. Cablevision System Corp.,*[10] held that, while CPLR 8001(a) does not bar compensation to a fact witness in excess of $15 per day and payment for travel expenses in excess of 23 cents per mile, a trial court erred, nonetheless, when it failed to charge the jury that the witness's testimony was suspect based upon the amount of the payment to the witness. The physician's fee to testify at trial was $10,000:

> In this case, the Supreme Court properly allowed the plaintiffs' counsel to cross-examine Dr. Krosser without limitation regarding the $10,000 payment that was made to him, and also properly permitted counsel to adequately address the issue in summations. The Supreme Court erred, however, in denying the plaintiffs' request for an explicit instruction to the jury regarding witness compensation.
>
> While the Supreme Court instructed the jury that it should consider bias or prejudice in determining the weight to be given to any particular witness's testimony, this general charge was insufficient under the circumstances. Just as a jury that hears testimony in a criminal trial from a witness who is testifying in exchange for a promise of leniency is given a specific instruction regarding the possibility of bias, we conclude that, in light of the important public policy considerations concerning fees paid to fact witnesses, more than the general credibility charge is also warranted where, as here, a reasonable inference can be drawn that a fact witness has been paid an amount disproportionate to the reasonable value of his or her lost time. In crafting an appropriate instruction, trial courts should bear in mind the general principles regarding fact-witness testimony heretofore discussed, including a fact witness's public duty to testify for the statutory fee of $15; the permissibility of voluntary compensation for the reasonable value of time spent in testifying; the goal of drawing the line between compensation that merely eases the burden of testifying and that which tends to unintentionally influence testimony; the inference, which may be drawn from the disproportionality of the payment to the reasonable value of lost time, that a fee for testimony has been paid; and the potential for unconscious bias that such a fee may create.[11]

PJI Includes Charge Based on *Caldwell*

Reflecting the Second Department decision in *Caldwell*, the New York Pattern Jury Instructions—Civil were revised to include a new instruction based upon that court's holding:

> Where a fact witness has received compensation in excess of that provided by CPLR 8001(a), the court may use the following instruction:

PJI 1:90.4 Compensation of Fact Witnesses

In addition to what I just told you about expert witnesses who give you their opinions about certain aspects of
the case, when a person like EF is subpoenaed to come
to court as a witness to tell you what he/she (saw, heard
or did) with respect to anything that happened relating
to the case and not as an expert, the subpoenaed witness
is entitled to receive $15 per day and 23 cents per mile
for travel to and from the court for each day he/she at-
tends. That amount of money may not fully compensate
the witness for loss of time from work or from business,
so the party who subpoenaed the witness may, but is not
required to, pay the person for the reasonable value of
the time away from work or the business lost in coming
to and from the court, waiting and testifying, as long as
the amount paid is not disproportionately more than
what is reasonable compensation for the time away from
work or business that the witness lost. A payment is disproportionately more than what is reasonable compensation if it is substantially, or significantly, more than such
reasonable compensation. If, on the basis of EF's testimony about how much he/she received and the work
time or business lost, you conclude that the amount was
disproportionately more than what was reasonable for
the loss of work time or business, you may take that into
consideration in deciding whether the amount paid to
EF influenced what he/she told you about what he/she
(saw, heard, did) in connection with what happened in
this case.[12]

Caldwell[13] in the Court of Appeals

On appeal to the Court of Appeals, that Court framed the issue on
appeal and its holding affirming the Second Department as follows:

At issue on this appeal is whether the testimony of a
subpoenaed fact witness, who receives a fee alleged
to be disproportionately in excess of CPLR 8001(a)'s
mandatory fee requirement for attendance at trial, is
inadmissible as a matter of law. We conclude that such
testimony is generally admissible, but that the trial
court should, in a proper case, charge the jury as to the
witness's potential bias, in light of the perceived exces-
siveness of the fee. Where, as here, the party that subpoenaed the witness offers no explanation for a fee that
is seemingly in excess of reasonable compensation for
lost time and incidental expenses, the trial court, upon a

timely request by an objecting party, must charge as to
the witness's potential bias.[14]

The Court gave a detailed recitation of the facts of the case and the
progress of the trial:

> In September 2006, defendant Communications Special-
> ists, Inc. (CSI), per its contract with Cablevision Sys-
> tems Corporation, began the installation of high-speed
> fiber-optic cable underneath Benefield Boulevard in
> Peekskill, New York. The work required CSI to cut a
> two-foot-deep and four-or-five-inch-wide trench along
> the entire length of the 3,000-foot street. CSI also dug 58
> one-foot-wide "test pits" in certain locations adjacent to
> the trench in order to locate pre-existing utility lines. CSI
> backfilled the trench and test pits but, at the time of the
> incident giving rise to this action, the street had not been
> re-paved.

> On October 11, 2006 at approximately 10:00 p.m., plain-
> tiff Bessie Caldwell, who resided on Benefield Boule-
> vard, took her dog out for a walk. She crossed Benefield
> Boulevard and walked the dog for a short distance. As
> she was crossing the street again, returning to her resi-
> dence, plaintiff tripped and fell, injuring her leg.

> Plaintiff and her husband (suing derivatively) com-
> menced this negligence action against, among others,
> CSI for creating a hazardous and unsafe condition in the
> road by failing to properly backfill the trench and test
> pits, failing to properly or adequately pave over those
> areas, and failing to install temporary asphalt. After
> CSI answered and the parties conducted discovery, the
> matter proceeded to a bifurcated trial with liability being
> tried first.

> Plaintiff testified that she stepped into a "dip in the
> trench" that caused her to fall. To rebut this testimony,
> CSI subpoenaed a physician who had treated plaintiff
> in the emergency room shortly after the accident. The
> doctor was called merely as a fact witness to testify con-
> cerning his entry in the "history" section of his consulta-
> tion note that plaintiff "*tripped over a dog* while walking
> last night in the rain." He testified consistently with his
> documented note. During cross-examination, plaintiff's
> counsel elicited from the doctor that CSI had paid him
> $10,000 for appearing and testifying. The doctor denied
> that his testimony was influenced by the payment, stat-
> ing simply that he was there to "testify to my records."
> His testimony consisted only of his verification that he

> made the entry into the emergency room record. No professional opinion was sought nor given. Plaintiff's counsel requested that the court strike the doctor's entire testimony or, in the alternative, issue either a curative instruction or a jury charge concerning monetary influence.[15]

The Court continued with the plaintiff's request for a charge tailored to the doctor's testimony:

> The following day, before summations, plaintiff's counsel asked that the court charge the jury that, pursuant to CPLR 8001, the doctor, as a fact witness, was entitled to a witness fee of $15 per day and $.23 per mile to and from the place where he was served with the subpoena. Defense counsel countered that the witness fee was the statutory minimum and that there was no prohibition against paying a fact witness for time missed from work. The court suggested that, rather than issuing a charge, the parties could address the issue during summation and the jury could draw whatever inference it wished from those facts. The court cautioned the parties against referencing the statutory criteria of CPLR 8001.

> After summations, where the parties addressed the doctor's fee payment in detail, the court gave the jury a general bias charge but made no specific reference to the doctor's testimony or the payment he received for appearing at trial. Following deliberations, the jury found CSI negligent, but that such negligence was not a substantial factor bringing about the accident. Supreme Court denied plaintiff's motion to set aside the verdict. The Appellate Division affirmed, holding that although CSI's "substantial payment" to the doctor did not warrant exclusion of his testimony, Supreme Court erred in failing "to adequately charge the jury regarding the suspect credibility of factual testimony by a paid witness," but that reversal was not required because the error was harmless.[16]

The Court explained its concern with the witness fee paid to the physician:

> We, like the Appellate Division, are troubled by what appears to be a substantial payment to a fact witness in exchange for minimal testimony. Such payments, when exorbitant as compared to the amount of time the witness spends away from work or business, create an unflattering intimation that the testimony is being bought or, at the very least, has been unconsciously

influenced by the compensation provided. While we are concerned by the amount the witness was paid for this minimal attendance and testimony, we conclude that the Appellate Division's order should be affirmed under the circumstances of this case.

CPLR 8001(a) provides that one who is compelled by subpoena to appear at trial is entitled to a $15 daily attendance fee and $.23 per mile in mileage fees. Although this is only the minimum that must be paid to a subpoenaed fact witness, that does not mean that an attorney may pay a witness whatever fee is demanded, however exorbitant it might be. Our courts and disciplinary rules have long acknowledged that "[t]o procure the testimony of witnesses it is often necessary to pay the actual expenses of a witness in attending court and a *reasonable compensation* for the time lost." "[T]here are [also] many incidental expenses in relation to the prosecution or defense of an action at law which can with propriety be paid by a party to the action."

What is not permitted and, in fact, is against public policy, is any agreement to pay a fact witness in exchange for favorable testimony, where such payment is contingent upon the success of a party to the litigation. Of course, that situation is not presented here. The doctor's testimony was limited to what he had written on his consultation note less than 12 hours after the accident and well before plaintiff commenced litigation. Nor can it be argued that the doctor tailored his testimony in exchange for the fee or that there is any record evidence that the doctor's consultation note was fabricated.

Plaintiff argues that, having been subpoenaed, the doctor had a legal duty to appear and a legal right to only a $15 attendance fee, and because he was paid in excess of that amount, Supreme Court should have stricken his testimony. That argument, however, is without merit since the fee set forth in CPLR 8001(a) is a minimum fee. Nonetheless, the payment of such a disproportionate fee for a short amount of time at trial is troubling, and the distinction between paying a fact witness for testimony and paying a fact witness for time and reasonable expenses can easily become blurred. A line must therefore be drawn "between compensation that enhances the truth seeking process by easing the burden on testifying witnesses, and compensation that serves to hinder the truth seeking process because it tends to 'influence' witnesses to 'remember' things in a way favorable to the side paying them."[17]

The Court concluded that a specific bias charge should have been fashioned by the trial court to address the compensation paid to the witness:

> In addition to asking the trial court to strike the doctor's testimony, plaintiff's counsel asked the court to charge the jury that, per the subpoena, the doctor was required by law to appear at trial and was entitled to a $15 attendance fee and $.23 per mile and "let [the jury] do with it what they will." This was tantamount to a charge request for a special jury instruction relative to the doctor's potential bias.
>
> We agree with plaintiff that Supreme Court should have issued a bias charge specifically tailored to address the payment CSI made to the doctor. Supreme Court generally instructed the jury that bias or prejudice was a consideration that it should consider in weighing the testimony of *any* of the witnesses, but this was insufficient as it pertained to CSI's payment to the doctor. To be sure, Supreme Court properly acted within its discretion in concluding that the fee payment was fertile ground for cross-examination and comment during summation. But because CSI did not even attempt to justify the $10,000 payment for one hour of testimony, Supreme Court should have also crafted a charge that went beyond the CPLR 8001 requirements. Supreme Court should have instructed the jury that fact witnesses may be compensated for their lost time but that the jury should assess whether the compensation was disproportionately more than what was reasonable for the loss of the witness's time from work or business. Should the jury find that the compensation is disproportionate, it should then consider whether it had the effect of influencing the witness's testimony. Of course, such a charge must be requested in a timely fashion. Additionally, it is within the trial court's discretion to determine whether the charge is warranted in the context of a particular payment to a witness, and to oversee how much testimony should be permitted relative to the fact witness's lost time and other expenses for which he is being compensated.
>
> We conclude that, although a more specific jury charge should have been given, Supreme Court's failure to issue one in this case was harmless. The dispute underlying the doctor's testimony was not whether he fabricated the contents of the consultation note. In other words, the substance of the doctor's testimony was such that the jury's

assessment was only tangentially related to the doctor's credibility.[18]

Conclusion

Since it may be another hundred years before the Court of Appeals weighs in on the issue, *Caldwell* is likely to be the final word on this topic for some time to come. Ironically, it looks as though the witness in the joke had it right all along: being paid for his time was permitted, while being paid for his testimony was not.

---

1.   For those too young to recall, this column's title was pirated from the 1952 Patti Page hit song "How Much Is That Doggie in the Window?"

2.   *See* 1988 Recommendations of the Advisory Committee on Civil Practice. Change comes slowly in this area. In 1840 the daily witness fee was 50 cents; thereafter, it was increased to a dollar and then, with the enactment of the CPLR in 1962, to $2. *See* Advisory Committee Notes.

3.   *Liebowitz v. State*, 95 Misc. 2d 183 (Ct. Claims 1978).

4.   *Bobrowsky v. Bozzuti*, 98 A.D.2d 700 (2d Dep't 1983) (citations omitted).

5.   *N.Y. State Dep't of Corr. Servs. v. C.S.E.A.*, 142 Misc. 2d 380 (Sup. Ct., Orange Co. 1989).

6.   *In re Robinson*, 209 N.Y. 354 (1913).

7.   *In re Robinson*, 151 A.D. 589 (1st Dep't 1912).

8.   *Id.* at 595.

9.   *Id.* at 600.

10. 86 A.D.3d 46 (2d Dep't 2011).

11. *Id.* at 55–56 (citations omitted).

12. N.Y. P.J.I.2d, Civil 1:90.4.

13. 2013 WL 451322 (Feb. 7, 2013).

14. *Id.*

15. *Id.*

16. *Id.* (citation omitted).

17. *Id.* (citations and parentheticals omitted).

18. *Id.* (citation omitted).

DAVID PAUL HOROWITZ (david@newyorkpractice.org) has represented plaintiffs in personal injury cases for over 24 years and is "of counsel" to Ressler & Ressler in New York City. He is the author of *New York Civil Disclosure* and *Bender's New York Evidence* (both by LexisNexis), as well as the 2008 and 2012 Supplements to *Fisch on New York Evidence* (Lond Publications). Mr. Horowitz teaches New York Practice, Professional Responsibility and Electronic Evidence & Disclosure at Brooklyn Law School. He serves on the Office of Court Administration's CPLR Advisory Committee, as Associate Reporter to the New York Pattern Jury Instruction (P.J.I.) Committee, and is a frequent lecturer and writer on these subjects.

This article originally appeared in the March/April 2013 *NYSBA Journal*.

ADR: A Smart Solution for Crowded Court Dockets

By Robert D. Lang

Perhaps no area has seen a greater rise in the use of mediation and arbitration than high stakes personal injury cases. Whether cases are in their earlier stages or on the trial calendar, both plaintiff and defense attorneys are increasingly using alternative dispute resolution (ADR) to resolve their cases. Personal injury litigation is particularly well suited to mediation, unlike business and commercial litigation, where there is often a greater common interest, if not collegiality, between counsel for the plaintiff and counsel for the defendant. The nature of these claims, other than in class actions, is such that the roles counsel play could easily be reversed, as both counsel are generally as experienced and comfortable representing the plaintiff in a commercial or business dispute as they are the defendant. This common ground helps communication between opposing counsel, which can lead to settlement without the involvement of a third party to facilitate negotiations. This is not the case for personal injury counsel.

One of the great untruths in personal injury litigation is that a lawyer never should be the first one to raise the prospect of settlement. Few statements are less accurate; lawyers well know that more than 90% of all personal injury cases settle. It is counterproductive to pretend otherwise. Moreover, it is sound business practice to consider settlement as soon as practicable because it reduces litigation costs and expenses. For the defense side in particular, the longer a case is pending the greater is the possibility that the defendant's officers and employees are no longer willing to testify for the defendant or have become ex-officers and ex-employees. What if an employee who would be asked to testify was fired for cause? If that cause is related to honesty, that is something that counsel for the plaintiff will be sure to probe and bring before the jury. Even if the employee is still with the company, that employee may have been transferred, perhaps across the country or to another country. Having that witness leave work to appear in trial is a costly and unnecessary proposition, if the reason is that the attorney refuses to discuss settlement with the adversary unless the adversary brings up the topic first. Clients are usually ill served by attorneys who refuse to broach the topic of settlement for fear of being considered weak or afraid. Fortunately, most attorneys now welcome the opportunity to use ADR to resolve their cases.

Glamour vs. Results

While one may debate whether law school adequately prepares graduates for the practice of law, and whether law school should be two or three years, most agree that law school fails to address one of the fastest-growing and most important areas of the law: alternative dispute resolution. Mediation and arbitration achieve faster, less expensive and comparable results to old-time, traditional litigation, with its numerous court appearances, conferences, hearings, trials and appeals. Yet some lawyers privately prefer to take a jury verdict for personal satisfaction. The lawyer has never lived who does not feel an adrenalin rush on hearing the words, "the jury is in." Many lawyers visualize that moment, based upon books, movies and TV. In film and television, when the foreman of the jury says, "We find the defendant guilty/not guilty," the whole world appears poised to hear the verdict. The camera swiftly moves to the faces of the victors and the vanquished. Especially regarding defense work, nothing binds a lawyer with the client more than a "DV"—defense verdict. To have the client and the claims examiner and supervisor in the courtroom when the jury returns a defense verdict is the closest most defense lawyers will come to the pantheon of great theater, which trial lawyers crave. The celebration immediately afterward, usually with adult beverages, further cements the relationship between the defense attorney, client and carrier.

Certainly no such moments of jubilation or despair occur when the arbitration award is received in the mail. To be sure, lawyers, and their clients will be happy or sad, but there is no great moment of total victory. More common is the low-key firm handshake or "job well done" email received from clients when arbitrations and mediations are concluded. An earlier and less expensive resolution of the case is not as glamorous as a jury trial, but, in many instances, it is the best way for an attorney to zealously represent the client's best interests.

Plaintiff's Bar vs. Defendant's Bar

In today's world, the ability to settle, not just try, cases can often be a most valuable asset for clients and carriers. However, personal injury litigators do not enjoy the collegiality of business and commercial litigators. Attorneys who typically represent plaintiffs in high-level personal injury cases are rarely, if ever, retained by insurance companies for self-insureds to represent defendants in those same cases. Likewise, the attorneys representing defendants in personal injury suits, who are customarily paid on an hourly or alternative fee basis, seldom represent plaintiffs in those same types of cases, where compensation is based upon a contingency fee. Indeed, some carriers require that their panel counsel agree *not* to represent any plaintiffs at all in personal injury cases. The resulting "opposite sides of the aisle" and "give no quarter" mentality of most plaintiffs' and defense counsel in personal injury cases can lead to skyrocketing legal fees and costs. Given these circumstances, the addition of a third-party neutral or mediator cannot only jump-start some negotiations but also lead the talks to a successful conclusion.

In personal injury cases, plaintiffs' counsel can have difficulty conveying to their clients the risks and problems in cases—especially when a relative or friend is whispering contrary advice in a plaintiff's ear, advice based on their memory of an entirely different personal injury case or a "made for television" courtroom drama. The entry of a mediator, often referred to as "Judge" and sporting more grey in his or her hair than the lawyers involved in the case, can often persuade reluctant plaintiffs to settle when their own attorneys are unable to do so.

There are attorneys who, although revered within their firm and among clients as "courtroom lawyers," and razor sharp on the rules of the evidence, recognize that they do not necessarily have the same high skill set when it comes time to settle the case. Courtroom lawyers who can be "compelled" to mediate a case allow clients and carriers to resolve the litigation earlier, with less expense and uncertainty. Attorneys who only deal with their adversaries as mortal enemies rarely fare well in the setting of a mediation. Mediators often encourage an atmosphere of dialogue and communication that promotes resolution of a case. Attorneys who can argue with their adversaries yet maintain cordial relationships with them—retaining some sense of humor—will do better at mediation.

Another consideration is the inevitable delays in courtroom litigation, with its attendant costs. For example, in many venues, it can be years between the time a case is placed on the trial calendar and when it is first called to select a jury. Even then, the actual start of a case may be delayed further if witnesses or counsel are unavailable—especially if some of the attorneys are already actually engaged in trial. On the plaintiff's side, a long wait is a big downside. For defense counsel and carriers, costs relentlessly accrue over time—another reason why mediation in personal injury cases is gaining traction.

The ADR Offensive

For the Plaintiff

Often, mediation can be used to hide a significant problem in a case, because it promotes conclusion of a matter before the adversary knows of the difficulty. For example, a plaintiff in a personal injury case may be unable to appear for deposition, a court hearing, or trial for any number of reasons, including deportation, incarceration, or drug or alcohol rehabilitation. Or it may be that a key witness has had a falling out with the plaintiff and, therefore, is no longer willing to cooperate and testify on the plaintiff's behalf. ADR can also conceal adverse medical histories. For example, a plaintiff may have a medical history which shows that the same body parts involved in the present lawsuit were the subject of prior claims and even testimony by the plaintiff. If these prior injuries cannot be explained adequately as being unrelated to the present injuries, plaintiff's counsel understandably want to avoid interrogatory answers, bills of particulars and testimony by the plaintiff becoming known to defense counsel. In all these scenarios, the timing of the offer to mediate is critical.

The moment of truth can also come for plaintiff's counsel when trial is near. Although excellent attorneys in their own right, many lawyers for the plaintiff prefer to hire outside trial counsel if aspects of personal injury cases are outside their immediate areas of expertise. However, with the retention of trial counsel comes a reduction of the fee which plaintiff's counsel will receive. Typically, a trial attorney will receive a contingency fee, one-third of the amount recovered. Thus, the plaintiff's attorneys may turn to private mediation to resolve the case so that, whatever the plaintiff recovers, the plaintiff's attorney will receive the full one-third amount and not have to share the recovery with another attorney.

To avoid tipping their hand to defense counsel, plaintiff's counsel can approach defense counsel and casually suggest that the case be mediated, maybe not even mentioning any particular reason. Or, plaintiff's counsel might suggest that several other cases with the same carrier be resolved on the same day or might make passing reference to "getting some money before the end of the year." Planting the seed of a mediated settlement before defense counsel are aware there may be a problem in the plaintiff's case can be an effective technique, benefiting the plaintiff and the plaintiff's attorneys.

Here is where art and skill can make all the difference. Plaintiff's counsel cannot appear too eager to mediate the case; otherwise, defense counsel, who are notoriously skeptical of plaintiffs, may suspect that the plaintiff's attorney is playing "hide the thimble." Any suggestion by the attorney for the plaintiff that the case be mediated, especially when the facts are such that an objective observer could conclude that the suit is anything but ripe for resolution, can raise suspicions. The attorney for the plaintiff will therefore try to set up a scenario where defense counsel will suggest the case be mediated. Or, the attorney for the plaintiff might innocently point out to the judge that perhaps the suit can be removed from the crowded docket if only the parties could bring themselves to agree on mediation, whether with a court-appointed mediator or a private mediator. No matter the particular words used, it is critical that the plaintiff's attorney not appear overly anxious, even though the plaintiff is intensely motivated to have the case settled before defense counsel becomes aware of the problems the plaintiff is seeking to veil.

For the Defense

Of course, defense counsel also may view mediation as a way to circumvent a weakness in their case. For example, a main defense witness may have been fired. Or a witness could have left the employer and no longer will cooperate. Perhaps compromising information is in the witness's personnel file. There are even circumstances where defense counsel knows, but counsel for the plaintiff does not, that a major defense witness will not or will fail to cooperate in the defense but may be eager to assist the plaintiff. The lawyer for the defendant can likewise pick up the phone or, when seeing his adversary in court, innocently suggest that the case be mediated (for any reason), perhaps stating that it is "time to clear up some inventory" or "time to get this case off the calendar." The point remains the same: when one side knows, but the other does not, that there is a significant problem in the case (often the situation), mediation can be an effective way to make sure the case is concluded without the adversary's knowing the problem.

Selecting the Mediator

All too often, attorneys rely on the recommendations of others in the critical step of mediator selection. It is all well and good for a lawyer to canvas the attorneys of the firm or ask colleagues for recommendations. However, those recommendations may fail to address critical relationships between the potential mediator and your adversary, and the prior track records that mediator has with your insurer or claims examiner. If the case proceeds to a mediation and does not settle, or does not settle on terms your insurer finds acceptable, a lawyer can expect questions from the claims supervisor as to why the particular mediator was selected. If that lawyer has nothing more to fall back on than the general reputation of the mediator, that response will likely be found inadequate—especially if the mediation goes poorly. A satisfactory response is that the attorney has had several cases with that specific mediator and those proceedings had good results; this answers the carrier's legitimate questions as to why a particular mediator was selected for this specific case.

Care also should be taken to ensure that the mediator is not a "personal favorite" of your opposing attorney. Although you do want a mediator who can be persuasive with your adversary, too close a relationship may give rise to the suggestion of partisanship, tilting the playing field in favor of your opponent. Learn which mediators are usually requested by your adversary and carefully weigh the pros and cons of agreeing to a mediator specifically recommended by the adversary.

One approach is to speak to your adversary at the beginning of the case and ask generally which mediators he or she uses and which mediators he or she seeks to avoid; in essence, share general information without making specific reference to the controversy at hand, before mediation is considered. Most lawyers learn to take note of their adversary's preferences and remember them when the time comes to agree upon a mediator for the case at hand.

Useful intelligence about which mediators to select or to avoid can be obtained by asking colleagues, often with other law firms, about prior cases they may have had with your adversary. If an attorney learns that the adversary prefers certain mediators over others, that intelligence can be used in creating strategies for mediating pending cases. It is important not only to know which mediators were used, but whether the mediations were successful. There is little purpose in choosing a mediator because he or she has a winning personality and fawns over you when your client is present at the mediation. The case cannot be settled if a mediator displays partiality. Whether the mediator, through various skills, wisdom and cajoling, can bring the parties across the finish line is critical. Everything else is, as they say, just "conversation."

With a particularly difficult case, it can be quite beneficial to recommend (or "reluctantly" agree upon) a mediator who has successfully concluded cases with your adversary. Keep in mind the prior track record of a mediator during the all-important selection process.

Mediating During Trial

Venues with favorable jury pools invite plaintiffs' lawyers to avoid mediation. One of the great variables in personal injury law is the jury. Lawyers in all fields agree that no one can predict what a jury will do, especially when potential jurors are drawn from backgrounds similar to those of plaintiffs in personal injury cases. One of the strongest cards that plaintiff's counsel can hope to play is that the jury will be sympathetic to the plaintiff's claims, especially on damages. Hoping to "ring the bell," some plaintiff's counsel therefore prefer not to engage in serious settlement discussions until the jury has been selected and opening statements given. They are keenly aware that insurance carriers for defendants in major personal injury cases are also mindful of the risks of submitting cases with large corporate defendants to sympathetic juries. To be sure, motions can be made to satisfy or reduce verdicts, and appeals can be taken. However, there is no certainty that such motions or appeals would be successful, and all of this militates against settling the case where a "good" jury for the plaintiffs is available or has been picked.

Although some attorneys therefore dismiss mediation as a viable option in such cases, the fact is that mediation is particularly helpful once the jurors are selected so that, with deference to Donald Rumsfeld, there are fewer "unknown unknowns." In many instances, the most effective and to-the-point mediations take place on the eve of trial or even during trial, with the case proceeding during the day and mediation taking place at night. Not only are there fewer variables—discovery has been completed and sometimes testimony is already under way—but since both sides are actually engaged in trial, the mediation quickly gets to the point and proceeds more swiftly, with less haggling. At this point, both sides know that the legal landscape may change tomorrow as witnesses are called and cross-examined.

Major personal injury cases require expert witnesses, certainly on damages but also on liability. Those witnesses called by the plaintiff and defendant include engineers, economists, actuaries, vocational rehabilitation experts, treating physicians and other experts. Many an attorney in the personal injury field has ruefully acknowledged that perhaps he or she would have been better off becoming a doctor, given the hefty fees these expert witnesses earn for testimony in court. Moreover, these fees have to be paid in advance and are not refundable, since a doctor has to sacrifice his or her entire workday to give testimony. Without such expert testimony, however, the case can fail on either side. Mediation is one of the best ways to have the benefits of expert testimony, without paying anew for the experts to appear in court. The expert's report, previously exchanged in discovery, can be utilized by either side in advocating its position. Substantial cost savings can be realized, with benefits to both the plaintiff's and defense counsel.

Arbitration

Several forms of alternative dispute resolution match well with personal injury cases. Arbitration is one. At first blush, one can assume that attorneys for the plaintiff would be loath to arbitrate any case, since they will be giving up their right to have the case heard and determined by the jury. This analysis is overly simplistic.

First, some plaintiff's counsel will not want their client's case to be heard by a jury because the jury pool may be more conservative than the sitting judge in the particular venue. In those instances, counsel for the plaintiff may not even request a jury trial. Rather, it will be defense counsel who, if given the option, would request a trial by jury.

Second, in many jurisdictions, the wait for trial is greater when the case is placed on the docket for jury trials. Depending on the jurisdiction and venue, the time between the case being called for trial in a jury as opposed to a non-jury setting may be years, not months. Since the attorney for the plaintiff is paid only when the case is resolved, whether by verdict or settlement, plaintiff's counsel has an incentive to ask that the case be tried before the court, and not before a jury. By the same token, insurance carriers may be more inclined to ask for a jury trial. The delay in resolution, particularly when there is a jury pool perceived to be favorable to the defendant, works against the plaintiff.

As far as defense counsel are concerned, although required to represent their clients zealously, they know that a jury trial takes longer to try than a non-jury case because of delays due to the scheduling of jurors. Indeed, the jury selection process—although quick in some jurisdictions—can take days or weeks in others. Jurors have to be available. A judge has to either sit in a room during jury selection or be available when rulings are needed on jurors. Lawyers will have to wait until the judge is available to make those rulings. All of this adds time. With plaintiff's counsel, their fee is based upon a percentage of the case's resolution; but defense counsel have the proverbial "meter" running when they are in court, waiting for the case to be called, waiting for jurors to be summoned, and during the selection process and challenges, whether for cause or peremptory. Offering to mediate or arbitrate and therefore eliminate the jury is not necessarily something that the plaintiff's attorneys will find objectionable; it may even be desirable to them, depending on the case.

Moreover, submitting a case to arbitration allows attorneys for the plaintiff the opportunity to sidestep potentially difficult problems which otherwise would take up time in court. For example, although the major players usually testify at arbitration, in many proceedings, each side will introduce evidence by affidavit and, with respect to medical evidence, provide medical reports rather than having the expert testify on the stand. If these major players were called as witnesses, either side might be able to score points by cross-examining such witnesses at trial. Arbitration avoids exposing weaknesses that could be revealed by the opposition's cross-examination.

High-Low Agreement
Nor is that all. In arbitration, lawyers for both sides can take into account the probable value of the case, based upon the venue and a likely jury pool, without undergoing the time and expense of a jury trial, and the uncertainty of what a jury may do. Often, the parties agree upon a "high-low" for the arbitration. One obvious benefit of a high-low agreement is that there is certainty on both sides. Plaintiff's counsel fear a defense verdict with no monies being paid to the plaintiff, or having a jury so dislike their client's case that it awards only a small figure. By having a guaranteed "low," the attorney for the plaintiff avoids such a situation.

The agreement on a "high" resolves the opposite problem. Defendants and their carriers fear a verdict which is higher than what is reasonably anticipated and which may withstand a motion to satisfy or reduce, or an appeal. Insurance carriers hold monies in reserve for outstanding claims, and one way for them to make certain that the reserve is adequate is by agreeing upon a "high." In complex personal injury suits, high-low arbitration agreements yield real and undeniable advantages for both sides.

From Mediation to Arbitration
The relationship between mediation and arbitration is such that sometimes one can flow into the other. For example, the parties mediate the case but are unable to bridge the final gap. Often, they will propose arbitrating the case but based on the high-low derived from the last demand and the last offer at the mediation. In such instances, the parties often will agree to arbitrate the case before the same individual who served as mediator. There are several reasons for this. One is that the mediator is already familiar with the case, having read the mediation submissions

and heard argument. Another reason is when an attorney believes that the mediator warmed to his or her arguments and therefore that attorney could have an advantage when the case is decided on the merits. However, some mediators decline to arbitrate cases they have mediated. Their reasons for doing so are various, including the concern that, having previously recommended a stated dollar figure for settlement after hearing the evidence, that opinion may change, and the attorney who, in essence, "relied" upon the earlier recommendation made in mediation, can hold the arbitration award against that mediator and therefore choose not to use that individual in future ADR.

Experts

The choice of doctors retained in complex personal injury cases can directly impact the choice of whether to litigate, arbitrate or mediate. The attorneys for the plaintiff do not have a free choice in selecting all of the expert witnesses. Treating physicians for plaintiffs, emergency room personnel, the plaintiff's personal or family physician, and those doctors who performed surgery typically "come with the case." All other experts, however, are selected by the attorney, whether the lawyer be for the plaintiff or the defendants.

In that selection process, due care is given for the professional background of the experts in medicine, biomechanical engineering, forensics, fire, vocational rehabilitation, and economics. The vetting of the experts is critical, as each side knows that the other is likely to check the experts' backgrounds and scrutinize the bona fides of their expertise. These credentials checks could uncover possible prior lawsuits against an expert. Attorneys for both sides will obtain and meticulously examine the testimony and reports the experts have given in the past.

Some lawyers lean toward experts with impressive academic and professional backgrounds, with curriculum vitae which can run for pages. These experts tend to stand up well on questioning of their expertise.

Experts with stellar academic credentials should be compared with others who, although qualified, may not have outstanding academic and professional pedigrees. However, when it comes time to testify at trial, many such experts have Teflon-like qualities, and it is difficult for opposing counsel to score points in their cross-examination. Undoubtedly, it would be best that the expert has both superior academic and professional qualifications and comes across to a jury as do iconic fictional doctors (such as Drs. James Kildare, Christina Yang and Steve Hardy).

Now comes the time for resolution of the case. The brilliantly written reports by experts with academic and professional credentials of the highest order help persuade the opposing side to lower its expectations and seek a settlement. But…not so fast! Lawyers may find that the extremely well-qualified experts they retained, although brilliant, do not relate well to jurors and can become unduly combative on the stand. In these circumstances, lawyers who retained combative doctors suggest, and strongly prefer, mediation or arbitration so that they can rely on the expert's well-written and well-crafted report rather than have the jury hear live testimony from a mercurial doctor.

One way to approach this subject, which requires some delicacy and finesse, is to "helpfully" suggest that everyone agree not to pay these doctors the exorbitant fees required for live testimony—often nonrefundable—and instead have each side rely upon the written submission of the expert.

However, what if counsel have retained experts who are beloved by juries, who can talk away a question and look at jurors with soft, wise, grandfatherly eyes (like a Dr. Marcus Welby or a Dr. Oz) knowing that whatever the shortcomings in the doctor's opinion, the jurors will like the doctor and believe the testimony? Clearly, this is a-game-within-a-game of courtroom acrobatics, tactics and strategies, in which each side seeks to maximize the strength of the expert and mask or minimize the weaknesses, and is using alternative dispute resolution and litigation concurrently to strengthen its position.

The Process

In settlement negotiations, attorneys scrutinize their opponents' body language and their tone of voice. But during mediation, the parties are separated. Typically, after each side has made an opening presentation to the mediator, the remaining proceedings go forward with one side sitting by itself in a room while the other side engages with the mediator in another break-out room. Although the attorneys will seek to anticipate the adversary's bottom line as numbers are proposed, to a large extent each side relies upon the mediator to find and, even more important, achieve, the client's settlement objective.

Depending upon the trust the attorneys place in the mediator, the lawyers may hold back on their final number, whether it be a demand or an offer. Other times, if there is a track record between the lawyers and the mediator, the lawyers may be more open and let the mediator know their final authority, in confidence that the mediator will not abuse that trust. In this regard, most private mediators realize that the key to their success is in achieving a settlement that will maximize their opportunity of being retained in the future. Mediators who betray confidences, give false expectations and, most important, fail to deliver, are rarely hired again, no matter how pleasing their personality.

There may also be instances where one side's expert is subject to a serious professional disciplinary proceeding or is about to have a malpractice suit reach trial. In these circumstances, that side may try to resolve the lawsuit in which the expert is slated to testify before, not after, the adversary becomes aware of the impending possible negative on that expert's qualifications. A call to the adversary suggesting mediation is one way to avoid the unpleasantness of having that expert cross-examined on the recent "problem."

Private mediators who are selected for personal injury cases are specifically chosen because they have knowledge, not only of the law, but of the value of personal injuries with particular emphasis on the county or district in which the case will be tried. Law clerks to federal judges usually have exceptional academic backgrounds, expert research skills, and they write brilliantly. When asked to value personal injuries, however, they will not perform as well. Law school teaches how to research issues of law, statutes, and regulations, but not how to put a dollar amount on redress for a quadriceps tendon rupture, acute tears of the posterior horn of the medial meniscus with multiple surgeries and possible future surgery. Accordingly, when a complex personal injury case comes before a judge at a settlement conference, the law clerk and law secretary may not prove to be the best resource for the judge (and litigants). That is why seasoned private mediators, rather than academically distinguished young law clerks and law secretaries, are better suited to resolving such cases.

Dramatic Differences Between Plaintiff and Defense Counsel in Personal Injury Lawsuits

As mentioned earlier, in litigation involving commercial or business interests, attorneys are capable of representing either side in the dispute. In a corporate takeover dispute, for example, Skadden may be representing the target company, opposing Wachtell, Lipton representing the corporation seeking to acquire; in their next encounter, their positions may be reversed, with Wachtell, Lipton representing the target company and Skadden representing the acquiring company. In this type of practice, lawyers are not wedded to one point of view, one strategy or one state of mind; they can represent either side of the transaction, with equal skill and fervor. The same is true in other areas of law, such as real estate, securities, banking and corporate transactions.

Not so in personal injury suits. The lawyers who typically represent plaintiffs scoff at the thought of representing insurance companies being sued because of an allegedly defective product, negligence or torts. Lawyers who represent defendants in personal injury cases rarely, if ever, represent plaintiffs, and complain that some lawyers will take any case where there is a significant injury and then try to conjure up facts to support a claim. Plaintiffs' attorneys grumble that the lawyers sent by defense counsel to court barely have authority to settle cases, state they are "handling someone else's" file and do little—other than delay proceedings. The attorneys for defendants counter that the lawyers sent to court by the plaintiff are young, inexperienced per diem stand-ins, who are paid just to cover the court conference, have little knowledge of the case and no settlement authority. Defense lawyers are paid on an hourly basis and are paid as the case proceeds, whereas plaintiffs' attorneys are not compensated based upon their time and are paid, if at all, only a share of the monies their clients receive.

From the sole standpoint of fees, the best result for a plaintiff's lawyer is a large sum of money for the client, one-third of which is kept by the lawyer, who has spent only a minimal amount of time on the case. The optimal financial result for defense lawyers is for their client to have paid little or no monies to the plaintiff, while defense counsel, with their hourly rate, have spent hours achieving that result.

Although collegial relationships can exist between attorneys for plaintiffs and defendants in personal injury cases, there is a definite divide, and a certain distrust by each side of the other. Indeed, although both plaintiff and defense lawyers may be active in bar associations, they often do not serve on the same committees, as they do not have the same interests. More often, each side will gravitate to its own bar association. Attorneys for plaintiffs join plaintiff-oriented bar associations such as the American Association for Justice (AAJ), while defense lawyers join the Defense Research Institute (DRI). Defense lawyers may join AAJ, but AAJ has committees, seminars, and litigation materials which are available only to those AAJ members who are part of the plaintiff's bar. Lawyers in "mixed" groups are less likely to let down their guard, especially since they may be thinking not only of their current case, but also the other pending cases in their offices against the same adversaries. It is no surprise that direct negotiation between such adversaries, when it comes time to settle cases, is neither smooth nor easy. Adding a mediator to the mix is often a necessary and welcome method by which such cases can be resolved.

Judges may try to settle cases in court. Although their interest is sincere, and they may sometimes succeed, there are several impediments to their efforts. First, some judges, particularly federal court judges, are reluctant to become involved in settlement discussions in cases they may later try. Settlement is, therefore, handled by magistrate judges and, in some jurisdictions, law secretaries or law clerks. The result is that the most knowledgeable jurists may be the least involved in major settlement efforts.

Second, judges usually seek to place a value on the case and persuade the parties that their evaluation is correct and should be accepted. However, the settlement process works better when the settlement figure evolves, rather than is imposed. If the plaintiff's attorney has evaluated the case at a certain figure for settlement purposes, or if the claims examiner on the defense side has reserved the case at a particular number, the fact that a judge may have a different number in mind may hinder a final settlement agreement.

Third, resolving a large personal injury case takes a great deal of maneuvering and time—which courts do not have. Often, mediations stretch over hours and may be conducted in sessions over several days. Due to budgetary constraints, the court system does not afford the time needed for long, extended settlement conferences. Private mediations, held outside the court, can start early in the morning, continue all day and into the night, if necessary, provided the parties are motivated and the opportunity to resolve the case is perceived to be obtainable, if only more time, cajoling, pushing and prodding—and giving and taking—can occur.

Private mediation is the best way to resolve larger multi-party personal injury cases for several reasons. Such cases often have multiple defendants—drivers of vehicles, manufacturers, inspectors, owners, managers, supervisors and subcontractors of all kinds. It is difficult to have meaningful settlement discussions unless all the parties are present. One of the only ways to have all the players together is in private mediation when the date is cleared in advance and the money people and claims supervisors with authority to settle are present.

Court-Ordered vs. Private Mediation

There is a significant difference between parties attending a compulsory court settlement conference or court-ordered mediation, as compared to those attending private mediation. In the former, the parties are required to appear, whether they wish to or not. One or both sides may not even be interested in talking settlement at that stage, for any number of reasons. They will appear at the settlement conference solely because they have been directed to do so by the court. That is a far cry from the attitude and motivation necessary to sit down and negotiate a settlement. Further, although public mediations may be less expensive than private mediations, in cases where the demand for settlement is seven figures, the cost of several thousand dollars for a private mediator is not a deterrent for either side.

In comparison, when the parties agree to private mediation, although they may speak confidently and longingly of having the case tried, they are actually sending the message that they are willing to expend significant effort to settle the case. Furthermore, since private mediators are paid meaningful fees, no side is going to pay for those fees and commit to having attorneys spend several hours negotiating unless each side is serious about trying to resolve the case. Committing to private mediation denotes a mindset that both sides are taking settlement seriously; the same cannot be said when both sides are required to appear for a court-ordered settlement conference.

Another reason why mediation helps settle personal injury cases is because the damage components are rarely clearly defined; they take time to sort out. The damages in a breach of contract case, for example, may be fairly straightforward. In a personal injury case, however, when it comes time to decide the value of past and future pain and suffering, nothing is exact, most of it is subjective, and everything is negotiable. Questions include whether, and to what extent, the plaintiff is truly disabled and unable ever to work again. Or will he or she be able to return to the workforce at some point in the future and, if so, in what capacity? When surveillance film of the plaintiff shows a supposedly injured person walking, driving and performing other activities, whether those restrictions are significant, temporary, or someone's wishful thinking must be assessed.

Evaluating the evidence and reaching an agreement on the value of the damages takes time, much discussion and comparisons of the opposing expert reports. This painstaking process is better suited to mediation than appraisal by a jury or a sitting judge. Complexities of quantifying injury into a dollar amount indicate mediation as the best way to resolve those important issues. Appraising damages in personal injury cases is neither simple nor direct. A full discussion and analysis of the multiple elements of damages in personal injury cases is required before a case can be resolved.

When a serious personal injury case is coming close to being called for trial on the court docket, the surest way to resolve the case is by spending hours and, if necessary, several days, in private mediation. Although it is possible to engage in settlement discussions while the trial is under way, the time and witness pressures are such that even the best multitasker is greatly challenged to both try the case and negotiate a settlement. Moreover, the meter will be already running for defense counsel, and checks will have been cut by both sides for experts, so the savings on litigation costs and expenses, which many parties seek to obtain by settling, will already be lost.

There are occasions where the attorney for the plaintiff may be perceived to have oversold the value of the case to his client, particularly at the time when the plaintiff hires the attorney. Or it may be that the value of the case was accurately assessed by the attorney for the plaintiff at the inception of the attorney-client relationship, but that later events have eroded its value. So, when it comes time for settlement, the plaintiff may balk, "Wait, you told me I had a great case, why are you changing your mind now?" A neutral, such as a former judge, sitting as mediator, can help persuade the plaintiff to agree upon a sum somewhat less than originally anticipated, especially if the plaintiff no longer has same great trust in the lawyer and/or the lawyer lacks the ability to persuade the client to appreciate the offer that is on the table.

Too often, a review of the case history reveals that no meaningful settlement negotiations have taken place between the time the action was commenced and its placement on the trial calendar. Not only are the parties not close to settlement, they are not even in the red zone. Oddly, much of the time near the end of negotiation is spent on the smaller dollars, since each side is looking for its own fair advantage. Plaintiffs do not wish to leave any money on the table, but the defense does not want to pay one dollar more than necessary. Resolving these final differences takes time and nuanced negotiations, sometimes over several days. Our overburdened court system lacks the critical resource time. Private mediators can place groups of lawyers in separate conference rooms or breakout rooms and maintain continued negotiations for hours.

Achieving finality is one of the biggest advantages of private mediation. If the case proceeds to trial and the plaintiff recovers a larger than expected verdict, the defense can appeal the verdict and, although that appeal may be unsuccessful, it may be another year before the plaintiff and plaintiff's counsel receive any money. An appeal on the defense side involves costs for printing the record on appeal or ordering the transcript of the trial proceedings as well as expenses of filing briefs. Insurance carriers may balk at these additional outlays. In private mediation, once the settlement agreement is signed, the settlement check is issued within a specified period of time.

Conclusion

In sum, litigation is designed to resolve disputes that the parties have been unable to resolve on their own. No one doubts that the courts are a useful and indispensable forum for dispute resolution. However, there are times when the process distorts the problem. Too often in litigation, the parties face each other and take on increasingly divergent positions, arguing that the accumulated evidence supports their respective positions. Mediation is quite the reverse, with the parties gradually moving toward one another, making compromises along the way, to arrive at a solution upon which both sides can agree. It has been wisely said that mediation is like making a soufflé, where sudden movements and loud noises are discouraged.

Going the route of private mediation, picking the right time to do so and the right mediator can achieve for the parties and their counsel what courts often cannot. That is the main takeaway from today's litigation in difficult, multifaceted personal injury cases, for those lawyers who wish to succeed, whether they represent plaintiffs or defendants.

ROBERT D. LANG (RDLang@Damato-Lynch.com) received his B.A. from the City College of New York in 1970 and graduated from Cornell Law School in 1973. He is a member of the firm of D'Amato & Lynch, LLP in New York City, where he manages the Casualty Department. The author would like to thank paralegal Sarah Dowson for her assistance.

This article originally appeared in the February 2014 *NYSBA Journal*.

PATHWAY TO THE PROFESSION: FROM LAW SCHOOL TO LAWYER

MARKETING YOU
AND
YOUR PRACTICE

Deal-of-the-Day Coupons
The Ethics of Discount Marketing by Lawyers

By Devika Kewalramani, Amyt M. Eckstein and Valeria Castanaro Gallotta

Legal Service Coupon Marketing

Deal-of-the-day and coupon marketing have gained in popularity with retailers, being offered via email, websites and other promotional tools. Lawyers seeking to access both broader and more targeted audiences are looking to promote their practices by offering discounted legal services and adopting group coupon marketing strategies as a way to reach new consumers seeking legal services. While there are differing views regarding the propriety of deal-of-the-day advertising[1] and the types of legal services best suited to discount marketing, the reality is that coupon programs for legal services are already widespread in certain marketplaces and regions. While lawyers may seek clients through these new marketing vehicles, they should be mindful of their professional and ethical responsibilities before engaging in this type of advertising activity. In addition, as technology and offer techniques evolve, new considerations arise.

Deal-of-the-Day
What's the Deal?

Group coupon marketing programs allow retailers to market products and services at a discount to consumers via websites that receive a portion of the retailer's profit. The retailer and the website separately negotiate the discounts to be applied. Subscribers to the website usually receive the offer via an email promoting currently available deals, noting certain restrictions or conditions, and providing the caveat that most deals are available for a limited time. Subscribers purchase the deal and are able to redeem a voucher or coupon provided by the website. Often, the offer is valid only if a certain minimum number of subscribers purchase the coupon. Typically, the website collects the cost of the coupon by credit card from the consumer, deducts a percentage of the gross receipts as its compensation and pays the balance to the participating retailer.

Legal Industry Coupon Programs

There are two types of popular legal industry coupon arrangements. The first is an ordinary coupon scenario where the subscriber buys a coupon for discounted legal services at the advertised rate with the promise that the rate applies to a specified number of hours of legal work. The subscriber separately pays the lawyer rendering services for the number of hours worked at the discounted rate. For example, the subscriber buys a $50 coupon that entitles him or her to receive five hours of a lawyer's time at a reduced rate. The second, and far more common, is the pre-paid coupon scenario where the subscriber pays the website up front for the entire value of the coupon for discounted legal services, regardless of whether the hours are actually worked or if the coupon is ever redeemed. For example, a lawyer offers an hourly rate discount of 50% for up to five hours, so the subscriber pays the full amount of $750 in advance.

Ethical Obligations in Legal Service Advertising

Legal services group coupon marketing implicates a broad range of ethics issues under the New York Rules of Professional Conduct[2] (the Rules) and the American Bar Association (the ABA) Model Rules of Professional Conduct (the Model Rules). The following Rules are some of the significant ones to consider:

- Rule 1.1 requires lawyers to provide competent client representation;

- Rule 1.5 prohibits lawyers from charging an excessive legal fee;

- Rule 1.7 requires lawyers to avoid conflicts of interest with current clients;

- Rule 1.10(e) mandates conflicts checking for new engagements against existing clients and previous engagements;

- Rule 1.15 proscribes commingling of client funds, requires segregation of client accounts and the safeguarding of client funds and other property;

- Rule 1.16(e) requires withdrawing lawyers to promptly refund any legal fees paid in advance but not yet earned;

- Rule 1.18 governs lawyers' duties to prospective clients;

- Rule 5.4 proscribes lawyer-nonlawyer sharing of legal fees and prohibits nonlawyers from regulating the professional judgment of lawyers whom they pay to render legal services for another;

- Rule 7.1 bars false, deceptive or misleading attorney advertising;

- Rule 7.2(a) forbids lawyers from compensating persons or organizations for a client referral;

- Rule 7.3 regulates solicitation of prospects by lawyers; and

- Rule 7.4 governs lawyers' identification of practice areas and specialties.

Structuring the Ethical Deal

State bar association ethics committees around the country are increasingly placing legal services coupon marketing programs under the ethics microscope. N.Y. State Bar Op. 897 (2011) (NY Opinion) concludes that it is permissible for lawyers to participate in daily deal websites but cautions lawyers to use such advertising carefully to avoid potential ethical pitfalls.[3] While several other states have approved lawyers' use of deal-of-the-day websites—subject to various limitations and conditions—some states prohibit legal service coupon marketing. For example, North Carolina, South Carolina and Maryland permit the use of properly structured legal services group coupon marketing deals, whereas Alabama, Arizona and Pennsylvania have found legal service group coupon marketing to be unethical and, as Indiana Bar Op. 1 put it, "fraught with peril."[4]

Recently, the ABA issued Formal Op. 465 (2013) (ABA Opinion), advising lawyers on using deal-of-the-day marketing programs while complying with the Model Rules.[5] Although the ABA Opinion provides warnings and guidelines regarding many of the same ethics issues analyzed by the NY Opinion, the ABA Opinion examines the issues under two different categories of group coupon arrangements, characterized as either "coupon" or "prepaid." The ABA Opinion concludes that while "coupon" deals can be structured to comply with the Model Rules, it identifies numerous issues associated with "prepaid" deals and is "less certain" that prepaid deals can be structured to comply with all ethical and professional obligations under the Model Rules. The particular ethics issues triggered by deal-of-the-day marketing websites are discussed below.

Improper Referral Payment, Fee-Splitting or Advertising Cost?

New York Approach

Rule 7.2(a) prohibits a lawyer from compensating a person or entity to recommend or obtain employment, or as a reward for having made a recommendation resulting in employment. Comment [1] to Rule 7.2 notes, however, that Rule 7.2(a) "does not prohibit a lawyer from paying for advertising and communications permitted by these Rules...." So, when a website collects the cost of a coupon from consumers of legal services and at the close of the deal-of-the-day deducts a percentage of the gross receipts as its compensation and pays the balance to the participating lawyer, does this constitute improper payment for a referral?

The NY Opinion found no violation of Rule 7.2 and agrees with South Carolina Bar Op. 11-05, which concludes that the money retained by the website is payment for "the reasonable cost of advertisements." The NY Opinion reasons that deal-of-the-day advertising does not run afoul of Rule 7.2(a) due to the lack of any individual contact between the website and the coupon purchaser, other than collection of the cost of the coupon by the website. The website takes no action to actively refer a potential client to a particular lawyer but merely charges a fee for carrying an advertisement, crafted by the lawyer, to interested consumers. The NY Opinion assumes that to the extent the percentage amount retained by various websites is a reasonable payment for this form of advertisement, there is no violation of Rule 7.2.

View of the ABA and Other States

The ABA Opinion reaches a conclusion similar to that of the NY Opinion, concluding that marketing companies that retain a percentage of payments obtain no more than payment for advertising and processing services rendered to lawyers who market their legal services, especially where lawyers structure the transaction as a "coupon" deal, since no legal fees are collected by the marketer. The ABA Opinion observes that the marketer's deducting payment up-front rather than billing the lawyer later for providing the advertised services does not convert the nature of the lawyer-marketer relationship from an advertising arrangement into a fee-sharing arrangement in violation of the Model Rules. The ABA Opinion caveats that the percentage retained by the marketer must be reasonable under Model Rule 7.2(b)(1).

The ABA Opinion also notes that many state bar associations have found lawyers' use of deal-of-the-day marketing arrangements to be permissible—that is, such promotions do not constitute fee-splitting with nonlawyers in violation of Model Rule 5.4. The underlying purpose of Model Rule 5.4 is to protect a lawyer's independent professional judgment by limiting the influence of nonlawyers on the attorney-client relationship. For example, North Carolina State Bar, Formal Op. 10 (2011) concludes that the portion of a fee retained by the website is merely an advertising cost, because "it is paid regardless of whether the purchaser actually claims the discounted service and the lawyer earns the fee." However, Alabama State Bar, Formal Op. 2012-01 (2012), takes a contrary position, finding that the percentage taken by the website is not tied in any manner to the "reasonable cost" of the advertisement. Thus the use of such websites to sell legal services is in violation of Rule 5.4, because legal fees are shared with a nonlawyer. Similarly, State Bar of Arizona, Formal Op. 13-01 (2013), observes that even if the portion retained by the website is reasonable, it constitutes improper fee sharing, because the consumer pays all the money directly to the website rather than the lawyer paying fees for advertising out of already earned fees.

Returns, Refunds and Retainers
New York Position

The NY Opinion observes that after a coupon is purchased, circumstances can arise where the coupon holder is unable to receive the full benefit of the legal services to which the coupon is entitled, thereby implicating Rule 1.5, barring excessive legal fees. For example, after the lawyer is paid by the website but before the purchaser receives the service, if the lawyer is unable to perform the work due to a conflict of interest under Rules 1.7 and 1.10(e) or lack of competence under Rule 1.1, then the lawyer must provide a full refund to the purchaser (including the portion retained by the website unless otherwise disclaimed). Similarly, where the buyer decides not to pursue the lawyer's services and discharges the lawyer, the lawyer must provide a full refund, subject to any quantum meruit claim for legal services performed prior to termination.[6] The NY Opinion also notes that in situations where a subscriber purchases a coupon but allows it to expire either by never seeking to use it or failing to use it before it expires or attempts to do so thereafter, the lawyer is "entitled to treat the advance payment received as an earned retainer for being available to perform the offered service in the given time frame."

Treatment by the ABA

The ABA Opinion agrees with the NY Opinion that the lawyer may retain the proceeds where coupon deals are purchased but never used. However, the ABA Opinion disagrees that lawyers must always return the entire amount of the purchase price, including any portion retained by the website, if legal services are not rendered for any reason whatsoever.[7] The ABA Opinion notes that while some states have concluded that retaining funds from an unredeemed deal constitutes an excessive fee under Model Rule 1.5, it differs with these states to the extent that lawyers had offered a "coupon" deal and disclosed that, as part of the offer, the cost of the coupon will not be refunded.[8] However, the ABA Opinion agrees that monies paid as part of a "prepaid" deal likely need to be refunded in order to avoid violating the Model Rules prohibiting unreasonable fees.

Contrasting "coupon" and "prepaid" deals, the ABA Opinion notes that for coupon deals, where the lawyer properly discloses as part of the offer that there is no right to obtain a refund of the purchase price of the coupon if the subscriber later has a change of heart, the right to compel a refund has been waived; whereas, for prepaid deals where the subscriber decides prior to its expiration not to proceed, the lawyer likely must refund unearned advance fees to avoid collecting unreasonable fees.

The ABA Opinion observes that where a lawyer cannot perform legal services required by the deal (either in coupon or prepaid deals) due to a conflict or other ethical impediment, the lawyer must provide a full refund to avoid receipt of an unreasonable fee. This duty to refund cannot be avoided through disclosure. Such a refund must be for the entire amount paid (i.e., including website fee), regardless of whether the lawyer is entitled to recoup any portion of the website fee. The ABA Opinion reasons that it would be unreasonable to withhold any portion paid by the purchaser if the lawyer's inability to render services is not the fault of the buyer. However, if a lawyer is not obligated to give a refund but chooses to, such as when a buyer allows a coupon deal to expire, the lawyer may refund only the portion of the payment received, provided this limitation is clearly disclosed at the time of purchase.

Avoid False or Misleading Advertising

New York View

The NY Opinion concluded that legal service coupon marketing must comply with Rule 7.1's strictures on attorney advertising: the daily deal advertisement must not be false, deceptive, or misleading (Rule 7.1(a)(1)); a written statement describing the scope of the service advertised for a fixed fee must be made available (Rule 7.1(j)); lawyers must render the service for the advertised fixed fee if the coupon buyer seeks that service within the specified time frame (Rule 7.1(l)); the offered discount must not be illusory and must represent an actual discount for the advertised service (e.g., an advertisement offering discounted services for five hours of legal work at $100 an hour for a total of $500 would be misleading under Rule 7.1(a)(1) if such lawyer's standard rate is $100);[9] the advertisement must include the label "Attorney Advertising" on the webpage and in the subject line of any related email (Rule 7.1(f)); and if the advertisement is "targeted" to a specific group, it becomes a solicitation and must comply with the rules on solicitation (Rule 7.3).

ABA Approach

The ABA Opinion notes that lawyers who choose to use deal-of-the-day marketing programs must properly supervise the accuracy of the content of the offers made to ensure they are not misleading or incomplete, in violation of the Model Rules. The ABA Opinion draws a distinction between advertising a "coupon" and a "prepaid" deal, observing that the latter likely presents greater obstacles because the public, particularly first-time or unsophisticated consumers of legal services, may not easily understand what legal services they require or are covered in an offer for "prepaid" deals for a specified service. The ABA Opinion cautions lawyers who offer "prepaid" legal services deals to carefully draft advertisements that clearly define the scope of the legal services offered, including whether court costs or expenses are excluded. In addition, the ABA Opinion advises that for both "coupon" and "prepaid" deals, lawyers should be explicit about the circumstances that may require a refund of the purchase price of a deal, to whom, and in what amount.

Absence of Attorney-Client Relationship

New York Perspective

The NY Opinion warns that because purchase of a coupon entitles the buyer to the described legal service, there is a risk that such an arrangement could be viewed, prematurely and improperly, as the formation of a client-lawyer relationship, before the lawyer has had any opportunity to check for conflicts of interests, determine if the described services are appropriate for the consumer, and if the lawyer is competent to render such services. The NY Opinion agrees with South Carolina Op. 11-05 that such a problem could be avoided with proper logistical arrangements and disclosures. The lawyer's advertisement on a deal-of-the-day website must disclose as part of the coupon offer that it is subject to a number of conditions: (1) before such a relationship is created the lawyer will check for conflicts and determine his or her competence to render services that are appropriate to the consumer; (2) if the lawyer decides that the client-lawyer relationship is untenable for such reasons, the lawyer must give the coupon purchaser a full refund; and (3) the lawyer must supply any other information preventing the offer from being misleading in any way. The NY Opinion adds that to the extent the client-lawyer relationship is actually formed, the lawyer must promptly describe the scope of the services to be performed and the fee arrangement pursuant to Rule 1.5(b).

Treatment by the ABA

The ABA Opinion alerts lawyers that they must be prudent and communicate the nature of the relationship formed, if any, by the purchase of a deal, in order to avoid creating any duties of confidentiality or to check for conflicts that may be owed to a "prospective client" (i.e., who consults about the possibility of forming a client-lawyer relationship regarding a matter) under Model Rule 1.18.[10] However, the ABA Opinion observes that the mere purchase of a deal for legal work does not automatically transform the buyer into a prospective client or a current client, entitled to the attendant duties owed by the lawyer. It notes that the lawyer's advertisement should explain that, until a consultation takes place, no attorney-client relation exists and no such relationship may ever be established if there is a conflict or the lawyer is unable to provide the representation. The ABA Opinion suggests disclosing on the website the use of a retainer agreement if the lawyer will require the potential client to execute one. It advises that the legal services promotions and other materials marketing the lawyer's services should contain language cautioning any consumer to review all purchase terms on the website, including whether the coupon is transferable. The ABA Opinion observes that not all legal services are appropriate for transfer or gift giving (such as "prepaid" deals), thereby obligating lawyers to properly evaluate the deal structure and the website to determine whether the offered legal service may be transferable.

Competence and Diligence

The ABA Opinion advises lawyers to limit legal services offered in such promotions to those they are competent to take on, and they should clearly disclose in the coupon offer any restrictions on the types of matters handled so that consumers can make informed decisions about purchasing the deal. Lawyers should also disclose that the matter covered by the coupon may become more complex than originally expected and may exceed the number of hours allotted under the coupon. The ABA Opinion adds that if the matter will require more time than is offered under the coupon, the lawyer must state how long it will take and at what rate, and be careful to limit the number of deals to be sold in order to avoid situations where the lawyer cannot manage matters promptly, diligently and competently.

Handling Advance Legal Fees

The ABA Opinion observes that deal offers are usually made through websites that collect payments, retain a portion thereof for their advertising services, and transfer the remainder to the lawyer, generally in a lump sum, reflecting the number of deals sold, without identifying individual buyers. So, whether this lump sum constitutes "legal fees... paid in advance" within the meaning of Model Rule 1.15(c) depends on the nature of the deal.

The ABA Opinion notes that for coupon deals, the coupon purchase merely establishes the discount applicable to the cost of future legal services. Therefore, no legal fees are involved unless and until a client-lawyer relationship is created, time is spent and the discounted legal fees are collected directly by the lawyer. Hence, the funds collected and forwarded by the website to the lawyer from the coupon sale are not legal fees and may be deposited into the lawyer's operating account. In contrast, with prepaid deals, the funds the lawyer receives from the website constitute advance legal fees because the website collects all the money the lawyer will be entitled to as set forth in the deal. Advance legal fees need to be deposited into a trust account and identified by the buyer's name. The ABA Opinion cautions that, in order to avoid improper handling of trust funds and fee sharing, lawyers should explain to the buyer of any "prepaid" deal what percentage paid is not a legal fee and will be retained by the website. In addition, lawyers who choose to offer a "prepaid" deal must make appropriate arrangements with the website to obtain adequate information about deal purchasers to properly comply with their duties to manage trust funds. The ABA Opinion cautions that despite the practical difficulties associated with tracking deal buyers and accounting for prepaid fees, even where lawyers use a website, they are still responsible for properly handling advance legal fees.

Avoid the Raw Deal

Clearly, legal services coupon programs trigger several important ethical issues. There may be new and different types of coupon arrangements that emerge, posing additional ethical concerns not yet identified. State bar associations thus far have taken divergent views on the propriety of such coupon programs. In light of these factors and other considerations, lawyers must carefully design and structure deal-of-the-day coupon offers to ensure any ethics issues are properly addressed.

1.   Krista Umanos, *Ethics, Groupon's Deal-of-the-Day, and the "McLawyer,"* 81 U. Cin. L. Rev. 1169, 1182–83 (2013).

2.   22 N.Y.C.R.R. §§ 1200 *et seq.*

3.   New York State Bar Ass'n Comm. on Prof'l Ethics, Op. 897, Marketing of legal services by use of a "deal of the day" or "group coupon" website (2011).

4.   North Carolina State Bar, Formal Op. 10 (2011); South Carolina Bar Ethics Advisory Comm., Advisory Op. 11-05 (2011); Maryland State Bar Ass'n Comm. on Ethics, Op. 2012-07 (2012); Alabama State Bar, Formal Op. 2012-01 (2012); State Bar of Arizona, Formal Op. 13-01 (2013); Pennsylvania Bar Ass'n, Advisory Op. 2011-27 (2011); Indiana State Bar Ass'n Legal Ethics Comm., Advisory Op. 1 (2012).

5.   ABA Comm. on Prof'l Ethics and Prof'l Responsibility, Formal Op. 465, Lawyer's Use of Deal-of-the-Day Marketing Programs (2013).

6.   *See* Rule 1.16(e); N.Y. State Bar Ass'n Comm. on Prof'l Ethics, Op. 599 (1989).

7.   *See* State Bar of Arizona, Formal Op. 13-01 (2013).

8.   *See* North Carolina Bar, Formal Op. 10 (2011); Maryland State Bar Ass'n Comm. on Ethics, Op. 2012-07 (2012).

9.   *See* N.Y. State Bar Ass'n Comm. on Prof'l Ethics, Op. 563 (1984).

10.   *See* Model Rule 1.18 and Comment [1] to Model Rule 1.18 ("Prospective clients, like clients, may…place documents or other property in the lawyer's custody…"); Indiana State Bar Ass'n Legal Ethics Comm., Advisory Op. 1 (2012) (the court could reasonably find that a person who has deposited money with the lawyer or lawyer's agent to form a client-lawyer relationship qualifies as a prospective client under Rule 1.18).

DEVIKA KEWALRAMANI is a partner at Moses & Singer LLP and co-chair of its Legal Ethics & Law Firm Practice group. She is chair of the Committee on Professional Discipline of the New York City Bar.

AMYT M. ECKSTEIN is of counsel to the firm in the Entertainment, Intellectual Property, Internet/Technology and Advertising practice groups.

VALERIA CASTANARO GALLOTTA is an associate in the firm's Litigation Department.

This article originally appeared in the May 2014 *NYSBA Journal*.

What Constitutes Attorney Advertising?

To the Forum:

I have been trying to develop an appellate practice and decided a few years ago to write a quarterly electronic newsletter discussing recent appellate decisions on issues that are of interest to my colleagues and potential clients. My thought was that the newsletter would give me an opportunity to demonstrate my writing and analytical abilities, and attract clients.

The newsletter (known as "The Able Law Firm Letter") targets attorneys and members of the business community who might refer business to my firm, and it includes my biographical and contact information. When I write about a case, I give the citation. I discuss the decision, its implications to the particular practice area and whether the decision is in my opinion correct. I never mention the names of the attorneys who handled the case. My plan is working and I have gotten several clients who tell me they decided to hire me because of the newsletter. Recently, I had a case in the Court of Appeals, which resulted in a major victory for me. I have decided to write about the case in my newsletter and plan on identifying the name of my client and highlighting the fact that I was the attorney who successfully handled the case.

A number of colleagues have suggested that my newsletter is attorney advertising, and that it is unprofessional for me to tout my victory by writing about it. Frankly, I do not think my colleagues are correct, but I am wondering whether it is possible that I am doing something wrong. I have also been told that even though my Court of Appeals decision is a reported case, I need the permission of my client to write about the case and identify its name.

Sincerely,
I.A.M. Able, Esq.

Dear I.A.M. Able, Esq.:

Your questions concerning The Able Law Firm Letter raise significant issues. First, are prior editions of The Able Law Firm Letter that merely discuss recent developments in the law "attorney advertising" pursuant to the Rules of Professional Conduct? Second, does the proposed forthcoming edition of The Able Law Firm Letter, in which you plan to tout your recent victory in the Court of Appeals, constitute attorney advertising? Finally, if that forthcoming edition is attorney advertising, are you required to obtain written consent from the client about whose case you intend to write?

Under Rule 1.0(a) of the Rules of Professional Conduct, a communication does not rise to the level of an "advertisement" unless it is "about that lawyer or law firm's services." As Professor Roy Simon, a leading commentator on New York ethics issues, wrote in his treatise (2013 ed.): If "a communication is not about either the lawyer making the communication or the services of the law firm making the communication, then it is not an advertisement" (at 22).

The principal advertising guidelines are in Rule 7.1. Comment 7 to Rule 7.1 states, in relevant part:

> Topical newsletters, client alerts, or blogs intended to educate recipients about new developments in the law are generally not considered advertising. However, a newsletter, client alert, or blog that provides information or news primarily about the lawyer or law firm (for example, the lawyer or law firm's cases, personnel, clients or achievements) generally would be considered advertising.

Professor Simon seems to concur with this view (at 1350).

Merely adding a lawyer's biographical information or contact information to a topical newsletter does not make the newsletter "about the lawyer or law firm's services." N.Y. State Bar Op. 848 (2010). Therefore, it appears that the prior editions of The Able Law Firm Letter are not "advertising" within the meaning of Rule 1.0(a).

However, the forthcoming edition of The Able Law Firm Letter (in which you intend to discuss your recent victory in the Court of Appeals) likely qualifies as an "advertisement" under Rule 1.0(a) because it touts your victory, rather than merely discussing the result in the case.

Rule 7.1 therefore applies to this communication. Rule 7.1 is extensive, and you should pay close attention to it. In particular, you should note the following:

Rule 7.1(a)(1) states that a "lawyer or law firm shall not use or disseminate or participate in the use or dissemination of any advertisement that contains statements or claims that are false, deceptive or misleading."

Rule 7.1(b) sets forth some categories of information that an advertisement may contain, including qualifications, names of "regularly represented" clients (provided they have given prior written consent), bank references, and range of fees.

Rule 7.1(c) states various matters that a lawyer may not include.

Rule 7.1(d) sets forth information that a lawyer may include, but only if the communication complies with Rule 7.1(e).

Rule 7.1(f) requires advertising to be prominently labeled as "Attorney Advertising" on the first page of a hard copy communication, on the home page of a website, and on a self-mailing brochure or postcard. It also states that, for a communication that is sent by email, "the subject line shall contain the notation 'ATTORNEY ADVERTISING'" (capitalization in the original).

The third part of our answer to your question deals with whether you must obtain your client's consent to write about your victory on the client's behalf. The answer here is probably not.

There are two rules that require an attorney to obtain the client's prior written consent for a communication that constitutes "attorney advertising": Rule 7.1(b)(2), which allows an advertisement to mention the "names of clients regularly represented, provided the client has given prior written consent"; and Rules 7.1(d)(3) and (e)(4), which allow for "testimonials or endorsements of clients, and of former clients," provided that "the client gives informed consent confirmed in writing."

In our view, neither of these applies to your forthcoming newsletter. Both rules appear to apply to client endorsements, whether implicit (Rule 7.1(b)(2)) or explicit (Rule 7.1(d)(3)). Many law firms list the names of representative clients to convey an implicit endorsement. That is, if XYZ Bank, or ABC Insurance Company, regularly engages the law firm, those clients are happy with the law firm's performance. Other lawyers like to use an explicit endorsement (e.g., Clarence Client says: "I.A.M. Able is the most able lawyer in town"). Both rules require that such endorsements be cleared with the client in advance, and that the client give prior written consent.

Because the forthcoming newsletter is not offering the client's name as a testimonial, but only as part of the truthful reporting about a decision by the Court of Appeals that is a matter of public record, the obligation to obtain the client's written consent is far from clear. The better reading of the Rules is that obtaining the consent is not required. The safer course under the Rules and (perhaps more important) for client relations is to obtain the consent anyway.

Sincerely,
The Forum by

Vincent J. Syracuse, Esq.,
Jamie B.W. Stecher, Esq., and
Matthew R. Maron, Esq.,
Tannenbaum Helpern Syracuse & Hirschtritt LLP

This article originally appeared in the September 2013 NYSBA Journal.

Our Evolving Profession
How Lawyers Increase Business Not So Different From Other Fields
By Brandon Vogel

Clients are key to any successful law practice. Acquiring and serving those clients well requires skills rarely taught in law school. Many attorneys, both solo practitioners and partners in large firms, know that from experience.

We asked three professional advisers to tell us what lawyers should do in pursuit of a successful legal practice in today's evolving profession. Here is what they told us:

Clifford Ennico: Be savvy

Words of wisdom from his Italian grandmother have resonated with Clifford Ennico throughout his 35-year legal career.

As a child, she told him, "If someone called me a donkey, I would laugh. If 10 people called me a donkey, I would buy a saddle and offer them rides."

In the late 1980s, Ennico was practicing corporate finance, venture capital and securities law. He realized that computer start-up companies had specific legal service needs.

His experience with technology law paid off handsomely as he gained 25 clients within a month.

"I had a learning curve, but I wasn't afraid to stretch a little," said Ennico, a solo practitioner in Fairfield, Connecticut. "Do not be afraid to be entrepreneurial."

"The key to success in any small business or legal practice is how you market," said Ennico. He said that lawyers working for an established law firm might be able to succeed without much marketing, but the partners will expect you to grow your client base. "Not marketing is not an option. You have to do it. Do it professionally, do it ethically, but do it."

Ennico suggested that lawyers use the back of their business card and bullet key points about themselves.

He also advised lawyers to market themselves, even if they have more clients than they can handle. He estimates that he spends 25 percent of his time marketing his practice by speaking at events and talking with the press.

At least once a week, he will get a referral from someone who heard him speak. "I talk about how to solve the problems of our clients," said Ennico. "That is what you as a lawyer are uniquely qualified to do."

"Every lawyer should have their own website and an email address connected to that website," said Ennico. "AOL and Yahoo email addresses instantly kill your credibility."

Ennico acknowledged that his website, which includes his fee schedule, might make him unpopular with some attorneys. "It is for the clients," said Ennico. "Clients know exactly what the fee is and are more willing to pay for representation because there are no surprises."

He recommends lawyers have something on their website that makes a client say, "I get it." He includes bullets of his most repeated services, as well as a list of what he does not practice.

"I don't want to waste my time or yours," said Ennico. He also includes on his website the line, "Call Me—I Don't Bite," to calm clients' fears about speaking with a lawyer.

Marian Rice: Be Visible

Garden City attorney Marian Rice, a partner at L'Abbate, Balkan, Colavita & Contini, LLP and co-chair of the State Bar's Law Practice Management Committee, said lawyers should determine their area of practice before seeking the best source of business for that area of practice.

If attorney referrals are the primary source of business, Rice recommends that attorneys join bar associations and become active in committees that include attorneys from every area of practice.

"Volunteering to perform needed tasks and then delivering as promised will earn you the respect and trust of your fellow members," Rice said.

Joining substantive law committees or sections in a chosen area of practice is also important to "keep you at the top of your game."

If the primary source of business is in the business community, Rice suggests that a lawyer may opt to become an active member of the local chamber of commerce or a charity to "show people that you are knowledgeable, diligent and responsive." However, Rice warns against spreading yourself too thin since the point is to build relationships.

Rice represents attorneys and is often retained by insurance companies to represent lawyers. "Speaking to lawyers on issues affecting their practice helps me to get in front of lawyers. When you speak on a panel, the audience can see you know what you are talking about," said Rice. "It's been an invaluable resource."

Carol Schiro Greenwald: Be Strategic

Carol Schiro Greenwald, owner of MarketingPartners, which helps lawyers grow their practice, said lawyers often do not have the sales skill-set. "Lawyers tend to be introverts and rational thinkers, whereas sales is very emotional. That's hard for a lot of lawyers," she said.

She said that lawyers rated highly by their peers do not necessarily bring in clients. "They judge each other on intellectual prowess. Clients do not ask how good you are as a lawyer. They assume you are a good lawyer," said Greenwald.

"You have to know your client's world," advised Greenwald. "Their financial planner knows their world; their attorney doesn't."

To better serve clients, she advised that elder law attorneys read *AARP Magazine* to stay current on trends and to be able to ask their clients interesting and relevant questions.

"If you are not following their world, you are going to miss a trend that affects your clients."

She also noted a real estate transaction that might be a first for a client is a routine event for an attorney. Clients do not understand court delays, she said.

Chemistry is key to a good lawyer-client relationship. "Clients ask themselves, 'Can I Trust You?' and 'Do I Like You?' It's a sales process in that you're going from a handshake with a stranger to a chemistry-and-trust-based relationship."

Lawyers should have a strategic plan when it comes to finding business. "Figure out what you like to do," advised Greenwald. "Pick a kind of law, then a kind of client. From there, create your ideal client. Do not network until you have figured that out."

Greenwald makes all of her clients join a group relevant to their practice.

"Most people go unprepared for networking events or are not sure what they might get out of it," said Greenwald. "Most events take four hours of your day. You have to do the research, you have to take notes and decide if it is worth going to. Always send a follow-up note with a reference about what was most important to you in the conversation."

"Any lawyer who chooses can learn to market themselves. It's not a personality thing," said Greenwald.

"Law requires you to research and be intellectually grounded and frame your arguments, as does marketing. It's the same skill-set in a different venue."

Brandon Vogel is NYSBA's Social Media and Web Content Manager.

This article originally appeared in the September/October 2014 NYSBA State Bar News.

Presentation Skills for Lawyers
Handling the Question & Answer Session
By Elliott Wilcox

*A*s the applause dies down, the emcee addresses you and says, "Thank you for speaking with us today—we really enjoyed it and received a lot of valuable information." Without warning, she turns to the audience and asks, "Does anyone have any questions for our speaker?" Urp. You didn't know they'd have a Q&A session after your presentation. What do you do?

If you're speaking to promote your firm or legal expertise, you will have to deal with question and answer sessions. Handle them well, and you'll appear to be the expert you say you are. Handle them poorly, and your expertise becomes suspect. Here are some tips for ensuring the success of a Q&A session.

Tell them in advance. If no one asks any questions, the Q&A session feels awkward for both the speaker and the audience. Usually, the audience didn't think of any questions because they didn't know they'd get the chance to ask them. You can fix this by telling them about the Q&A session at the beginning of your speech ("I'm sure some of you will have some questions about this subject. Please hold them until the Question and Answer session after my presentation, and I'll be happy to answer them then.") Alternative, ask your introducer to tell the audience about the Q&A session. ("After Shannon finishes speaking, she'll be happy to answer your questions.")

Prepare sample questions to prime the pump. Sometimes, even when you've notified them about the Q&A session, they're so stunned by your presentation that they forget to ask any questions. When that happens, kick-start the Q&A session with some sample questions. ("When I've presented this information before, someone in the audience usually asks, 'But does that tax provision also apply to LLCs?' It does, and here's why…") No one wants to be the first to ask a question. Jump-start the process, and they'll be more willing to ask questions.

Be prepared. Great! They're asking questions, just like you'd hoped. Now comes the hard part—you need to answer them. This will be the smallest portion of this article, but it's the most important. Just like the Boy Scouts, you must "Be Prepared." Know your subject matter and what questions to expect from your audience. If someone asks a question that you don't know the answer to, tell them you don't know. Promise to get back to them, and keep your word.

Repeat the question. If you speak to large groups, use a microphone, or record presentations for later broadcast, you should repeat the audience's questions. This helps everyone hear the question, and buys you a few additional seconds to compose your response.

Don't let one person dominate the Q&A. Remember the guy in law school who always dominated the classroom conversation? The class didn't like him then, and your audience doesn't like him now, either. How do you prevent one person from controlling the Q&A session? Offer to answer their questions after the presentation. Take only one or two questions from each person, to give everyone an opportunity to ask questions. Stop calling on that person.

You can even ask the emcee or meeting planner if anyone will give you problems during the Q&A. ("Oh yeah—Mr. Big always likes to heckle the speakers.") If so, ask for help—tell them to tap Mr. Big on the shoulder, pretend he's got a phone call, and walk him out of the room. They want your presentation to succeed, so they're usually willing to help. Just remember—you're onstage, so you're the one in control of the room. Don't cede your control to someone in the audience. Whatever you do, do it tactfully. Don't embarrass an audience member, unless they really, *really* deserve it. Chances are, they don't.

Don't offer advice that applies to only one specific instance. To head this off in advance, tell them you can't answer specific scenarios, since you won't be able to give a valuable answer without knowing all the facts. As always, remind them that they would best benefit from retaining private counsel to deal with specific legal issues. If someone is obviously trying to grill you about a legal problem they have, offer to meet with them privately after the presentation. ("This would take longer to answer than we have time for. Please meet with me after the meeting, and I'll be happy to speak with you then.") If it can't be answered during the Q&A period, it's probably a situation they need to retain your services for, anyway.

"I'll take two more questions." Give them a clue that the Q&A will end soon by saying you'll take two (or three) more questions. To ensure that the final question is worthwhile, try this technique: "Okay, this is going to be the last question. Please remember that I will be happy to meet with you afterwards for as long as I can. Now, let's finish with whoever has the absolute best question that will help the greatest number of people." When you phrase it like that, most people will drop their hands, and the remaining questions will usually be worthwhile.

Have a second close. Most Q&A sessions end on a low note. Take some advice from the bad guy in *Highlander*: "It's better to burn out than to fade away." Don't let the impact of your presentation dwindle away. Have a second closing comment prepared to deliver after you've answered the final question. This statement can be anywhere from 30 seconds long to a minute or so. It should remind them of the main point of your speech, and also end the presentation on a high note.

Handling the Q&A session can be difficult and a bit uncomfortable at times, but if you will do your research, be prepared, and follow these tips, you'll handle it with poise and polish. *Any questions?*

ELLIOTT WILCOX is a professional speaker and a member of the National Speakers Association. He has served as the lead trial attorney in over 140 jury trials, and teaches trial advocacy skills to hundreds of trial lawyers each year. He also publishes *Trial Tips*, the weekly trial advocacy tips newsletter available at www.trialtheater.com.

This article originally appeared in the January 2010 *NYSBA Journal*.

Presentation Skills for Lawyers
It's Not About You!
By Elliott Wilcox

*H*e's only been speaking for 10 minutes, but already you're sorry you re-scheduled that root canal appointment. So far he's discussed what his plans are for the board, who he wants to partner with, how he prepared for this position, and how he wants you to help him during his term as chairman. You sit in the audience, trapped, thinking to yourself, "So what? Who cares? I've got a billing quota to make, a brief due next Tuesday, and the temperature in here is freezing. Who cares about what you want?"

Sound familiar? We've all listened to speakers drone on about what they've done, what they want to do, how they want to do it, and who they want to do it with (or to).

Worse yet, some of us have done the exact same thing. Whether arguing a summation, presenting a community program, or speaking with our kids, we talked about what *we* want, rather than what our audience wants.

Let's be blunt: **audiences don't care what you want.**

It's not about you. Audiences are composed of people who care about what *they* want. They want to be healthier, happier, smarter, safer, and richer. They want to be better parents, investors, communicators, leaders, or lovers. They want to be more productive, more efficient, have more pleasure in their careers, and avoid the pitfalls and perils of public and private life. Audiences listen to speakers because they want us to enhance their lives.

Do you want to be a successful speaker? Do you want the audience to listen to your every word? Would you like your audience to think, act, or feel differently when you're done speaking? You need to begin by understanding one simple fact: **It's not about you.**

Tune into W.I.I.F.M. Don't start your speech by saying, "I would like…" or "I want…" Instead, start your speech by turning the dial to W.I.I.F.M. That is the radio station every audience member is tuned into: "What's In It For Me?" Remember, you're competing with all of the other ideas and concerns spinning through your audience's minds. They're thinking about their jobs, their families, what they have to do tomorrow, who they need to talk to, bills they need to pay, whether or not they turned off the iron before they left the house this morning, and a dozen other concerns. If you can't give your audience something of value, they tune you out and switch to one those competing thoughts.

Sit in your audience. Want them to pay attention? Start by thinking about your speech from your audience's point of view. What do they want to learn? What do they want to do differently? How can you help them improve? Tune into your audience's wants, needs, and desires. Ask yourself, if I was sitting in the audience, would I be interested? If I didn't know this speaker, would I care about what they have to say? Is this a worthwhile use of my time? If you answer, "No," ask yourself, "Why not?" Are you talking about what you care about, or are you talking about what they care about? Find out what your audience wants, and give it to them.

Provide more than they expected. If you are speaking to advertise your firm or your legal expertise, don't spend time talking about how great you are or how wonderful your firm is. **They don't care.**

Instead, talk about the benefits you can provide. Can you help their business save money? Can you protect them from potential lawsuits? Can you help them plan for retirement or to avoid a messy probate situation? That is what the audience cares about.

This approach even applies to jury trials. Do you want them to find the defendant liable? To tell the plaintiff he has no case? To find someone guilty? I bet you're already ahead of me by now: **they don't care about what you want.**

Think to yourself, "If I was sitting in the jurors' seats, why would I care about this case? What's in it for me?" When you can answer that question and tie it in to the outcome your client desires, you have a successful trial presentation on your hands.

So what do they care about? They want to walk out of that courtroom and feel they've done their civic duty. They want to think they've been fair. They want to know they've been just. Talk about what they want. Show them how their verdict prevents an injustice.

Remember: it's not about you. To present successfully, talk about what your audience cares about.

ELLIOTT WILCOX is a professional speaker and a member of the National Speakers Association. He has served as the lead trial attorney in over 140 jury trials, and teaches trial advocacy skills to hundreds of trial lawyers each year. He also publishes *Trial Tips*, the weekly trial advocacy tips newsletter available at www.trialtheater.com.

This article originally appeared in the February 2010 *NYSBA Journal*.

PATHWAY TO THE PROFESSION: FROM LAW SCHOOL TO LAWYER

PERSONAL DEVELOPMENT

Unexpected Career Transitions
By Gary A. Munneke and Deb Volberg Pagnotta

Introduction

Among the skills broadly defined as practice management skills, those dealing with career development and advancement are often overlooked. As lawyers, we are forced to address career issues when we are in law school, and on those occasions when, by intent or necessity, we make professional transitions in our professional employment. Yet many lawyers do not recognize that career skills are closely related to long-term success, however they define it, and personal satisfaction. Many lawyers deal with their careers only when circumstances arise that force them out of the status quo. And those who work in one firm or other employment setting for their entire professional lives may never confront these fundamental questions: What do I want to achieve in my career as a lawyer? What path should I follow to attain my goals? What skills will I need to attain my expectations?

This month, the Law Practice Management column turns to someone who has not only made her own career transitions, but who coaches lawyers in the career transition process. Deb Volberg Pagnotta is the president of Interfacet, Inc., a White Plains-based human management consulting practice. Her insights on career transitions are particularly relevant in an economic downturn, during which significant numbers of lawyers have been forced to come to grips with job loss in a market where new opportunities seem limited, and even lawyers who have not lost jobs personally have had to contemplate the possibility of professional dislocation. Ms. Pagnotta's insightful observations should connect with more than a few *Journal* readers.

"The One Less Traveled By"

In 1995, the year I turned 40, I was abruptly fired from my job as acting general counsel at a state agency. A new governor had just been elected, and the winds of change blew most of my law colleagues out of their jobs. I had been in public service for 12 years and had fully anticipated remaining there for at least 12 more.

Change did not sit well with me or my fallen colleagues, despite assurances from well-meaning friends and counselors that "this could be the best thing that ever happened to you." At the time, I remember tucking into my wallet a tiny copy of William Ernest Henley's poem "Invictus":

> Under the bludgeonings of chance,
> My head is bloody, but unbowed....

I am the master of my fate:
I am the captain of my soul.

This was to be my mantra; I was determined to march forward as the sole master of my fate, and forge my new future singlehandedly. Much to my surprise and distress, nothing turned out the way I had envisioned.

First, law jobs were not abundantly available, and, second, competition was fierce for the ones that existed. Reluctantly, I started a solo practice in employment law, focusing on discrimination. Within several years I joined a small firm in White Plains as an employment practice partner. In 1999, as my interests and client base shifted from litigation to counseling and training, I created a consulting practice, which provided corporate training on harassment, cultural diversity, and conflict resolution. These issues meshed well with my college studies in anthropology and linguistics. In 2000, when my law firm merged with another and my husband and I were in the process of adopting our daughter from China, I realized that it was time to reassess my work/life priorities. After much soul searching, I decided to give up the traditional practice of law to pursue my consulting practice exclusively. Now, almost 10 years later, I love my work; I make my own hours; and, amazingly, I am able to weave my various interests together daily.

The New Realities

Beginning in 2008 and continuing into 2009, lawyer layoffs from firms of all sizes have occurred in record numbers. In contrast to the years before the economic downturn, these lawyers face unique challenges in transitioning to new work. First, we face the harsh economic reality that law jobs themselves are decreasing, whether in firm practice, the government sector, or general counsel.[1] So, less soup is in the pot. Second, lawyers are used to being the advisors, the thinkers, and the doers, not the ones who are "done-to." Third, it is difficult to maintain optimism in a market where jobs are scarce, competition is great and the end is not in sight. Fourth, many, if not most, lawyers have developed a niche area of expertise. This creates a sense of limited opportunities, in their own and in others' perceptions. Fifth, lawyers often have pursued a legal career since youth, rendering this sudden, unwanted change additionally painful.

However, as my own career counselors told me, these challenges also present great possibilities. If you are a laid-off lawyer, or one who is contemplating an intentional career change, consider the following measures to assist you in following your unique path.

Finding Your Own Path

Carefully explore what you—not others—want to do. Many will offer advice on various options, but remember nobody else walks in your shoes. Take time to review what you liked and what you didn't like about your past work. Assess your real financial needs, and present assets. Make choices that are best for you.

Dealing With Circumstances

This may be an unexpected and devastating change for you, but it serves little purpose to assign blame or dwell on your misfortune. Imagine sitting in a boat, rowing as hard as you can across a sea tossed in a storm by angry waves. When you are swept inexorably in directions you did not anticipate and which you cannot control, you may feel overwhelmed. It would be futile to waste your energy rowing frantically to get back to where you started. Instead, your survival may depend on making your way out of the open waters and into a safe port where you can regroup and move on to new opportunities.

Your Choices Are Varied

You can work towards landing at an organization very similar to the one you recently left, with the goal of doing the exact type of work you've always done. Or, you can transpose your legal skills—the ones you enjoy—to other types of legal work. Were you doing commercial work? Your writing skills might serve you well in appellate work, legal journalism, or in-house counsel. If you love the advocacy of litigation, explore other types of litigation that are seeing an upswing. Perhaps bankruptcy, foreclosure, or employment law makes sense for you. Alternatively, you can use your diverse interests to create a niche practice of your own. Are you a sports buff? You could focus on sports law. A great reader? What about intellectual property law? Do you have an interest in adoption? Think about establishing a practice relating to the myriad aspects of reproductive processes. What about a scientific background in college? Consider patent law; technology is only increasing and legal issues relating to hardware, software and the Internet are blooming. Last, perhaps this is the time to leave law altogether. Your specific skills are transportable. This option may require additional education, and now might be the time to get that master's or Ph.D. that you've thought about over these years.

Seeking a Job Takes Time

You need to approach your job search as a job in and of itself. Allocate several hours a day, if not more, to the search. Assume it may take many months. Learn to network in the modern world. While fantasy is wonderful, the chances of simply being offered a perfect job immediately are small.

Reaching Out for Help

You need to use all the tools you can to enhance your chances and visibility. There is no shame in having been laid-off. Seek out law school classmates. Use your law school alumni and bar association networks. Let family and friends know you are exploring new options. If you belong to social groups, let people know you are looking. Learn new networking skills—specifically, begin to work with online social networks such as LinkedIn. Call on colleagues, or friends of colleagues, and other contacts for advice. It can feel depressing to call and ask strangers to talk with you, but framing the request as one for an "information interview" changes the dynamic. People really do like to help and talk and make contacts. When you call, ask for 20 minutes of that person's time, rather than an hour. This reduces pressure, and you will find most (although not all) contacts receptive. As basic as this sounds, follow up the interviews with a thank you e-mail or note.

Becoming Your Own Best Advocate

Use the tremendous skills—verbal, collaborative, competitive, written—that you have developed over the years since you graduated from law school. Use real time to craft reasonable, contemporary resumes and cover letters. Do not put off this process, no matter how daunting it might feel. Tailor these documents to the jobs you are seeking and focus on real-life skills and achievements. Review different resume styles and find the one that best suits your search.

Creating and Using Support Networks

Lawyers are used to being the counselors, but now is the time to seek counsel from others, whether close friends, partners or spouses, career coaches, or therapists. You do not have to do this on your own. Indeed, you cannot. Being laid-off inevitably shakes your sense of security and strength, no matter how much you know the cause is external not internal. As a lawyer, you have been in control, an advocate for others, or at the least, a wise counsel to your clients. You have had rules to follow, and you know how to play the game. Now, you must reinvent yourself, from the inside out. This takes time, patience and humor.

"Chun"

The Chinese Book of Changes, embodying Taoist philosophy, provides an apt hexagram entitled "chun" (difficulty at the beginning). This hexagram "connotes a blade of grass pushing against an obstacle as it sprouts out of the earth."[2] Career transition, particularly involuntary transition, is not easy at all. It feels chaotic, wildly unpleasant, and even, dare I say it, humbling. By recognizing the difficulties that accompany career change, you will be better positioned to move to a different place than you would ever have thought or imagined. While you cannot control outside events, you can learn from them and respond creatively and pro-actively.

As for me, since my own forced transition in 1995, I have replaced "Invictus" with a different poem. Hiking in Switzerland last year, all along the hiking paths, stones, fences, and trees were marked with white and red paint marked the trails, and these markers were peculiarly comforting and resonant to me; even though these markers did not designate precisely where I was hiking, they did tell me that I was indeed upon a path. Yet, I also know that there are times when the markers are uncertain, or altogether missing from the pathways, both in hiking in Switzerland and in our lives generally. On these occasions, "Invictus" offers little guidance on where to go. Instead, these words from "The Road Less Traveled," by Robert Frost, offer more hopeful but more realistic advice:

> Somewhere ages and ages hence:
> Two roads diverged in a wood, and I
>
> I took the one less traveled by,
> And that has made all the difference.[3]

---

1.   The U.S. Department of Labor has reported since June 2008 a steady decrease in legal sector jobs. Across the board, it is reported that, as Wall Street contracts, "the job losses will spread throughout the economy, with private sector job loss reaching 175,000 in [New York City] and 225,000 [New-York-statewide]." http://www.workforce.com/section/00/article/25/99/02.php. The economy clearly will get worse before it gets better.

2.   *The I Ching or Book of Changes*, Bollingen Series XIX, The Richard Wilhelm translation, rendered into English by Cary F. Baynes (11th edition 1974, Princeton University Press).

3.   "The Road Less Traveled" *in* Mountain Interval by Robert Frost (Henry Holt & Co. 1920).

GARY A. MUNNEKE (GMunneke@law.pace.edu) is a professor of law at Pace University School of Law in White Plains, where he teaches Professional Responsibility, Law Practice Management, and Torts. Professor Munneke is the Chair of the New York State Bar Association's Law Practice Management Committee, Co-Chair of the New York Fellows of the American Bar Foundation, and a member of the Board of Governors of the American Bar Association. The opinions included in this article represent the personal views of the author and do not reflect the policy of the American Bar Association or its Board of Governors.

DEB VOLBERG PAGNOTTA (dvpagnotta@interfacet.com) has been a lawyer since 1981. For the last 10 years, she has served as president of Interfacet, Inc.

This article originally appeared in the February 2009 *NYSBA Journal*.

Practical Skills: Money Management

By Stacy Francis

Times of transition are now the norm. Whether you are a recent law school graduate, a pink slip casualty, ready to reenter the workforce or an about-to-be-retired lawyer, this is an article you have to read.

It is more important than ever to master the practical skills of money management and get a firm handle on your finances. Here is some advice to get you on the right path...fast!

Law School Grad

Life is not so grand for newly minted law school graduates. We are in the fifth straight year of a depressed job market for new graduates. According to new U.S. Labor Department data,[1] the legal services sector added 2,700 jobs in August, the second highest single-month jump in the past year but still well below pre-recession employment levels. Instead of $150,000 a year salaries, many grads are earning as little as $25 an hour for contract work. At the same time expenses—especially in the Big Apple—continue to rise. Rents and home prices are at the highest levels we have seen in the last six years.

Don't Stop Learning Just Because You Are Out of School

When you needed to learn about contracts, you took Contracts. The same should be true about managing money. In fact, the practical skills of money management are much more important to your overall financial security than any course you took in law school.

Get smart and learn about money. Start with a book that is geared toward individuals in their 20s and 30s. Set yourself a goal to read at least one personal finance book a quarter.

Start an Emergency Fund

Before putting your student loan debt repayment plan in high gear, start to build an emergency fund. Put at least three months of living expenses in a high-interest savings account to ensure that you never have to move back home. Online savings accounts at Ally Bank and Capital One offer some of the highest interest rates. Remember that an emergency might occur due to a medical issue, job loss or unforeseen major expense. Please note, the release of the latest iPhone 5S is not an emergency.

Pay Off Your Debt

The average law school debt is upwards of $100,000 and it can even top out at $150,000. While your interest rate may be low, it is wise to start paying off your student loan debt now to ensure that you are not still making payments in 20 years' time. Be sure to make on-time payments; this will start to build your positive credit history.

Credit Score

While a credit score of 850 would not have gotten you into an Ivy League law school, it may help you get the job of your dreams. According to many employers, your credit score clearly defines how fiscally responsible you are and how you manage your obligations.

Be sure to pull your free credit report by visiting www.annualcreditreport.com. Review your report to make sure all information is accurate.

On Your First Day, Think About Retirement

Most likely you have not even had a chance to hang up your shiny new law school diploma, so retirement is most likely not on the top of your mind; however, it should be. The best time to start to plan for retirement is your first day of work. Sign up for your employer's 401(k) plan as soon as you are eligible. You can contribute up to $17,500 for the year. If you are not able to part with this much cash, be sure to contribute at least the amount required to get your employer's match.

Pink Slip Position

A sad part of working in the law field is that sometimes, despite your hard work and effort, you get laid off. All of a sudden you are without a paycheck and the security that comes with it.

Difficult as this may seem, a pink slip can give you the opportunity to re-assess your career. Which areas of law are you most passionate about? What aspects of your last position did you love or hate? What skills do you want to develop further?

An in-depth review of these questions and their answers will give you the direction you need to make smart moves with your career. The most lucrative investment vehicle you have is neither your investment accounts nor your home—it is your career. By mapping out a strategy that adds critical skills to your career portfolio, you will be adding major earnings potential.

Secure Heath Insurance

While your career plan and next steps are important, there are other vital decisions you need to make immediately. One of these critical decisions is regarding health insurance. You have the ability to maintain your current health insurance through COBRA. This may be a good option for you; however, it can be expensive. Another option is to get insurance through New York State of Health, New York's health plan marketplace.[2] This is an organized marketplace designed to help people shop for and enroll in health insurance coverage. Individuals, families and small businesses will be able to use the health plan marketplace to help them compare insurance options, calculate costs and select coverage.

American Express, Visa and MasterCard Are NOT Your Friends

Studies have shown that you are more likely to spend more if you use your credit card to pay versus paying cold hard cash. Resist the urge to whip out your credit card and if you do use your plastic, be sure to pay your balance in full every month. Pay your rent and mortgage first. Keeping a roof over your head is most important.

The "B" Word

Don't get turned off by the "B" word. Your budget plan is the path to financial security and the vacation, home and retirement of your dreams. Track your expenses for one month. Record what you pay right down to the newspaper, bagel and latte you grab on your way to an interview. Evaluate the results and pinpoint where you are spending your money. Cut out expenses that are unnecessary.

Roll Over Your 401(k)

Many job changers get burned because they leave their 401(k) at their old employer and forget about it. Be sure to roll over your 401(k) to a rollover IRA and rebalance your portfolio every year. Another option is to roll your 401(k) into your new employer's retirement plan. Strong arguments can be made on both sides. You need to weigh all the factors and make a decision based on your own needs and priorities.

Most individuals decide to roll their plan into a rollover IRA, as it generally offers more investment choices than an employer's 401(k) plan. You also may be interested in eventually converting your IRA to a Roth IRA. You'll have to pay taxes on the amount you roll over from a regular IRA to a Roth IRA, but any qualified distributions from the Roth IRA in the future will be tax-free.

Roughly 75% of 401(k) plans allow you to borrow money, making the option of rolling your 401(k) into your next employer's plan more appealing. If you roll over your retirement funds to a new employer's plan that permits loans, you may be able to borrow up to 50% of the amount you roll over, up to $50,000.

Returning to the Workforce

Whether it is because your kids are getting older, your partner lost a job or you are looking to get back into the career you love, returning to the workforce can be a major adjustment financially.

Rework Your Cash Flow

It is indeed a material world. However, don't let a "sudden money" mentality take hold of you now that more income is coming in the door. New cars, trips and even a larger home might be on your mind. Hold off on these purchases and maintain your pre-work level of spending.

Review your current budget and be sure to add new expenses such as child care, work clothing, dry cleaning and commuting costs. Be sure to calculate how much of a bite these new expenses will take out of your budget each month and make adjustments as needed.

Spending Accounts Save You Money in Taxes

Using a spending account is like getting a discount on certain expenses—not because the expenses are less, but because you are paying them with money that has not been taxed.

Medical Flexible Spending Plan

Medical costs have skyrocketed, so be sure to enroll in the Medical Flexible Spending Plan (FSA) at your new job. The limits are $2,500 per person, per employee for 2013.

Here are just some of the expenses that you can pay with your Medical FSA:

- Health plan copays and more

- Dental work and orthodontia

- Doctor's fees

- Eye exams and eyeglasses

- Contact lenses and saline solution

- Hearing aids

- Chiropractic treatment

- Laboratory fees

- Over-the-counter items

- Prescriptions

- Mental health counseling

Dependent Care FSA

If you have kids, most likely you will have additional child care costs. You can contribute up to $5,000 a year to this account. All contributions are pretax, thus reducing your taxable income and cutting the money due to Uncle Sam. You can use a Dependent Care FSA to reimburse you for the work-related cost of care for a child who is under age 13, or any other tax dependent, such as an elderly parent or spouse, who is physically or mentally incapable of self-care. Note that they must reside in the same principal residence as you.

Catch Up on Retirement

Many people reentering the workforce need to make up for lost time, because their retirement savings are nowhere near the levels they should be. The goal is to save as much of your new income as possible. Therefore, enroll in your company 401(k) or 403b plan on your first day of work, if you are eligible. Your contributions will be taken directly out of your paycheck—before taxes. This has the added benefit of lowering your taxable income and allowing you to pay less to the government come April 15th. Once you have maxed out your employer retirement plan, open an IRA. You can put $5,000 a year into your IRA and up to $6,000 a year if you are over age 50.

Review Your Benefits

Many employers offer plush employee benefits such as life and disability insurance. Understand your benefits and whether you need to supplement them with a private policy outside of work. Now that you are earning a salary, you need to make sure that you have insurance to replace income that would be lost to your family if you were to die or be unable to work due to health reasons.

You Are a Retiree...Finally!

Retirement can be the saddest or happiest day of your life. It is the extent of your preparation that will determine which it is for you.

Make Your Money Work for You

The investment selection in your retirement plan is more important today than ever. Many soon-to-be retirees have chosen conservative investments to be "safe." While this may seem like a wise choice, you should realize that this portfolio must last you another 25, or even 40, years. You must be careful about the "decumulation" phase and make sure that you have enough money to see you and your family through retirement. Choose an appropriate mix of stocks and bonds based on your age and risk tolerance. A fantastic resource to help you discover your hidden risk tolerance is Morningstar.[3]

Are You Ready to Retire?

Before you hand in your notice, make sure that you are well positioned for retirement. Do a retirement calculation. Do you know how much you need to have saved to live comfortably after retirement? About half of people queried in retirement confidence surveys think they'll need less than 70% of their pre-retirement income. However, we suggest that you have at least 90% of your pre-retirement wages.

Use a retirement needs calculator to determine how well you have prepared and what you can do to improve your retirement outlook. It is important that you periodically re-evaluate your preparedness. Changes in economic climate, inflation, achievable returns, and in your personal situation will impact your plan.[4]

Rome Wasn't Built in a Day and Not by One Person Alone

You only get one chance to retire successfully, but an experienced financial planner has been through this many times before. You will want to select a competent, qualified professional with whom you feel comfortable as well as one whose expertise and business style suits your financial planning needs.

The term "financial planner" is used by many financial professionals (and many non-professionals). Ask the planner what qualifies him or her to offer financial planning advice and whether he or she holds a financial planning designation such as the Certified Financial Planner™ mark.

Look for a Fee-Only Financial Planner

These advisors receive no compensation from any product recommended (like insurance or annuities) and do not represent any product or company. They never accept commissions, trails, cross-selling fees, referral fee arrangements, kickbacks, surrender fees, sales contests, "educational cruises" and vacations, or "free" gifts. For a fee-only advisor in your area visit the website www.NAPFA.org.

Conclusion

Transition is the new normal. You may not be able to predict or anticipate when and how change will come, but a firm financial foundation will help maintain stability—no matter what the future brings.

---

1.   *See* Tom Huddleston, Jr., *Legal Sector Adds 2,700 Jobs in August*, The AmLaw Daily, Sept. 6, 2013.

2.   https://nystateofhealth.ny.gov/.

3.   http://corporate.morningstar.com/us/documents/NASDCompliance/IWT_CurrentReport_RiskToleranceQuest.pdf.

4.   http://finance.yahoo.com/calculator/retirement/ret02/.

STACY FRANCIS is president and CEO of Francis Financial, Inc., a boutique wealth management and financial planning firm in New York City. A Certified Financial Planner, she attended the New York University Center for Finance, Law and Taxation. In 2013, she was listed as a National Money Hero by *CNN Money Magazine*.

This article originally appeared in the January 2014 *NYSBA Journal*.

Reflections on Transitions: Things I Have Learned

By Jessica Thaler

Have you ever felt as though you are having a bad day, bad week, bad month, bad year, bad decade? I found myself having all of the above simultaneously. I was unhappy at my job, going through a bunch of personal struggles and feeling very alone, estranged, disregarded, unsatisfied and lost. I was in my mid-30s, single and living in New York City, one of the most exciting and wonderful and lonely places you could possibly inhabit. I had a constant internal struggle between what I was "supposed" to be doing and how I was "supposed" to be living at that stage of my life, and disliking what I was doing and how I was living. I felt like I was constantly in an uphill battle with The Abominable Snow Monster of the North, who was constantly hurling meteor-sized snowballs at me.

"Work is just a means to live" was the motto my father said my grandfather lived by. As wonderful and enlightened as it sounds, in this day and age, with the advent of the computer, the Internet, the cell phone, Citrix, video conferencing, the Treo, the BlackBerry, the iPhone, email, cloud computing, virtual conference rooms, Skype and more, there is no longer a distinction between work time and family time. My grandfather was a hard worker. He came out of the Depression, working and building a very healthy nest egg for his wife and children despite his lack of formal education. (He got his high school diploma the year before I did, his pride hiding that fact from his children and grandchildren— only my grandmother knew the truth.) But his workday was early morning until early evening, not 48-hour stints in the office. His workweek was generally five days, not back-to-back weekends making one week flow undetected into the next. It was not awful if a person did not love what he or she did because work could be compartmentalized, as people knew there was an end to each workday and each workweek. Work as a means to an end was not a daunting statement.

The Plunge

At the time my father shared these words with me, I was struggling to find purpose in what I was doing and to find happiness and satisfaction professionally. I kept hearing my grandfather's words; I understood them intellectually, but they were not bringing me comfort or helping me get through the day. I wanted more out of my job and my career. I wanted to enjoy what I was doing each day because I was spending far too much time working not to. It was 2008. I left the firm I was working for to pursue my dream, but my timing was off. My expertise and client relationships were in banking and finance, an industry that was the heavy stone pulling the economy down, so, like many others, I found myself looking for a new job. And like many others finding themselves in transition, I found myself feeling like I was alone.

Every situation is different. Some people have money saved. Some have a spouse or other life partner who can help alleviate some of the financial pressures or provide the needed emotional support. Some choose to move home. Some pretend the transition is not happening. Some have a great deal of education. Some have little. Some are very senior level. Some are very junior. Some will choose to grab their passport and take off on a trip to restore the soul. Some will not be comfortable taking even one day off until they have found something. Some will become a hermit and speak to no one. Some will go to therapy or turn to religion for guidance. Some will speak to anyone willing to lend an ear. Some will spend their days working out. Some will spend them goofing off. Some will focus on all the home projects they had been meaning to do for years. Some will wake each morning and spend hour upon hour searching through websites for jobs. Some will attend conferences. Some will fill their schedule each day with coffee, lunch and drink dates—all in the name of networking. Some will have supportive family and friends. Some will want to divorce themselves from their family and friends. Some will become sleepless, get stomachaches and have their TMJ act up. Some will breathe deeply for the first time in years. Some will cry. Some will be angry. Some will look at it as a blessing. Some as a curse. For me, I was able to identify with and directly relate to many, if not most, of these people at some point during my transition.

Working Within and Without

Transition is discouraging. It can be very hard to stay positive. I have been in transition for a while now and, during that time, I set up my own firm. I get an unsteady flow of work from clients and other small and solo firms and have obtained a full-time contracting position for which I am grateful, especially when the ebb and flow of my practice starts to weigh on me. I have made it work. I have struggled, failed, fallen down and been scraped off the floor. I have spent hours talking to many people. I discovered that, upon first hearing that a person is in a job search, people are generally very sympathetic, offering drinks, hugs, advice, contacts and more. It is not that sympathy wanes as the months of searching go on but rather that people just do not know what more to say.

I have read countless books and attended numerous seminars trying to figure it all out. I do not have all the answers but I have made great strides in my outlook, which has significantly improved my access to opportunities, personal and professional relationships, as well as my physical and mental well-being.

When I first started to look for a position, I was in a very negative place, the victim, fighting for control over things I would never have control over, looking for answers and explanations where there were none. I have learned many things about control (or the lack thereof), about how things work (and do not work), about people and about myself. Someone recently commented that I appeared much calmer, happier, at peace and, after we spoke about what had changed in my life and my outlook, he smiled and asked, "So, you have finally accepted your situation?" I thought about it and answered, with a grin, "No, I have surrendered to it."

Whether characterized as surrender or acceptance, I have come to realize that the key is understanding that I can actually control only a small part of my transition. I can control what I do, how I present myself and how I take care of myself. I have little to no control over how I am perceived, even when I put my best foot forward, what assumptions people may make, what is going on with the economy, how many people I am competing against, the decisions a business makes concerning its hiring needs or the candidates it chooses. All I can do is to understand that a large part of the process is luck, collect rejections and know that after an indeterminate number of rejections, I will find something. In the interim, while I keep pushing, applying, interviewing and getting rejections, I need to take care of myself.

I have had many leads. I have had offers that I turned down and some that were reneged due to a change of financial circumstances of the company. I have quadrupled my already large network. I have joined every jobsite and every social networking site. I have gotten contract work. I have started my own business. I have spent multiple hours per day making calls; attending meetings; emailing; writing and rewriting my resume, my cover letter and my biography. Not being a coffee drinker, I have never visited as many different Starbucks as I have during this time of transition. I went from never having a cup of coffee to having a few each week. Despite being someone who does not enjoy working out, I have become a regular at the gym, if only to get out of the house for an hour or so each day. I have taken up drawing and painting again after not picking up a brush in more than 14 years despite having started college as an art major. I have learned to enjoy a quiet night at home and stopped filling my evening calendar to the brim. I have come to appreciate the day away from the City with "away" being the suburbs, as opposed to an alternative continent. I have spent the day with the TV on from 7:00 a.m. until midnight without knowing what I watched, as it was on only to provide the companionship and background noise I used to get by being in an office surrounded by others. I have started to learn that asking for help is okay. I have learned how to just say "thank you" when someone offers to pick up the tab, whether for a cup of coffee or for a meal, and not to feel guilty about it. I have gotten further involved with volunteer work—Make a Wish, the Red Cross, my alumni associations and more—figuring if I cannot feel fulfilled while making money, I will seek that fulfillment through doing good for others.

Fullness of Transition

Transition is a word I have used much more frequently since 2008, and I have recognized that it has many meanings. With regard to a career transition, it may mean a person is looking for a position after a layoff, after raising a family or after some other hiatus from working, generally; starting his or her own firm or business, or leaving one or the other; shifting to a different industry focus or type of organization or role; or entering or exiting from a profession. No matter the form transition takes, I have come to realize the experiences and emotions and methods for managing, prevailing or coping in the face of those experiences and emotions have many commonalities. It is scary, exciting, daunting, fun, frustrating, fulfilling and stimulating all at one time. What has gotten me through this process so far?

Accepting, or surrendering to, my circumstances. I have come to understand and embrace the reality that there is an element completely in the hands of the universe, the almighty, faith, karma, luck, or however else the unknown can be characterized, and it plays a large role in reaching the end goal of this transition process. I do need to take control of the things that I do have control over and take comfort in that fact. If I do everything I can actually do that I have control over, the only thing left to do is become comfortable with the fact that there is nothing more I can do other than wait for the stars to come into alignment. (If only I could control the stars.)

Allowing myself to feel down. This is not a call for martyrdom but rather a knowledge that transition is hard, very hard, and there will be good and bad days in the process. Both the good and the bad are to be expected. I try to remember that I am not made of steel, as much as that was a hard reality to grasp, having always prided myself and presented myself as someone who can handle anything thrown at me. However, accepting my vulnerability was liberating. It allowed me to say it is okay not to plan six meetings in a single day, to take a few days off from submitting job applications, to spend a few hours or a full day on the couch watching mindless TV, crying off and on, not answering the phone, to let my friends and family see my fears and then allow them to take care of me.

Forgiving people who do not know what to say to or do. People want to help. They care for me. But, not knowing what to say, they will often try to provide a pep talk or words of wisdom and inspiration. Although these words often feel empty, obvious and annoying, they do come from a good place, normally. I also have come to understand that they can stem from the other person's fear that he or she may end up in the same position as me and that they do not know how to tackle that fear or how they would possibly get through what I am managing my way through. If nothing else, these words often do work great as screensavers. Once I had compiled a list of proverbs so long that I was able to ensure the ability to change them monthly for the next three to four years, how did I avoid an unintended feeling of resentment for and frustration with these well-intended friends, family members and colleagues? I worked up the courage to tell people what I needed, whether it is meeting me at Starbuck's, for a quick lunch, a movie or just a hug. They do want to help. Most will be very grateful to know how they can help and be supportive.

Getting—even more—involved. Once people come to know of you as doer, as someone looking for networking opportunities, for ways to enhance your resume, you will be asked time and again to do one more thing, join one more committee, plan one more event, write one more article or speak on one more panel. With all the positives of this predicament, it did often leave me struggling to balance my sanity with what I thought I "should" do and trying to come through for everyone. I tried to set up rules as to how many things I would take on, meetings I would agree to and activities I would participate in daily, monthly and weekly, but I have found that nothing in my job search has been more beneficial than the volunteer work I have done, whether with professional organizations, nonprofits or otherwise. As a result, I quickly gave up on those rules. When I feel at my most overwhelmed and find myself struggling to prepare for, or even just get dressed for, yet another meeting, I remind myself that "you never know from where the next great opportunity will come." It has proven true time and again.

Realizing I am not alone. Although misery does love company, although we have all had the nights commiserating with colleagues and friends and although the occasional evening of venting can help me to feel better, I have learned that a "woe is me" mentality not kept in check will throw me quickly, and with added velocity, down Alice's rabbit hole, nothing to grab onto, walls too slippery to brace against, no cushion identifiable below, in the dark, hearing scary noises (sounding very much like insults) emanating from the abyss. I found the best thing to do is talk with people who are transitioning but who are also being proactive and those who have recently successfully transitioned. Those compatriots can provide a knowing nod and sympathetic smile when I am describing the latest sleepless night, my frustration that an opportunity fell through, my exasperation with feeling like my resume is in the void somewhere and my fear of an interviewer's unexplained silence. They will be less likely to walk me so close that I find myself teetering on the edge of the rabbit hole and more likely to ask why, exactly, it is that I am even looking into that hole again. They will help me see that hole ahead, recognize it is there, understand why it is appearing, and help me to steer in another direction. They will also understand the bumps and bruises I may have after a recent fall and may have a trick for alleviating the lingering pain and discomfort.

Knowing I am, and my situation is, not unique. It is not as harsh as it sounds. Despite always being praised for and encouraged to be unique, and in many ways I am very much my own person, and although my specific situation differs in degrees, the commonality I share with others in transition is just that—being in a state of transition. That process brings about uncertainty, vulnerability, stress and fear. As much as acceptance of this lack of distinction was a blow to my ego, when I finally accepted it, I was able to take a deep breath, recognize that there are others similarly situated who have survived this before, will survive it again and, because I also possess many of the same skills, education, resources, resilience, strength, perseverance, power, spirit, desire and drive, I too will survive. And, not only will I survive, I will succeed in my transition.

There Just Will Be Bad Days

Despite all the good, all the hard work and having a great screensaver, there are still those days that are just bad days. The days when I decide I will never work again. I will never be successful. I am a failure. I never deserved to get where I was prior to this transition. For me, those days tend to happen when a job opportunity falls through, whether after one or more interviews or, sometimes, after finding out it has been filled before even having had the opportunity to interview. It is the day when I am told "you're too senior" and "we need someone to hit the ground running" during two separate conversations regarding two similar positions at two different companies. It is when I am heading to a wedding, a baby or bridal shower or a birthday and want to get a gift, knowing I would have gotten a "better" gift if I were in a different financial position. Those days also happen after having a great meeting or interview, when I become so fearful of getting my hopes up, I begin convincing myself that it will not happen before the BlackBerry can even reset itself and start receiving the emails and texts that came through while on the interview.

I have to work hard to get myself through those days. I battle my demons. I know I will not get through every day unscathed. I am learning to have compassion for myself. I am figuring out what I need to feel safe and supported and to seek it out, to take care of myself, to put myself first when I need to, to allow myself to feel and to just be, and to know, at risk of using one of much dreaded proverbs, "this too shall pass."

Moving From Negative to Positive

I truly believe that this will pass and that this period of my life, although challenging in many ways, is part of the cycles that we all must go through in our lives. I believe that, at some point, having had the courage to go out on my own to build a practice, the ability and expertise to acquire and service clients of various sizes and structures in a multitude of industries, the resourcefulness and fortitude to find and maintain a full-time (and now very long-term) contract position that adds to my experience and supplements my income, the altruism and ambition to volunteer for (and often take a leadership role in) professional, philanthropic and other organizations, the initiative and sociability to expand both my personal and professional networks and the great appreciation for and the good fortune to have people in my life who have advised, supported, mentored, listened, assisted, comforted, encouraged and even just hugged me, will all work collectively not only to allow me to find a new job but also to permit me to find professional and personal satisfaction and fulfillment in and through that new job. Like Rudolph who turned his bad experience with The Abominable Snow Monster of the North into friendship, I know that I will look back at this time of transition with the knowledge that I embraced that which scared and challenged me, and transformed my experience into a positive one.

JESSICA THALER is a lawyer in New York City, practicing as a corporate-transactional generalist, counseling clients in connection with various types of corporate transactions including lending and finance, mergers and acquisitions, development and cooperation, services, real property and licensing, in the fields of sports, media, telecommunications, biopharmaceuticals, videogames and virtual worlds, entertainment, environmental, mobile advertising, technology and construction, among others. She is also a member of the New York State Bar Association and serves as the Chair of NYSBA's Committee on Lawyers in Transition, as Co-Chair of Membership of its Entertainment, Art and Sports Law Section and as an active member of the Sports Lawyers Association. Ms. Thaler is a graduate of UCLA, *cum laude*, and Fordham University School of Law.

This article originally appeared in the September 2012 *NYSBA Journal*.

What's in *Your* Transition Toolbox?
15 Essential Tools for an Effective Move Forward
By Amy Gewirtz

Derived from its root "transit," the word "transition" connotes movement. And movement implies action. Picture a commuter train carrying passengers from one destination to another.

As human beings, we are regularly moving, shifting, and repositioning ourselves and our career goals, ambitions and paths. Even when *contemplating* our next career steps, our brain, and its "wheels," are in motion (there's that train image again). Professional transitions can occur at any stage of your career, whether voluntarily or involuntarily. As a result, and given the challenges of today's uncertain economy and the restructuring of the legal profession, it's essential to have a full transition toolbox ready at all times to help prepare for a planned or unplanned transition. This article sets forth 15 essential tools to help those in transition move forward professionally.

Self-Assessment (Exercises/Assessments)

Taking the time to look inward to determine what is most important to you in your next career move is often the hardest, yet always the most critical, step. As Director of Pace Law School's New Directions for Attorneys program, which assists attorneys with their return to traditional law practice or an alternative legal career after stepping aside from the profession for some period of time, I am often asked how much homework is involved. My answer is always that the biggest piece of homework is the self-assessment. This task may start during the program but should continue well beyond the end of their participation in the program.

At New Directions, we present a workshop and exercises on self-assessment, but we also point out that self-assessment should be a lifelong exercise to be used as your life circumstances and personal and professional goals change. Whether you are experiencing a voluntary or involuntary transition, ideally your next move will be a good professional fit and in a place you would like to remain. Essential to the self-assessment is asking the important questions, such as: "What are your core values?" "What trade-offs are you able to make?" "Where have you been the most successful professionally and why?" "What skills have you developed during your career and other activities, whether professional or personal?" "Did you enjoy using those skills?" This is not an indulgence—

people are generally happier, and therefore more productive, when they are in a professional environment that suits them.

There are any number of self-assessment exercises available on the Internet that you can do on your own. Additionally, there are a number of other self-assessment tools such as the Myers Briggs Type Indicator (MBTI), The Highlands Ability Battery, and the Strong Interest Inventory, which are done with a counselor or coach certified to administer them and to evaluate the results. However you use the self-assessment tool, the key is to take this tool out of the toolbox and to use it.

Resume

Your resume is a living, breathing document and, as such, it should always be up-to-date and ready for a prospective employer. It is often the first impression you make on a prospective employer, and it must be *perfect*—no typos, grammatical errors, or unusual fonts. Ideally, it will reflect how your experience makes you a good fit for a position by including language that reflects (not necessarily parrots) the job description. A resume is not a one-size-fits-all document. Resume content and format will vary based on numerous factors, including the position for which you're applying, the particular experiences and skills you wish to highlight for that particular opportunity, and the career stage you're in.

If you are applying for different types of positions simultaneously— for example, a traditional position with a law firm and also a less traditional, law-related position—career counselors will often recommend having more than one resume, each of which is tailored to the position you are seeking. The traditional format is the reverse chronological resume in which your most recent employment is listed first. Another resume format is the functional, or skills-based, resume, in which you first list your skill sets rather than a reverse chronological order of your employment history. This type of resume may be a good choice for those who have had an employment gap or who are seeking to transition to an alternative legal career. Because this tool is so important, I recommend meeting with a career counselor or coach to see which format will work best for you.

LinkedIn Profile

If you don't already have one, you *must* create a LinkedIn profile. LinkedIn has a Help Center that offers webinars to help get you started, as well as a webinar on job search tips. To access these seminars, go to the LinkedIn home page at www.linkedin.com, scroll down to the bottom of the page, click onto Help Center, then type "LinkedIn Learning Webinars" in the search field. LinkedIn experts (searching the Internet is a great resource for finding numerous helpful resources about how to use LinkedIn) recommend that your profile be as complete as possible, which includes having a professional-looking photo. At the risk of sounding like a spokeswoman for LinkedIn, it is a fantastic tool for networking, job searching, and client development. Don't just create a profile—join groups such as law school alumni, bar associations, and affinity groups surrounding your areas of interest. Follow companies, invite people to connect with you (however, connect only with those you know or who may have been introduced to you by someone you know and respect) and ask for introductions to those who may be connected to an organization to which you recently applied for a job. There is enough to be said about the value of LinkedIn to fill several articles, but suffice to say, this is an indispensable tool.

Note: Attorneys who are currently employed but who wish to transition to another organization or opportunity may have valid concerns about signaling on LinkedIn that they are seeking another job. For those in this situation, googling "keeping your job search secret on LinkedIn" will yield a number of helpful articles.

Elevator Speech/Pitch

We've all heard of the "elevator speech," meaning what you can tell a fellow elevator passenger about yourself in the course of a 30-second elevator ride. I prefer a term that I heard an excellent career coach use at a recent NYSBA Lawyers in Transition program—"professional history." What you choose to include in your elevator speech may vary depending upon the environment (bar association event versus wedding) and the listener (prospective employer versus a neighbor).

In a professional setting, your elevator speech is basically a brief summary of your professional history and what you are transitioning toward. There are numerous approaches to developing your elevator speech, and many resources and examples may be found on the Internet. If you are consulting a career counselor or coach, creation of your elevator speech(es) should be made part of the conversation. Although it's commonly referred to as a "speech" or a "pitch," it should above all sound natural and not rehearsed or forced. You may want to practice it several times on a friend, trusted colleague, or career counselor.

Business Card

If you are currently employed, you will most likely have a business card identifying you as an employee of a particular organization. If you are between positions, however, you may not have one, or even see the need for one. Please get one. It is common practice to exchange business cards at professional and some personal events. The playing field is not level if someone hands you a business card and you either don't have one or you hand that person a resume. Even if you are not currently employed, get a very simple business card, on good card stock, white or ivory, with your name, and either "Counselor-at-Law" or "Attorney-at-Law," a phone number (that has a professional voicemail message—generally a cell phone) and an email address. Some people feel uncomfortable including their home address; that is fine, it does not need to be included. Increasingly, professionals are starting to include the link to their LinkedIn profile on both their business card and resume. Career counselors may have different opinions on this, but, if it is included, your LinkedIn profile should be fairly complete and be consistent with what's on your resume.

Facebook/Twitter

There are differences of opinion on the professional usefulness of Facebook and Twitter. That said, many organizations have Facebook and Twitter accounts on which they include the latest information about their organizations, as well as job postings. These are probably reason enough to establish Facebook and Twitter accounts and to have them in your toolbox. Much has been written about the "dangers" of including "too much information" on Facebook. Be warned: prospective employers are looking at your online presence and it should be as professional as possible. Google your name periodically to see what others see.

Smartphone

Many organizations have a 24/7 culture and thus have an expectation that their employees will have access to their email when they're away from the office. It is not enough simply to have a phone these days; and, in fact, having a phone that is *just* a phone, may date you and signal to a prospective employer that you are not current with technology.

Active Bar Status

If you've "retired" from the profession and are contemplating a return to traditional law practice, reactivate your license as soon as possible. You don't want to find yourself in a position in which you're being considered for a job opportunity and when you are asked if your license is current having to say no. You want to be able to say yes immediately.

Bar Association Membership

Bar association memberships make up another important tool in your transition toolbox. By definition, a bar association is populated with professional colleagues who can be excellent networking resources and sources of information about potential job opportunities and practice areas you may be exploring as part of your transition. Additionally, they offer continuing legal education classes that can bring you up to speed on the latest developments in a particular practice area. In a large bar association such as NYSBA, for example, there are committees and/or sections covering myriad practice areas and interests. Join one or more and assist with their panels and programs. Write posts for a committee blog. Get involved!

Networking Log

Since networking is such an important part of a transition, you will undoubtedly be meeting a number of people along your journey. It is very helpful to establish a system for keeping track of the contacts you have made, people to whom you've reached out, people to whom you'd like to reach out, dates of your outreach and follow up dates, results of your outreach efforts, and so on. Your system should be what works for you, whether it's an Excel spreadsheet or a chart. The format doesn't matter as long as you consistently review and update it.

An Accountability Wingman/Personal Board of Directors

It's important during a transition to surround yourself with people who support you and your decisions—the "yay-sayers" rather than the "nay-sayers." These are often friends, family and colleagues. They have your best interests at heart and want to see you succeed. As well-intentioned as they are, however, they are not always the best choices to help you maintain the discipline involved in a job search. It's important to find someone to whom you feel professionally accountable—someone whose opinions you respect and who will be firm in ensuring you adhere to whatever schedule you have established for your transition. The person should feel comfortable providing you with constructive criticism, and you should feel comfortable receiving it. You should develop a plan as to what goals you would like to accomplish and by when, and then establish a method of accountability to your wingman. A weekly email? A meeting once a month?

Similarly, a personal board of directors is a group of people who know and support you. The people you choose to be on that board will have various strengths, and you can look to them to assist you with different aspects of your transition. For example, one board member may be your personal motivator, an enthusiastic person who will inspire and energize you by reminding you of your strengths, and give you the confidence that you can be successful in this transition. Another may be someone with a large personal and professional network, who is happy to introduce you to those in that network for informational interviewing purposes. Yet another may be a meticulous writer with excellent legal research and writing skills. That's the person who will review your writing sample and resume.

Email Alerts

Email alerts are yet another essential tool for your toolbox. Whether for job postings tailored for criteria you specify, such as through www.indeed.com or Google alerts for topics in which you are interested or that relate to a position or organization to which you are applying, email alerts can be a wonderful resource when you are making a transition.

Current References

As with your resume, you will want to be sure you are ready to provide references to a prospective employer. Prepare a reference sheet with your name and contact information on the top, and the names of three or four references, their titles, organizations, contact information and the context in which they know you. If you have been out of the paid workforce for some period of time and are transitioning back, this may mean that you will need to reach out to colleagues or a supervisor from quite some time ago. Don't hesitate to do so; in most instances they will be happy to serve as a reference. When you reach out to them, be sure to remind them of projects you worked on together. If you are not able to find previous or current professional references, it is perfectly acceptable to list a fellow committee or board member, or your supervisor in a volunteer role you may have. The most important factor is that these are not character references; they are references from those who have seen your work ethic and skills.

Current Writing Sample

Some prospective employers may ask for a writing sample in connection with their application process. You will want to be sure you have one to submit. In general, it should be no longer than five to 12 pages. If the position is a traditional legal job, it should reflect legal analysis and proper citation. If you are using a writing sample from a prior employer, you should ask that employer for permission to use that piece and redact any identifying information. If you don't have a writing sample that you feel comfortable using, or if the last one you wrote was from a number of years ago, think about selecting a topic (legal or law-related) that is of interest to you and writing a short article about it. Even if you never submit the article for publication, the process of researching and writing it will get those wheels turning again. It may also generate an interesting conversation with a prospective employer as to why you chose that particular topic, the results of your research, and why you are arguing in favor of one position over another. Remember to be thoroughly familiar with the content of your writing sample when you go for an interview, as the interviewer may ask you about it.

An Action Plan

And last, but certainly not least, is an Action Plan. We've come full circle to the concept of transition as movement, motion, action. I started this article by noting that transition means moving from one state to another. I am going to end it by providing what I consider last transition essential—the Action Plan.

A transition can have so many moving parts that it can feel overwhelming. It's easy to become stuck because it can be so hard to know where to begin. One way to counteract that feeling is by taking action in an ordered, disciplined way. The first item on your Action Plan can simply be "Day 1, appointment 1—sit and think for an hour or two about what makes me happy." Reflect. Clean off your desk so that nothing is on it to distract you. It could be identifying a place, whether in your home, office, or a café, that you are now going to associate as your "transition planning" place. Pick your transition music, or turn off the music. Do whatever it is that gets you into the frame of mind in which you're determined to treat this transition process with the seriousness and attention it warrants. In New Directions, toward the end of the session we provide our participants with a 30-Day Action Plan Form that we encourage them to start completing even before they've finished the program. We encourage them to make unbreakable appointments with themselves—sacred time in which they are not to be disturbed, during which they devote time to their job search. You're reading this in January—what better time to make resolutions! And the first resolution is to fill your transition toolbox with these 15 essential tools.

AMY GEWIRTZ is the Director of Pace Law School's New Directions for Attorneys program. A graduate of Barnard College and the Benjamin N. Cardozo School of Law, she worked as an entertainment lawyer in theatre and for the Motion Picture Association of America. She shifted gears and began working as a career counselor at Cardozo and then Pace Law School, where she conceived the idea of a program for reentering attorneys. She is an active member of the NYSBA Committee on Lawyers in Transition.

Note: The views and recommendations are the author's own. Those reading this article should follow the advice that resonates with them.

This article originally appeared in the January 2014 *NYSBA Journal*.

Stepping Out on The Right Foot: Protect the Solo Practice by Protecting the Solo Practitioner

By Patricia Spataro

The benefits of being a solo practitioner are many. Perhaps the biggest risk in being a solo practitioner is isolation. The profession is demanding and can be stressful. Facing these demands and managing the stress alone can be daunting. Ensure your success by assessing and minimizing the risks. The best time to do this is before you open your doors to clients.

As the director of the lawyer assistance program for over 10 years I believe I may be in the best position to offer some words of wisdom. Not my wisdom but that of your colleagues who in the process of learning from their mistakes taught me a thing or two.

It is said that "if only" are the saddest two words anyone can mutter. Often the attorneys who called my office seeking help placed the following in the "if only" category. "If only I didn't ignore the warning signs", "if only I called sooner", "if only I managed my stress better". I am presenting them as words to the wise that might save your law practice, and even your life.

Insight One: Pay Attention to Early Signs That Something is Not Right

In general, mental health issues, such as problem drinking and depression, interfere with a lawyer's ability to fully function as person and as a lawyer. Maybe not at first, but certainly at some point an interference or interruption to life and law will emerge. The early warning signs can hint at the serious emerging issues.

These early warning signs can manifest in any area of a person's life. Depression can show itself in a simple and ignorable way, such as not wanting to socialize even though you once enjoyed being with colleagues, friends and family.

Harmless, maybe, but then the unshakable sadness makes it hard for you to concentrate, and your clients get frustrated by your procrastination. Your spouse starts telling you that you aren't yourself, you get irritated and sink further into depression and the personal and professional relationships become compromised.

You eat and sleep more than usual. Before you know it, your doctor is telling you that your blood pressure is dangerously high. Over time, every area of your life is touched by your depression, but you are not connecting all the dots.

Then a letter arrives from the grievance committee and it sits in the pile on your desk of the other documents you just can't seem to get to.

A drinking problem can run a similar course. You drink more to deal with stress. One day you almost miss a court date because you are hung over and cannot get out of bed.

Isolated incident … maybe … but, then, the start time for your first drink is at lunch instead of dinner and you argue easily with just about everyone in your life. Much to your surprise, you get pulled over on your way home from work and your blood alcohol content (BAC) is 0.28 and it is only 6:45 p.m.

Depression and procrastination go hand-in-hand, as does drinking too much and too often. Lawyers who procrastinate and are preoccupied are moments away from serious problems.

Insight Two: Manage Stress Before It Manages You

Everyone deals with stress, but not everyone gets to a place where it swallows them up. Stress can cause, or at the very least, exacerbate mental health concerns. This is one area where protecting the practice by protecting the practitioner is a "what comes first" dilemma. Managing your personal stress and stress related to your law practice.

Personal stress can effectively be managed by healthy life choices. Exercising and eating well are quickly dismissed as "who has time for that," but it has been shown over and over that those who are not overcome by stress, most often engage in these two healthy habits.

Practice stress can be managed by engaging with colleagues in a spirit of support. I know that the competitive profession of law isn't always amenable to this collegiality but those who have the greatest success in this profession do just this.

Establish a process by which you screen clients. The wrong clients will consume the majority of your resources and time and they will be the first ones to complain about your work. Don't fall into the trap of saying "yes" to everyone who walks through your door. Just about every solo who calls my office admits to being a "yes" person and cannot deny it causes them serious problems.

There are many more ways to manage personal and professional stress. Find the strategies that work for you and use them every day.

Insight Three: Make the Call to the Lawyer Assistance Program (LAP) Sooner Rather Than Later

"Making the call to LAP is the best thing I've done in a long time."

"Calling LAP saved my life."

"I wish I made this call sooner."

"You've given me many great ideas on how to deal with my situation."

These are common remarks we hear and the best thing I can do to persuade you to contact LAP is to share what your colleagues are saying about their experience.

Before you pick up your phone, let me remind you that the call is confidential. We understand and, perhaps most importantly, we do not judge. The fear of stigma and shame often stops a lawyer with a serious problem from making the call. We understand that it is hard to make the call, and we will put you at ease quickly.

Start your career off on the right foot. At the State Bar there are many resources and caring people who are committed to your success as a lawyer. Call the Lawyer Assistance Program at 800.255.0569.

Go to www.nysba.org/LAP to get help or to find out how to help a colleague.

PATRICIA SPATARO is the Director of the NYSBA Lawyer Assistance Program and can be reached at 800-255-0569.

This article originally appeared in the January/February 2014 NYSBA State Bar News.